ORDER AND JUSTICE IN INTERNATIONAL RELATIONS

Order and Justice in International Relations

Edited by

Rosemary Foot, John Gaddis,
and Andrew Hurrell

OXFORD
UNIVERSITY PRESS

OXFORD

UNIVERSITY PRESS

Great Clarendon Street, Oxford OX2 6DP

Oxford University Press is a department of the University of Oxford.
It furthers the University's objective of excellence in research, scholarship,
and education by publishing worldwide in

Oxford New York

Auckland Bangkok Buenos Aires Cape Town Chennai
Dar es Salaam Delhi Hong Kong Istanbul Karachi Kolkata
Kuala Lumpur Madrid Melbourne Mexico City Mumbai Nairobi
São Paulo Shanghai Taipei Tokyo Toronto

Oxford is a registered trade mark of Oxford University Press
in the UK and in certain other countries

Published in the United States
by Oxford University Press Inc., New York

First published 2003

British Library Cataloguing in Publication Data

Data available

Library of Congress Cataloging in Publication Data

Order and justice in international relations / edited by Rosemary Foot,
John Gaddis, and Andrew Hurrell.
p. cm.
Includes bibliographical references.
1. International relations. 2. Peace. 3. Security, International. 4. Justice.
I. Foot, Rosemary, 1948– II. Gaddis, John Lewis. III. Hurrell, Andrew.
JZ1308 .O73 2003 327.1′01—dc21 2002028264
ISBN 0-19-925120-7 (acid-free paper)
ISBN 0-19-925119-3 (pbk.: acid-free paper)

3 5 7 9 10 8 6 4

Typeset by Newgen Imaging Systems (P) Ltd., Chennai, India
Printed in Great Britain
on acid-free paper by
T.J. International Ltd
Padstow, Cornwall

Acknowledgements

This collection of essays originated from a seminar series held at the University of Oxford in the autumn of 2000. Originally, we did not envisage publishing the papers that were to be presented. However, the high quality of the presentations and the level of interest sustained in the series over the course of the term convinced us that the essays deserved to reach a wider audience.

We decided to commission two additional chapters, and held a workshop in May 2001 to strengthen the cohesion of the book and to re-examine its central themes. We also invited four discussants—Kalypso Nicolaidis, Jennifer Welsh, Laurence Whitehead, and Marc Williams—to comment both on individual papers and on the project as a whole. Their advice has proved invaluable and we would like to thank them for their important input into this collection. We are grateful, too, that one among them—Kalypso Nicolaidis—subsequently agreed to become a co-author of one of the specially commissioned chapters.

We have also benefited enormously from the assistance of Vivien Collingwood, a doctoral student at Nuffield College, who has done far more than was initially asked of her in helping to prepare these papers for publication. Her intellectual and practical contributions have proved vital in bringing this project to completion. Dominic Byatt of Oxford University Press has been very supportive of the project throughout and Michael James has proved to be a most efficient copy-editor. Dominic was instrumental in obtaining a number of serious, anonymous, reviews of the collection which have helped to sharpen the arguments that are presented here. We thank those colleagues in other academic institutions who agreed to take on this important and time-consuming task.

Funding for the various stages of this project has come from the Norwegian Foreign Ministry which has made a generous financial contribution to the Research Programme of the Centre for International Studies at the University of Oxford. We would like to thank the Norwegian government, the Programme Committee, and its Director for their support.

Rosemary Foot
John Gaddis
Andrew Hurrell
Oxford, March 2002

Contents

Notes on Contributors

KANTI BAJPAI teaches at the School of International Studies, Jawaharlal Nehru University, New Delhi. He specializes in international relations theory, international and regional security, nuclear proliferation, and India's foreign and security policies. At present he is completing a book on Indian grand strategic thought.

ROSEMARY FOOT is Professor of International Relations and the John Swire Senior Research Fellow in International Relations, St Antony's College, University of Oxford. Her latest book is entitled *Rights Beyond Borders: The Global Community and the Struggle over Human Rights in China* (Oxford University Press, 2000). Her research interests are in the fields of security studies and human rights, with special reference to the Asia-Pacific. She has been a Fellow of the British Academy since 1996.

JOHN LEWIS GADDIS is Robert A. Lovett Professor of History at Yale University and a Senior Fellow of the Hoover Institution. He has also taught at Ohio University, the United States Naval War College, the University of Helsinki, Princeton University, and the University of Oxford. Professor Gaddis has written a number of books on the Cold War, including *The United States and the Origins of the Cold War, 1941–1947* (Columbia University Press, 1972; second edition 2000); *Strategies of Containment: A Critical Appraisal of Postwar American National Security Policy* (Oxford University Press, 1982); and *We Now Know: Rethinking Cold War History* (Clarendon Press, 1997).

ANDREW HURRELL is University Lecturer in International Relations at the University of Oxford, and Fellow of Nuffield College. His major interests include international relations theory with particular reference to international law and institutions, and the international relations of Latin America, with particular reference to Brazil. Recent publications include *Regionalism in World Politics* (Oxford University Press, 1995; edited with Louise Fawcett); *Inequality, Globalization, and World Politics* (Oxford University Press, 1999; edited with Ngaire Woods); and, with Kai Alderson, *Hedley Bull on International Society* (Macmillan, 2000).

JUSTINE LACROIX is a doctoral candidate in political theory at the Université Libre de Bruxelles. Previously, she was a member of Jacques Delors' cabinet at the European Commission (1994–5), and a researcher at the Research and Policy Unit *Notre Europe* (1996–9). She has published two books: *Walzer: Le Pluralisme et l'Universel* (Michalon, 2001) and, with Jean-Marc Ferry, *La Pensée Politique Contemporaine* (Bruylant, 2000). Justine Lacroix holds a Diploma from the Institut d'Études Politiques de Paris and a Masters from the Université Libre de Bruxelles.

S. NEIL MACFARLANE is Lester B. Pearson Professor of International Relations at the University of Oxford, Professorial Fellow at St Anne's College, and until April 2002 was Director of Oxford's Centre for International Studies. His research focuses on the evolution of international relations in the Eurasian region and the role of international organizations therein, on conflict and conflict prevention in the newly independent states, and on the relationship between politics, peacekeeping, and humanitarian action. Recent publications include *International Politics and Local Conflict: Patterns of Intervention*, Adelphi Paper (Oxford University Press, for the International Institute of Strategic Studies, London, May 2002).

RANA MITTER is University Lecturer in the History and Politics of Modern China at the University of Oxford, and a Fellow of St Cross College. He was previously Lecturer in History at the University of Warwick. His publications include *The Manchurian Myth: Nationalism, Resistance, and Collaboration in Modern China* (Berkeley, 2000).

KALYPSO NICOLAIDIS is University Lecturer at the University of Oxford and a Fellow of St Antony's College. She teaches international relations, international political economy, European integration, and negotiation analysis. She has published on European integration, the World Trade Organization, trade and domestic regulations, negotiation dynamics, international regulatory cooperation and competition, international institutions and eastern Europe, and negotiation theory. Her forthcoming book, *Mutual Recognition Among Nations: Global Lessons from the European Experience*, attempts to draw lessons from European integration for the rest of the world.

JAMES PISCATORI is Fellow of Wadham College and of the Centre for Islamic Studies, University of Oxford. He has also held positions at the University of Wales, Aberystwyth; the Nitze School of Advanced International Studies (SAIS) of the Johns Hopkins University; and the Royal Institute of International Affairs, London. Professor Piscatori has written widely on Islam and international relations. His books include *Islam in a World of Nation-States* (Cambridge University Press, 1986), and, with Dale F. Eickelman, *Muslim Politics* (Princeton University Press, 1996).

SIR ADAM ROBERTS is Montague Burton Professor of International Relations at the University of Oxford, and a Fellow of Balliol College. Previously he held posts in the subject at the London School of Economics and St Antony's College, Oxford. His books include *Nations in Arms: The Theory and Practice of Territorial Defence* (2nd edn, Macmillan, 1986); with Richard Guelff, *Documents on the Laws of War* (3rd edn, Oxford University Press, 2000); and *United Nations, Divided World: The UN's Roles in International Relations* (2nd edn, Oxford University Press, 1993; edited with Benedict Kingsbury). He is a Fellow of the British Academy.

JOHN TOYE was the Director of the Institute of Development Studies at the University of Sussex from 1987 to 1997. He served in Geneva as Director of the Globalization Division of UNCTAD between 1998 and 2000. At present, he is a Visiting Professor at the Department of Economics, University of Oxford, and a Visiting Professorial Fellow of St Antony's College, Oxford. He directs the Centre for the Study of African Economies which is based at St Antony's College. He has published widely on development issues.

NGAIRE WOODS is Fellow in Politics and International Relations at University College, Oxford, and a Senior Research Associate of Oxford's International Development

Centre, Queen Elizabeth House. She is presently completing a book on the politics of the IMF and the World Bank, having recently published *The Political Economy of Globalization* (Macmillan, 2000), *Inequality, Globalization and World Politics* (Oxford University Press, 1999; edited with Andrew Hurrell), *Explaining International Relations since 1945* (Oxford University Press, 1996), and numerous articles on international institutions, globalization, and governance.

Abbreviations

ABIM	Angkatan Belia Islam Malaysia
ABM Treaty	Anti-Ballistic Missile Treaty
ACP	Asia, Caribbean, Pacific
AD	Anti-dumping
ASEAN	Association of Southeast Asian Nations
BIS	Bank for International Settlements
CAO	Compliance Adviser/Ombudsman
CCP	Chinese Communist Party
CIA	Central Intelligence Agency
CPSU	Communist Party of the Soviet Union
CSCE	Conference on Security and Cooperation in Europe
CVD	Countervailing duties
D-G	Director General
DSM	Dispute Settlement Mechanism
DSU	Dispute Settlement Understanding
EC	European Community
EEC	European Economic Community
EU	European Union
G-7	Group of Seven
GATT	General Agreement on Tariffs and Trade
HIPC	Heavily Indebted Poor Countries
IBRD	International Bank for Reconstruction and Development
ICT	International Campaign for Tibet
IDA	International Development Association
IFC	International Finance Corporation
IFIs	International financial institutions
ILO	International Labour Organization
IOC	International Olympic Committee
ITO	International Trade Organization
IMF	International Monetary Fund
INF Treaty	Intermediate-Range Nuclear Forces Treaty
MBC	Middle East Broadcasting Centre
MENA	Middle East and North Africa
Mercosur	Southern Cone Common Market
MIGA	Multilateral Investment Guarantee Agency
NATO	North Atlantic Treaty Organization
NGO	Non-Governmental Organization

NLF	National Liberation Front
PIN	Public information notice
PKI	Partai Komunis Indonesia
PLA	People's Liberation Army
PRC	People's Republic of China
PRSP	Poverty Reduction Strategy Paper
OECD	Organization for Economic Cooperation and Development
OED	Operations Evaluation Department (World Bank)
OSCE	Organization for Security and Cooperation in Europe
RSS	Rashtriya Swayamsevak Sangh (India)
SDT	Special and differential treatment
TNGO	Transnational Non-Governmental Organization
UN	United Nations
UNCTAD	United Nations Conference on Trade and Development
UNFICYP	United Nations Peacekeeping Force in Cyprus
UNSC	United Nations Security Council
WTO	World Trade Organization

Introduction

ROSEMARY FOOT

The study and practice of international relations records an unending search for an understanding of the relationship between order and justice. For most of the twentieth century, states and international society depicted the relationship as one of tension or gave priority to a view of order that focused on the minimum conditions for coexistence in a pluralist world where conflict was to be expected and, at best, temporarily contained. The pursuit of justice was seen as secondary, and often as a direct challenge to the maintenance of international order.

Three main developments at the end of that century prompted a reassessment of this position. First, the ending of the Cold War led to a renewed interest in the promotion of a just world order because of the presumed collapse of geopolitical and ideological confrontation, and the perception that certain sets of values concerning the well-being of human beings were now more widely shared. Second came a realization that the range of challenges that face us all required greater acknowledgement that we coexist in a single world and that effective and sustainable solutions to shared problems could not be achieved without a concern for justice. Third, globalization both deepened this sense of ideational and material interdependence, and empowered a new range of voices, including non-governmental and other groups within transnational civil society. Such groups were critical of the existing international order and especially of the negative consequences that globalization had brought in its wake. The murderous assaults on New York and Washington in September 2001 themselves sharpened awareness of the harmful effects of globalization: it became apparent how globalized networks had facilitated the work of a transnational terrorist organization, one that had come to conflate globalization with an unwanted Americanization of that globalized order.

This book represents an exploration of the meaning that this increasingly globalized world holds for questions of order and justice. It acknowledges the valuable and important expansion in the normative writing in international and political theory, and especially in writing on matters of global justice, that has recently taken place,[1] and seeks to make a contribution in this area of scholarship. However, its particular intention is to highlight the relationship between order and justice, to re-examine the connection between two ideas that are so crucial to the practical and theoretical understanding of international relations. Its approach is to show not only how international conceptions of the order/justice relationship have evolved over time, as reflected in major institutional settings and in the perspectives of major states and of other societal groupings, but also how that relationship is understood in the current era.

While this volume acknowledges that the terms of the order/justice debate have come to reflect a greater solidarist consciousness and ambition, and that there has been a revitalization of the liberal vision that order cannot be sustained in the absence of justice, it accepts too that it is essential to explore the depth and scope of this presumed solidarism. This is especially so in light of the evidence of the difficulty of acting on the basis of this more strongly articulated liberal position, and a continuing appreciation that the framing of order and justice remains contested territory. Whereas the early 1990s were a time of optimism and raised expectations with respect to the claims of justice, many have expressed disappointment and frustration at the position reached a decade or so later. Whether we turn to questions of humanitarian intervention, support for secessionist movements, promotion of universal human rights, protection of the global environment, or the maintenance of controls on weapons of mass destruction, 'really existing' responses suggest a thinness in this solidarism that deserves careful investigation.

These investigations are undertaken in the chapters that follow. International economists, historians, and international relations scholars offer views of the world from the perspective of countries or cultural and religious groupings on which they specialize or from inside the workings of institutions that they have come to understand well. The state-based essays take seriously national cultural traditions and provide a range of perspectives on order and justice at governmental and non-governmental levels, noting factors and experiences that have contributed to the shaping of those views and the degree of consensus that elite conceptions generate inside and outside of state borders. Those examining international organizations—at the regional EU or at the global level—consider whether these institutions, in their provision of a platform for normative debate or as producers of certain outcomes in world politics, have mediated successfully between these two concepts or have merely underscored the areas of disagreement on values and the consequences that flow from an unequal distribution of power in international society.

Since our approach requires no imposition of a single definition of order or justice on our contributors, the essays illustrate different, sometimes conflicting, conceptions. Several of the perspectives uncover the continuing attraction

---

[1] A number of the most helpful books in this area are contained in our select bibliography.

of traditional ideas of international order: that it should be based on the protection of societal difference and of values associated with the survival of the state system. Others investigate more expansive conceptions: ones that reflect the normative changes that have fostered a sense that the rights of the individual should take precedence over those of the state. When these chapters explore ideas of global justice, they uncover a variety of different voices including the claims of governments, of groups within particular political communities, and of those whose perspectives are no longer rooted in national territorial traditions. The authors examine both the formal procedural and the distributive notions of justice, together with ideas about what a just world order might look like. In these and other respects, our investigations contribute to an understanding of some of the political puzzles at the core of theoretical writing on these issues. How do we protect the pluralist communities that groups create for themselves and continue to value, while recognizing the justice claims of those beyond our own boundaries? How wide a global consensus on values does there have to be before we embark on the widespread promotion of these values? How can we define the legitimate scope of societal difference in the presence of universalizing processes? And who is the 'we' who is doing the recognizing, the promoting, and the defining?[2]

As suggested already, particular features associated with the last decade of the twentieth century have prompted us to revisit a relationship that has been of concern, at least in Western provenance, since the time of ancient Athens.[3] An important conjunction of processes and systemic change has served to give this topic a centrality that it has not enjoyed for some time.[4] The majority of the essays, however, underscore the importance of the insights that derive from a long historical treatment of the order/justice relationship. They recognize that historical experiences have been powerful in conditioning contemporary responses to notions of order and justice. The formative period of many modern states involved violence at the hands of both internal and external forces which often led to a premium being placed on order and on hierarchical structures as forms of control. For states that had undergone colonial or semi-colonial rule, it mattered a great deal that they reach a position where they could embrace those features of the Westphalian state system that enhanced their ability to maintain sovereign autonomy. China, India, Japan, and Turkey, among others, in earlier eras and in reference to what Hedley Bull described as their

---

[2] Andrew Hurrell's chapter is particularly relevant to an exploration of these questions. See too his 'Norms and Ethics in International Relations' in Walter Carlsnaes, Thomas Risse, and Beth Simmons (eds), *Handbook of International Relations* (London: Sage, 2002), esp. 147.

[3] It is notable that three of our authors—Kanti Bajpai on India, Neil MacFarlane on Russia, and Rana Mitter on China—point to the absence of a significant body of conceptual literature in these three societies on the relationship between international order and justice.

[4] For a valuable elaboration of ways to think about this conjunction see Ian Clark, *The Post-Cold War Order: The Spoils of Peace* (Oxford: Oxford University Press, 2001).

'badges of ... inferior status' demanded the renegotiation of unequal treaties, the removal of extra-territoriality, the opportunity for self-determination, and the ending of white supremacy.[5] The UN Charter's constraints on the use of force except in self-defence, and its strengthening of the principles of non-intervention and sovereign equality, were enormously attractive to states that perceived themselves as past victims of a wholly unjust world order. Inevitably, these ideas influence their current responses to such matters as international involvement in human rights issues, economic conditionality, or humanitarian intervention. Useful to them, too, both domestically and internationally, is their ability to make reference to this history of victimhood in order to ward off challenges that they would rather not face in the contemporary era.

Beyond matters of sovereign equality, such states also have a relatively long tradition of seeking justice through the development of a more equal economic order. This too has influenced their approaches to representational and distributional issues associated with the international financial institutions, the trade regime, and the United Nations. In the 1960s developing countries, focusing especially on the divisions between rich and poor countries, and referring directly to the inequalities identified from earlier eras, formed the Group of 77 at the first UN Conference on Trade and Development in 1964. A transfer of wealth via aid programmes was projected as a route to the development of the poor, an outcome that was to reflect the supposed common interests of both the First and the Third Worlds in more equitable development. By the 1970s, this search for consensus had given way to a more assertive formulation for a New International Economic Order that included demands for sovereignty over a state's own natural resources, stable and remunerative primary commodity markets, the regulation of transnational corporation activities, and increased influence in decision-making within the international financial institutions.[6] Decolonizaton had brought in its wake clear demands for distributional justice from rich to poor states, an objective that remains unfulfilled but is of continuing salience. Notably, however, the focus of these and earlier efforts, together with the continuation of the desire to maintain and strengthen the norm of sovereign equality, resulted in rather little concern for how that distribution—or lack of it, as it turned out—might affect impoverished individuals within states.

Weaker states, then, or those which saw themselves as most disadvantaged in the twentieth-century international system, have often been the loudest champions of inter-state justice in the context of a pluralist international order. On the other hand, those concerned with justice for individuals or for

[5] Hedley Bull, 'Justice in International Relations: The 1983 Hagey Lectures (1984)', in Kai Alderson and Andrew Hurrell (eds), *Hedley Bull on International Society* (Basingstoke: Macmillan, 2000), 209–11.

[6] Marc A. Williams, *International Economic Organisations and the Third World* (Hemel Hempstead: Harvester/Wheatsheaf, 1994).

minority groups often found their strongest sources of support in the industrialized world, as a result of the hold of liberalism as well as of the spillover of the demands made by political movements in the West calling for the removal of various sources of discrimination in their own societies. Arguments emanating from the women's movement, for example, came to make their mark on international aid policies in response to evidence that women's roles in development had been made invisible and aid programmes were failing to acknowledge that women often played the primary part in production.[7] Later, criticism turned to the differential impact that the World Bank and International Monetary Fund's (IMF's) structural adjustment programmes were having on women. This arose from the fact that it was predominantly females who were forced to take action to compensate for a reduced state role in such areas as education and health care.

The turn of attention to basic needs provision on the part of aid agencies represented a 1970s shift in thinking about how lending could best contribute to poverty alleviation, but also attested to a concern with the conditions of the most impoverished within societies. Explanations in academic and policy-making circles a decade later to the effect that policy failures owed much to the presence of kleptocratic or inefficient government rather than to the existence of structural barriers within the world economy further sharpened the focus on internal state institutions. The weakening of the Third World coalition itself added to this move away from international explanations as the basis for understanding the continuing poverty in the developing world. Combined with the orthodoxies of deregulation, privatization, and liberalization promoted during the Reagan-Thatcher era, these developments bolstered the idea that individual states should adopt the policies and establish the institutions that had brought such signal success in the developed world. As Ngaire Woods has put it: 'The shift in the argument about inequality from "structural barriers" to "policy choices" removed inequality from the realm of international politics and cast it instead into that of economics and public administration.'[8] The debate about order and justice and redistribution of wealth among states had been transformed in such a way as to give priority to the investigation of domestic, not global, conditions and towards ideas of internal 'good governance'. The stage had been set for a normative shift in which conditions within states and the experience of individuals and groups within particular societies had begun to attract greater attention.

Nevertheless, a normative development of this kind still had to be consolidated in the 1980s and the debates on economic justice outlined above were

---

[7] Ester Boserup was a pioneer in this field. See her book first published in 1970, *Woman's Role in Economic Development* (London: Earthscan, 1989).

[8] Ngaire Woods, 'Order, Globalization, and Inequality in World Politics', in Andrew Hurrell and Ngaire Woods (eds), *Inequality, Globalization, and World Politics* (Oxford: Oxford University Press, 1999), 15.

not typically the prime focus of international attention during the Cold War. Despite an increased concern with domestic economic practices and with the protection of the rights of minorities and of those individuals whose human rights were being abused, these matters were not consistently at centre stage— or, when they were, this predominantly reflected Cold War rivalries. During these decades, such rivalries had heavily conditioned the discussion of justice at the international level. In a world where political alignments were seen in zero-sum terms, preferential economic and political treatment had been directed to states that added strategic weight to one side or the other in the bipolar system, not to those who treated their domestic populations reasonably well. Important too was that the Cold War was primarily projected as a battle for the geopolitical survival of the state system in a nuclear-armed world. This was supposedly the 'high politics' of the era, whereas negotiation of trade rules or assistance packages was apparently 'low politics', whose successful outcomes primarily depended on the skills of those who managed the geostrategic order.

International order was bound up with the pursuit of stability and pre-dictability, setting up a disjunction between words and deeds particularly— though not solely—in the United States and former Soviet Union. As John Gaddis shows below, America defined itself as anti-colonial and in favour of self-determination, yet was frequently unwilling to risk supporting a national liberation movement that might draw inspiration from Marxist ideas. US administrations notoriously carried this even to the point where they would associate themselves with some of the most heinous agents of injustice. The European Community played its role in reinforcing the distinction between its version of stable and peaceful order in the western part of the continent and that prevailing in the Soviet-occupied, relatively impoverished east. In the former Soviet Union, too, as well as in China, despite a rhetorical commitment to revolution and national liberation, rather few practical attempts were made to upset the international order. Their levels of commitment to the Third World and to the international justice agenda tended to be connected to the state of the relationship with the US, or—after Sino-Soviet rivalry manifested itself— to the condition of that particular dyad. Thus, international order during the Cold War was projected as though it was somehow prior to justice; other social goals depended for their achievement on the establishment of stable political arrangements, and order became a goal in its own right.

1. ORDER AND JUSTICE IN THE POST-COLD WAR ERA

This sense of victimhood and desire for restitution in developing countries, and the beliefs that state-centric orders had provided a level of protection for many of the weaker and newer states and that balance of power mechanisms had placed some constraints on expansionist foreign policies, were attitudes that many held at the end of the Cold War era; and they have retained their attraction as understandings and principles in large parts of international society at the start of the twenty-first century. Nevertheless, alongside this desire to hold on to past principles associated with the institutions of the inter-state system, opportunities for reform and improvement also presented themselves. A concern to remove the deformities of those earlier times—such as structural inequalities in power, failures of popular representation, and the like—fuelled a series of expectations pointing in a liberal direction.

As noted earlier, the ending of the Cold War prompted many of these expectations and accelerated certain normative and material processes already under way, which had themselves encouraged a new exploration of the order/justice connection. The globalization of world order focused attention on the rise of issues beyond the capacity of the state to regulate on its own, and on the deepening and expansion of global norms in fields such as human rights, the environment, or economics. It also empowered a new range of voices, operating both domestically and transnationally. Assisted by the communications revolution, itself a crucial part of the globalization process, these new actors were able to put particular order/justice questions on the global agenda and even to produce political outcomes.

For many practitioners and normative theorists in international relations, these developments showed that a broader consensus in values had finally come into being, leading to a rise in optimism about what could be achieved in a world that had seen the end to the old ideological East-West division. Without the conditioning effect of the Cold War threat, the early 1990s seemed to be a period when issues other than those that had defined East-West relations could come to the fore for examination and possible resolution. The Gulf War coalition, UN Security Council unanimity, and a UN that was far more active in the management of peace and security than at any other period after 1945 were concrete manifestations of the significance of global structural change. Moves towards nuclear disarmament and further constraints on nuclear testing suggested that these most destructive of weapons could be removed from the international scene. The apparent triumph of the Western economic and political systems, together with the removal of the need to support undemocratic regimes as a short-term means of protecting local or regional security orders, further promoted the sense of a global consensus behind the pursuit of economic and political liberalism. A just world order from the perspective of powerful Western states or the international financial institutions (IFIs) such as the World Bank and the IMF came to be projected as attainable if liberal goals were pursued. The breakup of such states as the former Soviet Union or Yugoslavia reinforced the connection between self-determination and principles of justice. Only later would there be a reappraisal of the consequences for international order of moves in these directions.

The second development roughly coincident with the ending of the Cold War, tugging matters in a less optimistic direction, reflected a realization that progressively more porous state boundaries could have negative consequences. There was a perception, too, that states had become less able to cope with the myriad and complex problems that faced humankind. Globalization might be bringing some benefits but it was recognized to be increasing the scale of 'transnational harm',[9] whether we turned our attention to environmental issues, forced migration, transnational terrorism, organized crime, or the inequalities that the drive for economic liberalization and structural adjustment programmes were exacerbating.

If these processes were responsible for blurring the border between the domestic and the international, then what was undercut too were the arguments that justice could be sought only inside state borders; that international order and the inter-state system depended for their survival on the recognition of the value of protecting the sovereign status of diverse political communities through norms such as non-intervention and non-interference. Particular sets of justice claims soon arose as a result of the transnational qualities associated with such issue areas. Pressures to put in place regulatory arrangements that would reduce the areas of harm, or to agree an equitable arrangement for sharing the burdens of repair, increasingly shaped political action. Multilateral institutional cooperation became viewed by many as the most sensible way forward, prompting in at least one area of the world, as the chapter on the European Union (EU) shows, a discourse that emphasized EU experience in resolving the tensions associated with traditional state norms and in dealing with aspects of transnational harm inside the Union. The EU, then, could be a positive model for those beyond institutionalized Europe's boundaries as a body that had grappled with several difficult transnational issues.

The triumph of economic liberalism and the expanded remit of international organizations, like the effects of transnational harm, were developments that had more impact on the weaker states than on the strong. The IFIs, beginning in the 1980s, and the move from the GATT to the World Trade Organization (WTO) extended the reach of these bodies into the policy-making realm of the domestic societies with which they interacted, re-invigorating a sense of victimhood and inequality of treatment. As John Toye states, unlike the GATT, which did not request members to change any of their existing domestic legislation, the WTO requires domestic law to be brought into conformity with its rules. The WTO, moreover, makes regulations across a broad agenda in

---

[9] The phrase is used in Andrew Linklater, 'The Evolving Spheres of International Justice', *International Affairs*, 75 (1999), 474.

political settings where there are real disparities in negotiating strength and political and economic power, and unequal access to information and specialist advice during the conduct of complex trade negotiations. In bodies such as the World Bank and IMF, the performance criteria on which loans are conditioned have increased threefold or fourfold between the 1980s and 1990s. Good governance, deregulation, and structural adjustment programmes have deepened the level of intrusiveness in domestic societies, Ngaire Woods notes in her chapter, raising serious questions about the accountability of bodies that are not fully representative of their memberships or transparent in their decision-making procedures.

This questioning of the democratic deficit of global institutions goes well beyond a focus on those in the economic area, although it is a matter that is felt particularly keenly there. UN Security Council reform has been on the agenda for the last decade because of the possibilities for change in membership of the Council that appeared to have opened up with the ending of the Cold War. Of significance too, however, has been the development of a more activist UN in this period which, for many states without much political clout or which have not fully consolidated the process of state-building, has raised fears of an attack on state sovereignty from yet another direction. There are some signs, as Adam Roberts's chapter details, that the tensions between order and justice evident in the articles of the UN Charter and that, in the past, tended to accord priority to a state-based system of order have given way to a concern with individual justice, to support for humanitarian intervention in response to gross violations of human rights, and most recently to a concern with the promotion of democracy. Human rights law and the laws of war have prompted moves away from an international body of rules that focuses on the legal personality of the state to what has been described as 'world law' less closely tied to state consent, and which reflects a concern for individual justice in a world society of people.[10] The dilemma here, Andrew Hurrell contends in his chapter, is that these progressive moves are hobbled because they are promoted within institutions that still reflect hierarchy and difference, and are made on the basis of a still fragile solidarism.

Human rights, the environment, the accountability of institutions, among other matters that impinge on order and justice questions, owe their prominence in part to the concerns that state governments have been articulating, but also to the activities of non-state bodies. Undoubtedly, some political elites in the weaker states are disturbed about threats to state sovereignty, and it is this concern that has prompted their intervention in the justice-order debate. Some find themselves directly challenged by norms connected with

[10] David Armstrong, 'Law, Justice and the Idea of a World Society', *International Affairs*, 75 (1999), 547.

popular sovereignty and by the claims of ethnic or religious groups who have promoted their aims of increased autonomy or self-determination.

Beyond the state elites, however, social movements, NGOs—domestic and transnational—and influential individuals have also gained a role in the discourse at a level that would not have been thought possible in earlier decades. Such groups, using the techniques of networking that the technological revolution in the communications field has made possible, as well as the access that some states and organizations have offered for the presentation of their positions, have pushed their demands for the just resolution of issues that they hold dear. Sometimes they have done this in disregard of the justice claims of others or of the consequences for world order. They have brought issues relating to labour conditions, poverty alleviation, ecological sustainability, gender equity, good governance, and debt relief to the attention of powerful multilateral bodies and individual governments.[11] Religious and cultural groupings have also had an impact and have been equally successful in using the communications revolution to further their causes. Neo-liberals in India, Kanti Bajpai argues, see the growth in power of such non-state actors as inevitable in a globalizing world and as a major source of conflict in the contemporary global system. James Piscatori also points to the tension that can arise when new voices are granted authority. Although the effects of globalization are widely criticized in Muslim countries, it has also brought forth opportunities for resistance and constructed new bases of identity relating not to geography or territory but to religion and culture. The voices of counter-elites, though often disharmonious, are being heard and are setting the political agendas in the Islamic world and well beyond it, challenging intra- and inter-state orders in their calls for a redistribution of power or forms of political representation within countries as well as between them.

Although international NGOs have been around for decades and working in a diverse range of fields, their numbers have increased several-fold since 1945. Approximately half of all international social change organizations work on the three issues of human rights, women's rights, and the environment; and these, in particular, have grown in number.[12] The World Social Forum has now become an established and regular feature of international life and an increasingly authoritative source of ideas about how economic inequalities should be

---

[11] Robert O'Brien, Anne Marie Goetz, Jan Aart Scholte, and Marc Williams, *Contesting Global Governance: Multilateral Economic Institutions and Global Social Movements* (Cambridge: Cambridge University Press, 2000).

[12] Human Rights INGOs numbered 79 in 1983 and 168 in 1993; women's rights organizations were 25 in number in 1983 and 61 a decade later, and the environmental groups have increased from 26 to 90 over the same period. Margaret E. Keck and Kathryn Sikkink, *Activists Beyond Borders: Advocacy Networks in International Politics* (Ithaca, NY: Cornell University Press, 1998), Table 1, 11.

addressed. Such groups can have influence in a variety of ways: defining the issue and setting the agenda; influencing the discursive position of states and international organizations; affecting institutional procedures; bringing about policy change in the bodies that they are targeting; and sometimes actually changing behaviour on the ground.[13] Woods shows below that NGOs now receive more information from, and better access to, the IMF and World Bank than ever before, allowing some among them to exercise informal power and influence, a development that appears to represent a major contribution to international justice. However, alongside the concerns expressed about the accountability and legitimacy of the IFIs, similar questions have been raised about the NGOs themselves. Is it enough to view them as assets in the area of deliberative democracy, or does their representation function require their leaders to be chosen on the basis of open, legitimate, rules in an era when their power has been enhanced?

Justice claims, then, are coming from governments that perceive themselves to be disadvantaged, from official policy-making bodies that are receptive to pressures from non-state actors, from marginalized groups and individuals within world politics, and from those acting on the behalf of those so disadvantaged. Global norms that impinge upon both order and justice are being deepened and created by state and non-state groupings. Whether this adds up to a broad-based consensus on values, however, or even whether the body of claimants is pushing in parallel directions, has to be questioned. The profile of justice issues has certainly been raised, but what the promotion of justice requires, and how order and justice are to be related, remain problematic.

2. THE RELATIONSHIP BETWEEN ORDER AND JUSTICE

We have imposed no single definition of order or justice on those that are writing the chapters in this volume because we are sensitive to the argument that 'order and peace to one group of nations may be perceived differently by another'[14] and because of our desire to explore whether there is much depth to the notion of a greater sharing of normative understandings in a global society. Hedley Bull clearly has influenced some of our authors' discussions of order and justice because of the significance of his reflections on state-based orders, his focus on the expansion of international society, and exploration of

---

[13] Keck and Sikkink, *Activists Beyond Borders*, 25.
[14] T.V. Paul and John A. Hall, *International Order and the Future of World Politics* (Cambridge: Cambridge University Press, 1999), 2.

the so-called 'Revolt Against the West'.[15] For Bull, order related to the
security of life against violence, the sanctity of promises, and the stability of
possession.[16] Important too is Bull's distinction between world order and
international order. As he put it in the 1983 Hagey Lectures, 'the rights and
benefits to which justice has to be done in the international community are not
simply those of states and nations, but those of individual persons throughout
the world as a whole … It is a profound change in our perception of this matter that in the second half of the twentieth century the question of justice concerns what is due not only to states and nations but to all individual persons
in an imagined community of mankind'.[17] Bull continued to wrestle in the last
years of his life with the relationship between order and justice and with the
question of where to seek justice and how best to extend it to others, in the
context of his belief that we operated within a fragile international society.
Despite variation in perspective deriving from different historical experiences
and cultural settings, Bull seemed to acknowledge that there was an homogenizing process at work leading us in more solidarist directions. It is that
claim that we hope to investigate in the chapters that follow.

Much work in political theory continues to argue that it has to be the state
that attends to the justice claims of its citizens, in part because of that diverse
range of conceptions about what constitutes justice outside of state boundaries.[18] Many continue to argue that attempts to protect individuals and pursue individual justice are disruptive of inter-state order, a position with which
states such as China and Russia strongly agree. Not only is such a pursuit
viewed as potentially disruptive, but also has been depicted as a futile quest
because there is neither a global society nor a global surplus against which
claims for distributive justice can be lodged.[19]

Solidarists on the other hand take on these arguments directly. They contend that it is no longer morally tenable in a world of interdependence to
concentrate only on the interests of those within states and ignore our obligations to the whole of humanity. Individuals rather than states have to be the

---

[15] Important in these connections are H. Bull's *The Anarchical Society* (London: Macmillan,
1977) and H. Bull and A. Watson (eds), *The Expansion of International Society* (Oxford: Oxford
University Press, 1984).

[16] A valuable discussion of Bull's core ideas on order is contained in R. J. Vincent, 'Order in
International Politics', in J. D. B. Miller and R. J. Vincent (eds), *Order and Violence: Hedley
Bull and International Relations* (Oxford: Oxford University Press, 1990).

[17] Bull, 'Justice in International Relations', 220.

[18] See in particular John Rawls, *A Theory of Justice* (London: Belknap Press, 1971) and his
The Law of Peoples (Cambridge, Mass: Harvard University Press, 1999); Michael Walzer,
Spheres of Justice (New York: Basic Books, 1983).

[19] Molly Cochran elaborates upon these arguments in *Normative Theory in International
Relations: A Pragmatic Approach* (Cambridge: Cambridge University Press, 1999), Ch. 1.

starting point in the search for global justice.[20] Yet, as Andrew Hurrell argues below, such a formulation and the expectation of consensus around a coherent set of political and economic ideas plays down the extent to which a conflict of values still pertains in the global system. It neglects too the persistence of the perception that inequalities in power are behind these attempts to promote what has essentially been a liberal project at the end of the twentieth century and beyond, with its emphasis on notions of political legitimacy, self-determination, human rights, and relative avoidance of action to reduce global poverty. It is significant, for example, that all four of the Indian perspectives on order and justice laid out in Bajpai's chapter, though they are in disagreement on many matters, still retain a common suspicion of the most powerful actors in the global system. The emergence of the US as sole superpower, with a margin of superiority in all the underlying aspects of power—economic, military, technological, and geopolitical—over all the other major states combined,[21] has aggravated this sense of suspicion and imposition. As Chris Brown has put it, it has not been easy to differentiate between 'the impact on the world system of a victorious liberal internationalism and that of hegemonic America'.[22] Radical Islamists, Piscatori shows, certainly do not make that distinction. As Hurrell rightly reminds us, although power may be important to the advancement of justice claims, used in particular ways and overly concentrated it can also serve to undermine their legitimacy.

In the empirical investigations that follow Hurrell's exposure of the particular kinds of tension that surround justice claims, we find there are indeed different conceptions of order and justice still extant. Perhaps the narrowest—or most egoistic—conceptions of a just order are presented in the chapters by Rana Mitter and Neil MacFarlane. Mitter notes a Chinese preoccupation with establishing a strong country as a way to create order, and a desire as a next step to establish a Chinese-dominated Asian order. Close to this perspective is that of Kanti Bajpai's *Hindutvas* and their concern to achieve recognition of India as a great civilization-state as the basis for domestic and world order. It appears that the Chinese leadership has little interest in determining an overall framework of international order, but does remain concerned with shoring up orderly relations among states. Similarly, Neil MacFarlane, writing on Russia, notes a primary preoccupation with the re-establishment of order within the country as a reaction to domestic chaos and regional instability.

---

[20] See Charles Beitz, *Political Theory and International Relations* (Princeton: Princeton University Press, 1979).

[21] William C. Wohlforth, 'The Stability of a Unipolar World', *International Security*, 24/1 (1999).

[22] Chris Brown, 'History Ends, Worlds Collide', *Review of International Studies*, 25 (Special Issue, December 1999), 47.

As with the Chinese, Russians have a strong statist and pluralist conception of order: their views are egoistic rather than solidarist.

Neither Mitter nor MacFarlane views the Chinese and Russian espousal of Marxism-Leninism, or of rhetoric and sometimes behaviour that demonstrated commitment to a world socialist revolution, as significant in the shaping of their true attitudes to order and justice—even though their ideologies contained claims about substantive justice and represented a denial of the legitimacy of the Westphalian system. However, although we must acknowledge their self-centred perspective, when it came to the actual advancement of revolution the solidarist ideas their leaders espoused were important to some of the normative changes identified at the start of this Introduction. As David Armstrong has written, whatever Moscow's motives might have been, its espousal of the causes of anti-colonialism, the rights of the labour movement, opposition to racism, and support for feminist issues had an impact on international understandings of appropriate behaviour.[23] It generated and regenerated world attention to the injustices of the prevailing international order, forcing a response from the powerful and providing an opening for the weak.

Other chapters highlight state perspectives that are similar but not identical to those associated with Russia and China. Some reflect a less defensive stance and a more overtly flexible approach to the connection between particular forms of international and domestic orders. In the chapter on the Islamic world, for example, Piscatori argues that, for both pragmatic and normative reasons, many of the governing elites in this world perceive themselves as having adapted to, and as having derived benefit from, the ordering principles of the modern international society of states. Their tendency is to try to hold on to these ordering principles, especially in light of a growing challenge from radical Islamist groups totally dismissive of the current domestic and international orders. Nehruvians too are internationalist in their outlook and have found the Westphalian order to be compatible with their interests, even capable of improvement through the space it has provided for the articulation of the concept of non-alignment. Within the EU, there remains a powerfully articulated position that the survival and promotion of the state system should remain paramount, that justice is attainable only inside state or state-like borders, a conclusion which leads to the necessity for preserving traditional Westphalian norms. In this view, the EU is perceived as a buffer between the world within and that without.

---

[23] David Armstrong, *Revolution and World Order: The Revolutionary State in International Society* (Oxford: Oxford University Press, 1993), 156. Armstrong also notes that, in support of MacFarlane's argument, 'to protect their own power, their revolution, and as they saw it, the future of socialism, they had also to protect a doctrinal paradox: a revolution based upon an ideology that represented itself as the antithesis of the state had taken the concrete form of a state'. (120). Chinese leaders after 1949 soon faced the same paradox and eventually adopted similar tactics.

This pluralist or traditional conception is, however, challenged by more cosmopolitan understandings. An alternative European perspective, for example, has also been articulated: what our authors refer to as the 'post-national' paradigm which perceives a seamlessness between a just order within the EU space and the world community beyond it, and which claims that there should be no radical separation between these two spaces, only a difference in the levels of uncertainty and challenge that have to be faced. The chapters on the US and the UN suggest that solidarist ideas have come to have some purchase within these bodies too. The US, long concerned to maintain a state-based order that has served it well, nevertheless since the late 1970s has become more strongly committed to the promotion of international justice as it defines it. America found itself in the later stages of the Cold War and especially in the post-Cold War era in a position to pay more attention to certain specific justice claims, predominantly, as John Gaddis's chapter shows, to claims connected with self-determination and individual liberty. For Gaddis, the US-led NATO bombing of Serbia represented an implied promise that the US from then on would more likely come to the active assistance of those who were not just experiencing aggression but were also being brutalized at the hands of their own governments.

UN activism in the post-Cold War era similarly suggested a heightened international concern with what was going on inside the boundaries of states and a significant weakening of the domestic-external divide. In UN Secretary-General Kofi Annan's words, there was a need to make clear that in our contemporary reading of the UN Charter we were 'more than ever conscious that its aim is to protect individual human beings, not to protect those who abuse them' and that state sovereignty was being redefined to encompass the idea of individual sovereignty.[24] Adam Roberts illuminates this in noting the considerable number of cases of multilateral intervention in the period since the early 1990s in which humanitarian motives have been cited.[25] It is a perspective that Mahatma Gandhi would presumably have applauded—if it had been aligned with pacifist practices—given what Bajpai describes as his focus on the plight of individuals and concern for the emancipation of all humanity.

But solidarism of this kind which involves the merging of the domestic and the external realms does provoke understandable concerns. Woods's chapter on the major financial institutions shows how their enhanced attention to the conditions inside state boundaries has in turn given rise to demands for making these institutions more just in their procedural arrangements: more transparent, more participatory, and more accountable. The breach in the norm

[24] UN documents, A/54/PV/8, 22 September 1999.
[25] For further discussion of this see Nicholas J. Wheeler, *Saving Strangers: Humanitarian Intervention in International Society* (Oxford: Oxford University Press, 2000).

of non-interference and in favour of humanitarian intervention is partly at the root of developing country calls for the reform of the UN Security Council and for the suggestion that it too should be more representative of the larger membership. WTO intrusiveness provokes similar reactions and criticisms of the kind that John Toye outlines in his chapter. Whatever the actual results of the policies such bodies have adopted, these chapters remind us that they are being promoted on the basis of a presumed connection between order and justice. Good governance—involving economic, political, and legal criteria— is projected as capable of empowering the weak against corrupt, unrepresentative, and inefficient government, contributing to a level of justice for individuals that enhances world order. However, those that are on the receiving end of such policies do not readily interpret them in quite this way.

Such criticisms of powerful state-based institutions suggest that a trend that gives greater weight to the claims of justice and which emphasizes the connections of justice to order has not necessarily helped resolve how that connection should be made. The liberal position that justice has to be realized in a context of order and that order is best realized in meeting the demands for justice, and that paths to the reconciliation of the two have to be sought and can be found, often seems to be both too demanding and too vague.[26] In practice, such a reconciliation is difficult to bring about at the global level because of a conflict in priorities. For China and Russia, their governments believe this reconciliation involves recognition of their victim status and the need for affirmative action to allow them to claim a full and proper place in an international society of states. They both focus on justice for states and see promotion of changes in the current distribution of power in their favour as the key goal. Indian perspectives similarly reflect a desire for reducing the inequalities in state power, although they less often resort to the notion of past victim status as a means of legitimizing this demand. These countries are for engagement with major actors and the achievement of the power attributes that would allow them to claim a full place in international society.

In some Islamic societies, however, what seems to be emerging is something rather more complex and variegated: two, potentially or actually, conflicting axes—the territorial axis of order and the governance axis of justice—with different priorities being accorded to each by elites and counter-elites. And though the US might have moved more energetically in recent years to tip the balance in favour of justice, such a move seems more than capable of being re-examined—even reversed—in the more constrained political circumstances of post-11 September which has revealed in the starkest of forms US dilemmas when faced with order/justice questions.

---

[26] This is Bull's depiction of the liberal position in 'Justice in International Relations', 227.

In the Chinese and Russian cases, and in dominant Indian views—and even beyond these three—there appears, therefore, to be a privileged place for the state and for the role of great powers in the management of order, provided each of these polities is a member of that great power concert. Justice can be attended to only in these circumstances of order, and normative change has to be resisted where it can be seen as an attack on this inter-state order. They are united in their suspicions that the most powerful Western states will flout Westphalian norms in pursuit of their special interests, and will use international law and organization as tools of those interests. Similarly distrustful of the NGO, they tend to view such groupings as bodies either to be marginalized as much as possible or to be accommodated and co-opted. But, as many of the other chapters show—a perspective with which neo-liberals in India would agree—the NGO in its transnational and domestic forms is an established part of the contemporary landscape and plays an influential role in helping to keep the focus on justice claims. And, as Hurrell argues, a variety of new forces have led to the promotion of a much broader range of values than just those associated with the survival of the state system and great power management of the international order. These forces have to be acknowledged and require adaptation, an uncomfortable prospect for those who see themselves predominantly as lacking a sustained role in shaping the modern global system.

3. CHAPTER OUTLINES

The following ten chapters explore the connection between order and justice from several vantage points. In the first chapter, Andrew Hurrell enhances our conceptual understanding of order and justice and notes the abiding tensions inherent in that relationship. He takes issue with a traditional approach that has tried to separate order from justice and shows how the two are in fact inextricably intertwined whatever one's theoretical starting point. He also argues that the conditions of global social justice have been irrevocably changed by a wide range of social, political, economic, and technological forces. These changes make a retreat to pluralism—both in ways of thinking about justice and to the pluralist state-based model—impossible, which makes both morally compelling, but also materially necessary, the promotion of a much broader range of goals and values. Yet his conclusion is one that underlines the complexity of contemporary global society. Solidarist consciousness has to coexist with many aspects of the old Westphalian order: moves towards global justice are constrained because they bump up against a global political order that remains heavily structured around inherited pluralist mechanisms that are deformed by various sets of inequalities—of capacity, leadership, and advantage.

We turn next to an examination of how the order/justice issue is dealt with in particular institutional or sectoral contexts. In his chapter, Adam Roberts asks whether the UN and its members have achieved a substantive consensus on the content of international justice. He also explores how apparent clashes between order and justice have been addressed when they have arisen within a UN framework, which takes him into a discussion of state sovereignty and its breach in those cases where a state is deemed to be denying justice to those within its borders. His conclusions, which are specific to the UN, support the more general ones arrived at by Hurrell. Roberts argues that the underlying tension evident in the UN Charter between rules designed to bolster inter-state stability and those aimed at the promotion of justice persist. He also notes that the timing and location of interventions have not been determined by abstract considerations of justice but by a range of political and military factors. Despite the presence of such tensions in the UN's Charter and workings, he argues that the pursuit of various justice issues has long been seen as a legitimate part of UN activities and as one contribution the organization can make and has made to international order. UN interest in justice areas will be maintained, therefore, but controversy will continue to be generated about how it first selects, develops, and then pursues certain justice claims.

Ngaire Woods develops the order/justice discussion through a focus primarily on procedural justice within the international financial institutions. She argues that the processes adopted by these institutions are central to the debate about global economic justice, and thus it is essential to explore how these bodies make decisions and implement them. Her findings suggest that, notwithstanding recent, important, institutional reforms that have enhanced transparency and made the IFIs more open to a new range of 'stakeholders', these measures can address only in a limited fashion the core deficit in representation and accountability at the heart of these bodies. Addressing this deficit has been made more urgent by the IFIs' greater levels of intrusion into areas previously considered taboo, such as good governance, the rule of law, judicial reform, corruption, and corporate governance. Woods's prescriptions include greater openness in electing or appointing the heads of each organization, improved representation for member states, and further strengthening of internal surveillance mechanisms. However, she also cautions that the difficulties in reaching the goals of accountability and representation within such international organizations should in turn prompt a limitation on the range and scope of the IFIs' activities.

In his chapter on the international trade regime, John Toye places his main emphasis on matters of substantive justice. His general point is that all organizations that have just aims are least successful when the parties involved are unequal in resources or power. In his particular discussion of the trade regime, he argues that the transition from the GATT to the WTO has led to a 'judicialization' of trade cooperation through the WTO's dispute settlement mechanism (DSM). This development is likely to limit the prospects for growth in developing countries because of the trade regime's movement in the direction of preventing individual countries reneging on tariff concessions— under certain pre-specified conditions—to safeguard a domestic industry, as had been permitted under GATT rules. The substantive outcome will ensure, at best, the continuation, possibly even the worsening, of economic inequalities among countries, a state of affairs that will contribute to both disorder and injustice. For Toye, formal justice in the WTO's DSM is at odds with substantive justice since the inequalities of political and economic power between developing and developed countries have not been taken account of during the enactment of supposedly improved procedural rules.

The chapter by Kalypso Nicolaidis and Justine Lacroix represents a bridge between the institutional and the state perspectives on order and justice. It discusses the EU both as a regional organization with distinctive norms and practices and as a grouping of states that reflects particular traditions and views. The authors explore the approach to order and justice as practised both within the EU and externally, and describe two core paradigms which they label the 'national' and the 'post-national' models. The former is recognizably realist and state-centric in approach, even under the condition where allegiances can be said to have shifted to the European level. This paradigm implies that the pursuit of justice is still something that goes on within state or EU boundaries rather than beyond them, and that the focus of external behaviour should be the promotion of order via traditional power-political means and for traditional state-based normative ends. The post-national paradigm, however, reflects a cosmopolitan understanding of global society and behaviour that makes no separation between a European community of fate and a universal community of fate. The EU in this model can be viewed as a laboratory that faces and sometimes resolves problems that are the same as or similar to those that the world as a whole faces: refugees, socio-ethnic tensions, economic inequalities, and so on. This civic rather than military experience gives Europe the institutional and substantive knowledge that can legitimize actions that promote a global justice agenda. The authors subject this particular model to a test in three issue areas, searching for evidence of consistency in the way such issues are dealt with internally as well as externally. They do not find this consistency, leading to the conclusion that, while the EU may have the capacity to shape an order/justice agenda beyond its borders, its members have not yet agreed what that agenda should be.

The next chapters deal with national and cultural or religious conceptions of international order and justice. John Gaddis focuses on US grappling with the order/justice dilemma throughout the twentieth century. In practice, he states, the demands of order have superseded justice claims from the time of the administration of Theodore Roosevelt to the era of Richard M. Nixon. The turning point occurred in the wake of the 1975 Helsinki conference which led

the Carter and Reagan administrations to consider treating justice claims on a
par with concerns about order. The post-Cold War era took the US along a path
where it was willing to destabilize international order in the name of justice,
but Gaddis argues that it was not long before the over-optimistic expectations
that had been at the root of such a policy were dashed. Nevertheless, he notes
how difficult it is even in the current struggle against terrorism for the US to
disentangle order from justice, although Washington would prefer to pay
greater attention to the former rather than to the latter. Gaddis outlines what
he sees as two alternative strategies for dealing with the complexities that have
arisen as a result of trying to promote humane governance. The first is an
inside-out strategy that uses various tools of diplomacy in order to transform
those who need to improve their forms of governance; the second, alternative
strategy, to be used with those where reconciliation and transformation are
less likely, would be an outside-in model that seeks justice by a direct attack
on the legitimacy of the recalcitrant state in the expectation of outright surrender. Deciding upon the more appropriate approach is no easy task, but
Gaddis argues that, for political outcomes to be sustained and order and justice issues to be addressed, US hegemony needs to be coupled with legitimacy,
consent, and a modesty of aims.

Next, Neil MacFarlane argues that Russian perspectives on order and
justice—implicit rather than overtly articulated—are deeply rooted and are
basically inconsistent with liberal thinking. They strongly reflect the country's
geographical and historical experiences, which include violence at the hands
of external forces from both east and west and frequent disappointment of
claims to the equality of the Russian state in an emerging European international society. Somewhat paradoxically, there has also been a preference to
remain isolated from an international society that might erode Russian culture
or the state's capacity to control its citizens. The former Soviet Union's commitment to world proletarian revolution—the ultimate solidarist end involving a redistribution of wealth and power—soon waned, he states, and was
made subordinate to the perceived dictates of the state's and its leadership's
foreign policy. Similar preoccupations underpinned its embrace of national
self-determination or decolonization. Despite a brief solidarist flowering
during the Gorbachev era, leaders have remained wedded to the promotion of
a state-based order in which multipolarity prevails, multilateralism is to be
avoided, and the Russian loss of status is recovered along with its material
power. Russian leaders remain concerned with inter-state justice in the
context of a re-established domestic and Russian-led regional order, and
resistant to the idea of humanitarian intervention and the global promotion of
human rights.

Rana Mitter's chapter illustrates some of the same preoccupations as those
outlined in the chapter on Russia. He demonstrates that, until the late Qing,

the concepts of international order and justice were quite alien to China's imperial rulers. Since that time and through the Nationalist and Communist eras, however, China has perceived itself to be, and often projected itself as, the victim in an unjust world of aggressive and powerful states, particularly as it became a target of Western-led interventionist strategies. The unjust order imposed on China in the nineteenth and early twentieth centuries caused many among the modernizing elite to believe in a form of Social Darwinism. This belief provided a framework to understand why some states were in a position to impose the rules of the game while others had those rules imposed upon them. Contemporary Chinese perceptions of a just international order have been shaped by such past thinking, and encompass a strong element of restitution: China does not regard international society as a neutral forum and sees itself as having been denied its rightful place throughout its history as a modern state. Its leaders value power for its contribution to order; and justice claims, above all, start with the Chinese state itself rather than with the needs of a broader global community. Despite its current use of the language of international engagement, like Russia, it remains pluralist in outlook, resistant to the promotion of norms perceived as intruding in domestic affairs or which serve to attenuate the rights of states.

Unlike in China and Russia, however, where there has been considerable continuity of view between past and contemporary eras regarding order and justice, India has seen three or four dominant traditions of thought. The Nehruvian internationalists, Kanti Bajpai states, have proposed a 'Westphalia plus' system of order, where the 'plus' includes the concept of non-alignment and thus a role for weaker states in the building of order. The cosmopolitan Gandhians, on the other hand, emphasize the need to establish a just world order and focus on non-violent relations among individuals and other societal groupings as the moral basis of world society. The *Hindutvas*, or proponents of political Hinduism, accept the primacy of the inter-state system and perceive India's emancipatory struggle as being incomplete both domestically and internationally. They believe that the superiority of Hindu principles and practices will eventually become evident, leading to a 'Hinduized' and just regional or world order. In this regard, therefore, they accept that hierarchy is at the root of domestic and global order, but for them it should be based on the acceptance of the superiority of Hindu culture. A relatively new Indian voice, that of the neo-liberal globalist, perceives an international system that reflects more than anarchical relations among sovereign states. Instead, neo-liberals see international society as increasingly shaped by economic interdependence, they view war as dysfunctional, and believe human security will steadily be given priority over national security. In comparing the four traditions' attitudes towards state sovereignty, the use of force, the utility of rules and institutions, and inequality, Bajpai places these perspectives along a continuum that at one end shows some compatibility with the Westphalian concept of order and justice, and at the other reflects more solidarist interpretations. He also outlines what a just order would look like from the four perspectives and notes that a three-way conversation is taking place on these attributes of order/justice between the Nehruvians, the increasingly influential *Hindutvas*, and the nascent neo-liberals.

If Indians are grappling with the implications of alternative conceptions of order and justice, the Islamic world as a whole, James Piscatori shows in his chapter, shares in that experience. Many Islamic states in recent and earlier eras had found a degree of comfort in accommodating themselves to an international society that recognized sovereign equality and believed that treaties should be adhered to and war avoided. Indeed, for such states the effects of globalization are not all bad either, for it has given them opportunities for the consolidation of state power as state elites have taken advantage of new communications technologies to strengthen their links with their constituencies. However, other effects of globalization have been less benign for such elites. One impact has been to shift allegiances from territorially based political communities to those based on religious or cultural identity, which has undermined commitment to this state-centric international order. Still another has been to amplify the voices of previously marginalized groups, leading to the growth of new critical social movements within and across Islamic countries, many of which attack globalization in terms that reflect criticisms made outside the Muslim world. Some radical Islamists among these groups are seeking nothing less than the overturning of prevailing international and domestic orders as a response to what they see as the widening of inequalities, world domination by an exploitative, aggressive, and militantly secular US, and the manipulation or co-option of Muslim leaders within this Western hegemonic order. The outcome of this varied and complex process is extraordinarily difficult to predict. A prominent feature is, as Piscatori argues, that space has been created for the emergence of a new and possibly transformational Islamic civil society which directs its attention principally to the reform of Muslim societies themselves. This move has led to the promulgation of insistent justice claims, difficult to satisfy on the basis of the current political arrangements.

4. SOLIDARISM UNDER CHALLENGE

The more explicit concern in the post-Cold War era with establishing a just world order may rely on the kinds of social movements referred to in some of the chapters above, and their efforts to keep the issue of justice on the political agenda. It may also rely on the most representative of all the international organizations, the UN, to advance the rhetoric and pursue material actions. Alternatively, it could remain prominent through the actions of bodies such as the EU as it draws on its own experience—both successes and failures—in approaching many of the problems that contribute to global anxiety. But the concern will be sustained too by the self-evident fact that states on their own cannot cope with the many instances of transnational harm that confront us and which underline the weakening of the boundaries between the domestic and external realms. For these reasons, those engaged in the study of global politics, as well as those who have to practise it, will sustain their interest in the relationship between order and justice and will continue to grapple with that relationship in the context of a global system that has gone beyond privileging the concerns of the society of states, yet has not entered into a world society based on a consensus of values.

The evidence drawn from our essays illustrates how difficult the road is of those who seek to find broad-based agreement on the order and justice principles that could inform and underpin world society. Nor do these chapters illustrate wide areas of concurrence on how order and justice are to be related. National political and historical experiences and widely varying levels of development contribute to these different perspectives. The result is that some states try to hold fast to traditional Westphalian norms whereas other formal or informal bodies embrace more revolutionary conceptions that transcend or reject ideas about the state as the site of both order and justice claims. In light of the spectrum of views presented here, therefore, it would be imprudent to claim that liberal visions of order and justice have triumphed over more particularist formulations. This underlines the importance of what Andrew Hurrell has argued: that there is a need to pay attention to and build upon some notion of fair process before we can attend to wider concerns, and especially to process that is rooted in the exercise of legitimate rather than hegemonic power.

Indeed, it is ideas about the distribution and legitimate exercise of power that provide some common ground in the essays that make up this volume. The clearest area where there is some overlap in perspective about a just world order relates to long-articulated concerns about inequalities in all forms of power and its exercise on behalf of a particular and incomplete justice agenda. Different groups representing diverse constituencies will be engaged in articulating this perception, aided in that task by the resources they have at their disposal, the access provided for their views, and the degree of unity in their approach in their separate areas of interest. If the promotion of democracy, human rights, and self-determination has been the focus of attention for some of the powerful voices at the end of the twentieth century, these essays suggest that the privileged position of these ideas has not and will not go unchallenged. Nor does it remain certain that they will maintain that privileged ranking in the future.

1

Order and Justice in International Relations: What is at Stake?

ANDREW HURRELL

John Rawls's famous claim that 'Justice is the first virtue of social institutions' has, when applied to international relations, faced the perennial realist rejoinder that international life has never had very much to do with the pursuit of virtue or of justice.[1] As Gilpin puts it, 'Anarchy is the rule; order, justice, and morality are the exceptions'.[2] This debate has taken different forms at different times but the tension between solutions to the problem of order and solutions to the problem of justice has shaped and structured a very great deal of international thought.[3]

This chapter addresses three questions:

1. In what sorts of ways has the relationship between order and justice been understood within International Relations?
2. Are traditional strategies of reconciling order and justice adequate?
3. If, as will be argued, they are indeed inadequate, how should we think about international justice and the problem of order in a globalized world?

1. TRADITIONAL UNDERSTANDINGS OF ORDER AND JUSTICE

Many analyses of social order, whether in International Relations (Bull) or social theory (Elster), begin with a beguilingly simple distinction.[4] On the one

[1] John Rawls, *A Theory of Justice*, rev. edn (Oxford: Oxford University Press, 1999), 3.

[2] Robert Gilpin, 'The Richness of the Tradition of Political Realism', in Robert O. Keohane (ed.), *Neorealism and Its Critics* (New York: Columbia University Press, 1986), 304.

[3] Martti Koskenniemi, 'The Police in the Temple. Order, Justice and the UN: A Dialectical View', *European Journal of International Law*, 6 (1995), 325–48.

[4] Hedley Bull, *The Anarchical Society: A Study of Order in World Politics*, 2nd edn (Basingstoke: Macmillan, 1985), especially 3–21; Jon Elster, *The Cement of Society: A Study of Social Order* (Cambridge: Cambridge University Press, 1989), 1–16.

hand, social order can be understood in the sense of stable and regular patterns of human behaviour. In this depiction it is contrasted with chaos, instability, or lack of predictability. On the other hand, social order requires the existence of a particular kind of purposive pattern that human agents have infused with meaning, that involves a particular set of goals, objectives, or values, and that leads to a particular outcome. Beguilingly simple because, of course, order as fact and order as value are very hard to disentangle.[5]

If order is to be understood in terms of some purposive pattern, what sorts of purposes, goals, and objectives might be relevant? In 1969, Raymond Aron posed the question of international order in the following manner: 'under what conditions would men [*sic*] (divided in so many ways) be able not merely to avoid destruction, but to live together relatively well in one planet?'[6] For Aron, living 'relatively well' was to be viewed in distinctly minimalist terms. Order was understood as 'the minimum conditions of coexistence' that might obtain in the anarchical system of states. He took states to be the principal agents of order, hence making international order and global order for all practical purposes synonymous. And he proposed a definition of order which deliberately sought to avoid any discussion of shared values or the necessary conditions for the promotion of some shared vision of how global society might ideally be organized.

A few years later Hedley Bull defined order as 'A pattern [in the relations of human individuals or groups] that leads to a particular result, an arrangement of social life such that it promotes certain goals or values'.[7] Although a little more optimistic than Aron, Bull's analysis of these 'certain goals and values' also pointed in a constrained and minimalist direction. As is well known, Bull's study of order in world politics concentrated on the common framework of rules and institutions that had developed within the anarchical society of states and that prescribed patterns of behaviour which sustained the basic goals of

---

[5] There are, of course, many other approaches to the study of order in International Relations. Some analysts, for example, focus less on regular and persistent patterns and on the attitudes of agents towards those patterns and more on the political, economic, or social forces and structures responsible for producing the patterns. We understand the behaviour of the parts by uncovering the logic of the whole and the laws that shape that logic. This approach is captured in many usages of the terms 'the global capitalist order' and 'the liberal post-cold war order'. A further very influential approach seeks to make sense of the immense complexity of global society by identifying the underlying micro-mechanisms and logics that permit cooperation to take place and social order to be created. This interest-driven, rationalist approach has been dominant within institutionalist theory. See, for example, Karol Soltan, Eric M. Uslaner, and Virginia Haulfer (eds), *Institutions and Social Order* (Ann Arbor: University of Michigan Press, 1998).

[6] Raymond Aron, as reported in Stanley Hoffmann, 'Conference Report on The Conditions of World Order', *Daedalus*, 95/2 (1966), 456.

[7] Bull, *The Anarchical Society*, 3–4. See also Stanley Hoffmann's definition: 'the norms, practices, and processes that ensure the satisfaction of the basic needs of the social group in question'. 'Is there an International Order?', in *Janus and Minerva* (Boulder, CO: Westview, 1987), 85.

international social life. It was a necessarily limited and fragile society whose three primary goals were the preservation of the society of states itself, the maintenance of the independence of individual states, and the regulation—but not elimination—of war and violence amongst states and societies.[8]

On this view, inter-state cooperation and international institutions could never be expected to provide a stable and universal peace but only to mitigate the inevitable conflicts that would arise from the existence of a multiplicity of sovereignties. The correct question with regard to the study of world order was not: how might human beings create forms of international society or schemes of international cooperation that embodied all their aspirations for justice or which universalized some particular conception of the good society?, but rather: how might states and other groups do each other the least possible harm and, in an age of total war and nuclear weapons, survive as a species? So the core goals of international social order were survival and coexistence; and the political framework for the attainment of this pluralist order was the system or society of states—Great Powers, balances of power, diplomacy, deterrence, and so on.

The narrowness of this conception of order undoubtedly reflected the intense ideological and geopolitical conflicts of the cold war. But it also drew upon a deep-rooted tradition in Western thought which had long viewed international society in pluralist or minimalist terms. This minimalism and deep scepticism regarding 'idealist' aspirations does not depend on the view that international life is somehow destined to remain an arena of perpetual conflict; nor does it depend on the argument that there is an absolute and eternal divide between 'domestic order' on the one hand and 'international anarchy' on the other. After all, Morgenthau's political realism was just as much a response to events on the streets of Weimar Germany as it was to the failings of the League of Nations in Geneva. Rather, it reflects a powerful sense of the fragility of all social order, including within the developed and prosperous West. The core intuition is that Hobbesian 'diffidence' or fear is extremely difficult to dislodge, especially in social settings characterized by great inequalities of power, weak institutions, and deep societal differences. Thus, the structure of power and interests, the extent of inequality, the divergences of cultures and value systems, and the rigidities of political language make the resolution of many conflicts difficult, if not impossible. All politics, but especially world politics, is the arena for struggles amongst differing social and political ideals, and the character of competition for power between these rival

---

[8] For a detailed analysis of Bull's view, see Kai Alderson and Andrew Hurrell (eds), *Hedley Bull on International Society* (Basingstoke: Macmillan, 2000), Chs 1–3. For a broad and far reaching discussion see N. J. Rengger, *International Relations, Political Theory and the Problem of Order* (London: Routledge, 2000).

views—and the manner in which power is deployed—will remain *a*—but not necessarily *the*—central focus of enquiry.

One reason for this limited conception of order and even more constrained view of justice therefore was a pessimistic view of power politics and of the political difficulties of sustained cooperation. But a second reason was a deep scepticism about claims regarding the existence of consensus and shared values across international and global society. All communities and polities have to find ways of dealing with diversity and value conflict. Conflict is, after all, intrinsic to all morality, and even within a single value system conflicts arise: how different principles are to be related to one another; how shared principles are to be applied to the facts of a particular case. For international society the problem has always run much deeper, and the creation of any kind of universal society of states or any other kind of world society has had to face up to the existence of fundamental differences in religion, social organization, culture, and moral outlook. These difficulties may be based on what Sen calls 'the empirical fact of pervasive human diversity',[9] or may reflect, as for Isaiah Berlin, a belief in the plurality, contradictoriness, even incommensurability of human goods. But they underscore the degree to which diversity is a basic and common feature of humanity. The clash of moral, national, and religious loyalties is not the result of ignorance or irrationality but rather reflects the plurality of values by which all political arrangements and notions of the good life are to be judged. It has been a persistent illusion of liberals and Marxists that modernization and development will lead to a convergence of social, cultural, and ethical outlooks.

From this perspective, we are condemned to minimalism by the constraints on effective and sustained cooperation and by the ways in which power and values interact. Thus even very broadly shared values and conceptions of justice will tend to reflect or to reinforce the interests of particular states at particular times. This was, of course, central to Carr's brand of realism, as well as to Marxist understandings of the place of moral values in political life. As Morgenthau put it: 'The appeal to moral principles in the international sphere has no universal meaning. It is either so vague as to have no concrete meaning that could provide rational guidance for political action, or it will be nothing but the reflection of the moral perceptions of a particular nation.'[10]

For classical realists the answer is a retreat to power and to the analysis of the order and orders produced by competing powers, above all the balance of power. For international society theorists such as Bull, the answer is a double move involving both order as fact and order as value: on the one hand, to

---

[9] Amartya Sen, *Inequality Reexamined* (Oxford: Oxford University Press, 1992), xi.
[10] E. H. Carr, *The Twenty Years' Crisis, 1919–1939*, 2nd edn (London: Macmillan, 1946); Hans Morgenthau, *American Foreign Policy* (New York: Knopf, 1951), 35.

uncover the basic minimal conditions under which it is possible for social order to obtain; and on the other, to trace the degree to which the state system has constituted some kind of minimalist society. But within both ways of thinking it is a logical step to separate questions of order from questions of justice; to suggest that questions of justice can be meaningfully addressed only after some modicum of society exists; and to stress the tensions that will continue to exist between them. As Bull puts it: 'Order in social life is desirable because it is the condition of the realisation of other values ... International order, or order within the society of states, is the condition of justice or equality among states and nations.'[11] Or Kissinger: 'If history teaches anything it is that there can be no peace without equilibrium and no justice without restraint.'[12]

Although highly influential, there are serious difficulties with this way of treating order and justice. In the first place, it has always involved many silences and many problems. The value of order is not placed within any general ethical account or framework.[13] Order as analysed by Bull, Kissinger, or Kennan implies an ethical view and hence a view of justice: to argue that certain goals should be pursued is to suggest that it is right to pursue them and that those who do so act justly. However, these particular goals are not argued for in a clear and consistent manner. Nor are they coherently related to other values. For example, what does justice require when the political or geopolitical constraints aren't quite as tight? How should we resolve disagreements between order and other values? When might the values of this minimalist inter-state order legitimately be overridden in the interests of justice?

Second, the retreat to power as the final arbiter of all politics and the removal of all concern with morality manifestly fails. As Hoffmann pointed out, the meaning of the alleged trumping claims of realism—defending the national interest, even guaranteeing national survival—are necessarily contested and involve a range of normative assumptions, most importantly about the value of the national community whose interest is being defended.[14] More generally

---

[11] Bull, *The Anarchical Society*, 93.

[12] Henry Kissinger, *The White House Years* (London: Weidenfeld and Nicolson, 1979), 55.

[13] See Ian Harris, 'Order and Justice in "The Anarchical Society"', *International Affairs*, 69 (1993), 725–41. As Koskenniemi puts it: 'The very need for and definition of order are normative statements in their own right: conceptualizing "order" in terms of stability or peace or the "securing of the elementary needs of the relevant group" creates an axiological system with a normative premise.' Koskenniemi, 'The Police in the Temple', 329.

[14] Stanley Hoffmann, *Duties Beyond Borders: On the Limits and Possibilities of Ethical International Politics* (Syracuse: Syracuse University Press, 1981). For the classic normative critique of international life as a Hobbesian war of all against all in which morality plays no role, see Charles Beitz, *Political Theory and International Relations* (Princeton: Princeton University Press, 1979), Part 1. Unmasking the necessarily normative character of mainstream theory has been a central claim of post-positivist writing. See, for example, Steve Smith, 'Is the Truth Out There? Eight Questions about International Order', in T.V. Paul and John A. Hall (eds), *International Order and the Future of World Politics* (Cambridge: Cambridge University Press, 1999).

we should remember Weber's telling critique of reducing all politics to 'power politics', a move which reveals 'a most wretched and superficial lack of concern for the *meaning* of human action, a blasé attitude that knows nothing of the tragedy in which all action, but quite particularly political action, is in truth enmeshed'.[15]

Given these well-known difficulties, we need to move quickly from a discussion of order versus justice and instead consider how order *and* justice are to be related *within* different, and often conflicting, conceptions of world order. If we do this, can we retell the pluralist account giving greater play to the links between order and justice? Where, if anywhere, do values and ethics come in? Or is the Westphalian order, as Philip Allott suggests, truly a morality-free zone?[16] Three kinds of arguments are commonly deployed, albeit in different ways and in varied combinations.

In the first place, some writers appeal to the unavoidable centrality of an ethics of statecraft. Moral politics, on this view, should be closely tied to the practice of statecraft and to Weber's ethic of responsibility that will inevitably dominate the choices of political leaders. On the strong account of this position, there are no overarching global principles of justice that apply to foreign policy. Political morality is the art of successfully navigating very stormy seas and prudence becomes the supreme political virtue. But, even if there are some shared principles of justice, acting upon them in the face of the contingency and perverse consequences that characterize political action will still involve a great deal of prudential judgement, pragmatic adaptation, and painful trade-offs amongst competing goals. In Chapter 6 John Gaddis provides several examples in US foreign policy of precisely this prudentialist approach to order and justice.

Second, many see states, but not necessarily any particular state, and the apparatus of state sovereignty as providing a container for pluralism and a framework for the protection of diversity. What animates this claim is the idea that peoples, nations, and communities have an identity and seek the protective and expressive power of the state to further that identity. If state sovereignty provides the basic institutional framework, it is self-determination—most commonly national but often shading into cultural and religious—that has come ever more to provide the political power and the moral meaning to the idea of

[15] Max Weber, 'The Profession and Vocation of Politics', in Peter Lassman and Ronald Speirs (eds), *Weber: Political Writings* (Cambridge: Cambridge University Press, 1994), 354–5. Similar problems arise from the institutionalist attempt to draw an excessively clear-cut distinction between a rational logic of consequences and a norm-following logic of appropriateness that has become so influential in political science. How we calculate consequences is often far from obvious and not easily separable from our understanding of legal or moral norms.

[16] Philip Allott, 'The Concept of International Law', in Michael Byers (ed.), *The Role of Law in International Politics: Essays in International Relations and International Law* (Oxford: Oxford University Press, 2000).

living in a world of states and an international society. It shapes all discussion about the identity of the actors and about the character and moral purposes of those actors. In a post-imperial age it is a fundamental feature of the discourse by which claims to political authority and to the control of territory are articulated and justified. To this pluralism is often tied the related argument that justice belongs inside national borders and that it is only identification with a national community that can foster meaningful citizenship and provide a secure basis for both grounding and implementing conceptions of social justice.[17]

And third, pluralists emphasize that the limited and fragile institutions of international society do indeed provide a morally significant means of promoting coexistence and of limiting conflict in a world in which consensus around more elaborate forms of cooperation does not exist. The defence of this image has always rested on the requirements of effectiveness and on the limits of actual consensus. The law of the jungle may not be deflected by very much, but, for the pluralist, in the absence of any firm reason for believing in the viability of transforming international society this little will always remain morally highly significant.

Whether one stresses the power-political conflictual side of the argument or the more principled liberal-pluralist side, there are still many powerful voices who would emphasize that order-justice issues are really about the politics of pragmatic case-by-case modi vivendi between and amongst political collectivities, with the apparatus of the state system still providing a fundamental framework for the management of power and the mediation of difference. Indeed, it is striking to note that a more or less traditional vision of international society is defended by some of the most important contemporary political theorists, most notably John Rawls.[18] Other examples include Robert Jackson's powerful reworking and extension of the case for normative pluralism and of the rules and institutions of the state system as providing the framework for that pluralism.[19]

More importantly for this volume, a pluralist and limited international society is viewed by many major states as the only acceptable framework for understanding order and justice. As we move through earlier waves of what Bull termed 'the revolt against Western dominance', we can note the extent to which those Third World leaders who had so vehemently denounced imperialist international law and society came to appreciate its benefits, as had French, Soviet, and Chinese revolutionary leaders before them.[20] Being mostly weak,

---

[17] See the discussion of the state-centric paradigm in Chapter 5.

[18] John Rawls, *The Law of Peoples* (Cambridge, MA: Harvard University Press, 1999).

[19] Robert Jackson, *The Global Covenant: Human Conduct in a World of States* (Oxford: Oxford University Press, 2000).

[20] See Hedley Bull and Adam Watson (eds), *The Expansion of International Society* (Oxford: Oxford University Press, 1984).

it made great sense for them to buy into the political advantages that sovereign statehood provided and such—fragile—protection as international legal rules might afford. Moreover, external support and access to the instruments of juridical statehood played major roles in the battle for domestic survival.[21]

As the chapters on India, Russia, China, and the Islamic world—or at least some parts of it—suggest, claims for justice and for just treatment are still overwhelmingly made in terms of respect for non-intervention and state sovereignty; for equal treatment of different cultural and religious traditions within a state-based framework; for equal rights of entry and of participation in the Great Power club; and for some degree of restitution for, or at least understanding of, past injustices inflicted during the imperialist era. We see a persistent and very powerful protest against the ways in which a normatively more ambitious but Western-dominated international society and Western-dominated globalization are both undermining the inherited pluralist order and the protections that it provided. And finally, and in direct consonance with traditionalist understandings, we see frequent claims that the maintenance of political order within conflict-prone societies and regions may often have to trump liberal Western preferences for human rights or self-determination. Whilst such claims are no doubt often self-serving and whilst 'political order' may sound an old-fashioned topic within the lexicon of Western political theory, it is easy to see why it remains a fundamental value in areas where violence and division continue to characterize everyday political life.

2. THE INADEQUACY OF TRADITIONAL UNDERSTANDINGS

As the Introduction to this volume discusses, the end of the Cold War witnessed a dramatic rise in support for the idea that international society could, and should, seek to promote greater justice, as in the broadening agenda of human rights, the apparent determination and capacity to deal with brutality within states, and the proclaimed responsibility of a revitalized international community to come to the aid of victims of aggression. In addition, there were increasingly powerful arguments throughout the 1990s that order itself depended on the satisfaction of justice claims: for example, that peace was bound up with the ending of autocratic, undemocratic, and oppressive regimes, or that greater equity was a central requirement of global sustainability.

Instead of being merely a catch-all phrase to indicate a concern with ethics and morality, a more coherent global justice agenda can be identified, both

---

[21] See Christopher Clapham, *Africa and the International System: The Politics of State Survival* (Cambridge: Cambridge University Press, 1996).

within recent practices of world politics and in the explosion of academic writing on international normative theory: the notion that all individuals should receive the treatment that is proper or fitting to them; the idea that international legal rights, duties, and entitlements should be respected and acted upon and that wrongdoing be punished wherever it occurs; and the broader notion that the major international and global social, political, and economic institutions that determine the distribution of benefits and burdens should be organized and, if necessary, restructured in accordance with principles of global social justice.

It is critical to remember that this set of developments came on top of a much broader and more far-reaching increase in the normative ambition of international society that had been gathering pace throughout the twentieth century. The narrow conception of what international society could, or should, aspire to, and the privileged place that it gave to a limited power-political order built around the sovereign state, has long faced an array of powerful critics. But in the course of the twentieth century it was challenged by more far-reaching, maximalist, or solidarist conceptions of order. What states and peoples deem it legitimate to expect from international society, or from the much appealed-to international community, has increased exponentially. Thus a minimally acceptable notion of order is increasingly held to involve the creation of international rules that deeply affect the domestic structures and organization of states, that invest individuals and groups within states with rights and duties, and that seek to embody some notion of a global common good. As we shall see in the next section, this has involved a shift in the normative structure of world politics both towards a more strongly solidarist conception of international society and towards the theory and practice of a model of transnational governance.

But what has driven these changes? Does the expansion of justice claims merely reflect another liberal moment? As the wheel turns and as the power-political, economic, and ideological determinants of world politics appear ever more ineluctable, will these claims simply be left on the margin of world politics? Or have they become more firmly entrenched? The core argument of this section is that a retreat to pluralism is impossible: pluralism both as a way of thinking about justice and as a limited model of state-based international order.

There are five sets of reasons for the expanded normative ambition of international society. In the first place, it reflects material developments and changing understandings of hard pragmatic interest. The goal of minimal order has become less adequate given the range and seriousness of the problems and challenges facing all states and societies. The rising costs of major war; the growth of economic, ecological, and social interdependence; and the degree to which individual societies depend on each other have dramatically increased the demand for international cooperation. It is both an everyday intuition and the stuff of countless articles and speeches that globalization creates problems that can be solved only by stronger, deeper, and more effective forms of international cooperation.

Second, various more specific implications follow from this rather trite general claim. The management of globalization necessarily involves the creation of deeply intrusive rules and institutions and debate on how different societies are to be organized domestically. This is a structural change. If states are to develop effective policies on economic development, environmental protection, human rights, the resolution of refugee crises, the fight against drugs, or the struggle against terrorism, then they need to engage with a wide range of international and transnational actors and to interact not just with central governments but with a much wider range of domestic political, economic, and social players. If you want to solve problems in a globalized world, you cannot simply persuade or bully governments into signing treaties; you are therefore inevitably drawn into becoming involved with how other people organize their own societies.

In addition, the move towards the coercive enforcement of international norms, involving both the use of force and economic sanctions and conditionalities, makes it very difficult to exclude arguments about legitimacy and hence about justice. As the struggle against terrorism shows, even hegemonic states can find that multilateralism and international law provide an instrumentally valuable means of both legitimizing their own use of force and delegitimizing other forms of political violence. And finally, even if created for pragmatic and instrumental purposes, institutions act as platforms for ongoing normative debate, for the mobilization of concern, and for debating and revising ideas about how international society should be organized. Although often driven by instrumental and functional logics, international institutions can shape, and not merely reflect, communities of interest. Once formed, such communities may then provide the framework for crystallizing consensus on the content of global justice claims. Thus, however much practitioners and social scientists insist on analysing international institutions solely in terms of the provision of international public goods, normative issues cannot be kept out of the picture. Hence, as Ngaire Woods suggests in Chapter 3, it is significant that debates about the effectiveness and efficiency of global financial institutions have had to engage in arguments about accountability, legitimacy, and procedural justice. And finally, we have good reason for believing that international institutions themselves have acted as powerful agents for the diffusion and socialization of norms.

A third factor behind the increased normative ambition of international society reflects changes in the organization of domestic society and in the powerful transnational ideological forces that have shaped those changes. Thus the legitimacy of governments—democratic and authoritarian—has come to depend on their capacity to meet a vastly increased range of needs, claims, and demands. In part this has involved increased expectations of the role of the state in economic management, something that remains substantially true even in an era of deregulation, privatization, and globalization. In part it reflects changed notions of political legitimacy and broadened understandings of self-determination, of human rights, and of citizenship rights. In addition, although it may be true, as realists tell us, that the international system tames and socializes revolutionary regimes, it is also true that each of the great social revolutions of the modern era has left an indelible mark on the dominant norms of international society.[22] Contrary to the impression given by most International Relations texts, international norms do not float wholly free from the domestic and transnational structures within which states are embedded.

Fourth, there has been the steady growth of demands that the norms of international society should express not just pragmatic or material interests but also common moral purposes. In some cases this stems from the drive to universalize that is inherent in most of the world's most developed ethical systems, religious or secular. In others it is tied to the belief that globalization and increased interdependence have given a greater reality to the previously abstract notion of sharing a single world and have helped to foster a cosmopolitan moral consciousness, however embryonic and fragile it may be. And in still others, it comes from the ways in which conceptions of justice shape foreign policy. Given the current distribution of power, it is of great importance that the US frames its foreign policy not in a realist language of hard interest but instead within an ideology of justice, albeit one that reflects its own historical values and traditions. Especially in times of conflict, whether during the Cold War or the struggle against terrorism, it has sought to impose and to act upon a Manichean view of the world derived from its own conceptions of global justice. As John Gaddis points out in Chapter 6, this intertwining of interests and values has united liberal and conservative traditions of US foreign policy.

Fifth, there is the role of power. Change in normative structure is closely bound up with power and the distribution of power, within the state system but also within the global economy and transnational civil society. Power played a major role in many of the great international institutional developments of the twentieth century, most notably the creation of the UN and the Bretton Woods economic institutions in the 1940s. And one of the most important questions of the post-cold war period concerns the extent to which the increased incorporation of liberal economic and political norms into international law and the

---

[22] This interaction is explored in David Armstrong, *Revolutions and World Order* (Oxford: Oxford University Press, 1993).

practices of international institutions reflects and reinforces a new age of Western hegemony.

There is no question, then, that power matters. And yet it is highly misleading to view normative expansion solely as a process of imposition by powerful states. The nature of power is seldom straightforward and the translation of crude material power into effective political action is complex. This is nowhere more true than when it comes to the creation and institutionalization of new norms. Thus the revolt of the colonial world against Western dominance did involve a surprisingly successful shift in many dominant legal and political norms, for example those relating to conquest and colonialism, nonintervention, self-determination, and racial equality. In addition, even at those moments when hegemonic imposition seems most clear-cut, the reality has turned out to be more complex, as detailed historical work on institution-building in the immediate post-1945 period has shown or as liberal analyses of the particular character of contemporary US hegemony suggest.[23] Most importantly, as the density and complexity of the international legal system increases and as globalization opens up new channels of transnational political action, so the process of norm creation becomes harder for the powerful to control. Thus, apparently weak states have been able to use the institutional platforms and to exploit already established patterns of legal argument to promote new and often far-reaching legal rules and institutions—as with the International Criminal Court. A good deal of the process of normative expansion has been driven by non-state groups and by transnational and transgovernmental coalitions, most conspicuously in the areas of human rights or the environment.[24]

Taken together, these forces and factors suggest that it is no longer possible to accept Martin Wight's classic distinction between domestic society as that arena within which understandings of the good life might be debated, developed, and, potentially, realized, and international relations as condemned to remain for ever an arena of 'mere survival'.[25] To take only the most obvious example, 'mere survival' in relation to the protection of the global environment depends fundamentally on how societies are organized domestically and on how their various conceptions of what the good life entails—their 'comprehensive doctrines', in Rawlsian terms—can be brought together and reconciled. Material and moral circumstances have therefore pushed international

---

[23] G. John Ikenberry, *After Victory: Institutions, Strategic Restraint and the Rebuilding of Order after Major Wars* (Princeton: Princeton University Press, 2001).

[24] See, for example, Thomas Risse, Stephen C. Ropp, and Kathryn Sikkink (eds), *The Power of Human Rights: International Norms and Domestic Change* (Cambridge: Cambridge University Press, 1999).

[25] Martin Wight, 'Why Is There No International Theory?', in Martin Wight and Herbert Butterfield (eds), *Diplomatic Investigations* (London: Allen and Unwin, 1966).

society inevitably beyond Nardin's practical association—'an association of independent and diverse political communities, each devoted to its own ends and its own conception of the good'.[26] They also decisively undercut the strong pluralism of Rawls. What possible sense can one make of Rawls's concentration on bounded political communities whose basic structure is defined in terms of 'self-sufficient schemes of cooperation *for all the essential purposes of human life*'?[27]

3. IF WE CANNOT RETREAT TO PLURALISM, WHERE CAN WE GO?

For many people it is impossible to deduce general principles of global justice that could be applied to the whole world because of the absence or weakness of an international community or society within which they could be situated and to which they could be applied. What is the international or global community that can legitimately define and promote applicable principles of global justice? Here we need to consider whether the same forces and factors that have blocked the retreat to pluralism may also provide a basis for a meaningful dialogue on conceptions of global justice or even a framework for the successful promotion of global justice.

In this section I suggest that the normative structure of international society has evolved in ways which help to undercut the arguments of those who take a restrictionist position towards global economic justice. There is now a denser and more integrated network of shared institutions and practices within which social expectations of global justice and injustice have become more securely established. But, at the same time, our major international social institutions continue to constitute a deformed political order, above all because of the extreme disparities of power that exist within both international and world society. This combination of density and deformity shapes how we should think about the relationship between order and justice.

Those who seek to refute the restrictionist or rejectionist view of global justice and of the scope of duties beyond borders consider the broad range of changes that have occurred within each of the three arenas of social order: civil society, the state, and the market economy. Those changes are most commonly gathered together under the heading of 'globalization'. For all the problems of definition, globalization involves the dramatic increase in the density and depth

[26] Terry Nardin, *Law, Morality and the Relations of States* (Princeton: Princeton University Press, 1983), 9.
[27] John Rawls, *Political Liberalism* (New York: Columbia University Press, 1993), 301; emphasis added.

of economic, ecological, and societal interdependence, with 'density' referring to the increased number, range, and scope of cross-border transactions, and 'depth' to the degree to which that interdependence affects, and is affected by, the ways in which societies are organized domestically.

Let us look first at economic globalization. The increasing integration of markets—not just cross-border transactions but also integrated transnational production structures—seems intuitively to have important normative implications and to buttress claims for moral cosmopolitanism. For moral cosmopolitans, globalization has eroded the boundedness of political communities whose particular cultures, traditions, and ways of living are given so much weight by communitarians. It has also given a new reality to the sense of sharing a single world and to the nature of plurality, connection, and finitude.[28] The circumstances of justice and the nature of social cooperation have been altered so fundamentally that we are entitled, indeed compelled, to transpose many of our understandings of social justice that apply within the state on to the international or transnational level.[29]

But there are real problems with such arguments. In part these have to do with empirical work showing the limits of economic globalization and the extent to which it is neither self-evidently new nor any more far-reaching than in the past. More importantly still, we are faced with the old difficulty of relating empirical accounts of an increasingly unified world to normative accounts of the emergence of a world community.[30] However dense and intense economic exchange may be, it does not translate easily or automatically into a shared awareness of a common identity, a shared community, or a common ethos. This is especially true given the massive inequalities within contemporary global capitalism. There is also a real danger of tying notions of moral community too closely to networks of economic interaction when so many of the world's most vulnerable people are precisely those who are excluded or marginalized from integration processes that are misleadingly described as 'global'. Much of the rhetoric of an economically globalizing and unifying world, then, fails to distinguish between three senses of the idea of unity: as interdependence and interconnection; as uniformity in the character of the states and societies that make up the global system; and as consciousness of a shared humanity or commitment to some shared set of purposes.

What of transnational civil society? This term refers to those self-organized intermediary groups that are relatively independent of both public authorities

---

[28] Onora O'Neill, *Towards Justice and Virtue: A Constructive Account of Practical Reasoning* (Cambridge: Cambridge University Press, 1996), Ch. 4.

[29] See, for example, Thomas Pogge, *Realizing Rawls* (Ithaca: Cornell University Press, 1989).

[30] Chris Brown, 'International Political Theory and the Idea of World Community', in Ken Booth and Steve Smith (eds), *International Relations Theory Today* (Cambridge: Polity Press, 1995).

and private economic actors, that are capable of taking collective action in pursuit of their interests or values, and that act across state borders. The roles of such groups within international society have increased very significantly: first, in the formal process of norm creation, standard-setting, and norm development; second, in the broader social process by which new norms emerge and find their way on to the international agenda; third, in the detailed functioning of many international institutions and in the processes of implementation and compliance; and finally in direct participation in many governance activities—disbursing an increasing proportion of official aid, engaging in large-scale humanitarian relief, leading efforts at promoting democracy or post-conflict social and political reconstruction. In all of these areas the analytical focus has been on transnational networks—for example, knowledge-based networks of economists, lawyers, or scientists—or transnational advocacy networks which act as channels for flows of money and material resources but, more critically, of information, ideas, and values.[31]

Transnational advocacy groups, social movements, and transnational networks have undoubtedly played very important roles in the changing politics of global justice and in processes of norm development and institutionalization. Beyond this, very important claims have been made about the normative potentiality of global civil society as an arena of politics that is able to transcend the inside-outside character of traditional politics and to fashion and provide space for new forms of political community, solidarity, and identity.[32] Sometimes the emphasis is on global civil society as a relatively autonomous self-organized public sphere in which genuine deliberation among competing positions can take place and through which some notion of international public reason can be developed. In other cases, global civil society and its linked network of 'domestic' civil societies feed positively into state-based order through the provision of legitimacy and consent and into market-based order as the repository of the trust and other forms of social capital without which markets will not function. But on both views global civil society represents a pluralist and open arena for the negotiation of rules and norms based on genuine and unforced consent. It serves as a regulative ideal but one whose potential can be gauged from the changing real practices of world politics.

But, as with markets, there are very real problems and limits and a need to counter a certain romanticization of the potentialities of transnational civil society—although not, as is the current danger, to go too far in the other

[31] See Margaret E. Keck and Kathryn Sikkink, *Activists Beyond Borders: Advocacy Networks in International Politics* (Ithaca: Cornell University Press, 1998).

[32] See, for example, Richard Falk, *On Humane Governance: Toward a New Global Politics* (Cambridge: Polity, 1995), and *Predatory Globalization: A Critique* (Cambridge: Polity Press, 1999); and Mary Kaldor, 'Transnational Civil Society', in Timothy Dunne and Nicholas Wheeler (eds), *Human Rights in Global Politics* (Cambridge: Cambridge University Press, 1999).

direction. Civil society is, after all, an arena of politics like any other in which the good and thoroughly awful coexist, in which the pervasive claims made by social movements and NGOs to authenticity and representativeness need to be tested and challenged, and in which outcomes may be just as subject to direct manipulation by powerful actors as in the world of inter-state politics. Whilst state action may be shaped by global civil society, it is often state action that is crucial in fostering the emergence of civil society in the first place and in providing the institutional framework that enables it to flourish. And, very critically, state power is increasingly determined by the ability of governments to work successfully within civil society and to exploit transnational and transgovernmental coalitions for their own purposes. There is always a danger of global civil society becoming an arena of politics which states and other economic and social organizations seek to dominate and exploit precisely in order to legitimize their own claims to power.

What, finally, of the changing character of international society itself? Here I think that we are entitled to argue that the normative structure of international society has evolved in ways which help to undercut the arguments of those who deny the existence of a global justice community or who take a restrictionist or strongly pluralist position towards global justice. Morgenthau's claim that 'the appeal to moral principles in the international sphere has no universal meaning' is simply wrong: perhaps its meaning is not universal but it is certainly widely diffused across the global system. There is now a denser and more integrated network of shared institutions and practices within which social expectations of global justice and injustice have become more securely established.

The normative structure of international society has moved significantly in the direction of greater solidarism. Four dimensions of change are especially important. The first has to do with the *content* of norms. In contrast to mere coexistence, the norms of this more solidarist law involve more extensive schemes of cooperation to safeguard peace and security—for example, prohibiting aggression or broadening understandings of what constitutes threats to peace and security; to solve common problems such as tackling environmental challenges or managing the global economy in the interests of greater stability or equity; and to sustain common values such as the promotion of self-determination, human rights, or political democracy. The second dimension concerns the *source* of these norms. In a traditional pluralist conception, the dominant norms are created by states and depend directly on the consent of states. In a solidarist conception, the process of norm creation is opened to a wider range of actors, both states and non-state groups; and there is an easing of the degree to which states can be bound only by rules to which they have given their explicit consent—a move from consent to consensus.

The third dimension has to do with the *justification and evaluation* of norms. Alongside the old idea that actors create and uphold law because it provides them with functional benefits, the post-1945 period has seen the emergence of a range of internationally agreed core principles—respect for fundamental human rights, prohibition of aggression, self-determination—which may underpin some notion of a world common good and some broader basis for evaluating specific rules.[33] This may be viewed in terms of the surreptitious return of natural law ideas or of a philosophically anchorless but nevertheless reasonably solid pragmatic consensus—but note Berlin's remark that the return of the ancient notion of natural law in the twentieth century was driven not by *faith in* but rather *fear of* mankind.[34] And the fourth dimension has to do with moves towards the more effective *implementation* of these norms and the variety of attempts to move beyond the traditionally very 'soft' compliance mechanisms and to give more effective teeth to the norms of this more ambitious society.[35]

This model of a solidarist society of states captures a great deal of the aspirational progressivism of international lawyers and of Western liberal opinion. But its attraction is by no means limited to Western states; and it can be seen in the constant appeals to the existence of an 'international community' capable of fulfilling a broader range of political and moral purposes. As this increasingly solidarist legal order has developed, so a crucial ambiguity begins to open up around the idea of states as the principal agents of world order. Within the pluralist world, states could be understood as 'agents' simply in the sense of those acting or exerting power and of doing so for themselves: 'The law of nations is the law of sovereigns', as Vattel famously put it.[36] But the expanding normative agenda of solidarism has opened up a second and different meaning of agency: the idea of an agent as someone who acts for, or on behalf of, another. Within the solidarist order states are no longer to act for themselves as sovereigns but rather, first, as agents for the individuals, groups, and national communities that they are supposed to represent—hence the move towards sovereignty as responsibility—and, second, as agents or interpreters of some notion of an international public good and some set of core norms against which state behaviour should be judged and evaluated.

Change has not only involved inter-state institutions but has also seen the emergence of transnational governance structures. One argument here points simply to the increasingly active role of firms and NGOs in the process of

---

[33] See the discussion of the United Nations in Chapter 2.

[34] Quoted in Michael Ignatieff, *Isaiah Berlin: A Life* (London: Chatto and Windus, 1998), 250.

[35] One might add that it is the increased density of solidarist institutions, together with ongoing powerful processes of globalization which have fed into the upsurge of debates about cosmopolitan democracy. See, for example, Daniele Archibugi, David Held, and Martin Kohler (eds), *Re-imagining Political Community: Studies in Cosmopolitan Democracy* (Cambridge: Polity, 1998); and the discussion of the post-national paradigm in Chapter 5.

[36] Emerich de Vattel, *The Law of Nations*, trans. Joseph Chitty (London: Steven and Sons, 1834), xvi.

norm creation, whether as lobbyists within individual states or as participants directly within international regimes and institutions. A second argument concentrates on the role of non-state actors as the generators of norms that are then taken up and assimilated into international legal structures. The third, and most radical, position highlights the emergence of private authority structures that exist largely independently of the framework of both municipal and international law: private systems of arbitration and dispute settlement, privatized rule production resulting from technical standardization, internal regulations within transnational firms, and private regimes governing particular sectors of the global economy.

It is, then, far from obvious that international institutions cannot move different states and societies towards 'shared understandings of the meaning of social goods', to use Michael Walzer's phrase.[37] Shared and institutionally-embedded understandings as to what constitutes justice and injustice are no longer confined within national communities. There has been created a shared international political culture within and around shared institutions, albeit fragile and often fractured. In examining the changing structure of international society we surely are dealing with 'an identifiable set of institutions whose impact on the life chances of different individuals can be traced'[38] or, in Rawls's terms, with political, social, and economic arrangements that 'define men's rights and duties and influence their life prospects, what they can expect to be and how well they can hope to do'.[39]

The *density* of international and world society has undoubtedly increased along both solidarist and transnational dimensions, reflecting changes that are unlikely to be easily reversed. And yet the elements of *deformity* are equally evident. We are not dealing with a 'now vanished Westphalian world', in Allen Buchanan's words, but rather with a world in which solidarist and cosmopolitan models of governance coexist, usually rather unhappily, with many aspects of the old Westphalian order.[40]

In the first place, there is deformity in terms of the distribution of advantages and disadvantages: in the way, for example, security is defined and the choices taken by institutions and states as to whose security is to be protected; or, very obviously, in the massive inequalities of the global economic order; or in the past and present consumption of ecological capital. Second, there is deformity in terms of who sets the rules of international society. Institutions are not, as some liberals would have us believe, neutral arenas for the solution of common problems but rather sites of power, even of dominance. The vast majority of

---

[37] Michael Walzer, *Spheres of Justice* (New York: Basic Books, 1983).
[38] David Miller, *Principles of Social Justice* (Cambridge: Harvard University Press, 1999), 5.
[39] John Rawls, *A Theory of Justice* (Cambridge: Harvard University Press, 1971), 7.
[40] Allen Buchanan, 'Rawls's Law of Peoples: Rules for a Vanished Westphalian World', *Ethics*, 110 (2001), 697–721.

weaker actors are increasingly 'rule takers' over a whole range of issues that affect all aspects of social, economic, and political life. Third, there is deformity in terms of the very different capacity of states and societies to adapt to the demands of a global economy, combined with the extent to which the economic choices of developing counties are, if not dictated, then certainly shaped by the institutions dominated by the strong and often backed by coercion in the form of an expanding range of conditionalities. And finally, deformity is evident in the limited capacity of international law and institutions to constrain effectively the unilateral and often illegal acts of the strong. In this sense we are not moving beyond sovereignty but rather returning to an earlier world of differentiated and more conditional sovereignties.

These characteristics do much to explain whose claims to justice are heard and picked up. Indeed, it is very striking that, for many Western states after the Cold War, 'justice' was taken uncontroversially to mean human rights, defence against murderous dictators, and democracy and political self-determination. It is also noteworthy that many of those who celebrated thevalues of a global liberal order proclaimed the virtues of democracy within states but steadfastly ignored calls for the democratization of decision-making within international institutions. Still more telling has been the deafening silence regarding either social and economic rights or global distributive justice. In 1998, for example, some 588,000 deaths were due to war; 736,000 were due to homicide and social violence; but starvation and preventable disease claimed around 18 million lives. Since the end of the Cold War 200 million deaths have been due to poverty-related causes.[41]

But how does deformity play into the discussion and analysis of order and justice? In the first place, it seriously complicates the search for shared principles of justice and for convincing ways of grounding those principles. For some, it is precisely human reason and its universality that provide both the foundation of moral argument and the best hope that it can be acted upon globally. The normative theorist begins with his or her best considered judgement based on reasons that are suitably coherent and generalizable. Whatever people may actually believe, he or she seeks to find good reasons why they should alter their beliefs and their patterns of behaviour. Showing that certain values are widely accepted in social practices is not the same as providing valid arguments as to why they are justified.

But even many of those who wish to start with their own 'best considered judgements' as to what justice requires and who seek to build theories of justice around universal principles that would be chosen by any rational individual do not end the story there. Thus, for example, Rawls insists that the

---

[41] See Thomas W. Pogge, 'Priorities of Global Justice', in Thomas W. Pogge (ed.), *Global Justice* (Oxford: Blackwells, 2001), 6–23.

theorist's considered judgement be related to the values that are available within the political or moral culture of a given society—the idea of a so-called reflective equilibrium—and that valid principles of justice must be publicly justifiable. And yet there are very serious difficulties. What do we mean by reason? Whose reason?[42] What precisely are the values and moral culture of this international society against which we seek to justify particular claims, especially when the international and transnational public spheres available are characterized not just by density but also by serious deformity? What meaning can be attached to even the purest and most serene universalist voice—whether of the Kantian liberal or of the religious believer—calling from the mountain if those to whom it is addressed do not believe themselves to be part of even the thinnest and most fragile shared community?

For others, normative theory should begin with the norms and values that exist within particular communities. Theory should uncover, interpret, and critically develop understandings of morality that exist within specific international historical and cultural contexts. On this view, as Miller puts it, 'There are no universal principles of justice. Instead, we must see justice as the creation of a particular political community at a particular time, and the account we give must be given from within such a community'.[43] As suggested above, the density of transnational and international normative structures has developed to the point where such an approach can indeed provide a viable and valuable basis for thinking about international and global justice. But, again, there are difficulties. Why should any consensus that emerges from so self-evidently unequal and fractured a global society be taken as the legitimate basis for normative deliberation and argument? Perhaps we can indeed point to the increasingly solidarist character of international law, as, for example, in the shifting and more permissive attitudes towards humanitarian intervention. But we also know that, despite the doctrinal emphasis placed by international law upon state consent, there is a great deal of coercion, coercive socialization, and crude imposition that lies behind the emergence of a new norm or support for a particular UN Security Council (UNSC) resolution.

So from whichever point one starts, the search for shared principles of justice will need to inquire into the social and political conditions that make for a meaningful global moral community and the degree to which they correspond to what actually exists or is likely to exist. At a general level these might include: some acceptance of equality of status, of respect, and of consideration; some commitment to reciprocity and to the public justification of one's

---

[42] Alasdair MacIntyre, *Whose Justice? Whose Rationality?* (London: Duckworth, 1985). For MacIntyre, '...the legacy of the Enlightenment has been the problem of an ideal of rational justification which it has proved impossible to attain' (p. 6).

[43] David Miller, 'Introduction', in David Miller and Michael Walzer (eds), *Pluralism, Justice, and Equality* (Oxford: Oxford University Press, 1995), 2.

actions; some capacity for autonomous decision-making on the basis of reasonable information; a degree of uncoerced willingness to participate; a situation in which the most disadvantaged perceive themselves as having some stake in the system; and some institutional processes by which the weak and disadvantaged are able to make their voices heard and to express claims to unjust treatment.[44]

The degree to which unequal power and deep value conflict continue to undermine these conditions has implications for how we might think about global justice.[45] First, it seems highly unlikely that any single ideology or world view will provide an overarching framework or meta-narrative for values and ethics in the twenty-first century—global liberalism, for instance. Instead debate, deliberation, and contestation over issues of justice will take place in a wide variety of spheres and domains involving a wide variety of actors: states, NGOs, firms, international organizations. Second, the participants will continue to come from a wide variety of cultural, religious, and linguistic backgrounds. One does not have to believe in clashing civilizations or incommensurability to believe that human diversity and value conflict remain important and that perspectives on issues of international order and justice vary enormously from one part of the world to another. This may be because of 'cultural differences' in the strong sense; but, as several of the chapters in this volume illustrate very powerfully, it is more often the result of differences in national and regional histories, in social and economic circumstances and conditions, and in political contexts and trajectories. But, whichever is the case, the premium is on understanding those different world views and appreciating the difficulties of communication. Cultural and historical complexity also make it difficult to read off judgements in particular cases from general or universal moral laws: a great deal of the debate over values and ethics in the twenty-first century will necessarily have to be context-rich and interpretative.

Finally, and most importantly, it remains vital to distinguish between justice and fairness in relation to process and procedure, and justice and fairness in matters of substance. Fair process matters more than substantive consensus: or, rather, it is the most plausible route to reaching substantive agreement given the depth and pervasiveness of value conflict and, even more, given the ease with which international law and institutions are contaminated by the special interests and particular values of the powerful. The most viable form of global moral community will continue to be one that is built around some minimal notion of just process. Why? First, because of the framework of shared meanings and the shared moral culture that have actually been developed in and

---

[44] See Chapter 4 on the trade system for a discussion of how substantive inequality impacts negatively on fair process and procedure.

[45] I owe many of the ideas in this paragraph to Laurence Whitehead's comments at the Nuffield Place authors' workshop and to many conversations on these matters.

around international society; second, and more foundationally, because of the universality of ideas about fairness of process: hearing the other side, providing arguments for one's actions, finding some mechanism for adjudicating between conflicting moral claims. This view of global justice sees reason and rationality not as abstract and universal but rather as developing 'naturally from necessities of social life, that is from the inevitably recurrent conflicts which must be resolved if communities are to survive'.[46] Global justice is not something that can be deduced from rational principles, nor can it be reflective of a single world view, religious or secular; it is, rather, a negotiated product of dialogue and deliberation and therefore always subject to revision and re-evaluation.

But deformity is not just a problem in the search for shared principles of justice and for a persuasive way of grounding such principles. It also feeds directly back to the question of order and thus to the traditional arguments with which this chapter began. There are clearly many ways in which order and justice can be brought together productively in international life: in the well-established links between democracy and peace; in the degree to which 'order-based' institutions can serve as a locus of shared values and the framework for the promotion of those values—as suggested in Chapter 5; and in the extent to which any stable order—domestic, regional, or international—requires legitimate authority. An order that is based on crude coercion or the simple exercise of hegemonic power is unlikely to endure. It will be excessively costly for the hegemon; inefficient and ineffective as a means of dealing with the complex problems associated with globalization; and likely to generate the very oppositional behaviour that realists tell us is the eternal characteristic of international politics.

And yet problems remain, above all because of the degree to which the elements of deformity, however normatively distasteful, are still crucial to the structures of political order that obtain in international life. The continuing tensions between order and justice derive from the instability of legitimate authority in international life; from the extent to which even elaborate institutions rest on an underlying distribution of power, whether balanced or hierarchical; and from the degree to which nation-states still see the necessities of conflict and insecurity as justification for pursuing their own conceptions of order and justice.

At the global or systemic level a great deal follows from what Cassese calls 'the end of a magnificent illusion',[47] namely, that the UN Charter system could provide an effective answer to the use of aggressive force and an effective instrument for the management of other conflicts. Equally illusory is the idea that this failure was somehow due to the Cold War and that the end of the

---

[46] Stuart Hampshire, *Justice is Conflict* (London: Duckworth, 1999), 25.
[47] Antonio Cassese, *Violence and Law in the Modern Age* (Cambridge: Polity Press, 1988), 33.

Cold War would open up a new age of international security cooperation. Of course the *collective element* in security management has expanded very significantly, as in the role of regional alliances or coalitions, international peace-keeping forces, and UN authorizations of the use of force. It is certainly the case, as Adam Roberts points out in Chapter 2, that this increased collective action has involved important shifts in understanding how order and justice are related. And yet we cannot ignore the irrelevance of the UN to many conflicts, the continued centrality of the balance of power in many regions of the world, and the many cases of domestic or regional instability where such peace as exists seems to depend 'not so much on the authority of a central power, or the law or a sense of community, but rather on an unstable balance of power amongst groups prepared to use force'.[48]

And where the international community has acted in pursuit of shared goals and values in the post-cold war period, this action has depended to an uncomfortable extent on the political interests of the US and its allies and on the military capabilities that they have been willing to deploy. The classic realist doubt reappears: not simply that international law and institutions are unable to constrain effectively the unilateralist tendencies of the most powerful, but rather, and far more profoundly, that international political order itself may require action by the hegemon or by major powers that can never be wholly regulated and controlled from within the legal order. This is true of action at the 'order' end of the spectrum, for example, in the struggle against terrorism or weapons of mass destruction. But it is just as true of actions at the 'justice' end, designed to promote and enforce shared conceptions of justice, as in the effective exercise of humanitarian intervention even in cases where full legal authorization may not be obtainable.

A further way in which the deformity of global politics relates to order concerns the link between the distribution of political and economic power and the functioning of even elaborate institutions. In some cases, the successful development of effective institutions reflects the existence of some broad underlying balance of power, as within the EU or the WTO. In other cases it is unequal power or hierarchy that plays the crucial role. Although realism has long given pride of place to balances of power, hierarchy and inequality have played an equally important role. They were central to the old pluralist order: Great Powers could promote order both by managing relations between themselves—through diplomacy, conferences, missions, joint interventions—but also by exploiting their own unequal power over subordinate states within their spheres of influence, alliance systems, and, most importantly, imperial systems. This conception of order remained extraordinarily powerful and influential throughout the

---

[48] Pierre Hassner, 'Force and Politics Today', in Pierre Hassner, *Violence and Peace: From the Atomic Bomb to Ethnic Cleansing* (Budapest: CEU Press, 1997), 38.

twentieth century and continues to be. Thus, for example, the Cold War 'order' and the long peace of 1945–89 were constructed in very traditional fashion around attempts to regulate the balance of power between the superpowers—through arms control agreements, summits, and mechanisms of crisis management—and through the exploitation of hierarchy—through the mutual, if tacit, recognition of spheres of influence and the creation of an oligarchical non-proliferation system designed to limit access to the nuclear club.[49]

Moreover, even as the idea of sovereign equality gained ground and as international institutions expanded so dramatically in both number and scope, hierarchy and inequality have remained central. Sometimes the 'ordering' role of hierarchy is formalized, as in the special rights and duties of the permanent members of the UNSC or the weighted voting structures of the IMF or World Bank. More often it can be seen in powerful political norms, as in the practice of ad hoc groupings and contact groups to deal with particular security crises; or the role of the Group of Seven in attempts to manage not just global economic issues but a great deal more besides; or the way in which international financial management is dominated by closed groups of the powerful, as in the Bank for International Settlements or the Financial Stability Forum.

This pattern reflects the need for concentrations of power. The fundamental problem with models of dispersed sovereignty is that, whilst they correctly acknowledge the dangers of centralized power, they fail to perceive the necessity of such power for social order and the promotion of common moral purposes. This is most obviously true in the field of international security. But it also applies to economic order and, by extension, to economic justice. Think, for example, of the need for effective states with sufficient legitimate power and authority to tax transnational corporations or to enforce equitable burden-sharing in the management of financial crises. Equally, however normatively attractive, models of cosmopolitan democracy at the level of international institutions and of deliberative democracy within civil society have as yet failed to explain how they will deal with the management of unequal power and the need to secure effective power for democratically agreed purposes. At the global level and within many regions, the question of political order remains unsolved and unresolved.

4. CONCLUSION

The argument has unfolded in four stages. First, I suggested that the conditions of global social justice have been irrevocably changed as a result of a

[49] See John Gaddis, *The Long Peace* (Oxford: Oxford University Press, 1987).

wide range of social, political, economic, and technological forces. These conditions undermine earlier efforts to distinguish order from justice and to base international order on a limited pluralist state-based arrangement. They also make the promotion of a much broader range of goals and values both morally compelling and materially necessary. Second, I argued that the normative structure of international society has evolved in ways which help to undercut the arguments of those who take a restrictionist position towards global justice. There is now a denser and more integrated network of shared institutions and practices within which social expectations of global justice and injustice have become more securely established. But, third, our major international social institutions continue to constitute a deformed political order, above all because of the extreme disparities of power that exist within both international and world society and the consequent degree to which this privileges the imposition of particular understandings of what constitutes global justice.

Finally, I have argued that this combination of density and deformity seriously complicates the search for shared principles, for convincing ways of grounding those principles, and for bringing order and justice together. The global political order remains heavily structured around inherited pluralist mechanisms that are, by any standards, deficient and deformed, certainly when measured by the values to which international society aspires but very often even by the more minimalist goals and values of the earlier period. In this sense we have not escaped from the tensions between order and justice, nor are we likely to do so any time soon.

2

Order/Justice Issues at the United Nations

ADAM ROBERTS

Since its foundation in 1945, the United Nations has recognized that peace is a matter not just of order but of justice. Already enshrined in the Charter, this recognition has been reflected in numerous declarations and activities of UN organs and agencies. The fact that the UN and its members have been committed to both order and justice has had positive aspects, and has been a key element in the UN's survival over more than half a century. The organization's concern, not just with the maintenance of order between existing states but with a wide range of justice-related issues, helps to explain its modest but nonetheless unprecedented degree of success. It contributed to the process of decolonization. It has helped to secure the interest of peoples and governments in the organization. It has resulted in some remarkable developments in the rhetoric, practices, and decisions of UN bodies.

The contrast with the League of Nations (1920–46) is striking. Although the League did have a limited involvement in certain justice-related issues, for example in the fields of labour rights and prohibition of slavery, it was associated, to a dangerous extent, with the territorial status quo of 1919. It could do little to answer the criticism that the peace was unjust, and it was powerless to respond to criminal conduct by states within their borders. For these as well as numerous other reasons, it could never command anything like the UN's near-universal membership and widespread popular support. The League's failure to be associated with justice, as well as its incapacity to maintain order, helps to explain its decline into insignificance during the 1930s.

As will be seen, principles of order and justice can often conflict with each other. Yet they do not always do so. Practically all concepts of international order are based, implicitly or explicitly, on some idea of justice. Similarly, all ideas of international justice encompass the idea that it is only through progress in righting wrongs—ending colonialism, reducing inequality, upholding human rights and democracy—that a secure and lasting peace can be obtained. Moreover, it is wrong to view justice issues as necessarily challenging the sovereignty of states. Most states, for most of the time, have worked on the assumption that justice issues are not a threat to themselves though they may be for others. Some justice issues are entirely compatible with the state system, either because they are explicitly concerned with justice for states or because the elements of justice that they enshrine—for example, the individual's right to life—may be widely viewed as best secured within the framework of the state. The UN has therefore been on apparently sure ground in upholding both order and justice.

However, the logical and practical problems of being committed simultaneously to order and justice in international relations are considerable. Some of these problems spring from the fact that 'justice' means different things to different peoples. This capacious term can refer to the actual or claimed rights of states, of peoples, and of individuals. There have been strong differences of opinion between states as to which particular justice issues should have priority: for example, whether civil rights are more fundamental than economic ones; whether the UN should be involved in supporting multi-party democracy within states; and whether state sovereignty can ever be violated in order to stop terrible injustice. Principles of justice can sometimes conflict with each other as well as with the principle of order.

Order/justice issues have naturally been the subject of heated debates and divided votes.[1] Debates on them in and around the UN have had several unsatisfactory aspects. They have been marked by a disturbingly high ratio of rhetoric to serious content. Throughout the history of the UN era, states and UN bodies have been accused of inconsistency, hypocrisy, double standards, and turning blind eyes to injustice and atrocity. They have been guilty of all these charges, though not all of them, not all of the time, and not on all issues. There even have been doubts, not always publicly articulated, about whether the UN should be preoccupied with a wide range of justice-related issues.

A central question has to be faced. Can an emphasis on justice lead, not just to unsatisfactory debates, but to war? For centuries, leaders have used the language of justice when resorting to war.[2] The UN era has been no exception. There are two main ways in which UN-based proclamations of justice can play a part in triggering war. The first involves some distortion of justice issues: when states and other organizations make claims based on international justice, they tend to be selective about which particular principles and claims they highlight, and which they sweep under the carpet, reinforcing the human propensity for self-righteousness and even violence. The second way does not necessarily involve distortion: if certain principles of justice are widely proclaimed by states and international bodies but no effective action is taken to implement them, this can lead to calls to arms by regional states,

---

[1] Voting figures in the UN General Assembly are noted in several footnotes below.

[2] See David A. Welch, *Justice and the Genesis of War* (Cambridge: Cambridge University Press, 1993).

national liberation movements, or even by terrorist groups. Armed action arising in either of these ways tends to provoke a military response, which may
also be in the name of justice.

The UN is not an institution to which people should look if they want logic,
consistency, clarity, and simplicity. The UN system as it has evolved since 1945
is a sprawling collection of states, conferences, and bureaucracies, and has
been through many incarnations over time. One cannot expect total intellectual
coherence and consistency from it. Sometimes it has been hard to get people
in one part of the system to speak to, let alone with the same voice as, those in
another. The UN is not an international actor in its own right. However, it has
many important roles in international society, especially, so far as order/justice
questions are concerned, as an agency which is involved in the development,
articulation, and even sometimes implementation of international legal and
political norms.

Three central questions are explored in this chapter. (1) What have been
the main landmarks in the evolution of views at the UN on order and justice?
(2) Have the UN and its members achieved a substantive consensus on the
content of international justice? (3) How have apparent clashes between order
and justice been addressed when they have arisen within a UN framework?
Particular attention is devoted to the evolution of views on whether the sovereignty of states can be infringed, and foreign military intervention viewed
as legitimate, in those cases where a state is deemed to be denying justice to
its inhabitants.[3]

Since a huge array of justice-related issues has been raised in various UN
bodies, selectivity in addressing these questions in this chapter is unavoidable.
There are two especially egregious omissions. The first concerns the
International Court of Justice (ICJ). One of the six principal organs of the UN,
its Statute was adopted in 1945 at the same time as the UN Charter, and all
UN member states are parties, as also is Switzerland. The successor to the
Permanent Court of International Justice, established at The Hague in 1922,
the ICJ is empowered to issue binding decisions in cases between states which
have consented to its jurisdiction. It also provides advisory opinions when
requested to do so by competent international organizations. In the period
from its foundation in 1946 to February 2002, it delivered 74 judgments in
contentious cases and also delivered 24 advisory opinions. Its judgments have
addressed such matters as land frontiers and maritime boundaries, non-use of
force, non-interference in the internal affairs of states, diplomatic relations
and immunities, the right of asylum, rights of passage, and economic rights.

---

[3] On 'humanitarian intervention', see also the fuller exploration in Adam Roberts, 'The
So-Called "Right" of Humanitarian Intervention', *Yearbook of International Humanitarian Law
2000*, III (The Hague: T.M.C. Asser Press, 2002), 3–51.

It has played a key role in certain inter-state disputes; but its work is basically restricted to those disputes which contending states can agree are of a kind which can usefully be resolved in a court. A notable feature, especially since the early 1970s, has been the willingness of post-colonial states to take disputes to the ICJ.[4]

The second serious omission is that this survey does not encompass justice in relation to international development, trade, and finance.[5] In this area different UN bodies have adopted different approaches, which have also changed significantly over time; and there has been a particularly striking disjunction between some UN rhetoric and aspiration on the one hand and what actually happens on the other. A visit to the headquarters in Geneva of the UN Conference on Trade and Development (UNCTAD) has at times felt like a visit to a temple of a failed faith. Whatever its achievements, which include substantial work in information and research, UNCTAD has not delivered on all the hopes invested in it in 1964.[6] Likewise, not too many hopes are now invested, if they ever were, in the grand abstraction of the New International Economic Order, proclaimed by UN General Assembly resolution in 1974.[7] The UN system in all its many aspects remains involved in addressing global economic inequality.[8] However, there is widespread scepticism about the capacity of the UN to introduce a general transformation of what are perceived as the dominant structures of economic power.

This short survey, which is illustrative, not comprehensive, is divided into four sections.

(1) *The UN Charter*
    Charter provisions
    The Charter and the question of intervention
(2) *Development of justice-related principles at the UN*
    Decolonization
    General Assembly documents on principles of international order
    Human rights law
    The laws of war

[4] Useful surveys of the ICJ and its work include Arthur Eyffinger's lavishly illustrated *The International Court of Justice 1946–1996* (The Hague: Kluwer Law International, 1996) and Shabtai Rosenne, *The World Court: What It Is and How it Works*, 5th edn (Dordrecht: Martinus Nijhoff, 1995).   [5] On economic issues, see Chapters 3 and 4.
[6] These hopes were reflected in the resolution establishing UNCTAD, GA Res. 1995 (XIX) of 30 December 1964, adopted without a vote.
[7] 'Declaration on the Establishment of the New International Economic Order', GA Res. 3201 (S-VI) of 1 May 1974; the accompanying Programme of Action, GA Res. 3202 (S-VI) of same date. Both were adopted without a vote.
[8] See, for example, 'Agenda for Development', GA Res. 51/240 of 20 June 1997, adopted without a vote by a special meeting of the UN General Assembly.

1. THE UN CHARTER

Charter Provisions

The UN Charter, signed on 26 June 1945, contains principles and rules that are strongly in favour of order, especially as regards non-use of force by states. However, those principles and rules also put emphasis on justice. This dualism in the Charter between order and justice has contributed to the complexity of debates on the tangled question of whether there is a right of intervention within states when they fail one or another test of justice.

The rules in the UN Charter as they relate directly to international order are widely and rightly seen as fundamentally non-interventionist in their approach. Taken as a whole the Charter essentially limits the right of states to use force internationally to cases of (1) individual or collective self-defence and (2) assistance in UN-authorized or controlled military operations.

In the Preamble, the famous opening words 'We the peoples' indicate that the focus and *raison d'être* of the body is not the system of states as such but people. The Preamble's principal justice-related clauses specify a joint determination:

to reaffirm faith in fundamental human rights, in the dignity and worth of the human person, in the equal rights of men and women and of nations large and small, and to establish conditions under which justice and respect for the obligations arising from treaties and other sources of international law can be maintained, and to promote social progress and better standards of life in larger freedom, AND FOR THESE ENDS ... to employ international machinery for the promotion of the economic and social advancement of all peoples.

Likewise, the Charter's Article 1, on Purposes, contains strong commitments to justice in each of its three substantive paragraphs:

1. To maintain international peace and security, and to that end: to take effective collective measures for the prevention and removal of threats to the peace, and for the suppression of acts of aggression or other breaches of the peace, and to bring about

by peaceful means, and in conformity with the principles of justice and international law, adjustment or settlement of international disputes or situations which might lead to a breach of the peace;

2. To develop friendly relations among nations based on respect for the principle of equal rights and self-determination of peoples, and to take other appropriate measures to strengthen universal peace;

3. To achieve international co-operation in solving international problems of an economic, social, cultural or humanitarian character, and in promoting and encouraging respect for human rights and for fundamental freedoms for all without distinction as to race, sex, language, or religion ...

The strongest and most frequently-cited prohibitions on intervention are those in Article 2, which is on principles. Article 2(3), less often cited than 2(4), contains a cryptic reference to justice in expounding the principle: 'All Members shall settle their international disputes by peaceful means in such a manner that international peace and security, and justice, are not endangered.' The reference to justice was inserted at the initiative of a number of small states which feared that the Great Powers could conduct a policy of appeasement to their detriment, as with the 1938 Munich Agreement.[9] It thus foreshadowed a key element in the UN conception of justice: respect for the rights of small states. This was also embodied in Article 2(4), which sets out the basic non-interventionist principle:

4. All Members shall refrain in their international relations from the threat or use of force against the territorial integrity or political independence of any state, or in any other manner inconsistent with the Purposes of the United Nations.

Article 2(7) adds to this by placing certain limits on the freedom of action of the UN itself in relation to states:

7. Nothing contained in the present Charter shall authorize the United Nations to intervene in matters which are essentially within the domestic jurisdiction of any state or shall require the Members to submit such matters to settlement under the present Charter; but this principle shall not prejudice the application of enforcement measures under Chapter VII.

At the very least, Articles 2(4) and 2(7) create a strong presumption against forcible military interventions by member states and a weaker one against intervention by the UN. However, subsequent parts of the Charter have a less statist character than the rules on non-intervention might suggest. There were specific commitments to take action on human rights in Articles 13, 55, 56, 62, 68, and 76.

---

[9] Bruno Simma (ed.), *The Charter of the United Nations: A Commentary* (Oxford: Oxford University Press, 1994), 105–6.

The Charter's emphasis on such issues did much to establish that the UN was no mere trade union of states, as the League had often seemed to be. In addition, care was taken by the UN's founders to ensure that the dreadful mistake of the League's creation was not repeated. The Covenant of the League of Nations had originated as an integral part of the peace treaties concluded at the end of the First World War—treaties that soon came to be seen as unjust. The UN Charter was a free-standing agreement, not so tainted by association with injustice.[10]

A striking feature of the international debate leading up to the Charter was the emphasis on social and economic as well as political rights. This had its background in the New Deal and in the growing strength of welfarism and the left in many countries. The inclusion of the language of human rights and justice in the UN Charter, sometimes thought to have been a largely American achievement, was in fact the result of pressure from many states, including the Soviet Union, which had its own vision, or at least rhetoric, of a system of global justice beyond the confines of existing sovereign states.[11] The British, in numerous wartime documents about international organization from the Declaration by United Nations of 1 January 1942 to the British drafts of the UN Charter preamble in 1945, consistently favoured the commitment to social matters and human rights.[12] One reason why the British supported the inclusion of the statement of purposes and principles in the Charter was that they wanted a strong Security Council, free to act in a variety of situations.

The Charter's extensive attention to justice was appropriate to the peculiar period of world history which was ushered in at the end of the Second World War. For most of the period of the UN's existence there were two Cold War superpowers which (1) subscribed to overtly anti-colonial ideologies, and favoured the ending of European colonial empires, (2) supported the proposition, at some level of rhetoric if not always of political practice, that the system of states was unsatisfactory and needed to be reformed, and (3) accepted in some form the rhetoric of human rights. Against this background, a Charter which had simply established a club of existing states without reference to any larger issues of justice could never have been agreed, let alone survived.

---

[10] Part of the Charter's Article 53, the 'enemy state clause' does discriminate against Germany and its allies in the Second World War. Although still technically in force, for all practical purposes this clause has long been a dead letter and has not seriously damaged support for the UN in the countries concerned.

[11] Ruth B. Russell, *A History of the United Nations Charter: The Role of the United States 1940–1945* (Washington, DC: Brookings Institution, 1958), 777–9.

[12] See for example Llewellyn Woodward, *British Foreign Policy in the Second World War*, II (London: HMSO, 1971), 212, 217; P. A. Reynolds and E. J. Hughes, *The Historian as Diplomat: Charles Kingsley Webster and the United Nations 1939–1946* (London: Martin Robertson, 1976), 166, 167; *Foreign Relations of the United States, 1942*, I (Washington, DC: Government Printing Office, 1960), 21, 23.

The Charter and the Question of Intervention

Does the UN Charter, despite its fundamental non-interventionism, leave any room for any doctrine or practice justifying military intervention within a state against the wishes of its government and on grounds relating to claims of justice—as distinct, for example, from self-defence? This question can encompass not only the much-discussed issue of humanitarian intervention but also intervention to support self-determination struggles or to uphold the observance of a wide variety of international norms against states which are deemed to be violating them.

There are two main bases in the Charter for arguing that, in exceptional circumstances, there may be some room for forcible intervention within states on justice-related grounds. The first way in which the Charter may leave room for intervention arises from its above-quoted references to fundamental human rights, proclaimed to be central purposes of the UN in the Preamble and in Article 1. These provisions inevitably raise the question, not addressed directly in the Charter, of what should be done if the most fundamental human rights and humanitarian norms are openly flouted within a state. These clear enunciations of the UN's purposes must also have some effect on how to interpret the final phrase of Article 2(4), with its prohibition on the threat or use of force by member states 'against the territorial integrity or political independence of any state, or in any other manner inconsistent with the Purposes of the United Nations'.

The second way in which the Charter may leave scope for intervention concerns the possibility of such intervention under UN Security Council auspices. In general, Chapter VII of the Charter is much less restrictive than had been the equivalent provisions of the Covenant of the League of Nations (1919) about the circumstances in which international military action can be authorized. Under Article 39 the Security Council can take action in cases deemed to constitute a 'threat to the peace, breach of the peace, or act of aggression': in practice, a range of justice-related issues within states can encompass or coincide with any or all of these threats. Articles 42 and 51 leave the Security Council a wide range of discretion regarding the type of military action that it can take. In addition, Article 2(7) implicitly recognizes the possibility that the Security Council could authorize enforcement measures partially or wholly within a sovereign state. Article 25 places member states under an obligation 'to accept and carry out the decisions of the Security Council in accordance with the present Charter'. All these provisions, coupled with those in Chapter VII, suggest that in certain circumstances the Security Council may be within its powers in authorizing intervention in a state on, for example, humanitarian or human rights grounds; but they are far from suggesting that states have such a right in the absence of Security Council authorization.

2. DEVELOPMENT OF JUSTICE-RELATED
PRINCIPLES AT THE UN

Decolonization

The Charter's provisions foreshadowing the process of European decolonization were opaque. This was the result of compromise between the states principally involved in drafting the Charter, some of which were firmly anti-colonial
while others, Britain and France among them, still had hopes of hanging on to
large parts of their extra-European empires. Although the word 'decolonization'
was not used, the Charter's emphasis on the sovereign equality of states and its
provisions regarding non-self-governing territories (Chapter XI) and international trusteeship (Chapter XII) contained an implicit assumption that the days
of European colonialism were numbered.

Similarly, the deliberately cautious phrase 'equal rights and self-determination
of peoples' in Article 1(2) came to be seen as a legitimation of the principle of
decolonization. The Charter's framers had avoided using the term 'national self-
determination', which had come to mean that each 'nation'—that is, a people
sharing a number of common attributes—is entitled to form a state. Since the
principle of 'national self-determination' had caused numerous problems in
Europe in the inter-war years and was associated with conflict and failure, it is
not surprising that different terminology was used.

Through these Charter provisions, however cautious, and also through its
subsequent actions, the UN came to be associated with the most important
single process in international relations since the Second World War: the fission of empires into states. Largely because of this fission, the UN's membership almost quadrupled between 1945 and 2000, from 51 original members
in 1945 to 189 as at 31 December 2000.

Already in 1960, as the process of decolonization was gathering pace, the
General Assembly passed the 'Declaration on the Granting of Independence
to Colonial Countries and Peoples'. This was the first of a series of declarations interpreting the Charter provisions on the relationship between order and
justice. It proclaimed in its first substantive article: 'The subjection of peoples
to alien subjugation, domination and exploitation constitutes a denial of fundamental human rights, is contrary to the Charter of the United Nations and
is an impediment to the promotion of world peace and cooperation.'[13]

For the most part, the form that decolonization took was not based on the
proposition that specific ethnic groups should form states but rather on the

---

[13] 'Declaration on the Granting of Independence to Colonial Countries and Peoples', GA
Res. 1514 (XV) of 14 December 1960, adopted with 89 in favour, none against, 9 abstaining,
and 1 absent. *GAOR*, 15th session, supplement no. 16, UN doc. A/4684 (1960), 66.

proposition that existing political and territorial units within empires should acquire self-government. Already in 1960 the above-mentioned Declaration on Colonialism expressed this approach in remarkably dogmatic terms: 'Any attempt aimed at the partial or total disruption of the national unity and the territorial integrity of a country is incompatible with the purposes and principles of the Charter of the United Nations.'[14] For all its limitations, this approach was probably a better basis for decolonization than would have been a principle that permitted wholesale redrawing of boundaries.

As the post-colonial majority in the UN grew during the 1960s, it pressed hard for further acts of decolonization, particularly in Africa, reinforcing the perception of the UN as supporting colonial liberation. Not the least of the UN's contributions to the process of decolonization was that it provided a place in which new or reconstituted states could be received into the international community, recognized, and treated as formal equals of other states. Furthermore, because the UN was associated with the cause of decolonization, it was less difficult than it might have been for new states to accept the existing framework of international organization and law. Such acceptance would have been more problematic had the UN been seen as grudging or hostile to the causes of colonial, and later post-communist, liberation. The UN's anti-colonial stance was by no means free of excesses. The British in particular criticized the way in which, in the General Assembly and its committees, all problems in colonies were blamed on the colonial rulers; and British representatives repeatedly attacked the double standard by which overseas rule was condemned but dictatorial rule within states was ignored. Yet in general the UN rode the wave of decolonization successfully.

General Assembly Documents on Principles of International Order

The UN General Assembly has considered and approved certain declarations of a general character interpreting the Charter provisions on the relationship between order and justice. Most of these documents, including the five cited below, date from the period from 1965 to 1981. In those years, a strong coalition of post-colonial states, often assisted by the Soviet bloc, emphasised predominantly statist and non-interventionist ideas and values.

Some initial efforts at general expositions about order and justice took a different tack. For example, a Chilean proposal in August 1950 sought to place on the agenda the admirably entitled item 'Strengthening of democratic principles as a means of contributing to the maintenance of universal peace', accompanied by a 34-point explanatory memorandum, super-Kantian in tone, calling for the establishment of an 'international democratic pact'. It was

---

[14] 'Declaration on the Granting of Independence to Colonial Countries and Peoples', Article 6.

withdrawn. It was premature and could not survive in the hostile environment of the worst years of the Cold War.

The period between 1960, when the Declaration on Colonialism was adopted, and the end of the Cold War was one in which post-colonial states formed a majority in the General Assembly, and through coalitions such as the Non-Aligned Movement and the Group of 77, created in 1961 and 1964 respectively, were keen to exercise their power there. This was the period in which key documents touching on order and justice were adopted by the General Assembly. Third World initiatives, as Ian Brownlie has written, were often 'intended to establish new legal concepts or to give legitimacy to existing political concepts'; but they did not seek to supplant existing legal concepts generally, and in any case Western diplomatic influence had 'continuing effectiveness'.[15]

In December 1965 the UN General Assembly adopted its first detailed formulation of the principle of non-intervention, the 'Declaration on the Inadmissibility of Intervention in the Domestic Affairs of States'.[16] This included the following statements:

1. No State has the right to intervene, directly or indirectly, for any reason whatever, in the internal or external affairs of any other State. Consequently, armed intervention and all other forms of interference or attempted threats against the personality of the State or against its political, economic and cultural elements, are condemned...
5. Every State has an inalienable right to choose its political, economic, social and cultural systems, without interference in any form by another State.

In October 1970, the General Assembly followed this with the 'Declaration on Principles of International Law concerning Friendly Relations and Co-operation among States in Accordance with the Charter of the United Nations'.[17] The most comprehensive of the elaborations of the Charter provisions relating to peace and security, this document reiterated the above-quoted formulations of a fundamentally non-interventionist character, even strengthening them by saying 'No State *or group of States* has the right to intervene ...'.[18] However, it went

---

[15] Ian Brownlie, 'The Expansion of International Society: The Consequences for the Law of Nations', in Hedley Bull and Adam Watson (eds), *The Expansion of International Society* (Oxford: Clarendon Press, 1984), 367.

[16] The full title is 'Declaration on the Inadmissibility of Intervention in the Domestic Affairs of States and the Protection of Their Independence and Sovereignty', annexed to GA Res. 2131 (XX) of 21 December 1965, adopted with 109 in favour, none against, 1 abstaining, and 7 absent. *GAOR*, 20th session, supplement no. 14, UN doc. A/6014 (1965), 11–12.

[17] 'Declaration on Principles of International Law concerning Friendly Relations and Co-operation among States in accordance with the Charter of the United Nations', annexed to GA Res. 2625 (XXV) of 24 October 1970, adopted without a vote. *GAOR*, 25th session, supplement no. 28, UN doc. A/8028 (1971), 121–4.   [18] Emphasis added.

on to address the right of self-determination in such terms as to suggest a right to assist at least some peoples seeking self-determination:

Every State has the duty to promote, through joint and separate action, realization of the principle of equal rights and self-determination of peoples, in accordance with the provisions of the Charter...
Every State has the duty to refrain from any forcible action which deprives peoples referred to above... of their right to self-determination and freedom and independence. In their actions against, and resistance to, such forcible action in pursuit of the exercise of their right to self-determination, such peoples are entitled to seek and to receive support in accordance with the purposes and principles of the Charter.

This statement has many limitations. First, there is much scope for debate about what constitutes a 'people' and which peoples might be considered appropriate candidates for self-determination. The document appears to confine its concern to self-determination struggles in colonial territories. Second, the document, like the 1960 Declaration on Colonialism, also contained a strong reaffirmation of the territorial integrity of sovereign and independent states. Third, it was left unclear what forms of support peoples seeking self-determination were entitled to receive. Despite such limitations, the statement left an opening for a possible future defence of intervention in those cases in which there was a self-determination issue at stake.

In December 1970, less than two months after it passed the Friendly Relations Declaration, the UN General Assembly approved the 'Declaration on the Strengthening of International Security'.[19] It contains, particularly in paragraphs 4 and 5, strong reaffirmations of existing norms regarding state sovereignty and non-intervention. However, its paragraph 18 calls on all states to 'render assistance to the United Nations and, in accordance with the Charter, to the oppressed peoples in their legitimate struggle in order to bring about the speedy elimination of colonialism or any other form of external domination'. Paragraph 22 makes a connection between human rights and peace, stating that the General Assembly

Solemnly affirms that universal respect for and full exercise of human rights and fundamental freedoms and the elimination of the violation of those rights are urgent and essential to the strengthening of international security, and hence resolutely condemns all forms of oppression, tyranny and discrimination, particularly racism and racial discrimination, wherever they occur...

The 'Definition of Aggression', approved by the UN General Assembly in December 1974, is similar to the three above-mentioned declarations in that

---

[19] 'Declaration on the Strengthening of International Security', GA Res. 2734 (XXV) of 16 December 1970, adopted with 120 in favour, 1 against, and 1 abstention. *GAOR*, 25th session, supplement no. 28, UN doc. A/8028 (1971), 22–4.

it is fundamentally non-interventionist.[20] Article 5(1) states: 'No consideration of whatever nature, whether political, economic, military or otherwise, may serve as a justification for aggression.' However, its Article 6 leaves substantial scope for the Security Council to authorize the use of force; and Article 7 explicitly echoes the Declaration on Friendly Relations when it refers to 'the right to self-determination, freedom and independence, as derived from the Charter, of peoples forcibly deprived of that right' and 'the right of these peoples to struggle to that end and to seek and receive support...'.

The generally non-interventionist thrust of such UN documents reached a curious high-water mark in the fifth and final one considered here, the 1981 UN 'Declaration on the Inadmissibility of Intervention and Interference in the Internal Affairs of States'. A remarkably state-centred text, it proclaimed *inter alia* 'The duty of a State to refrain from the promotion, encouragement or support, direct or indirect, of rebellious or secessionist activities within other States, under any pretext whatsoever, or any action which seeks to disrupt the unity or to undermine or subvert the political order of other States' and 'The duty of a State to refrain from the exploitation and the distortion of human rights issues as a means of interference in the internal affairs of States, of exerting power on other States or creating distrust and disorder within and among States or groups of States'. Many important states including the US voted against this declaration.[21] Indeed, the declaration can be read as a riposte to President Ronald Reagan's emerging policy of supporting armed opposition movements deemed to be fighting for liberty in countries under communist tyranny.[22]

Can any rough and ready generalization be made regarding the directions taken by formal interpretations of the UN Charter in the Cold War years? The non-intervention rule was widely seen as fundamental and was presented as reflecting the demands of justice as well as of order. However, there were also some conflicting trends and disjointed moves which pointed, often ambiguously, in the direction of accepting the legitimacy of intervention in support of some, but only some, oppressed and threatened populations. The problems of southern Africa and the Israeli-occupied territories provided the main focus

[20] 'Definition of Aggression', annexed to GA Res. 3314 (XXIX) of 14 December 1974, adopted without a vote. *GAOR*, 29th session, supplement no. 31, UN doc. A/9631 (1975), 142–4.

[21] 'Declaration on the Inadmissibility of Intervention and Interference in the Internal Affairs of States', annexed to GA Res. 36/103 of 9 December 1981, adopted with 120 in favour, 22 against, 6 abstaining, and 9 absent. Those voting against were mainly Western developed states. *GAOR*, 36th session, supplement no. 51, UN doc. A/36/51 (1982), 78–80.

[22] Reagan had been inaugurated as US President on 20 January 1981. For an extreme expression of the Reaganite view that the US was entitled to support anti-communist resistance movements in the name of democracy, freedom, and US national security, see Constantine Menges, *The Twilight Struggle: The Soviet Union v. The United States Today* (Washington, DC: AEI Press, 1990).

62 *Adam Roberts*

for this development. In UN doctrinal debates, so far as other regions and issues were concerned, statism ruled. There would be major changes in the 1990s, but emanating more from Security Council practice than from General Assembly doctrine.

Human Rights Law

In the years since 1945, many legal developments have made the actions of governments subject to international scrutiny and, ultimately, to certain forms of international pressure. In fields ranging from arms control to the environment there are international standards by which the conduct of states can be evaluated. The body of law that most directly embodies justice-related concerns and that has made the largest inroads into state power is human rights law. Global developments in this field have been negotiated almost entirely in a UN framework.[23] In an organization consisting of sovereign states, some of them dictatorships, the issue has naturally been controversial and difficult. Yet the achievement in securing global consensus around a modest but far from empty body of rules has been considerable.

In the UN's early years, when there was a strong pro-Western majority in the General Assembly, several important steps were taken to put flesh on the bones of the Charter's commitment to human rights. On 9 December 1948 the General Assembly adopted the Genocide Convention, which specifies that any contracting state 'may call upon the competent organs of the United Nations to take such action under the Charter of the United Nations as they consider appropriate for the prevention and suppression of acts of genocide ...'.[24] This was a clear indication that an extreme issue relating to fundamental justice may entitle the UN to take coercive action against a state.

On the following day, 10 December 1948, the General Assembly adopted the Universal Declaration of Human Rights.[25] Although not a treaty, and technically no more than a non-binding declaration, it came to be seen as an

[23] For a succinct survey of the origins and growth of the UN's multi-faceted involvements in human rights issues, see Tom J. Farer and Felice Gaer, 'The UN and Human Rights: At the End of the Beginning', in Adam Roberts and Benedict Kingsbury (eds), *United Nations, Divided World: The UN's Roles in International Relations*, 2nd edn (Oxford: Oxford University Press, 1993).

[24] 1948 Genocide Convention, Article VIII. The text was adopted in GA Res. 260 (III) of 9 December 1948, adopted with 56 in favour and 2 absent (Costa Rica, El Salvador). The Convention entered into force on 12 January 1951. For a critical view of the provisions and working of the Convention, see Leo Kuper, *Genocide: Its Political Use in the Twentieth Century* (New Haven: Yale University Press, 1982), esp. 36–9, 174–85.

[25] 'Universal Declaration of Human Rights', GA Res. 217A (III) of 10 December 1948, adopted with 48 in favour, none against, 8 abstaining (Byelorussian SSR, Czechoslovakia, Poland, Saudi Arabia, South Africa, USSR, Ukrainian SSR, Yugoslavia), and 2 absent (Honduras, Yemen). *GAOR*, 3rd session, Part I, UN doc. A/810 (1948), 71–7.

authoritative interpretation of the Charter. At the time, it was vigorously opposed by the Soviet Union and other states as an infringement of sovereignty. After 18 years of bargaining in a much-changed UN came the two 1966 human rights covenants, respectively on Economic, Social, and Cultural Rights, and on Civil and Political Rights, both of which entered into force in 1976. There was also a huge range of treaties on such matters as refugees (1951), elimination of racial discrimination (1965), equal status of women (1979), torture (1984), and rights of the child (1989).[26]

These agreements had momentous implications, not just for the relations between citizen and state but also for the conduct of international relations. For good or ill, they strongly reinforced the view that a government's treatment of its citizens was a matter of legitimate international concern. They also provided mechanisms whereby a range of human rights issues could be pursued. Most dramatically, the 1984 UN Convention on Torture incorporated provision for what is commonly, if loosely, called 'universal jurisdiction'. This treaty was the basis of the judgment of the House of Lords on 24 March 1999 in the Pinochet case, that in principle the former Chilean President could stand trial outside his own country in respect of crimes committed in it. The decision marked a recognition that human rights standards were beginning to make inroads into the rival principle of sovereign immunity. However, serving ministers still retained some immunity from the jurisdiction of foreign courts.

While the development of human rights law and policy in the UN era has been impressive, it has also been deeply flawed. Three problems in particular merit attention here. First, the debates in UN fora have sometimes framed human rights issues in divisive and even misleading ways. A case in point in some 1960s discussions was the presumed dichotomy between economic and social rights—championed by the Soviet Union and many Third World states— and civil and political rights—championed particularly by Western states. It gradually came to be recognized by most states that both types of rights are not merely valuable but inherently compatible. As Amartya Sen and others have pointed out, political freedoms and independent media can assist in the satisfaction of the most basic economic rights and can help stir action against the evil consequences of droughts and other disasters.[27]

Second, a great deal of time in the 1970s and 1980s was spent at conferences which attached the language of rights to matters which were not best addressed in that manner. The so-called 'right to disarmament' was a case in

---

[26] The main agreements in the field are usefully collected in Ian Brownlie, *Basic Documents on Human Rights*, 3rd edn (Oxford: Clarendon Press, 1992).

[27] See for example the detailed studies pointing to this conclusion in Jean Drèze and Amartya Sen (eds), *The Political Economy of Hunger* (Oxford: Clarendon Press, 1990): Volume 1: *Entitlement and Well-Being*, 6–7, 23–4, 146–89; Volume 2: *Famine Prevention*, 145, 153, 159–60, 190–1.

point. Rhetoric on such matters offered excellent opportunities for the expression of self-righteousness, the attribution of blame, and the conduct of political warfare generally.

Third, states have been consistently reluctant to create strong UN-based machinery for monitoring of human rights or to fund the various bodies that have been created. There have simply been too many governments, especially dictatorships of various kinds, that have no wish to be challenged. The General Assembly has consistently been parsimonious about funding the activities of the numerous human rights bodies it has established. In particular, the Office of the UN High Commissioner for Human Rights, established in 1993–4, has been kept on a short financial leash. This is the Geneva-based body charged with implementing the complex and frustrating procedures for considering reports about the human rights situation in individual countries. When in March 2001 Mary Robinson threatened to resign as the second holder of the post of UN High Commissioner for Human Rights, her principal stated ground was the 'constraints' of the UN system, including particularly the lack of financial resources. She complained that her office received only about $20 million from the UN's annual budget of over $1 billion. Although she agreed to stay on for one further year, there has been little sign of a change of heart in the General Assembly. The extensive UN implementation machinery in respect of human rights agreements is widely viewed as ineffective.[28]

Has all the UN-based law-making and institution-building in the human rights field created a genuine global consensus on the subject? There is a consensus of a kind. The modern law in this field, as expressed in the two 1966 covenants and other documents, is no mere Western creation but the product of hard negotiations involving Western, Communist, and post-colonial states. The 1993 Vienna Conference on Human Rights proclaimed, with only modest elements of compromise, that 'the universal nature of these rights and freedoms is beyond question'.[29] Human rights have become an important part of the dialogue between states: even China, a powerful one-party state with ample reasons to be cautious about the matter, has taken some hesitant steps towards accepting that dialogue on its human rights performance is legitimate.[30]

[28] Useful critical surveys of the functioning of the existing regime are Philip Alston and James Crawford (eds), *The Future of UN Human Rights Treaty Monitoring* (Cambridge: Cambridge University Press, 2000) and Anne F. Bayefsky (ed.), *The UN Human Rights Treaty System in the 21st Century* (The Hague: Kluwer Law International, 2000).

[29] From the first paragraph of Article 1 of the Vienna Declaration and Programme of Action, adopted by consensus by representatives of 171 states on 25 June 1993 at the World Conference on Human Rights, Vienna.

[30] China signed the 1966 UN Covenant on Economic, Social and Cultural Rights in October 1997 and ratified it in March 2001; it signed the Covenant on Civil and Political Rights in October 1998 but had not ratified it by March 2002. On the background, see Ann Kent, *China, the United Nations, and Human Rights: The Limits of Compliance* (Philadelphia: University of Pennsylvania Press, 1999) and Rosemary Foot, *Rights beyond Borders: The Global Community and the Struggle over Human Rights in China* (Oxford: Oxford University Press, 2000).

Is the global consensus on human rights real? Fundamental principles of existing international human rights law that have considerable power and appeal include equality of sex and race, and the prohibition of torture. Yet even these run into problems in many states. Indeed, states have been selective about how they apply human rights principles in their domestic and foreign policies; and the language of human rights does run into genuine difficulties in many societies. Furthermore, human rights can become a weapon of political warfare, as was amply evident at the 2001 UN Conference on Racism.[31]

Could a more substantive international agreement on human rights emerge? Two possible approaches have been put forward. Professor Onuma, a Japanese international lawyer, has suggested what he calls an 'intercivilizational' approach. He argues that, even if contemporary concepts of human rights are largely Western in their origin and are subject to different interpretations, there is a need further to develop them and in particular 'to seek common standards and frameworks of human rights which are based on today's political, economic and social realities, as well as diverse civilizational underpinnings'.[32] He is on strong ground when he addresses the manner in which human rights norms are advocated and implemented. For example, he trenchantly criticizes certain human rights NGOs for West-centric narrowness and selectivity. However, he is on weaker ground when he implies that existing treaty law may be less important than a possible future consensus, as in his statement that 'existing international instruments on human rights are no more than a first clue to identify transnational and intercivilizational human rights'.[33] This approach risks leaving the impression that human rights are ill-defined pending their possible eventual emergence in intercivilizational form. By contrast, Andrew Hurrell has recommended a more cautious approach. Recognizing that human rights structures and practices have developed impressively but at the same time remain riven by political conflict and moral dispute, he suggests that 'the first commitment needs to be to forging and upholding a *procedural consensus*: an agreement between states over the framework of international rules and institutions by means of which clashes of interest and conflicting values can be mediated and through which accommodation might be possible'.[34] Hurrell's diagnosis, like Onuma's, confirms the conclusion that, while the UN has embarked on the road of seeking

[31] World Conference against Racism, Racial Discrimination, Xenophobia and Related Intolerance, Durban, 31 August–7 September 2001. Declaration adopted 8 September 2001 following numerous disagreements.

[32] Yasuaki Onuma, 'Towards an Intercivilizational Approach to Human Rights: For Universalization of Human Rights through Overcoming of a Westcentric Notion of Human Rights', *Asian Yearbook of International Law, 7* (Dordrecht: Kluwer, 1997), 37.

[33] Onuma, 'Towards an Intercivilizational Approach to Human Rights', 38–46, 78.

[34] Andrew Hurrell, 'Power, Principles and Prudence: Protecting Human Rights in a Deeply Divided World', in Tim Dunne and Nicholas J. Wheeler (eds), *Human Rights in Global Politics* (Cambridge: Cambridge University Press, 1999), 300.

genuine international consensus on human rights, the destination has not yet
been reached.

Because of the lack of a universal international consensus on how human
rights norms should be implemented, some of the more effective international
human rights regimes are regional, not global. The system based on the 1950
European Convention on Human Rights functions effectively because the
states concerned have similar outlooks on key issues, because its provisions
have become part of the domestic law of the states concerned, and because
individual redress can be sought in the European Court of Human Rights,
established in 1959. Perhaps the nearest equivalent in another continent is the
Inter-American Court of Human Rights, established in 1978. The UN has a
long way to go to achieve anything remotely comparable.

A striking feature of the UN's involvement in justice-related issues generally
and human rights in particular is the way in which it has stimulated the growth
and activity of a huge array of non-governmental organizations (NGOs). Many
NGOs have seen their role as assisting the further development of the law and
also putting pressure on states to observe commitments by which they are
already bound. At the 1993 Vienna Human Rights Conference the participants
included representatives of more than 800 NGOs. Even at the 1998 Rome
Diplomatic Conference on the Establishment of an International Criminal
Court, which, being a treaty-negotiating conference, had a more formal and
narrowly focused function, 135 NGOs attended as observers. The UN and
NGOs have operated in unspoken and sometimes conflicting conjunction, seeking to ensure observance of certain limits on the untrammelled power of states.
This is part of what some have seen as a larger process in which states are losing some of their authority upwards—to supranational authority—and some of
it downwards—to citizens and local communities.[35]

One principle of justice enshrined in human rights instruments has proved
particularly open to contentious interpretation. Article 1 of both of the 1966
UN Human Rights Covenants declares 'All peoples have the right of self-
determination. By virtue of that right they freely determine their political status and freely pursue their economic, social and cultural development'. This
reassertion of the Charter principle of 'self-determination of peoples' appears
to be both emphatic and universal in its application. However, the question of
which peoples are appropriate candidates for self-determination and which
are not remains difficult, as does the question of whether 'self-determination'
implies a right to separate sovereign statehood. There is some evidence that in
UN-centred discussions since the early 1990s the right of self-determination

---

[35] See, for example, Hisashi Owada, 'Justice and Stability in the International Legal Order:
An Essay in Legal Analysis of the Contemporary International Order', *The Japanese Annual of
International Law*, 39 (Tokyo: Japan Branch of International Law Association, 1996), 18. At that
time Owada was Japan's Permanent Representative to the UN.

has undergone changes of meaning and nuance. It was often mentioned in UN debates in the 1960s and 1970s in terms that implied a right of statehood for some, including the inhabitants of Israeli-occupied territories and of colonial hangovers in southern Africa. It was emphatically not a right for all. It appears to be undergoing a process of subtle reinterpretation as a right to a degree of self-rule and even a right to democracy, but not necessarily a right to independent statehood.[36]

Since the mid-1980s the UN has become more associated than before with the cause of multi-party democracy. It has supported elections as a means of resolving certain internal conflicts; it has become deeply involved in planning, organizing, and monitoring elections in numerous countries; and in at least two cases—Haiti and Sierra Leone—the Security Council has given legitimacy to those who sought to restore a democratically elected government that had been deposed in a military *coup d'état*. The developing association between the UN and democracy, however tentative and incomplete, confirms the far-reaching implications of the UN's preoccupation with human rights and other justice-related issues.

The Laws of War

In its early years, the UN was involved only in a minimal way in the field of the law of armed conflict—*jus in bello*. This was partly because of a belief that the UN's job was to eliminate war altogether, not to mitigate its effects. In 1946 the General Assembly did affirm the principles of international law recognized by the Charter and judgment of the Nuremberg tribunal.[37] However, in over four decades of negotiations it failed to agree to a text spelling out what those principles actually were, largely because states found it difficult to address the touchy question of a soldier's right to disobey superior orders if they are illegal.[38] In 1948, as noted above, the General Assembly adopted the Genocide Convention, which belongs equally to human rights law and the laws of war. However, the UN's involvement remained limited. The 1949 Geneva Conventions and some subsequent agreements on the laws of

---

[36] Discussed further in Adam Roberts, 'Beyond the Flawed Principle of National Self-Determination', in Edward Mortimer with Robert Fine (eds), *People, Nation and State: The Meaning of Ethnicity and Nationalism* (London and New York: I. B. Tauris, 1999).

[37] GA Res. 95 (I) of 11 December 1946, adopted unanimously.

[38] The tortured draft of one of the International Law Commission's inconclusive attempts to spell out the Nuremberg principles can be found in *Yearbook of the International Law Commission 1950*, II (New York: UN, 1957), 374–8. The problem of defining the Nuremberg principles has largely been overtaken by the adoption of the 1998 Rome Statute of the International Criminal Court. See esp. Articles 25 (individual criminal responsibility), 27 (irrelevance of official capacity), 28 (responsibility of commanders and other superiors), and 33 (superior orders and prescription of law).

war were negotiated by states outside a UN framework: key coordinating roles were played by the Swiss government and the International Committee of the Red Cross. The Geneva Conventions introduced provisions for what is sometimes called 'universal jurisdiction' in respect of grave breaches, but this had only limited effects. It did not turn out to be a general licence to states to issue international arrest warrants for foreigners suspected of war crimes. This became particularly clear in an ICJ case brought by the Democratic Republic of the Congo (DRC) against Belgium, which had issued an international arrest warrant *in absentia* against the DRC's foreign minister on the grounds of grave breaches of the Geneva Conventions and crimes against humanity. The alleged crimes had been committed outside Belgium and neither perpetrator nor victims were Belgian citizens. In its decision of 14 February 2002 the ICJ decided that the DRC's foreign minister, who in the meantime had ceased to hold ministerial office, had had immunity from criminal jurisdiction and that the arrest warrant should therefore be cancelled.

In the decades after 1949 the UN did gradually become more involved in the laws of war. Some of the early activities in this area were minor and at arm's length: it was a UN specialized agency, UNESCO, that provided the framework for negotiating the 1954 Hague Convention for the Protection of Cultural Property in Armed Conflict. In the late 1960s the UN General Assembly, and through it the UN more generally, became much more active in this field. In 1968 the General Assembly adopted unanimously a much-acclaimed resolution on 'human rights in armed conflict' which established its interest in the field, created a useful link with human rights which brought the subject into the UN's competence, and was to play a key part in stimulating the further development of the law. Important as it was, this resolution was not free of that element of hypocrisy so often detected in the work of international bodies. It *inter alia* called on 'all States which have not yet done so to become parties to the Hague Conventions of 1899 and 1907 ...'.[39] Out of the 58 states supporting this resolution which were not parties to the key treaty concerned, 1907 Hague Convention IV, only one—South Africa—actually followed up, ten years later. The disjunction between what states vote for in the UN and what they actually do was evident.

The UN's involvement in the field, which proceeded side by side with a tendency in international diplomacy to relabel the laws of war as 'international humanitarian law applicable in armed conflicts', has had limited effects. From 1967 onwards, the numerous General Assembly and Security Council

[39] GA Res. 2444 (XXIII) of 19 December 1968, 'Respect for Human Rights in Armed Conflicts', adopted with 111 in favour, none against, and none abstaining. GAOR, 23rd session, supplement no. 18, UN doc. A/7218 (1969), 51. Subsequently, apart from South Africa, only Fiji (in 1973) became a party to the Hague Convention IV; but, having joined the UN only in 1970, it had not voted for the resolution.

resolutions on Israeli conduct in the territories occupied in 1967 (discussed further below) achieved little. As far as treaty-making is concerned, the UN interest in the field has not supplanted the coordinating role of states and other bodies, and many treaties since 1968 have, as before, been negotiated outside a UN framework. However, certain treaties were negotiated in UN committees and/or conferences, including the 1976 Convention on Environmental Modification Techniques and the 1980 Convention on Certain Conventional Weapons. The Security Council's role in establishing the criminal tribunals for the former Yugoslavia (1993) and Rwanda (1994), and the General Assembly's role in preparing the way for the conference which drew up the 1998 Rome Statute of the International Criminal Court, are strong evidence of the UN's commitment to implementation of international humanitarian law. In 1999, these aspects of UN activity were also reflected in the issuing of three sobering reports relating to the protection of civilians against the effects of armed conflict generally,[40] the failure to prevent the genocide in Rwanda in 1994,[41] and the failure to prevent the mass killings at Srebrenica in Bosnia in 1995.[42]

The UN's involvement in laws of war matters relates to its roles in relation to international order in several distinct ways. The most significant are as follows: (1) there is a hope, expressed in a number of Security Council resolutions, that the prosecutions will help to deter the commission of similar crimes in the future; (2) the establishment of criminal tribunals, particularly the Yugoslav one, has reinforced views that justice against war criminals is a critically important part of peace-building after a civil war, since blame for atrocities can thereby be attached to named individuals rather than to entire ethnic groups; and (3) the UN Security Council, as seen at the end of the next section, has on a number of occasions felt obliged to authorize military action when fundamental norms of the laws of war have been repeatedly violated by a party to a conflict.

3. EPISODES INVOLVING ISSUES OF ORDER AND JUSTICE

Rhodesia and South Africa

There were two notable exceptions to the thrust of the UN's general pronouncements and resolutions of the 1960s and 1970s condemning interference in the internal affairs of states. The UN Security Council determined that

---

[40] 'Report of the Secretary-General to the Security Council on the Protection of Civilians in Armed Conflict', UN doc. S/1999/957 of 8 September 1999.

[41] 'Report of the Independent Inquiry into the Actions of the United Nations during the 1994 Genocide in Rwanda', attached to UN doc. S/1999/1257, New York, 16 December 1999.

[42] 'Report of the Secretary-General pursuant to General Assembly resolution 53/35: The Fall of Srebrenica', UN doc. A/54/549 of 15 November 1999.

two particular situations that were largely internal, in both of which a critical issue was racial domination by a white minority population, constituted threats to international peace and security. It made such determinations in respect of Rhodesia in 1966 and South Africa in 1977, in both cases taking action— namely, sanctions—under Chapter VII of the Charter.[43] In neither case did the Security Council authorize direct external military intervention within the state concerned, but it did appear to accept that domination by a minority and refusal to take into account the wishes of the majority population were factors which helped to justify taking measures under Chapter VII. Thus the Security Council's approach, even though stopping short of direct military intervention, seemed to recognize the primacy of justice in these very special situations.

The UN General Assembly was also active against Rhodesia and South Africa, not least through its important acts of recognition of national liberation movements. However, as an arena in which self-righteousness flourishes, and assuming too easily that it had a monopoly on international justice, the General Assembly sometimes made mistakes even in respect of these territories. Its tendency to engage in shrill and ineffectual condemnations of the activities of great powers, especially the US, was manifested in successive resolutions condemning the US 'constructive engagement' initiative in southern Africa in the 1980s led principally by Chester Crocker. A very long General Assembly resolution on Namibia passed in September 1986 '*Strongly rejects* the policies of "constructive engagement" and "linkage", which have served to encourage the racist régime of South Africa to continue its illegal occupation of Namibia, and calls for their abandonment so that United Nations resolutions and decisions on the question of Namibia can be implemented'.[44] Great rhetoric, but within four years, due partly to the Crocker mission, Namibia was independent and a UN member.[45]

While the General Assembly strongly supported action against Rhodesia and South Africa, it resisted any doctrine that might imply any general right to take action against oppressive governments. The UN's member states, by defining the problems there as illegitimate and racist final remnants of European colonialism, avoided any implication that their own subject peoples might have a right of secession.

[43] SC Res. 232 of 16 December 1966, imposing sanctions on Southern Rhodesia; and SC Res. 418 of 4 November 1977, imposing an arms embargo on South Africa.

[44] 'Question of Namibia', GA Res. S-14/1 of 20 September 1986, adopted with 126 in favour, none against, and 24 abstaining including the US and many other Western states.

[45] Long negotiations under US mediation led to agreements on Namibia and Angola signed in New York on 22 December 1988 by Angola, Cuba, and South Africa. The Namibia agreement provided *inter alia* for a ceasefire and elections under UN supervision and for methods of reaching agreement on a date for the final withdrawal of the South African administration and its forces. Elections were held on 1 November 1989. Namibia achieved independence on 21 March 1990 and was admitted to the UN on 23 April.

Overall, the UN's involvement in the affairs of Rhodesia and South Africa helped to consolidate the interest of post-colonial states in the UN and it served a valuable purpose in keeping these issues on the agenda. The UN did itself no harm by being closely associated with the causes of racial equality and majority rule.

The Israeli-occupied Territories

Ever since the Israeli conquest of the West Bank, Gaza, and the Golan Heights in the Six Day War in 1967, the UN has been deeply involved through commissions, committees, and a stream of resolutions from the Security Council and the General Assembly on the subject. These have raised in sharp form numerous justice-related issues. The resolutions have stressed the unacceptability of permanent acquisition of territory through force, the need for a negotiated peace, the applicability of the 1949 Geneva Civilians Convention to the occupation, and opposition to a range of Israeli practices in the territories, including the establishment of settlements.

Some of these resolutions and other UN actions were carefully considered and achieved virtually unanimous support. However, other resolutions betrayed a tendency to engage in political warfare. The General Assembly's approach was often strident and denunciatory, most notably in the notorious and subsequently abandoned 1975 resolution equating Zionism with 'racism and racial discrimination'.[46] This had the effect of forcing Israel into the same category as South Africa. Some Arab states voting for the resolution, including Syria, had killed more of their own citizens than were ever killed in the Israeli-occupied territories.

A fateful effect of the UN resolutions on the Israeli-occupied territories was that they were widely interpreted in the Arab world as establishing that the Israeli occupation was completely illegal and had been so proclaimed by the highest decision-making bodies in the world. This view was far from being the whole truth. There are questions about the legal standing of General Assembly resolutions, especially when not strongly supported; and in fact those proclaiming the Israeli occupation as illegal per se had received only modest support. Resolutions of both the General Assembly and the Security Council recognized that an Israeli withdrawal must follow from negotiation and be part of a process of mutual recognition—a process which would require the participation, usually not forthcoming, of Arab states and the Palestinian political leadership. However, the simple view that the occupation

---

[46] GA Res. 3379 (XXX) of 10 November 1975, adopted with 72 in favour, 35 against, 32 abstentions and 5 absent; revoked by GA Res. 46/86 of 16 December 1991, adopted with 111 in favour, 25 against, and 13 abstentions.

had been proclaimed illegal prevailed, contributing to political hostility and hampering the conclusion of peace agreements.

A further effect of the strong expressions of view in a UN framework has been that it is even more difficult than it would have been anyway, due to the veto and other factors, for the UN to be an effective interlocutor in negotiations on the future of the occupied territories. UN demands for a comprehensive solution on the basis of defined principles prevented the UN from managing the pragmatic and piecemeal negotiations necessary to any actual settlement. By contrast, the US, while justly criticized for its often uncritical support of Israel, emerged as the only power capable of managing effective negotiations between Israel and its neighbours. Results included the 1974 Israeli-Syrian disengagement agreement, the 1978 Camp David accords between Egypt and Israel, the 1993 Washington Agreement providing for limited Palestinian self-rule, and the 1994 Israel-Jordan peace treaty.

The UN's roles in the Israeli-occupied territories have had both positive and negative effects. Some UN actions may have strengthened the hand of those Israelis who favoured conducting the occupation with restraint and on the understanding that it was temporary. However, the UN efforts have exposed in sharp relief certain hazards that can accompany an emphasis on justice. In particular, the idea that the fruits of military conquest should never be recognized and made permanent, while central to UN ideas of a just international order, can make it hard to achieve a peace based on political compromise and may have contributed to the extreme difficulty of reaching a general peace agreement in the Arab-Israel conflict. The occupied territories have remained a poisonous issue, and from 1967 to 2002 have contributed to a political atmosphere, not confined to the Middle East, in which terrorist movements of exceptional ferocity can flourish. The seriousness of the problem of the occupied territories has frequently led UN bodies, as in a 1985 General Assembly resolution, to temper 'unequivocal' condemnations of terrorism with clauses urging states to 'contribute to the progressive elimination of the causes underlying international terrorism and to pay special attention to all situations, including … those involving alien occupation, that may give rise to international terrorism …'.[47] This was open to interpretation as tending to excuse or even justify terrorism, and contributed to suspicions that the UN, by using or abusing the language of justice, was failing to address terrorism seriously.[48] While some later resolutions were more genuinely unequivocal, many UN resolutions and much rhetoric in a UN framework did undermine the idea,

---

[47] GA Res. 40/61 of 9 December 1985, adopted without a vote.

[48] For a vigorous critique by the US State Department's Legal Adviser, see Abraham D. Sofaer, 'Terrorism and the Law', *Foreign Affairs*, 64 (Summer 1986), esp. 903–6.

important to the UN, that there must be principled limits to the use of force. The language used at the UN could be taken as implying that justice trumped all other considerations.

The Helsinki Process

UN principles on order and justice can have an impact on diplomatic processes in which the UN is not directly involved. A good example was the Conference on Security and Co-operation in Europe (CSCE). The pattern was set in the first phase of CSCE negotiations in 1971–5. Certain justice-based provisions of the UN Charter and of other UN-based treaties and procedures permeated every part of the 1975 Helsinki Final Act. In one of the many references to justice, Principle VII of the document stated: 'The participating States recognise the universal significance of human rights and fundamental freedoms, respect for which is an essential factor for the peace, justice and well-being necessary to ensure the development of friendly relations and co-operation among themselves as among all States.'[49] The Helsinki package, whatever the Soviet motives in accepting it, did much to legitimize dialogue about human rights both within and between the countries involved; and the resulting Helsinki process contributed something to the end of communist rule in eastern European states and the Soviet Union in 1989–91.

Justice Issues in Interventions during the Cold War

At various times in the Cold War Western states often complained that any interventions they launched were routinely condemned, whereas the General Assembly did not adopt equally strong resolutions on certain cases of interventions by certain other states. Some of the Western complaints betrayed incomprehension of the strength of UN criticisms. After the Suez disaster in 1956, British officials complained that the UN was concerned with order, not justice. This reflected British anger that the UN Security Council and General Assembly had been more effective in stopping the Suez intervention than in taking action on the Soviet intervention in Hungary; and that the UN had failed to show understanding of the stated purpose of the Franco-British military action against Egypt, namely, the restoration of claimed international rights in Egypt. Sir Ivone Kirkpatrick said in an article published in March 1957, shortly after his retirement as Permanent Under-Secretary of the Foreign Office: 'A United Nations which is concerned only to prevent the use

[49] Conference on Security and Cooperation in Europe, *Final Act* adopted at Helsinki on 1 August 1975, Cmnd. 6198 (London: HMSO, 1975), 5.

of force, but which has neither the will nor the capacity to cause truth and justice to prevail, constitutes a positive incitement to lawlessness and injustice.'[50]

The UN General Assembly's failure to criticize the Indian invasion of Goa in 1962 reinforced criticisms of the organization. However, the retrocession of colonial enclaves did undeniably present the UN with a series of tricky problems. Another notable silence followed the Soviet-led occupation of Czechoslovakia in 1968: the Czechoslovak government, acting under duress, asked that the matter not be discussed.

The Indian intervention in East Pakistan in 1971 was defended in the Security Council by both India and the Soviet Union, partly on the grounds of justice. Human rights and other justice-related issues were made urgent by the repression by Pakistan's armed forces, which had led to a flow of 10 million refugees to India. The Indian Foreign Minister, in the course of his plea to the Security Council, emphasized key justice-related issues.[51] This did not cut much ice with the Western powers, especially the US, which appeared to be more interested in strategic stability and pressed ahead with ceasefire resolutions. The Soviet Union, which strongly supported India, used the veto to prevent these ceasefire resolutions from being passed. Nor did India's plea for justice get much support in the General Assembly, where a resolution was passed calling for a ceasefire.[52]

The General Assembly routinely condemned a number of interventions, including the Indonesian invasion of East Timor (1975), the Moroccan invasion of Western Sahara (1975), and US-led interventions in Grenada (1983) and Panama (1989). It also criticized certain interventions by the Soviet Union and its allies, namely, the Vietnamese invasion of Cambodia (1978) and the Soviet intervention in Afghanistan (1979). It paid little heed to the justifications made by interveners. Where there seemed to be a conflict between the morality of states and the morality of individual justice, the morality of states generally prevailed: the Vietnamese invasion of Cambodia in 1978, criticized in numerous General Assembly resolutions from November 1979 onwards, left the UN with the choice of which regime to recognize: the old genocidal one or the new one which was the illicit child of intervention. In choosing the

---

[50] Sir Ivone Kirkpatrick, 'Must the UN Collapse?', *The Sunday Times* (24 March 1957). The previous month a Foreign Office memorandum entitled 'The United Nations: A Stocktaking' had been even more critical of the UN on these grounds. See FO-371/129903, UN-2251/27 of 7 February 1957. I am indebted to Dr Neil Briscoe for this information, which appears in much fuller form in his Oxford doctoral thesis on Britain and UN peacekeeping (2002).

[51] He made specific reference to paragraph 22 of the Declaration on Strengthening International Security. UN, SCOR, 26th year, 1613rd meeting, 13 December 1971, 23.

[52] GA Res. 2793 (XXVI) of 7 December 1971, adopted with 104 in favour, 11 against, 10 abstentions, and 6 absent. The states opposing a ceasefire were India, the Soviet Union, and allies.

former course, it appeared to prefer the morality—if it can be called that—of states. Non-interventionism seemed to be the dominant principle.

International Interventions in the 1990s and Beyond

Since early 1991, the UN has been involved in intervention in a new and different way, and more through the Security Council than the General Assembly. There are some common elements. In numerous crises the Security Council specified certain conditions that were to be observed by a state or parties to a conflict. These conditions were generally about justice: return of refugees, observance of human rights law and the laws of war, assistance to humanitarian workers, and the return of democratic governments which had been ousted in a *coup d'état*. In several cases, following resolutions on these matters, there was multilateral military action by armed forces from outside the country concerned. In all these cases such action, whether or not specifically authorized by the UN, and whether or not with the consent of the government of the host state, had a stated purpose of implementing the relevant UN resolutions. Something along these lines happened in northern Iraq (1991), Bosnia and Herzegovina (1992–5), Somalia (1992–3), Rwanda and Haiti (1994), Albania (1997), Sierra Leone (1997–2000), Kosovo (1998–9), and East Timor (1999).

The UN's involvement in justice-related issues in the 1990s has not been limited to these cases. In central America, emphasis on human rights has been an important part of peace settlements, especially in Guatemala, and in these contexts the UN role has been seen as an advocate, though not efficient protector, of human rights.

It is a strange paradox that the UN, which until the 1980s was so closely associated with the principle of non-intervention, has in many ways and many instances become associated with intervention. The UN's focus in the post-Cold War era on justice-related issues and its increased willingness to contemplate or tolerate intervention have many causes. It would be idle to assume that it is a simple story of increased preoccupation with international justice. The timing and location of interventions has been determined, not by abstract considerations of justice, but by a range of political and military calculations which have included consideration of the likelihood of effective military resistance. Factors of interest have been ever-present. For example, in most crises of the 1990s an interest in ensuring that refugees do not flood into neighbouring countries has resulted in an active policy of bringing about change in the refugee-producing society: refugee issues have powerfully driven the increased international emphasis on human rights and humanitarian norms. This is one of the numerous ways in which old-fashioned state interest has formed an unholy alliance with norms of justice.

The interventionism of the 1990s and early twenty-first century, in which UN institutions and UN-backed norms have played a significant part, has achieved some significant results. Not the least of these is that large numbers of refugees and internally displaced persons were able to return to their homes, including in northern Iraq, Haiti, Kosovo, and East Timor. In Bosnia in 1995, outside intervention played some part in the military pressure that led to the ceasefire and the Dayton settlement. However, many of the interventions, including those in northern Iraq, Somalia, and Haiti, experienced difficulty in establishing a stable political order. Such cases serve as a reminder that, while an international presence may sometimes help in the process, both justice and order must have local roots if they are to endure.

4. CONCLUSIONS AND GENERAL ISSUES

In the UN era, the contrast between precepts of justice and realities of politics, always striking in international relations, has continued. However, there have been distinctive new elements. Serious efforts have been made to create elements of a global consensus about certain justice norms and even about their implementation; to hammer out differences between various national and intellectual traditions; and to develop an institutional role for the UN itself as well as for regional organizations. The UN is now strongly associated with the view that an enduring peace, between or within states, should be based on ideas of justice. These conclusions explore some issues raised by these distinctive elements.

From the negotiation of the UN Charter onwards, the interests and ideologies of major powers, including the permanent members of the Security Council, have shaped the UN's preoccupation with a wide range of issues connected with justice, including issues that affect the citizen's relations with the state. Interest and justice have not inhabited separate categories. However, from 1945 onwards, the UN's articulations of principles of order and justice, including in the field of human rights, have not been the result of dominance by a single hegemonic power but the product of hard bargaining between states with different outlooks and traditions. Granted this fact, the extent of accord, especially in the field of human rights, is remarkable. It is equally remarkable that the collapse of the Soviet empire, and other changes since the end of the Cold War, have not led to a sense that all the justice-related agreements negotiated with active Soviet participation in the Cold War years are now out of date.

However, the continued existence of deep differences in outlook between states suggests the need for caution before we rush to any conclusion that international norms relating to justice, for example in the sphere of human rights, are part of a teleological process leading inevitably to a superior and more stable international system.

The underlying tension, evident in the Charter itself, remains between a set of rules designed for inter-state stability and a set of general norms aimed at justice. Indeed, it has been made much more acute by the development of an extensive body of law giving flesh and even teeth to previously vague norms. The continuing tension is evident in the unresolved debates on whether there is a right of humanitarian intervention; in the perennial difficulty of the question—raised frequently by the negotiation of peace agreements aimed at ending armed conflicts—whether amnesties for former war criminals can ever be appropriate; and, above all, in the willingness of states and individuals, including terrorists, to take up arms against a perceived international injustice. The UN era has witnessed the growth of numerous doctrines justifying the use of force in the name of justice. The virtues of Burkean prudence, the case for pursuing political goals by non-violent means, and the importance of restraints on the use of violence which would apply in both peace and war have sometimes received insufficient attention both inside and outside UN fora.

A striking feature of the UN era, arising particularly from the UN's involvement in justice-related issues, has been the increased role of NGOs, including in UN conferences and decision-making. Also certain other bodies such as the International Committee of the Red Cross have increased an already well-established presence. In some cases such bodies have been a formal part of UN conferences, in others they have influenced them from the fringes. At times they can be a scourge of the UN, as in their criticisms of the adverse effects of sanctions on the Iraqi population. NGOs have also had a powerful effect in keeping issues on the agenda and in drawing attention to the gaps between what states say and what they do. In some instances, as with the 1997 Ottawa Convention on Anti-Personnel Mines and the 1998 Rome Statute of the International Criminal Court, they have contributed significantly to the conclusion of radical and controversial inter-state treaties. The role of NGOs and similar bodies is viewed with a degree of scepticism by some states: for example, China sees them as an essentially Western phenomenon, and the US, having been critical of the role of NGOs in the negotiating process for both the above-mentioned treaties, remains hostile to the resulting texts. Yet the role of NGOs is now a reality which serves as a reminder that states, and inter-state bodies, are far from being the only actors in international relations.

Throughout the organization's history, UN bodies have been right to keep certain justice-related issues alive and on their agenda, and to press for their eventual resolution. Cases in point include southern Africa and East Timor. In such territories, supporting order and the status quo at the expense of justice would have been grotesque. Yet the UN's proper emphasis on justice does come at a price: in some cases it may exacerbate a crisis. Conflict resolution and preventive diplomacy, even in the hands of the most skilled negotiators, are not cure-alls. Where, as over East Timor or the Israel-Palestine conflict, both sides are deeply attached to their goals and associate them with principles of justice, attempts at negotiated solutions frequently lead to explosions of violence.

The most marked changes in justice-related issues since the end of the Cold War in 1989–91 have concerned implementation. There have been serious national and international efforts at implementation of humanitarian and human rights norms, including assistance in democratic development and election monitoring. However, implementation remains a weakness of the UN emphasis on justice. States generally have been reluctant to give serious money or legal teeth to some of the main UN bodies concerned with monitoring and implementation. In some extreme emergencies, as in Rwanda in 1994, states have also been reluctant to act militarily in support of such rights. It is progress that since 1990 the UN has been more willing than before to establish tribunals to punish extreme violations of international humanitarian norms and to authorize or tolerate military action against certain offending states provided that they have special claims on the attention of major states and are not too powerful themselves. The fact that even former heads of government and state—such as Jean Kambanda of Rwanda, Augusto Pinochet of Chile, and Slobodan Milosevic of Yugoslavia—have not been immune from legal process confirms how significant the development of justice-related norms and procedures has been. A difficulty with the new emphasis on implementation is that it is inevitably selective and reinforces frustration in some parts of the world when perceptions develop that certain injustices—for example, in the Israeli-occupied territories—have not been put right.

The attitude of the US to the UN's emphasis on justice and to the concern about implementation is profoundly ambivalent. The UN is seen as a useful forum for what the US does well: coalition-building. However, it is also a place where great powers, including the US, can be and frequently are criticized and through which the US, even more than most countries, can be dragged into military interventions in support of international principles, in circumstances where its interests are not obvious. The UN's declaratory but sometimes ineffectual role can force the US into schizophrenic policies: for example, supporting an arms embargo on the countries of former Yugoslavia in the Security Council while simultaneously conniving in the arming of Croatia. The US fears the supranational element in some of the UN's justice-related work, and is especially nervous that the International Criminal Court might prosecute its servicemen.

The UN is by no means universally associated with justice. The Security Council's arms embargo in the Yugoslav wars of 1991–5 was widely criticized as assisting the Belgrade government, the principal denier of justice to Croatia and Bosnia. There and elsewhere, UN peacekeeping has sometimes been impartial between the attacker and the victim. The killings in Rwanda in 1994 and at Srebrenica in 1995, both of which occurred in countries where UN forces were present, cast a shadow over the UN's pretensions to stand for justice. Economic sanctions, so often used by the UN in the 1990s, can be a blunt and cruel instrument, and the UN's use of them against Iraq has led to huge criticism. The structure of the Security Council denies proper representation to certain major states. Sooner or later the UN will have to address the difficult conundrum of its own democratic deficit. There may be doubts as to whether any kind of directly elected democratic control over the operations of the UN itself is possible or desirable. An extensive and rigorous culture of accountability, with all aspects of UN activities subject to professional evaluation, may provide one approach to the problem.

Despite its incompleteness, and the problems it has caused, the UN's espousal of justice-related issues has taken root and will not disappear. A realist health warning must be added: the watchful concerns of states with power and the pursuit of interest endure. However, the realist reductionist fantasy, seeking to avoid the grand rhetoric of global justice and find the minimum conditions of coexistence, has had its day. No states take a position explicitly privileging order over justice. A wide range of justice issues is perceived by most states to be not merely a legitimate part of UN activities but an important contribution to international stability.

The question for member states is not whether the UN should be involved in justice-related issues but which ones should be emphasized, how they should be pursued, and how clashes over them should be mitigated. There have been momentous developments on these matters in the years since 1945, exemplified by the fact that interventions within states, with some degree of authorization from the Security Council and justified in terms of justice as well as order, are now tolerated by the community of states, even if they are nervous about embracing a general doctrine approving such practice. There remains the question of which particular justice-related issues should be the main focus of further development in the twenty-first century. Democracy and principled limits on the use of political violence are two interesting but of course problematical candidates.

3

Order, Justice, the IMF, and the World Bank

NGAIRE WOODS

Debates about global economic governance bring the tensions of reconciling order and justice in world affairs into sharp focus. Every economic order makes some claim to justice. Free-market capitalism is said to reward the hard-working and entrepreneurial. Centrally planned economies are said to protect the poor and unfortunate. Equally, at the international level debates rage about order, justice, and the role of governments. What should the IMF, the World Bank, or the World Trade Organization do? What 'public goods' should they produce? Whose interests should they further? And to whom, in the end, are they accountable? Every international organization is built upon some understanding of international order and the requirements of stability in world affairs. So, too, each is underpinned by a vision of justice that guides the broader purposes of the organization and imbues it with legitimacy in carrying out its day-to-day work. But the demands of order and justice in the global economy are extremely difficult to define.

Achieving order in a globalizing economy is becoming ever more complex. International flows of capital, investment, goods, services, information, and corporate organization are increasing in quantity and speed. Managing the global economy was never an easy task, and in the twenty-first century it is one fraught with more fragilities and instabilities than ever before. This was dramatically demonstrated by the economic consequences of the terrorist attacks on the US on 11 September 2001. As stock markets plunged and national airlines faced bankruptcy, policy-makers were forced to reassess the issue of how to intervene effectively in a global economy. Even before September 2001, the experiences of the 1990s had proven that a crisis in Thailand could provoke a financial collapse in Russia that would itself reverberate rapidly into the corridors of an investment fund in Greenwich, Connecticut. When the US hedge

This chapter draws on an article previously published by the author, 'Making the IMF and World Bank More Accountable' *International Affairs*, 77/1 (2001).

fund Long Term Capital Management wobbled in 1998, it threatened to bring down America's largest banks and with them stability in the world economy.

Equally difficult and complex are the requirements of justice in a globalizing world economy. State borders now provide even less of a buffer than they did previously to justice claims in international affairs. Poverty, for example, has become a major issue on the global economic governance agenda, even though in some countries its causes should be located at the domestic rather than the international level. Equally, claims for gender equality spill over into the international community as groups within countries address international fora in search of redress. Certain states have become ever more subject to the imposition of economic conditionality and external intervention in matters of domestic governance. All of these considerations throw into sharp focus the issue of who should be accountable to whom and for what in the international system.

The work of the IMF and the World Bank powerfully reflects the changes described. Created immediately after the Second World War, both institutions originally embodied the then strong consensus against interventionism as expressed in Article 2(7) of the Charter of the United Nations: 'Nothing contained in the present Charter shall authorize the United Nations to intervene in matters which are essentially within the domestic jurisdiction of any state ... '. Yet in recent years the work of both the IMF and World Bank has expanded to include programmes and policies that affect a wide range of people, groups, and activities within states as much as, if not more than, among states. The work of the Fund and Bank now roams into areas that were previously considered taboo, such as good governance, the rule of law, judicial reform, corruption, and corporate governance.

For many developing countries, the new role and scope of the IMF and World Bank threaten to reduce the role and accountability of national governments. This is problematic in a world in which globalization is already eroding government capacity. Developing countries regularly face negative economic shocks that are not of their own making, be it in respect of commodity prices or trade access. 'Contagion' in global capital markets adds the further risk that a country might be dragged into a serious financial crisis, regardless of the soundness of its own policies. In a crisis, most developing countries have to turn to the IMF and the World Bank for assistance. Yet, far from restoring or bolstering their sovereignty, multilateral assistance comes at the price of further international intrusion. The price paid by governments for assistance, in addition to interest payments, is conditionality, which requires them to reform their economies and societies at a fundamental level. For these reasons, over two-thirds of countries in the world have become more deeply affected than ever before by the work of the IMF and World Bank. Unsurprisingly then, in recent years, both institutions have been subject to greater scrutiny. Critical attention has focused on both their contribution to order and their impact on justice in the global economy.

Critics allege that the IMF and the World Bank are bad for both order and justice. They argue that the institutions' prescriptions for liberalization and privatization exacerbate inequality within states and leave developing countries yet more vulnerable to industrialized countries' protectionism and instability. They argue that the Fund and the Bank represent the interests of powerful industrialized country groups and exacerbate global injustice. Supporters of the institutions, on the other hand, point out that these bodies are limited by their resources, by the political preferences of their major shareholders, and by the reluctance of borrowing governments seriously to implement the whole range of reforms necessary to bring about equitable development. They argue that, although the institutions are flawed, they are probably the best hope we have for both order and justice. Supporters remind us that, at minimum, the IMF and the World Bank are multilateral and universal organizations. They permit all countries to have some say, even if decision-making power is weighted. Furthermore, the institutions are accountable to their entire membership.

Critics and supporters of the Fund and the Bank highlight both what the institutions do and how they do it. The agencies are alternatively criticized or praised for the outcomes of their work in alleviating or exacerbating poverty. So, too, they are criticized or praised for their structure and procedures. Some hold up as a model of efficiency the small Executive Board and weighted voting power of the IMF and the World Bank. Others criticize the same as secretive, unequal, and unjust.

The underlying premise of this chapter is that the outcomes reached by the IMF and the World Bank are inextricably linked to the processes they each adopt. Put simply, the mission of each institution is determined by a political process that mediates, or should mediate, a wide range of views about what is just and unjust, what works and what does not. Countries rarely agree on these things; indeed, economists rarely agree with each other. Where they agree on the goals of economic policy, they often disagree about which policies would best achieve those goals. And where economists agree about policies, they often disagree about the order and priority of the policies that are to be implemented. For these reasons the processes used to determine what the IMF and the World Bank do and how they do it are central to the debate about justice.

This chapter focuses on how the IMF and the World Bank make decisions and implement them. It does this by asking: to whom are the institutions accountable and how? The answers highlight the tensions involved in balancing the needs of order, efficiency, and stability on the one hand, and justice, equity, and legitimacy on the other. It may seem desirable for the ends of 'justice' that a decision about global policy is taken in consultation with virtually everyone and every government in the world economy. Yet the requirements of order and efficiency will often mean that the decision has to be made in a more timely and less costly way. Sometimes in the work of the IMF and the World Bank there are trade-offs between order and justice. Interestingly, however, there are several areas in which the procedural demands of order and justice seem to be converging.

The first section of this chapter outlines the decision-making structure in the IMF and the World Bank as planned by their founders back in 1944. The second section discusses the defects in this structure, highlighting how it skews accountability and whom it leaves out. Section three analyses recent attempts to make the institutions more inclusive and more accountable. The conclusion offers some recommendations for improving the institutions and sounds a warning about the limits of procedural justice and accountability at the international level.

1. DECISION-MAKING IN THE IMF AND THE WORLD BANK: TO WHOM ARE THE INSTITUTIONS ACCOUNTABLE?

Like many international organizations, the IMF and the World Bank face complex problems of legitimacy when they try to answer simple questions such as: who do they represent, to whom are they accountable, and how? Within democratic political systems, there exist a wide range of mechanisms to ensure that the government has the consent of the governed. These include a number of mechanisms for representation and voice, but also ways by which policy-makers are held to account and the abuse or misuse of political power is prevented.[1]

'Procedural justice' in domestic politics is ensured through measures such as elections, ombudsmen, and judicial review. The aim is to make sure that, overall, governments abide by the rules of the game and that political actions are predictable, non-arbitrary, and procedurally fair. Decision-makers are supposed to be answerable, and this means that rules and parameters on the exercise of power have to be enforced. For all these reasons, accountability within public institutions is an integral part of our conception of 'justice'.

Unlike democratically elected governments, international institutions cannot claim that their actions are legitimized by the existence of elections, judges, ombudsmen and so forth. Decision-makers within the international institutions do not face the same range and depth of constraints that exist

---

[1] Andreas Schedler, Larry Diamond, and Marc Plattner (eds), *The Self-Restraining State: Power and Accountability in New Democracies* (Boulder, CO: Lynne Rienner, 1999).

in domestic societies. Rather, international organizations grapple with an unwieldy structure of government representation. In the past, when such institutions were required to perform a narrow range of technical functions, the consequent problems of representation and accountability were less acute. Today, however, the international financial institutions (IFIs) are being required to perform a much broader range of tasks directly affecting a wider range of people. This makes their decision-making procedures all the more important.

The basic structure of decision-making in the IFIs works through representatives of governments. At the top of the system are the boards of governors—the ministers of finance or development, central bank governors, and their equivalents—who meet just once per year and are supposed to oversee and maintain overall control of the institutions. However, the day-to-day operations and main work of the institutions are overseen by representatives of member states who sit on the executive boards of each institution. The executive directors, as they are called, have a dual role: to represent a country or a group of countries and collectively to manage the organization. Executive directors appoint and can dismiss the head of each organization who in turn controls the management and staff.

The chain of representative accountability described is in practice a long and imperfect one. Flaws in each link highlight how weak the relationship between most member governments and the IMF and the World Bank are. Simply put, member governments—with the obvious exception of the US—are too far removed from the workings of the representative body—the executive board—which in turn exercises too little control over the staff and management of the institutions for its role to be described as an exercise of vertical accountability.

2. WHY DO THE IMF AND THE WORLD BANK NOT SEEM ADEQUATELY REPRESENTATIVE OR ACCOUNTABLE?

A first core problem in the structure of the IMF and the World Bank is one of flawed representation. The board should reflect governments who are members of each organization. Yet representation is inadequate in two respects. In the first place, the board does not adequately represent all members, and it particularly fails adequately to represent countries with the most intensive relationships with the institutions, for example the African members. A second aspect of the problem is that representatives on the boards of the institutions are too distant from the governments they represent and stakeholders most affected by the work of the institutions. Let us examine each of these arguments in turn.

Representation on the Executive Boards is Too Unequal

The board of executive directors ('the board') is the vital link from countries—and voters—to each of the IMF and the World Bank. Yet only the largest member countries—the US, Germany, France, Japan, UK, Saudi Arabia, Russia, and China—are directly represented by their own executive director. All other economies are grouped within constituencies represented by just one executive director. This means that most national governments have only the weakest link to the formal deliberations and decision-making processes of the institutions. For example, in the IMF 21 Anglophone African countries, at least eleven of whom have an 'intensive-care' relationship with the institution and all of whom are deeply affected by its work, are represented by just one executive director and have a voting share of only 3.26 per cent. In the World Bank, the same group of countries plus the Seychelles are likewise represented by one executive director and have a voting share of 4.07 per cent. Further exacerbating this lack of representation is the fact that these countries also lack influence in the informal processes of consultation and decision-making within both the IMF and the World Bank.

When the board makes decisions, each country has voting power exercised by the executive director representing it. In each institution, this voting power depends upon a country's 'quota', which is determined by a formula that attempts to translate relative weight in the world economy into a share of contributions and votes—and, in the IMF, access to resources. The formula has been criticized for some time and its technical elements have recently been reviewed for the managing director of the IMF.[2] The real problem with quotas and voting power, however, is that they were created to govern institutions with very different world roles from those played by the IMF and the World Bank today.

Voting shares in the World Bank and the IMF are allocated according to rules formulated in 1944. At that time, members of both institutions were expected to be both contributors and borrowers, with the exception of the US. European countries expected to draw both upon the IMF for assistance in crises and on the International Bank for Reconstruction and Development (IBRD, later part of the World Bank group) for post-war reconstruction and development. Hence, 'shareholding members' were also 'stakeholders' in the work of the institution. Furthermore, the accountability of the IMF was

---

[2] See the Report to the IMF Executive Board of the Quota Formula Review Group (Washington, DC: IMF, 28 April 2000). For earlier critiques see: Nancy Wagner, *A Review of PPP-Adjusted GDP Estimation and its Potential Use for the Fund's Operational Purposes*. IMF Working Paper (Washington, DC: IMF, 1995); and Ariel Buira, 'The Governance of the International Monetary Fund', in Roy Culpeper and Caroline Pestieau (eds), *Development and Global Governance* (Ottawa: International Development Research Centre, the North-South Institute, 1996).

largely 'constitutionalist', with its duties and actions carefully prescribed by its Articles of Agreement. Neither the Bank nor the Fund were given an explicit mandate to enter into policy conditionality and to attempt to alter the economic structure of a member's economy in a far-reaching way. These founding presumptions of the IMF and the World Bank were rapidly superseded by events. The role of the World Bank, then actually the IBRD, was transformed in 1947 when the Marshall Plan was announced to deal with reconstruction in Europe. This left the World Bank lending exclusively to developing countries. In the 1970s, the IMF's role changed dramatically when the Bretton Woods system of exchange rates collapsed. By the 1980s, both institutions had become heavily involved in conditionality and policy-based lending. Over this time, the membership of both institutions more than trebled as decolonization brought a host of new, independent states into their midst. The result of these changes has been dramatically to expand the number of 'stakeholders' in the institutions. The original stakeholders made large contributions to the basic capital of the institutions. A subsequent group of stakeholders—'non-concessional borrowing countries'—are those who pay most of the running costs of the institutions through loan charges. A further—overlapping—group of stakeholders are those whose cooperation is vital if the IMF and the World Bank are to fulfil their respective purposes. This now embraces a much wider, indeed universal, category of countries.

By 2000, in the wake of the financial crises of the 1990s, the powerful industrialized members of the IMF and the World Bank had cast the institutions into the role of ensuring 'forceful, far-reaching structural reforms' in the economies of borrowing members in order, among other things, to correct weaknesses in domestic financial systems and ensure growth and poverty alleviation.[3] The result is not only that borrowing members have a high stake in the institutions but that equally the institutions have a high stake in gaining a deep political commitment to change in borrowing member countries. Yet the stake of countries whose commitment is now being sought is not reflected on the executive boards of either the Fund or the Bank; indeed, it has even been diminished.

When the IMF and the World Bank were created, there was a clear and explicit concern to ensure some equality among members to reinforce the 'universal' and 'public' character of the institutions as opposed to giving them a structure that simply reflected economic and financial strength in the world economy.[4] This was achieved by giving every member of the institution 250 'basic votes',[5] to which were added weighted votes apportioned on the basis

    [3] IMF, *The IMF's Response to the Asian Crisis* (Washington, DC: IMF, 1998).

    [4] Joseph Gold, *Voting and Decisions in the International Monetary Fund* (Washington, DC: IMF, 1972), 18, 173–4.

    [5] Keith J. Horsefield, *The International Monetary Fund, 1945–1965: Twenty Years of International Monetary Cooperation*, I (Washington, DC: IMF, 1996).

of the quota—mentioned above. In this way two kinds of stake were acknowledged: to a degree, every member had both an equal stake in the institution and recognition of its specific contributions and influence. As I have argued elsewhere, this balance, explicit in the foundation of the institutions, has subsequently been dramatically eroded. The proportion of 'basic votes' to total votes has diminished from its high point of 14 per cent of all votes in 1955 to around 3 per cent in both the Fund and the Bank.[6] Yet, if anything, the role of basic votes should have increased as the stakes in the institution changed in the ways described above.

The Executive Boards Do Not Adequately Hold the Staff and the Management to Account

Once it is established that member states are represented in the IMF and the World Bank purely through the executive board, it can be seen that these boards are also the only way in which, formally, the institutions can be held to account by their members. This requires scrutiny of the quality and depth of oversight and control exercised by the executive boards over the work of each institution. In each of the Fund and the Bank, the board is expected to appoint and oversee the senior management and work of the institutions. However, in practice, the board rarely holds the management and staff of the institutions tightly to account. Executive directors seldom have the time or information properly to scrutinize decisions, for several reasons.

In the first place, it is difficult for members of the executive boards to prepare positions on all countries, papers, and issues brought to board meetings. Many executive directors are in the job only for a short time. Indeed, in some multi-country constituencies there is regular and short-lived rotation of the executive directorship. In the second place, the executive board is not assisted in playing an active role by the staff and management of each institution, who seldom divulge internal disagreements to the board, tending instead to attach 'considerable importance' to presenting a unified view in board discussions.[7] A third feature of the executive boards is that many decisions are taken, or agreement reached on them, prior to board meetings. As reports on both the Fund and the Bank aver, real debates over policy and issues are conducted outside of the board.[8] Controversial cases and stand-off debates are rare. A loan, for example, that did not meet with US approval would seldom be presented

---

[6] Ngaire Woods, 'The Challenge of Good Governance for the IMF and the World Bank Themselves', *World Development*, 28 (2000), 28.

[7] IMF, *External Evaluation of IMF Surveillance*, Report by a Group of Independent Experts (Washington, DC; IMF, 1999), 34; World Bank, *Report of the Ad Hoc Committee on Board Procedures* (Washington, DC: World Bank, 26 May 1992).

[8] IMF, *External Evaluation* and World Bank, *Report of the Ad Hoc Committee*.

to a board for discussion. Before getting that far, in most—but not all—cases staff and management would have been in dialogue with those whose agreement was necessary for the loan to go through. Finally, it has been argued that the executive board's limited oversight is also due to the fact that directors are protective of the countries they represent, and expect—and reciprocate—similar deference from their colleagues on the board. Hence, in the words of the External Evaluation into Surveillance, what is supposed to be 'peer pressure' in fact becomes 'peer protection'.[9]

The Heads of Both Organizations are Selected by a Non-transparent Process that Excludes Most Member Countries

A further, very obvious way in which the IMF and the World Bank seem inadequately representative or accountable to their membership lies in the appointment of the heads of each organization. Appointed by the executive boards, it is to these heads of the organizations that all staff must eventually account. Yet in neither the Bank nor the Fund is there an open and transparent process of appointment, whether aimed at achieving political representation or technical excellence. Rather, a 50-year-old political compromise means that in each organization the head is appointed by convention according to the wishes of the US in the case of the World Bank and of Western Europe in the case of the IMF. This process came under scrutiny during the appointment in spring 2000 of the managing director of the IMF, when Germany's first favoured candidate failed to win support from other major shareholders. This resulted in much adverse press and policy attention, not so much to the personalities involved but to the evident lack of transparency and accountability in the selection process. Although both institutions have established committees to propose improvements in the appointment procedure, until the US and European countries are prepared to give up their privilege change in this procedure will not occur.

The Role of the IMF and the World Bank has Expanded, their Decision-Making Structure and Accountability has not

The problems of accountability highlighted above have all been magnified by the increase in and transformation of the activities of the IMF and the World Bank. Previously, the need to respect the sovereignty of member governments limited their range of activities. However, both now reach deeply into policy-making within member governments, going well beyond the delicately respectful parameters set out in the original Articles of Agreement. Specifically,

---

[9] IMF, *External Evaluation*, 34.

as Devesh Kapur has argued, both the IMF and the World Bank embrace areas of policy that it was inconceivable for them to touch prior to the 1980s. The expansion can be tracked by measuring how numbers of 'performance criteria' on which loans are conditional have increased: in a sample of 25 countries, there were between six and ten measures in the 1980s, as contrasted with around 26 measures in the 1990s.[10] Equally, if not more revealing, is the way the number of programme 'objectives' being included in loans and programmes has increased, with countries now being required to undertake actions such as mobilizing, redefining, strengthening, or upgrading government processes in an ever wider range of areas.

The new conditionality is dramatically deepening and broadening the purview of the IFIs within member countries. No longer are they engaged in merely monitoring specific macroeconomic policy targets in the context of a crisis, or specific project loans and conditions. Both institutions are now engaging governments in negotiations that cover virtually all issues of economic policy-making—and beyond, with good governance extending into the rule of law, judicial reform, corporate governance, and so forth. This new, wide-ranging domain of advice and conditionality directly affects a wider range of policies, people, groups, and organizations within countries. Yet the IMF and the World Bank were not created or structured to undertake or to be accountable for such wide-ranging activities. They were created to deal with a narrow, clearly stipulated range of technical issues. For this reason, at their birth it was decided that they should deal with member countries only through the treasury, finance ministry, central bank or suchlike of a country and that only a representative of these agencies could sit on the boards of the institutions[11]—which is still true today.

Meanwhile, the work of both the IMF and the World Bank has broadened and deepened far beyond the purview of the finance ministries or central banks with whom they are negotiating. This means that, through conditionality and loan agreements, the Fund and the Bank are making finance ministries or central banks formally accountable for policies which should properly lie within the scope of other agencies and for which those other agencies are domestically accountable. We would expect policy affecting the distribution of health care, for example, to be the responsibility of the minister of health, a public figure who we could expect to be answerable to voters and to his or her society at large. Yet, as the Fund and the Bank intrude further into these

---

[10] Devesh Kapur, 'Expansive Agendas and Weak Instruments: Governance Related Conditionalities of the International Financial Institutions', *Journal of Policy Reform*, 4/3 (2001); and Devesh Kapur and Richard Webb, *Governance-Related Conditionalities Of The International Financial Institutions* (Geneva: UNCTAD, 2000).

[11] See in the Articles of Agreement of the IMF (Article V, section 1) and the World Bank (Article III, section 2).

kinds of decisions, the risk is that the line of accountability they establish with the finance ministry or central bank will override other agencies and local or democratic accountability.[12]

A further implication is that, while in theory different agencies within government compete for and debate competing priorities and goals, negotiations with the Fund and the Bank heavily sway these debates, subjecting broad areas of policy to the narrower focus, priorities, and analysis of central banks and finance ministries, even though neither necessarily have the desire, mandate, accountability, or expertise to evaluate and formulate policy in respect of these broader issues. In a subtle way, this point is underscored by a remark in the 'External Evaluation into IMF Surveillance' report, where the evaluators found that 'the most favourable appraisals came from those whose lines of work bore close similarities to the Fund's—central banks, and, to a lesser extent, finance ministries'.[13] Turned on its head, this statement emphasizes the degree to which the Fund's core mandate remains that shared with central bankers. Yet, at the same time, the institution is now formulating directions for policy in areas outside of this formal mandate and expertise.

In the extreme, the problem becomes that succinctly expressed by Martin Feldstein in response to the IMF's intervention in East Asia: 'The legitimate political institutions of the country should determine the nation's economic structure and the nature of its institutions. A nation's desperate need for short-term financial help does not give the IMF the moral right to substitute its technical judgements for the outcomes of the nation's political process.'[14] The accountability problem underscored here is: who makes particular policy decisions? By whose rules? And under whose scrutiny?

3. IMPROVING PROCEDURAL JUSTICE IN THE IMF AND THE WORLD BANK

Aware of the criticisms they face, and also frustrated by their limited effectiveness in implementing wider policy reform, both the IMF and the World Bank have begun more explicitly to recognize a wider range of stakeholders in their work. Both institutions have undertaken a number of steps to make themselves more accountable to such stakeholders, including more transparency, new mechanisms of horizontal accountability, and working more closely with

---

[12] Of course, the external line of accountability does not always produce the outcomes desired by the IFIs, as argued by Paul Collier, 'Learning From Failure: The International Financial Institutions as Agencies of Restraint in Africa', in Schedler *et al.*, *The Self-Restraining State*, 313–30.   [13] IMF, *External Evaluation*, 35.

[14] Martin Feldstein, 'Refocusing the IMF', *Foreign Affairs*, 77/2 (1998), 27.

non-governmental organizations. The implications for accountability are worth examining.

Transparency

First and foremost among the steps taken by the institutions in improving their own accountability is an increase in transparency. Both the IMF and the World Bank now publish a large amount of their own research and explanations of what they are doing—and to what effect—on their websites. They are also pressing governments to permit greater disclosure and publication of policies and agreements made with governments, which are confidential if the government so wishes.

Transparency is crucial to improving the accountability of both institutions. It makes it possible to hold them to account by opening up their express objectives, advice, and agreements. At the same time, however, some important limitations deserve noting. First, there are still many gaps in what is publicly available to date. For example, the World Bank has an excellent independent unit of evaluations, the Operations Evaluation Department (OED), yet not all of its publications are available to the public. In the IMF, internal review documents are not available. These omissions are important, for the outside scrutiny of such documents not only adds to the external accountability of the organizations but also ensures that such reviews are taken seriously within the institutions themselves.

A second issue raised by the new penchant for transparency is its cost. Often underestimated by major shareholders pushing for greater transparency are the high costs of collecting, editing, and publishing information. Of course, such costs are borne in large part by borrowing members of the institutions, since they add to the running costs of the institutions and thereby to their loan charges. Third, if not carefully considered and balanced, transparency of selected data, policy, or considerations rather than all of them can distort decision-making or perceptions of it. Most importantly of all, however, transparency provides the most important and necessary—but not sufficient—means for the IFIs to be held accountable.

Ensuring Member Governments are Accountable to their Own People for Policies Agreed with the IFIs

A second part of the new transparency policies of both the Fund and the Bank has been to promote transparency within countries with whom they work. The rationale here is that, while the IFIs advise and assist member countries, it is governments in those countries that are accountable for all policies, both to global markets and to their own people. Of course, this formulation glosses over the fact that some governments see little choice but to accept Fund or Bank advice and assistance, having resorted to the IFIs for assistance precisely because they have no alternatives. The transparency being pursued by the IMF involves releasing their documentation and agreements with countries, with the agreement of the member governments concerned. The result has been the publication of information such as Public Information Notices (PINs) following about 80 per cent of its Article IV consultations, and publishing Letters of Intent (LOIs) and related country documents that underpin Fund-supported programmes with respect to about 80 per cent of requests for or reviews of Fund resources.

Going yet further, in some cases the IMF and the World Bank now require governments to consult more and to be actively accountable to their own people. At the behest of their largest contributors, both IFIs are requiring governments wanting enhanced debt relief under the Heavily-Indebted Poor Countries (HIPC) initiative to produce a plan as to how they intend to reduce poverty. The plan, labelled the Poverty Reduction Strategy Paper (PRSP), must be 'nationally owned' and produced in consultation with 'civil society'. Uganda and Mauritania were the first to qualify for enhanced debt relief under this programme, having each had a pre-existing well-developed plan for poverty reduction. Bolivia also qualified early by producing an interim PRSP on the basis of a 'national dialogue' already undertaken which set out future plans for reducing poverty and for engaging civil society in the formulation of its full PRSP.[15]

The new disclosure and consultation measures highlight the sensitivity of the IFIs to concerns about accountability, not just within the institutions but also within countries with whom they are working. Significantly, the Fund and the Bank have ceased to describe their interlocutors in member countries exclusively as 'national authorities'. Rather, the World Bank writes of 'development partners'[16] and the IMF of 'authorities and civil society' and of the need for its programmes to enjoy 'ownership by the societies affected'.[17] Along with this recognition has come the opening up of new mechanisms through which these groups can question or probe the legitimacy of the IFIs' assumptions and recommendations.

Agencies of Horizontal Accountability

The terms 'constitutionalism' and 'democracy' have been used to contrast different kinds of accountability.[18] For example, in the US political system,

---

[15] For an updated list of countries preparing PRSPs, see http://www.imf.org/external/np/prsp/

[16] World Bank, *Partnership for Development: From Vision to Action* (Washington, DC: World Bank, 1998).

[17] IMF, 'The IMF in a Changing World', remarks by Horst Köhler, Managing Director, given at the National Press Club (Washington, DC, 7 August 2000).

[18] See comments by Richard Sklar on Guillermo O'Donnell, 'Horizontal Accountability in New Democracies', in Schedler *et al.*, *The Self-Restraining State*, 53–8.

while democracy is served by the US Congress, constitutionalism is served by the Supreme Court. This simple contrast usefully highlights the way 'horizontal' or 'sideways' accountability can enhance vertical accountability by contributing agencies and processes that exist to monitor and to enforce the mandate, obligations, rules, and promises of institutions.

Within the IFIs, several agencies and processes have recently emerged with the aim of enhancing horizontal accountability. For example, the IMF has commissioned three independent external evaluations in the past decade and has published their reports, and has now created an office for independent evaluation.[19] Much more established is the World Bank's OED, which reports to the executive board. The OED rates the development impact and performance of all the Bank's completed lending operations, as well as the Bank's policies and processes, and reports its findings to the board. In 1993, in the context of a broad review of the Bank's disclosure policy, access was opened up to the OED's 'Annual Review of Evaluation Results' and summaries of evaluation reports ('Précis') for selected projects. Since that time, much more of the OED's work has become publicly available.

A more powerful and unprecedented step towards greater horizontal accountability was taken in the World Bank in 1993, when the executive board created an Inspection Panel. The Panel opens up the possibility for complaints to be made by any group able to show that: (1) they live in the project area—or represent people who do—and are likely to be affected adversely by project activities; (2) they believe that the actual or likely harm they have suffered results from failure by the Bank to follow its policies and procedures; (3) their concerns have been discussed with Bank management and they are not satisfied with the outcome. The three-person Inspection Panel has powers to make a preliminary assessment of the merits of a complaint brought by a group, taking into account Bank management responses to the allegations. Subsequently, it can recommend to the Board that a full investigation be undertaken, and make recommendations on the basis of such an investigation. The executive board retains the power to permit investigations to proceed and to make final decisions based on the Panel's findings and Bank management's recommendations. The Inspection Panel thus enhances the power of the executive board as well as of a wide group of affected 'stakeholders' in the Bank's work.

The most highly publicized of recent cases is that of the Western Poverty Reduction Project in Qinghai, China. The case resulted from a complaint filed by the International Campaign for Tibet (ICT), a US-based NGO acting on behalf of local people, which claimed that the project would harm Tibetan and Mongolian people. The final report of the Inspection Panel found that the

---

[19] See IMF, *Report to the IMFC on the Establishment of the Independent Evaluation Office and its Terms of Reference* (Washington, DC: IMF, 12 September 2000).

Bank had failed to comply with some of its own policies, including those on the environment, indigenous peoples, and disclosure of information.[20] The case became a notorious one in the media, mobilizing US and international Tibet campaign groups as well as environment lobbies and supporters of indigenous groups.

Behind the media glare of such cases, a number of serious questions of governance emerge as to the role and implications of such inspections, as highlighted in retrospect by one of the expert consultants who advised the Inspection Panel in the China case. Robert Wade points out that an initial problem with the Panel is that its 'image of success is to find projects out of compliance'. He then writes that

since almost any project can be found to be out of compliance if one pushes hard enough, and since there is no limit to the cases that affected groups can bring—assisted by Washington-based NGOs—the Bank is likely to be deluged with Inspection Panel investigations.[21]

The problems hinted at here are worth examining further, for they touch on the core question of how widely or narrowly 'accountability' should be defined and what kind of breach should trigger an enforcement action.

If the 'triggering mechanism' for inspection is unlawfulness, this not only presumes that actions that are legal must also be legitimate in the eyes of the citizenry but opens up the risk that minor 'legal' infractions can be used as a weapon for much larger political purposes. This point has been made in a study of accountability whose author, alluding to the Clinton-Lewinsky scandal, reminds us that 'minor legal infractions can be used by partisan opponents to thwart the clearly expressed preference of the public-at-large'.[22] In other words, beware of the fact that agencies of horizontal accountability can be abused.

The warning about the abuse of inspections or horizontal accountability agencies is an important one because inspections cost money and take time. Wade reports that the East Asia department of the Bank spent about $3 million on work responding to the Panel's investigation of Qinghai, in addition to the extra costs incurred by the Chinese government. The cost of the extra work that the East Asia region proposed as a consequence came to another $2.5 million. The cost of that which the Panel report calls for is estimated at

[20] World Bank, *China Western Poverty Reduction Project Inspection Panel Report* (Washington, DC: World Bank, 2000) and see http://www.worldbank.org/eap/eap.nsf/

[21] Robert Wade, 'A Defeat for Development and Multilateralism: The World Bank has been Unfairly Criticised over the Qinghai Resettlement Project' (full manuscript unpublished, short version published in *Financial Times*, 4 July 2000).

[22] See comments by Philippe Schmitter on Guillermo O'Donnell, 'Horizontal Accountability in New Democracies' in Schedler *et al.*, *The Self-Restraining State*, 59–62.

around \$4 million, or 10 per cent of the total loan. Wade reports that this cost, and the fear of an inquisitorial process, means that Bank staff are now refusing to contemplate projects involving involuntary resettlement or indigenous peoples, because they cannot compete with other sources which do not have to take into account such high additional costs. This, he implies, is ultimately to the detriment of the disadvantaged groups that the Bank is setting out to assist.[23]

An alternative model of accountability, which avoids some of the problems above, is that provided by the new Office of the Compliance Adviser/Ombudsman (CAO) of the International Finance Corporation (IFC) and the Multilateral Investment Guarantee Agency (MIGA). This new ombudsman's office was created in June 1999 after consultations with shareholders, NGOs, and members of the business community. The aim was to find a workable and constructive approach to dealing with environmental and social concerns and complaints of people directly affected by IFC- and MIGA-financed projects. The CAO and her staff are independent of the Bank and IFC and report directly to the president of the World Bank. The emphasis of the office's work, however, is very much dialogue, mediation, and conciliation. Other than the power to make recommendations, the CAO has no formal powers. Indeed, the draft operational guidelines of the office state: 'The ombudsman is not a judge, court or policeman.'[24]

In the absence of enforcement powers, one must ask whether an ombudsman can really be considered a mechanism of accountability. Clearly the CAO office provides for transparency and monitoring, and these are vital to accountability. It also provides for a very light form of indirect enforcement. For this reason, it avoids the costs associated with the Inspection Panel, highlighted above, and possibly also the incentive for users to abuse the process of accountability in the pursuit of other goals. However, it remains to be seen whether this mechanism has enough power to hold decision-makers to account. More generally, such mechanisms cannot be seen as sufficient in and of themselves to patch up the accountability of international institutions. They operate alongside the forms of vertical accountability outlined above, affording another 'check' on IFI officials.

The experiments in compliance enforcement being undertaken in the World Bank and IFC highlight how little horizontal accountability exists for the IFIs. Obviously, the primary agencies that should hold the institutions to account are their member governments, through bolstered and improved forms of vertical accountability. However, both IFIs are now working in a world political

---

[23] Wade, 'A Defeat for Development'.
[24] *Operational Guidelines for the Office of the IFC/MIGA* (Washington, DC: World Bank), at http://www.ifc.org/cao

system in which groups within and across countries are becoming more effect-ive at demanding more account of the work of international organizations, both through governments and directly from the organizations concerned. It is for this reason that horizontal accountability has become a large plank in both IFIs' responses to those who criticize their unaccountability. A further part of this response has been to engage more directly with their critics and in particular with non-governmental organizations.

Engagement with Non-governmental Organizations

In recent years both the IMF and the World Bank have begun to recognize non-state actors and non-governmental organizations (NGOs). The trend was acknowledged in 1999 by the then US Secretary of the Treasury in discussing the Fund's modus operandi:

It should become more attuned, not just to markets, but the broad range of interests and institutions with a stake in the IMF's work. Just as the institution needs to be more permeable for information to flow out, so too must it be permeable enough to let in new thoughts—by maintaining a vigorous ongoing dialogue with civil society groups and others.[25]

Both the Fund and Bank make much more information and analysis available to NGOs. The World Bank's NGO-World Bank Committee, established in 1982, has become more active. Both the Bank and the Fund now consult with lobbying organizations in Washington DC, with grass-roots organizations in member countries, trade unions, church groups, and such like. These contacts are taking place at regional, country, and local levels. World Bank regional directors and IMF resident representatives are being told to seek out and main-tain such contacts. At the annual and spring meetings, both institutions have been actively involved in more dialogue and meetings with a select group of transnational NGOs (TNGOs). In addition to these measures that increase transparency and consultation, the institutions have also moved more recently to permit some level of local participation by non-state actors, such as in the PRSPs being required of countries seeking enhanced debt relief.

It is worth stressing that NGOs have not become the major 'stakeholders' in the institutions: they have not acquired control or a formal participatory role in decision-making except at the behest of their own governments. However, where 'Northern' NGOs have allied with or used political leverage in major shareholding countries—at any rate in the US—they have exercised consid-erable informal power and influence. Indeed, in such cases, the position of

---

[25] Lawrence Summers, 'The Right Kind of IMF for a Stable Global Financial System', remarks to the London Business School, 14 December 1999 (US Treasury: LS-294).

some NGOs starts looking much stronger than that of many smaller developing countries, whose formal right to participate in decision-making is diluted
by the problems of representation described earlier. For this reason, the recognition of NGOs as stakeholders has led to a vociferous debate about the
accountability and legitimacy of the NGOs themselves, in particular among
developing country governments.

In further analysing this debate it is useful to distinguish local or 'Southern'
NGOs within borrowing countries, and transnational or 'Northern' lobbying
organizations, usually based in Washington DC or one of the G-7 capitals. The
implications of developing relations with each are somewhat different for the
accountability of the IFIs.

Engagement with Southern NGOs

Local or Southern NGOs are stakeholders in a direct sense of the term: they
represent groups directly affected by the programmes and policies of the IFIs.
Their inclusion in discussions and strategy formulation is required because of
the way in which the activities of the IFIs have broadened. Both IFIs recognize that, to quote the World Bank, 'policy reform and institutional development cannot be imported or imposed'.[26] In countless publications, both IFIs
recognize that wider participation and ownership is required for policies to be
successfully implemented.[27] For these reasons, the IMF and the World Bank
are encouraging both their own local representatives and government officials—such as in the PRSP process outlined above—to develop consultative
links with local NGOs. At the same time, NGOs now have access to the complaints procedures described above, namely, the World Bank Inspection Panel
and the IFC Ombudsman.

However, new relations with Southern NGOs do not resolve the problems
of accountability faced by the IFIs, even if they add some positive elements.
Neither the Fund nor the Bank has been structured as an agency of forceful,
far-reaching domestic reforms. Their governance structure gives them neither
the necessary elements of legitimacy nor accountability for such tasks. They
are being forced for practical and political reasons to look beyond their
traditional and narrow points of contact with 'national authorities'—finance

---

[26] World Bank, *Annual Review of Development Effectiveness* (Washington, DC: World Bank,
1999).

[27] See World Bank, *Sub-Saharan Africa: From Crisis to Sustainable Growth* (Washington,
DC: World Bank, 1989); *Governance and Development* (Washington, DC: World Bank, 1992);
Governance: The World Bank's Experience (Washington, DC: World Bank, 1994); *The World
Bank Participation Source Book* (Washington, DC: World Bank, 1996), and *Annual Review*.
IMF: *Good Governance: The IMF's Role* (Washington, DC: IMF, 1997); *External Evaluation
of the ESAF*, Report by a Group of Independent Experts (Washington, DC: IMF, 1998); *A Guide
to Progress in Strengthening the Architecture of the International Financial System*
(Washington, DC: IMF, 2000).

ministries, central banks and the like—to the wider 'civil society'. However, such relations should not divert attention from the core lack of accountability to developing country governments. Are the IFIs beginning to step around governments and themselves attempt to persuade societies to support certain kinds of reform? The problem here is that the government itself should be the agent of persuasion. And borrowing governments will not be able to persuade their own societies to accept changes required by international institutions in which they—developing country governments—cannot claim to have an effective voice.

Relations with NGOs also bring problems of accountability and legitimacy of their own. Foremost is the question of which 'civil society groups' ought to be consulted or recognized. As Jan Aart Scholte has documented in the case of the IMF, some non-governmental groups, such as business groups, are being consulted much more than others.[28] This poses the question: to whom are local NGOs accountable, and for what? Until now, both the IMF and the World Bank have been pursuing relations with NGOs in an ad hoc and reactive way. However, as Charles Abugre and Nancy Alexander have noted, one needs to consider more systematically criteria such as the effectiveness, representativeness, internal decision-making structure, membership, and accountability of groups being so consulted.[29] The problem of accountability in local NGOs is further heightened where they are given a more active role in the implementation or formulation of policy. In such cases, the accountability of local NGOs ought to be compared with that of local government agencies. In the 1980s and early 1990s it was sometimes too readily assumed that the former were preferable; in the World Bank's work in Africa this led to criticisms of the Bank for undermining the capacity of governments in the region.[30] A decade later, it has become more obvious that using NGOs to bypass government institutions risks thwarting 'institution building' and 'state modernization'.

A final problem concerning relations with Southern NGOs is the question of who shapes and influences the modalities and processes of consultation with such groups. In the PRSP process described above no framework was spelled out. There is nevertheless a risk that certain kinds of consultations become recognized in a de facto way as preferable to others, *not* on the grounds that they enhance existing mechanisms of local accountability but rather on the grounds that they please the political sensitivities and preferences of major

[28] Jan Aart Scholte, 'The IMF Meets Civil Society', *Finance and Development*, 35/3 (1998), 42–5.
[29] Charles Abugre and Nancy Alexander, 'Non-Governmental Organizations and the International, Monetary and Financial System', *International Monetary and Financial Issues for the 1990s*, IX (Geneva: UNCTAD, 1998).
[30] Abugre and Alexander, 'Non-Governmental Organizations', 114.

shareholders in the IFIs. In other words, there is a risk that a new 'Washington consensus' on the politics of participation and consultation will be forged, and that this will pay insufficient attention to the complex social and political arrangements which give life to accountability at the local level.[31]

Nonetheless, the vociferous debate about NGOs and their lack of accountability risks being overplayed in the context of Southern NGOs. Certainly, they now have access to more information, and transparency is a powerful step towards holding governments and institutions to account. NGOs are also, with government approval, being consulted more regularly. In the World Bank and the IFC they have the right, although not necessarily the resources, to access the new complaints procedures. These steps, however, do not amount to a transfer of decision-making power or substantial influence. Indeed, the argument has been made that Southern NGOs should be strengthened and used more efficiently by developing-country governments, (1) in order to enhance their own information and analysis regarding the IFIs; (2) as a bargaining counter, in alliance with Northern NGOs, to put pressure on major shareholders, who face demands from their own publics to pay attention to NGOs; and (3) to counter the power of Northern NGOs.[32]

New consultation mechanisms with NGOs in borrowing countries highlight problems of order and justice within countries and the need for more democratic and inclusive processes within those countries. They do not, however, provide an immediate unproblematic solution. Nor do the new forms of consultation resolve problems of accountability both within the IFIs and in relation to their government interlocutors. Indeed, these problems may well be exacerbated by new developments in the IFIs' relations with the other category of new lobbyists and stakeholders: Northern NGOs.

Engagement with Transnational and Northern NGOs

TNGOs do not have the same stake in the IFIs as directly affected local groups. In defining their 'stake' in international organizations, one needs to consider their broader place in global governance. Even there, they are not part of the state-based system of representation in world politics. But politics is not just about representation, it is also about debate; and in international politics, NGOs open up and contribute to an active debate about the IFIs and their policies. Their role is to speak for different views and interests that are

---

[31] For the original statement of the Washington consensus, see John Williamson, *Latin American Adjustment: How Much Has Happened?* (Washington, DC: Institute for International Economics, 1990). For subsequent analysis see: Moises Naim, 'Washington Consensus or Washington Confusion?', *Foreign Policy*, 118 (2000), 86 ff.; Joseph Stiglitz, *More Instruments and Broader Goals: Moving Towards the Post-Washington Consensus* (Helsinki: WIDER/ United Nations University, 1998); and Robin Broad and J. Cavanagh, 'The Death of the Washington Consensus?', *World Policy Journal*, 16/3 (1999).

[32] Abugre and Alexander, 'Non-Governmental Organizations'.

not necessarily expressed through the formal channels of representation, that is, to act as lobbyists for particular interests relevant to notions of justice, development, the environment, and so forth. In more academic terms, the argument for the place of NGOs in an international 'deliberative democracy' is voiced by theorist James Bohman: 'In the case of a political setting where there is no public to whom appeal can be made or institutions in which voice is important, international institutions and the NGOs that attempt to influence their procedures and standards themselves can function as a public to whom equal access of political influence is guaranteed and open.'[33]

The accountability problem posed by TNGOs lies first and foremost in the question: to whom are they themselves accountable? Most TNGOs are accountable in various ways to at least three constituencies: their member-ship—actual and potential, and predominantly Northern; their major funders and/or clients, which include governments and corporations; and in many cases NGO partners, some in the South. Overall, there is a tendency for such TNGOs to be primarily accountable to Northern groups, funders, and partners. For this reason, a long-standing concern about TNGOs has been that they magnify Northern views—both outside of governments and through governments—in the international organizations, adding yet another channel of influence to those peoples and governments who are already powerfully represented.

The risk here is that TNGOs further distort the inequalities of power and influence already emphasised in this chapter. As Abugre and Alexander found: 'Activism by US NGOs has probably expanded the already disproportionate role of the US in the IFIs, especially the World Bank.'[34] Similarly, where TNGOs deploy their considerable resources and expertise in representing and assisting local groups bringing cases to the Inspection Panel, it is not always the case that the interests of those being represented are the same as the interests of those to whom the TNGO is primarily accountable—members and funders. The TNGO has an incentive to favour an outcome that maximizes publicity and sup-port for itself. Yet in some cases the quieter, compromise decision may well do more for the group they claim to represent.

The difficulty for critics is that, whilst the work of many TNGOs has undoubtedly magnified Northern influence in the IFIs, other TNGOs have used their influence with the US government—both Congress and the Executive—and other G-7 governments effectively to campaign for greater transparency, disclosure, and new forms of horizontal accountability, which are of interest to all stakeholders. Hence, some TNGOs have assisted in enhancing the accountability of the IFIs, even while at the same time further undermining

---

[33] James Bohman, 'International Regimes and Democratic Governance: Political Equality and Influence in Global Institutions', *International Affairs*, 75 (1999), 511.

[34] Abugre and Alexander, 'Non-Governmental Organizations', 116.

the relative power and participation of both developing countries and Southern NGOs.

The devil with TNGOs lies not so much in the detail as in the objectives, priorities, and constitutions of the organizations. Some TNGOs working on and with the IFIs are fully aware of the risks mentioned and steer clear of them by prioritizing multilateralism, local accountability, and capacity-building in developing countries. In so doing such groups are implicitly respecting the claims of more directly affected stakeholders to have priority in holding the institutions to account. TNGOs that do not so delimit their priorities, it is argued here, are wrong to claim that their stake in the institutions gives them a right of account.

4. CONCLUSION

In recent years, policy-makers and demonstrators across the world have joined in criticizing the injustices and inefficiencies of the present structure and work of the IMF and the World Bank. The institutions have been called upon to become more transparent and inclusive to a new range of 'stakeholders'. This chapter has probed the limitations of these measures as solutions to the core deficit in representation and accountability lying at the heart of the institutions. They are supposed to represent, and to be directly accountable to, their member governments through their executive boards. Yet there are deep flaws in this structure. Furthermore, as the activities of the Fund and the Bank expand, causing them to intervene more and more deeply into the affairs of their members, the deficit in their representativeness and accountability becomes more problematic.

The implications for reforming the institutions are several. The head of each organization should be appointed or elected through an open and legitimate process that clarifies whom they represent and to whom they are accountable. The representation of member states needs to be improved. Specifically, developing countries need greater recognition on the boards of the organizations. That said, however, the overall representativeness and accountability of executive directors needs strengthening. They need better links back to their own governments and peoples. It is equally important that they play a stronger role in overseeing and directing the work of each institution. Alongside these measures, positive steps towards independent evaluation, inspection, and transparency are improving the procedural fairness and justice of the IMF and the World Bank.

Although improvements can be made to procedural justice, it is worth ending with a reflection on its limits in international organizations. Ultimately, although the IMF and the World Bank can be made more accountable to the governments and peoples most affected by their lending and policies, there are limits to how representative and accountable an international organization can be. The arguments made in this chapter raise a profound issue concerning how far-reaching the activities of relatively unaccountable agencies should be.[35] In his essay on whether international institutions can be democratic, political theorist Robert Dahl warns that we should be 'wary of ceding the legitimacy of democracy to non-democratic systems'.[36] His point is that domestic political systems have a potential to be democratic and accountable in a way that international organizations cannot. The implication is that the IMF and the World Bank should be reined in from far-reaching policy conditionality. Their activities should be limited to those for which they can claim to be effectively representative and accountable.

[35] I am grateful to Devesh Kapur for spurring me to think about this issue.

[36] Robert A. Dahl, 'Can International Organizations Be Democratic?', in Ian Shapiro and Casiano Hacker-Cordon (eds), *Democracy's Edges* (Cambridge: Cambridge University Press, 1999), 33.

4

Order and Justice in the International Trade System

JOHN TOYE

The reconciliation of order and progress, including social justice, is a nineteenth century agenda. Its intellectual parents were the Saint-Simonians, Auguste Comte and the Positivists, and the scientific socialists. The aftermath of the French Revolution convinced them that, while progress was desirable and reaction was impossible, *the pursuit of social justice was politically and socially disruptive of order*. Therefore, people with special knowledge of society should be empowered to direct what should be done for the good of all.[1] However much today, after the end of the Cold War, democracy and its triumph are trumpeted, this older ideal of technocracy—that power should be exercised by experts, who know how to reconcile justice with order—is still alive and well in political affairs. The spread of democracy has been accompanied by a growing interest in 'agencies of restraint', devices by which certain aspects of economic policy can be removed from the regular political arena and by which democratic governments try to commit themselves to refrain from acting on matters of economic importance and leave decisions to supposedly impartial experts.[2]

---

[1] Comte refers to such people as 'scientists', but he held that 'legists' had a supporting role to play within the scientific elite because they had the skill of making regulations, which was indispensable in the construction of a new social system. See H. Stuart Jones (ed.), *Auguste Comte: Early Political Writings* (Cambridge: Cambridge University Press, 1998), 74, especially note e.

[2] The most famous example of this in trade matters is the 1934 decision of the US Congress to delegate the setting of tariff levels to the office of the president, who was less accountable to particular electoral constituencies. I. M. Destler, *American Trade Politics: System under Stress* (Washington, DC: Institute for International Economics, 1986), 1–4; Judith Goldstein, 'International Institutions and Domestic Politics: GATT, WTO and the Liberalization of International Trade', in Anne O. Krueger (ed.), *The WTO as an International Organization* (Chicago: Chicago University Press, 1998); but see also Richard T. Cupitt and Euel Elliott, 'Schattschneider Revisited: Senate Voting on the Smoot-Hawley Tariff Act of 1930', *Economics and Politics*, 6/3 (1994), which takes a different view of the impact of constituency economic interests. Similar measures after the Cold War include safeguarding the independence of central bankers, thereby taking national interest rate policy out of the hands of the elected politicians.

Technocracy is also on the rise in international affairs, including in international trade. The new World Trade Organization (WTO), which has been created since the end of the Cold War, is distinguished from its predecessor, the General Agreement on Tariffs and Trade (GATT), in part by the greater scope of decision-making it allows to various kinds of legal technocrats. Most academic observers have regarded this change as a self-evident improvement. This chapter asks: will this recent judicialization of trade disputes lead to the reconciliation of justice and order in the international trade system? Its conclusion is that the great economic and political inequalities between nations prevent this (1) when formal justice is dispensed in an incomplete legal system and (2) when the rules to be administered do not recognize these inequalities as a difference relevant to the issue of substantive justice.

I begin with a fundamental distinction between justice as an ideal and justice as a legal organization, that is, as a system of legislature, courts, and sanctions. Historically, justice as an organization came first. At least in medieval England, 'justice' meant a form of organization whose purpose was the enforcement of law and the promotion of public order. The law was mainly custom and practice, and the decisions that the justice organization enforced, while somewhat effective in relation to order, were arbitrary in relation to any modern ideal of justice. The ideal of justice in public organizations became influential, even insistent, centuries later as an intellectual critique of the actually existing justice organizations. Its key exponents were Locke, Beccaria, Rousseau, and Bentham. The fruits of this critical spirit can be seen in eighteenth century constitutions that enshrined 'due process' and outlawed compulsory self-incrimination, double jeopardy, and the widespread use of cruel and unusual punishments.

Initially, the main point upon which I wish to insist is that ideals of justice in society, having started out as criticism, in the end require their own justice organizations if they are to have an effect in the world. For the US constitution, for example, the new justice organization was the Supreme Court.[3] The new ideal of justice could realise itself—or not—according to the institutional features of this new justice organization: how its judges are appointed, whether they can be dismissed, whether decision is by simple majority, what rules of interpretation they adopt—strict construction, role of precedents, and so forth—whether the costs of supplicants are paid by the court, and so on. It is these factors that determine what, in the real world, any ideal of justice actually delivers. No ideal of justice in society can be worth more than the new justice organizations to which it gives birth, and the devil is always in the detail.

---

[3] Bentham described the US as 'that newly-created nation, one of the most enlightened, if not the most enlightened, at this day on the globe', although he also criticized the looseness of the drafting of the Declaration of Independence. Jeremy Bentham, *An Introduction to the Principles of Morals and Legislation* (London: Athlone Press [1780] 1970), 309–10.

Andrew Hurrell has said that, from the point of view of justice, all international organizations suffer 'deformity'. It is certainly true that they are incomplete as legal systems, lacking a legislature, courts that can compel recognition, and centralized sanctions, and that this affects the quality of the justice that they deliver. However, additionally, *all* justice organizations, regardless of whether they are municipal or international, have common features that put them at a distance from most ideal forms of justice. They all:

- use up resources for which someone, somewhere, has to pay, and in regulating these costs legal technocrats face a clear problem of moral hazard;
- take time to come to judgment, during which time the offence continues unpunished;
- generate judgments that are unpredictable, even under a legal regime of strict precedent, because of the open texture of legal rules;
- produce miscarriages of justice, from time to time finding in favour of the violator of the law instead of for the victim of the violation;
- and therefore operate with least success when the parties between whom justice is to be done are unequal in resources, power, or culture.[4]

So, in discussing order and justice in the international trade system, I shall look not only at ideals of justice in international trade but also at the justice organizations that these ideals have entailed. In particular, I shall consider the justice arrangements of the WTO, embodied in its dispute settlement understanding (DSU).

1. FREE TRADE: JUSTIFICATION AND CRITICISM

'Free trade' is one of those brilliant eighteenth century ideas that contained a powerful moral principle that was critical of old practices. The moral justification of free trade was utilitarian. It was that, regardless of differences between countries in terms of natural and human resources, unrestricted trade between them would necessarily generate a higher level of welfare in all the trading countries. Subsidies to national producers, navigation laws, and all the paraphernalia of mercantilism were not only harmful to the welfare of other countries—that was intended and to be expected—but were *also harmful to the welfare of the country that employed them*. That was something that mercantilists neither intended nor expected.[5] This is, incidentally, one of the

---

[4] On the sense of injustice and the role that inequality plays in sustaining it, see Judith N. Shklar, *The Faces of Injustice* (New Haven: Yale University Press, 1990), 83–126.

[5] On the problems of using the term 'mercantilism' in historical studies, see Donald C. Coleman, 'Eli Heckscher and the Idea of Mercantilism', in Donald C. Coleman (ed.), *Revisions in Mercantilism* (London: Methuen, 1969).

most robust of economic theorems.[6] It was made the intellectual foundation
for British policy in its period of world hegemony, namely, *unilateral* removal
of tariff barriers, followed up by bilateral free trade accords.[7]

'Justice' as an abstraction has at least three layers. One layer is simply the
notion of there being some appropriate assignment of rights and duties within
societies, including international societies. Another layer is that of general
theories of how such an assignment might be determined, and this includes
utilitarian, contractarian, intuitionist, and other theories. Yet another layer is
that set of distinct and partially overlapping common sense norms of justice,
all of which seem quite reasonable in themselves but which in part conflict.
They cause both the moral dilemmas that we encounter in everyday life and
the difficulties of coming to just legal judgments. Now, the justice of free trade
is argued from a well-elaborated utilitarian general theory, based on the principle of maximizing aggregate net benefits.[8] That theory, however, does not
always sit well with the other principles of justice from the third layer of
specificity—norms such as non-discrimination, distributional equality, universality, reciprocity, and maximum liberty, all of which can be applied as
ideals of justice in international trade. Utilitarians regard these justice norms
as socially useful rules but as essentially subordinate to the principle of utility. In contractarian theories of justice, however, these specific justice norms
are both more prominent and more integrated into the theoretical structure.
Unfortunately, in many discussions of trade, this somewhat complex layering
of theories and norms of justice is often reduced to the misleadingly simple
dichotomy of free trade versus fair trade.[9]

In response to the free trade argument, Friedrich List proposed that *the case
for free trade had to be modified if some nations were still developing*. He
completely accepted the case for free trade in the context of universal peace,

---

[6] It does, however, assume that market prices reflect social costs, so that theoretical debates
about free trade centre around possible cases of market imperfection; Jagdish N. Bhagwati,
'Free Trade: Old and New Challenges', *Economic Journal*, 104/423 (1994), 232. There is also
the question of how equally the gains from trade are distributed between the countries that trade.

[7] Goldstein, 'International Institutions and Domestic Politics', 139.

[8] 'An action then may be said to be conformable to the principle of utility ... (meaning with
respect to the community at large) when the tendency it has to augment the happiness of the
community is greater than any it has to diminish it.' Bentham, *An Introduction to the Principles
and Morals of Legislation*, 12–13. This principle of 'maximum aggregate net benefit' does not
take account of the distribution of benefits and disbenefits or the equality of rights or liberty;
John Rawls, *A Theory of Justice* (Oxford: Oxford University Press, 1972), 22–33. In its modern
form, however, utilitarianism does concern itself with whether the gainers from an action do
actually compensate the losers, and not merely whether hypothetically they could do so. I am
grateful to Dr Vijay Joshi of Merton College, Oxford for reminding me of this point.

[9] For a discussion of legal justice, see H. L. A. Hart, *The Concept of Law* (Oxford: Oxford
Clarendon Press, 1961), 153–63. For a useful review of norms of fairness in international trade,
see Steven M. Suranovic, 'A Positive Analysis of Fairness with Applications to International
Trade', *The World Economy*, 23/3 (2000).

a global moral community, and a world government, that is, if the world could be treated as a single society. However, he argued that the existence of nations had to be taken seriously in considering the justice of free trade.[10] According to List, the moral communities of civilization were embodied in nations. He defined prosperity not as the possession of material wealth, but as the ability to support invention, the arts, and the sciences.[11] It was these that would underwrite the sustainability of material wealth, *and they could be gained only if agrarian states became industrialized, if necessary behind tariff barriers.* In his own words, 'the system of protection, inasmuch as it forms the only means of placing those nations which are far behind in civilization on equal terms with the one predominating nation ... appears to be the most efficient means of furthering the final union of nations, and hence also of promoting true freedom of trade'.[12]

Without protection for the less developed, List claimed that free trade would serve best the purposes of the most economically advanced nation. It was a doctrine that would perpetuate any hegemonic nation's political and economic dominance because it would allow the emerging industries of any potential antagonist, on which its safety would depend in wartime, to be destroyed by the economic competition that free trade would permit.[13] The morality of free trade was the morality of cosmopolitanism, but, in a world of unequal and potentially antagonistic national states, it was a doctrine that would entrench the national interests of the one predominating nation.

List challenged the doctrine of free trade by challenging the utilitarian norm of maximum aggregate net benefit. His argument rested on an implicit appeal to the norms of distributional equality and maximum liberty. He thereby opened up the debate on the variety of principles of justice that could be applied to international trade. This variety itself further suggested that there was a possibility of self-interest entering into the adoption of a particular principle. List suggested that the choice of justice norm by the hegemonic state could be, and indeed was, self-interested. There are three prongs to his argument:

1. nations do not confront each other as economic equals but in a world where one nation exercises hegemony;
2. the hegemonic nation gains legitimacy for its dominance by prescribing an ideal of a just world order to the economically weaker nations; and

[10] Similarly, modern contractarians have argued that persons have to be taken seriously when defining social justice. 'Utilitarianism does not take seriously the distinction between persons'; Rawls, *A Theory of Justice*, 27.

[11] Friedrich List, *The National System of Political Economy* (Fairfield NJ: Augustus M. Kelley [1885] 1977), 208–9. [12] List, *The National System*, 127.

[13] List, *The National System*, 130–2. This view is also to be found in Stephen D. Krasner, 'State Power and the Structure of International Trade', *World Politics*, 38 (1976), 322. It is quite odd that the 'polarization effect' is often cited as a potential drawback of creating a regional free

3. any such ideal must be limited by the economic—and military—interests of the hegemonic nation.

He therefore concluded that the ideal of a just world order propagated by a hegemonic state could not and should not be accepted uncritically by the non-hegemonic states.[14]

2. NATIONAL LABOUR STANDARDS AND THE ILO AS A JUSTICE ORGANIZATION

In the late nineteenth century, Germany's national development, partly under List's influence, involved both industrial tariffs and the creation of a welfare state.[15] In order to recruit workers into the national endeavour of industrialization, Bismarck created social security systems, actively supported by the German Historical School of economists and their Union for Social Policy. This produced a major problem of justice in the international trading system. The greater the nation's efforts to create a truly national economic community at home, the less competitive it became in international trade, at least in the short run before greater social cohesion is able to improve the investment environment.[16] Germany's share in international trade was vulnerable to competition from the US, which also adopted industrial protection but did not provide social security for its workers, and had no need to as long as millions of continental European workers wanted to emigrate to America.

---

trade area, but it tends to get lost in discussions of global free trade. A notable exception to this is Alan V. Deardorff, 'Rich and Poor Countries in Neoclassical Trade and Growth', *Economic Journal*, 111/470 (2001), 277–294.

[14] See List, *The National System*, 397–8. List's view here differs from the most familiar Marxist formulation of the role of the state as a mere emanation of a capitalist world order; Milton Fisk, *The State and Justice: An Essay in Political Theory* (Cambridge: Cambridge University Press, 1989), 219–22. Marx thought that the worldwide expansion of bourgeois society and its capitalist mode of production, under the banner of free trade, was unstoppable—except by proletarian revolution. 'The cheap prices of its commodities are the heavy artillery that batters down all Chinese walls ... in one word, it [bourgeois society] creates a world in its own image'; (Karl Marx, 'The Communist Manifesto', in David Fernbach (ed.), *The Revolutions of 1848* (London: Penguin [1848] 1973), 71. Unlike List, Marx never took nations seriously, or their international organizations.

[15] There was a positive correlation between the adoption of tariffs and economic growth for ten countries, including Germany and the US, in the period 1875–1914; Kevin H. O'Rourke, 'Tariffs and Growth in the Late 19th Century', *Economic Journal*, 110/463 (2000), 456–7. Correlation does not imply causality, but this scepticism also applies to modern correlations of growth with trade openness.

[16] This is one of the sources of the free trade *versus* fair trade debate; George F. DeMartino, *Global Economy, Global Justice: Theoretical Objections and Policy Alternatives to Neoliberalism* (London: Routledge, 2000), 203–15. I am grateful to Dr Ha-Joon Chang of Cambridge University for his helpful comments on the original version of this paragraph.

The continental European states, by contrast, faced revolutionary political movements that threatened political order in the name of liberating the working class, and had to address the injustice that, the more vigorous they were in legislating social reform, the more they placed their national firms at a disadvantage in international trade. Only if all nations would agree to level their labour standards upwards could revolution in Europe be staved off and free international trade be reconciled with 'fair' international trade, according to norms of reciprocity and non-discrimination. The new organization to tackle this injustice was the International Labour Organization (ILO). Adumbrated before the First World War, it was established as part of the Versailles postwar settlement under the threat posed by the Bolshevik revolution in Russia.[17] Compared with the League of Nations, it was a successful international organization.[18] Its work was, however, overtaken by events. In the inter-war years, the emergence of much greater distortions in the international trade system overshadowed the problem of unequal labour standards.

On 8 July 1916, Democratic Congressman Cordell Hull had argued in the House of Representatives for the establishment of 'a permanent international trade congress'. Its function would be to consider 'all international trade methods, practices, and policies which in their effects are calculated to create destructive commercial controversies or bitter economic wars, and to formulate agreements with respect thereto, designed to eliminate and avoid the injurious results and dangerous possibilities of economic warfare, and to promote fair and friendly trade relations among all the nations of the world'.[19] This vision united order and justice in trade relations, but it was based on the idea—reflected in the third of President Wilson's Fourteen Points—of the removal, so far as possible, of all economic barriers to trade. The stock market crash of 1929 began a decade of tariff raising, starting with the infamous Smoot-Hawley tariff in the US, plus discriminatory trading arrangements organized around regional currency blocs that practised the beggar-my-neighbour tactics of competitive currency devaluation. This experience destroyed popular confidence in the possibility of a return to the previous automatic and self-regulating

---

[17] The function of the ILO was to raise 'the common standard of the conditions of life, so that those nations which lead the world on social reform may not be placed at an undue disadvantage by those which compete with them by the exploitation of their labour ... '; James T. Shotwell, 'Introduction' to *The Origins of the International Labour Organization*, I (New York: Columbia University Press, 1934), xix. Despite its defeat in 1918, Germany was extremely keen to be allowed to join the new ILO, for obvious reasons.

[18] It had a unique structure in that international negotiations were conducted through a tripartite mechanism, which involved representatives not only of national governments but also of each country's employers and trades unions. This built up a national consensus for change in the course of an international negotiation. The disadvantages of the ILO were that progress was very slow, and the labour standards conventions agreed often pertained to highly specific working practices and technologies that were, in any case, rapidly becoming uneconomic.

[19] Cordell Hull, *The Memoirs of Cordell Hull*, I (London: Hodder and Stoughton, 1948), 81–2.

arrangements. It provoked new ideas on the reconciliation of economic order with economic justice and of the justice organization that could best deliver it. After 1933, 'There began to crystallize ... a conception of "economic order" that included norms, rules and frameworks for ... decision-making on a multinational level—this to supply the deficiency of the liberal ideal, in which the key legal, institutional and "moral" context was simply taken for granted'.[20]

The ILO served as a model for the American designers of the new United Nations system.[21] To regulate international trade, a new specialized agency, the International Trade Organization (ITO), was negotiated at Havana in 1947–8. It did not come into being because the US government failed to ratify it. This was because what the US government negotiators agreed to in Havana was not in the end acceptable to its own domestic business community, and the Truman Administration belatedly realized in 1950 that, without business support, ratification was politically impossible. In this curiously accidental way, the GATT—which was only a temporary agreement pending the ratification of the ITO—became the main justice organization in the field of international trade for nigh on 50 years. The ILO continued its task of seeking voluntary harmonization of national labour legislation, but that of rolling back discriminatory trade taxes—tariffs—was left to GATT.

3. GATT AS A JUSTICE ORGANIZATION

What ideal of justice inspired GATT? The purposes of GATT reflected the new American world hegemony. The US was much more ambivalent about unadulterated free trade than Britain had been when it exercised world hegemony. This ambivalence produced a distinctly different ideal of justice and order in international trade from free trade. It is known as 'embedded liberalism'. The moral basis of the new ideal was open multilateralism, derived from the norms of non-discrimination and reciprocity. Its claim to 'fairness' was that it required sharing both the benefits of any other country's tariff reductions *and* the burdens of any other country's 'need' to reimpose tariffs to safeguard its domestic industry. It inclined to free trade in that it aimed to facilitate multilateral and reciprocal tariff reductions. At the same time, 'contingent protection' was also provided for, that is to say, opportunities for individual countries to renege on tariff concessions under pre-specified conditions to

---

[20] Neil De Marchi, 'League of Nations Economists and the Ideal of Peaceful Change in the Thirties', *History of Political Economy*, 23, Annual Supplement (1991), 144.

[21] The idea of a small central UN secretariat and a large number of specialized agencies arose from favourable perceptions of the ILO compared with the failed League of Nations.

avoid 'injury' to domestic industries adversely affected by tariff reduction—there were, indeed, more clauses of GATT devoted to reneging than there were devoted to free trade! In short, 'embedded liberalism', made manifest in the GATT rules, was from the start an attempted compromise between the application of utilitarian theory and of other norms of justice, and between free trade and various different notions of fairness in trade.[22]

Existing levels of tariffs were intended to be reduced by mutual agreement in successive GATT 'rounds' of multilateral negotiations.[23] These agreements did indeed reduce industrial tariffs substantially, and this contributed to the expansion of world trade at a rate between 1.7 and 1.8 times faster than the expansion of world output between 1950 and 1994.[24] GATT tariff reductions were achieved by reaching a consensus among the near-equal rich countries.[25] The developing countries remained outside this virtuous circle.[26] From 1955 special treatment was granted to developing countries, allowing them to protect particular industries and to plead balance of payments reasons for adding to quantitative restrictions on trade.[27] They were glad to do this at the time. The tragedy was that, in general, they were not using these exemptions to carry out an effective development strategy, but only opportunistically, to grow some visible but chronically uncompetitive industries. They were rarely

[22] Goldstein, 'International Institutions and Domestic Politics', 139, 146–9. According to Ruggie, '... that multilateralism and the quest for domestic stability were coupled and even conditioned by one another reflected the shared legitimacy of a set of social objectives to which the industrial world had moved, unevenly but "as a single entity". Therefore, the common tendency to view the post-war regimes as liberal regimes, but with lots of cheating taking place on the domestic side, fails to capture the full complexity of the embedded liberalism compromise'. John Gerard Ruggie, 'International Regimes, Transactions and Change: Embedded Liberalism and the Postwar Economic Order', *International Organization*, 36/2 (1982), 398. Ruggie borrowed the term 'embedded' from Karl Polanyi, *The Great Transformation: The Political and Economic Origins of Our Time* (Boston: Beacon Press [1944] 1957). The treatment of tariff reductions as 'concessions' which must be reciprocated is a vestige of mercantilist thinking.

[23] The eight GATT 'Rounds' were Geneva (1947), Annecy (1949), Torquay (1951), Geneva II (1956), Dillon (1960–1), Kennedy (1964–7), Tokyo (1973–9) and Uruguay (1987–94).

[24] See Angus Maddison, *Dynamic Forces in Capitalist Development: A Long-run Comparative View* (Oxford: Oxford University Press, 1991), 50, 75. Tariff reductions were only one of several favourable factors in output growth, however, as the slowdown of growth in the second sub-period indicates. Fixed exchange rates, national full employment policies, and cheap petrol prices were also important favourable influences in the period up to 1974, and falling transport costs were present throughout. The growth of trade faster than output is evidence of that tariff reduction stimulated a more refined specialization within industrial sectors and even within industrial firms. Ruggie, 'International Regimes', 400–1.

[25] Developing countries did not participate actively in any of the GATT Rounds until the Uruguay Round; Krueger, *The WTO as an International Organization*, 5, n. 9. While developed countries have greatly reduced tariffs on products of mutual interest, they maintain tariffs that are comparatively high on products of export interest to developing countries. Bhagirath Lal Das, *The World Trade Organisation: A Guide to the Framework for International Trade* (London: Zed Books, 1999), 69.   [26] Ruggie, 'International Regimes', 413.

[27] Mari Pangestu, 'Special and Differential Treatment in the Millennium: Special for Whom, and How Different?', *The World Economy*, 23/9 (2000).

using them to shield a time-phased programme of development that would create competitive industries with the capability to export. There were a few, but hugely significant, exceptions to this: after 1965, the Asian economic 'tigers'. These apart, the developing world suffered static losses to its economic welfare inflicted by its own tariffs, but did not reap the dynamic gains that would have been possible from their more intelligent use.

Furthermore, the arena of tariff reduction among the developed countries was limited to industrial products. Until 1987, agricultural tariffs were never even on the tariff-reduction agenda since developed countries were agreed on protecting their own agricultural sectors. This was the legendary era of butter mountains and wine lakes in Europe and huge grain surpluses in the US, the result of the foolish policies of the EEC and the US of subsidizing farm production rather than farm incomes. The excess production had to be disposed of, and the methods of disposal often forced down the world prices of food products and damaged the livelihoods of farmers in developing countries.

From the justice perspective, it is noteworthy that GATT's free trade disciplines were mild since its rules were mainly based on negative prescription. They did not require states to do something that GATT specified. They required them to refrain from actions contrary to the twin GATT principles of eliminating discrimination in trade and halting tariff increases. GATT never insisted on a maximum tariff rate or on a particular rate of indirect tax on imports. It asked states only to refrain from increasing tariffs and from taxing imports differently from domestic production. In addition, the clauses in GATT that permitted countries to renege on tariff reductions included safeguard measures against serious injury and other measures against material injury. Anti-dumping (AD) and countervailing duties (CVD)[28] were permitted, the intention being to penalize trade distorting practices according to the norm of reciprocity. They were quickly adapted by the US and a few other leading industrial countries to be instruments of unilateral protectionism. The Tokyo Round tried to eliminate this by greater legal clarification, but the use of the AD-CVD mechanism for protection grew rapidly in the 1980s, with the US, the EC, Australia, and Canada between them bringing 96 per cent of all cases, and some of the larger middle-income countries getting in on the act in the 1990s.[29] It seems that this surge of abusive AD-CVD actions was stimulated because the very legal clarifications that were designed to eliminate them in fact conferred some legitimacy on them.[30]

---

[28] Duties that 'countervail' subsidies granted by the government of the exporting country, deemed to be a non-tariff barrier to trade.

[29] P. K. Matthew Tharakan, 'Political Economy and Contingent Protection', *Economic Journal*, 105/433 (1995), 1551; Bhagwati, 'Free Trade', 237.

[30] Howard P. Marvel and Edward J. Ray, 'Countervailing Duties', *Economic Journal*, 105/433 (1995), 1593.

Contrary to Hull's vision of the union of justice and order, the abuse of reneging provisions helped to swell the number of trade disputes. Overall, legal proceedings in GATT were initiated in over 200 cases. However, the legal force of the GATT rules remained moot. There was no provision for disputes to go to the World Court, and enforcement in national jurisdictions was impossible except in the few countries that had incorporated the GATT rules into their domestic laws. What remained was legal proceedings within GATT. These could be stymied by the countries found to be in contravention of the rules, who could block the adoption of the panel reports that found them guilty and thereby prevent their own punishment. Enforcement came from periodic unauthorized unilateral retaliation by large countries, especially US Section 301, but this blatantly breached the norm of non-discrimination.[31] For the rest, order in international trade depended on members' sense of being under a legal obligation and/or care for their national reputations.

The mere threat of AD-CVD actions had a harassment value because they were costly to contest.[32] It was used to secure so-called 'voluntary export restraints' (VERs) on textile exports from developing countries.[33] The textile industry is the obvious first step on the path of industrialization, but poor countries were denied the economies of scale that they could have gained by exporting to developed country markets. Restraints on textile exports were exceedingly damaging to the economic welfare of the developing countries, but they were either untouched or positively recognized by GATT. This breach of the non-discrimination norm was accepted by developing countries themselves as part of a larger implicit bargain in which their current account deficits, worsened by trade restriction, were met by off-setting flows of official financing from OECD country donors or, in more familiar terms, by foreign aid.

Perhaps it is too sweeping to say that the injustice was accepted by the developing countries. In the euphoria of decolonization, there was one moment when

---

[31] It has been argued that being bound by 'international obligation may reduce the incentive to punish a cheater outside GATT, thereby raising the gain from cheating … It is possible for international obligation to exert forces reducing cooperation …'. Dan Kovenock and Marie Thursby, 'GATT, Dispute Settlement and Cooperation', *Economics and Politics*, 4/2 (1992), 96.

[32] 'Frequent investigations, even if the complaints are finally rejected, amount to a kind of harassment of the defendants because of the uncertainty and expenses such actions create.' Tharakan, 'Political Economy', 1551. See also Marvel and Ray, 'Countervailing Duties', 1583–4; and Destler, *American Trade Politics: System under Stress.*

[33] Ruggie, 'International Regimes', 411. 'Most governments … [negotiated] a "voluntary" export restraint with the presumably reluctant exporter who had been previously "softened" by threats of emergency action under GATT (Article XIX). The 1962 Cotton Textiles Arrangement (later the Multi-Fibre Agreement) was a VER administered by the GATT, although it was clearly a new form of trade discrimination.' (Harry G. Johnson, *Economic Policies Towards Less Developed Countries* (London: Allen and Unwin., 1967), 21–2). After nearly 40 years, it still has not been fully phased out, although it is now planned to end in 2005. See Sam Laird, *Multilateral Market Access Negotiations in Goods and Services*, CREDIT Research Paper No. 00/4 (Nottingham: University of Nottingham), 4–5.

an alternative seemed feasible and when List's argument that free trade was not optimal when some of the world's nations still had to develop was given an organizational basis. In 1964, UNCTAD—the UN Conference on Trade and Development—was established, but in a curious form. This new international organization was largely financed by developed countries (Group B) in order to support the claims of injustice of all the others: the Group of 77 developing countries. Then, during the 1980s, the instrument of redistribution chosen by UNCTAD—international commodity agreements (ICAs)—proved to be something of a broken reed.[34] It turned out that petrol power was—and is—the only effective economic lever to move the OECD countries, and the oil producers lacked solidarity with the non-oil-producing developing countries. That is why Adam Roberts could describe UNCTAD headquarters in Geneva as 'the temple of a failed faith'.[35]

4. THE TRANSITION FROM GATT TO THE WTO

The bargain between OECD and developing countries on balance of payments support in exchange for trade access restrictions broke down in the 1980s in the wake of the oil price shocks, the debt crisis, and the arrival of Reagan, Kohl, and Thatcher. A ceiling was put on foreign aid, and when private capital flows dried up after the 1982 Mexican debt crisis the current account deficits of developing countries had to be contracted by means of internationally inspired stabilization and structural adjustment policies.

The Uruguay Round, the last GATT Round, was launched in 1986. Part of the work of this Round remained in the traditional mode, namely, further major industrial tariff reductions and a strengthening of non-discrimination in government procurement. In addition, a start was made, at long last, on bringing agriculture and textiles into the arena of tariff reduction negotiations, albeit in the form of writing a post-dated cheque. Moreover, a host of new issues of interest mainly to the developed countries were introduced into the international trade regime, even though agriculture is still far from being fully liberalized. Finally, the Uruguay Round engineered the birth of a new trade system under the aegis of a new justice organization, the WTO.

[34] Gilbert suggested that ICAs are not infeasible per se, but that the collapse of the International Tin Agreement in 1985 led to a loss of confidence in ICAs among producers and that this undermined their willingness to work at resolving the operational difficulties of ICAs. Christopher L. Gilbert, 'International Commodity Agreements: an Obituary Notice', *World Development*, 24/1 (1996), 17.

[35] An excessively dismissive evaluation of UNCTAD is in David Henderson, 'International Agencies and Cross-Border Liberalization: the WTO in Context', in Krueger (ed.), *The WTO as an International Organization*, 110–11.

How does the WTO differ from its predecessor? The institution breaks new ground in five key ways:

1. One strand of the change concerns the nature of the agenda. The overall aim has broadened from non-discrimination and the reduction of trade barriers to the adoption *of policies in support of open markets generally*. New agreements have been added concerning trade in goods, such as agriculture, sanitary and phyto-sanitary—plant hygiene—standards, textiles and clothing, technical barriers to trade, and trade-related investment measures. Other agreements on 'new issues' apply to trade in services, intellectual property rights, and the removal of various non-tariff barriers.
2. The WTO is potentially much more intrusive on national policies because it is now *making rules* across this substantial new agenda, whereas before GATT used only negative prescription.
3. These rules now override the pre-existing national laws of members. In 1947, GATT required countries to comply with its provisions only to the extent that they were not incompatible with domestic law at the date that the Agreement came into force: this is known as 'the GATT grandfather clause'. The WTO now requires countries to change existing domestic laws that conflict with the obligations of WTO membership.
4. A new Trade Policy Review Mechanism requires members to give regular public accounts of the state of their compliance with their obligations.
5. Under GATT, trade disputes perforce had to be dealt with by informal diplomacy, with the aim of dispute avoidance and reconciliation. Now, the WTO has a strengthened dispute settlement mechanism (DSM).[36] The status in international law of the reports of dispute investigation panels has changed. Under GATT it remained obscure. It is now much clearer that any ruling obliges all WTO members to bring their practices into conformity with the rule upheld by the adjudication. There will, therefore, now be an accumulating case law where observance will be mandatory on all members.[37] Members are not allowed to discuss the Appellate Body's decisions but must abide by them under the threat of trade sanctions.[38]

These five institutional innovations, taken together, have two general effects: (1) they make considerable inroads on what were matters of domestic governance before the coming into force of the Uruguay Round agreements, and

---

[36] The full text of the Understanding on the Settlement of Disputes is given in John H. Jackson, *The World Trade Organization: Constitution and Jurisprudence* (London: Pinter for Royal Institute of International Affairs, 1998).

[37] Jackson, *The World Trade Organization*, 85–9.

[38] 'The last resort … is the possibility of suspending the application of concessions or other obligations under the covered agreements on a discriminatory basis vis-à-vis the other Member, subject to the authorization by the DSB [Dispute Settlement Body] of such measures' (Article 3, Clause 7).

(2) they further 'judicialize' the process of trade cooperation in the expectation that this will simultaneously improve order in the trade system and render it more just.

5. THE WTO DISPUTE SETTLEMENT UNDERSTANDING

That a more powerful mechanism for the settlement of international trade disputes should have blossomed in the early 1990s is somewhat surprising. It has been argued that an open world trade structure is most likely to occur during periods when a hegemonic state is in its ascendancy.[39] Given that the US's relative dominance has declined since 1945, this would imply that the trade dispute settlement mechanism would tend to weaken, not strengthen. To all appearances, the opposite has happened. GATT's dispute settlement process broke down in the 1950s, when America was at the height of its relative power. In fact, the US itself had a very bad record of compliance with GATT panel judgments.

The new DSM restores and strengthens the original GATT dispute settlement process by making it more automatic and introducing specific time limits on procedures. Requests for panels on alleged violations are approved more automatically, as are the panel reports, the Appellate Body reports, and the authorizations of retaliation. Instead of requiring a positive consensus to proceed, they now need a negative consensus to fail to proceed. These changes have allowed about 160 cases to be handled during the first five years of the WTO, roughly three times the previous level. Developing countries have been involved in more cases, about 25 per cent of the new total.[40] This has been taken as a sign that the DSM is working well. However, although the formal justice of the institution has improved, formal justice can be at odds with substantive justice, and this I claim has been the case with regard to one issue of fundamental importance to developing countries.[41]

Where, then, is there any lack of justice for developing countries? Let me begin with the formal justice of the WTO as it impinges on developing countries. For them, there remain serious deficiencies at every stage of the WTO dispute settlement process, from inception to judgment, granting remedy and enforcement. These deficiencies arise from the interaction of the standard features of a legal process—its cost, absorption of time, and uncertainty of

---

[39] Krasner, 'State Power', 323.

[40] Das, *The World Trade Organization*, 7; Gary P. Sampson, 'The World Trade Organization After Seattle', *The World Economy*, 23/9 (2000), 1112–13.

[41] Formal justice is the equal application of the existing rules of an institution in its legal or administrative processes. Hart, *The Concept of Law*,156–8; Rawls, *A Theory of Justice*, 58–60.

outcome—with the incompleteness of international legal machinery and the great inequalities of wealth and power that currently exist between nations. In particular:

- given the substantial cost of bringing a WTO case in terms of legal and diplomatic person time, poor countries are deterred disproportionately from doing so;
- only governments can bring cases to the DSM, and poor governments will be disproportionately deterred by the prospect of antagonizing more powerful countries on whom they depend in non-trade matters, such as defence or foreign aid;
- by convention, no compensation is paid by the loser for a violation after a process that can still take over two years to complete, a fact that bears more heavily on poor states than on rich ones;
- if a country does not take measures to comply with its WTO obligations, there is no centralized sanction. The only sanction is retaliation. Since all economic sanctions are costly to the initiator, the ability of a poor country to sanction a rich one is much less than in the reverse.[42]

Thus, even if we assume an identical propensity to violate WTO rules among developed and developing countries, and perfect formal justice in the panels in reaching their judgments on cases, developing countries will win fewer cases than they lose and will be less assured of remedy in those that they do win. The norms of distributional equity, universality, and reciprocity are not satisfied in this outcome.

This effect would be reinforced if, in addition, the developed countries were to be tempted to exploit the advantages that they enjoy in this legalistic environment. Wealthy states can better afford to hazard their resources in the hope of a successful outcome to the dispute process, even when there is no actual violation. We have already seen how a few advanced countries were able to create harassment under the GATT rules on AD and CVDs. More extensive rules plus increased judicialization widens the scope for oppressive litigation by rich countries, which the poorer party cannot afford to contest and for which there is no remedy.[43] While most of such suits would not be upheld, some surely would be, given the open texture of all legal rules.

The fact that the improved administration of formal justice in the WTO nonetheless produces an outcome biased against developing countries is one

---

[42] Das, *The World Trade Organization,* 397, regards this as a 'serious limitation' of the DSU. On these major systemic deficiencies, see Bernard M. Hoekman and Petros C. Mavroidis, 'WTO Dispute Settlement, Transparency and Surveillance', *The World Economy,* 23/4 (2000).

[43] The fact that developing countries have started to bring disputes to the DSM does not detract from this point if, as seems to be so, these are disputes mainly with other developing countries. Jackson, *The World Trade Organization,* 74.

reason to doubt the benefits of the recent judicialization of the Organization. More serious is the coincidence of judicialization with the adoption of new rules that, on one key issue, embody substantive injustice. The Uruguay Round introduced new rules on the use of CVDs.[44] In a further attempt at legal clarification, reneging is now permitted in the face of some subsidies but not others. Three kinds of subsidies—to R & D, to disadvantaged regions, and to the costs of complying with environmental regulations if available to all firms or industries regardless of their status as exporters—are now not actionable with CVDs. The remainder are actionable according as they inflict 'material injury'. If subsidies are 'specific'—to an exporting enterprise or industry or to an exporting group of enterprises or industries—they can be countervailed if they cause material injury. The definition of 'material injury', already weak, was further diluted.[45] Participation in this subsidies code, which developing countries could and did decline to join under the Tokyo Round rules, has now ceased to be voluntary. It is now mandatory on all WTO members, although some have fixed transition periods before full compliance.

The effect will be to outlaw the sorts of industrial subsidies that have been used successfully in the past to accelerate the growth and development of poor countries. It has been said that the Asian miracle growth of the period 1965–95 could never occur again under WTO rules. It seems clear to me that the phenomenal growth of the Asian tiger economies did depend on selective departures from pure free trade regimes. Contrary to the opinion of most orthodox economists, the Asian miracle demonstrated that an intelligent long-term development strategy, based on interventionist departures from free trade that are genuinely selective and temporary, can be made to work. Indeed, if the right conditions can be created, it can be made to work spectacularly well.[46] What is not so clear, however, is that the Annexes to the WTO Agreement absolutely prohibit *all* the instruments of such a strategy. The change from GATT to WTO does bring tighter restrictions, particularly the clear outlawing of specific subsidies, but it also leaves some gaps unplugged that an imaginative and ingenious developmental state might want to try to exploit for its purposes.[47] Much

---

[44] Although ADs and CVDs are analytically and legally distinct, they are linked in practice. In most US cases they are sought jointly by the complainant industry and granted together by the US ITC [International Trade Commission]. This is evidence that they are being used for protection and not for their original purpose of removing trade distortions; Marvel and Ray, 'Countervailing Duties', 1587–8.

[45] Robert E. Baldwin, 'Imposing Multilateral Discipline on Administered Protection', in Krueger (ed.), *The WTO as an International Organization*, 311.

[46] Robert Wade, *Governing the Market: Economic Theory and the Role of Government in East Asian Industrialization* (Princeton, NJ: Princeton University Press, 1990) and Ha-Joon Chang, *The Political Economy of Industrial Policy* (Basingstoke: Macmillan, 1994), 91–129.

[47] Yilmaz Akyüz, Ha-Joon Chang, and Richard Kozul-Wright, 'New Perspectives on East Asian Development', *Journal of Development Studies*, 34/6 (1998), 30–2.

will depend on how the dispute settlement mechanism actually works, and it is in the hands of the legal technocrats how activist they decide to be.[48]

My concern is that, even if they do not choose to be legal activists now, as time passes and as the DSM gets into high gear they will take that route, which the WTO rules would clearly permit. If and when they do, *the interpretation of the Annexes will increasingly prohibit all protection of infant industries in developing countries*. This will slam the door on a vital means of economic catching up, which at least some poor countries are capable of using, and so serve to solidify the existing unequal worldwide distribution of wealth and income. Although perfectly consonant with criteria of reciprocity and non-discrimination, the consequences will be unjust in terms of distributional equity, universality, and maximum aggregate net benefit.

6. THE WTO AS A MEMBERSHIP ORGANIZATION

When critics raise this issue, or other issues concerning the substantive justice of the WTO rules, they are often answered with an implicit appeal to the norm of reciprocity. The WTO arrangements cannot be unjust, it is said, since every nation voluntarily agreed to them when applying to join the WTO, and voluntary agreement to an act implies that the gain and the loss from it are at least equivalent. Is this an adequate reply?

In weighing this rebuttal, one must bear in mind the evolution of the community of nations. For all the talk of the demise of the nation-state, it has in fact been multiplying fast. The members of the UN in 1945 were 51. Now there are about 190. Moreover, as a result of that quadrupling the disparities between the strongest nations and the weakest nations have multiplied. These new states necessarily emerge on to a stage where the international action is already well advanced. They do not face a moral or legal tabula rasa on which they can, jointly with others, inscribe a new compact. To believe otherwise is to take fiction for fact.

In fact, not every member nation did participate in shaping the constitution of the WTO. Formally, it was agreed between the 76 nations that negotiated the Uruguay Round. Others have had to queue to join a done deal and, in negotiating their admission, are forced to take the rough with the smooth.

---

[48] Amsden argues that the new WTO rules leave ample room for developing countries to pursue industrial strategies that use subsidies; Alice H. Amsden, *Industrialization under New WTO Law* (Geneva: UNCTAD, 2000). This is true, but the problem is that the developmental use of subsidies requires them to be temporary, selective, and conditional on the performance of the beneficiary firm; see William H. Kaempfer, Edward Tower, and Thomas D. Willett, 'Performance Contingent Protection', *Economics and Politics*, 1/3 (1989), 272. If the selection criteria include *export performance*, it will be difficult to avoid the charge of giving a 'specific' subsidy.

As of 1 January 2002, a further 68 nations had been admitted, and applications from a further 27 were still outstanding. It is significant that these negotiations for admittance do not take place with the membership as a whole, but with individual existing members. The entry of China to the WTO was negotiated by the US Administration, for example.[49]

Did all of the 76 nations that were GATT members in 1994 shape the WTO rules? Well, yes and no. They may have been formally in the Uruguay Round negotiation, but states differ vastly in the actual leverage they can exert in such negotiations. A few states or groups of states had negotiating strength, but most of them had little and sat on the sidelines. That was the situation at the birth of the WTO, and it continues to be the case. Formally, all WTO members are equal. Unlike the IMF and the World Bank, the WTO does not have an unequal voting structure, in which rich countries control a share of the vote that is much greater than their share of world population. It appears as if the poor countries, which form the majority, *could in principle outvote the rich countries*. Why does this not happen? Because the WTO, like the GATT before it, does not take decisions by voting. Instead, it 'finds consensus'. Finding consensus is an informal procedure in which the Director-General invites some members to participate in a 'green room consultation'. These discussions with selected members go on until the Director-General thinks he has found a basis for consensus, which he brings for approval to the WTO Council plenary session. At this stage countries decide whether a consensus exists.

This informal procedure allows the inequalities that exist between members to come into play. There are two main sources of disparity: information about what agreements will benefit your country, and the power to influence the outcome of the informal negotiation.

The information access problem comes down to a simple economic question. Can your country afford to maintain an embassy in Geneva? If it cannot, it is unlikely that you will be able to follow the trade negotiations, let alone take part in them.[50]

Then, if your country's resources are inadequate, what international help is available to assist it to acquire and process trade-related information? There is in fact very little. The regular WTO budget provided $741,000 in 1998 for technical assistance and training, about $7,000 for each developing country member.[51] Of aid donors' total expenditure on technical assistance, only about 2 per cent is trade-related.

Since the inauguration of the WTO in 1995, the problem of understanding which outcomes will be more in your interests is aggravated by the great

---

[49] See Chapter 8.
[50] Sampson, 'The World Trade Organization after Seattle', 1100.
[51] Sampson, 'The World Trade Organization after Seattle', 1100, n. 7.

broadening of the trade agenda. The effects on a country of a round of mutual tariff reductions is fundamentally calculable, albeit by economists using general equilibrium models. The effects of a change of standards, by which a whole range of a country's export products may be suddenly deemed substandard, is very much harder to forecast, to calculate, and to negotiate.

A country's informal negotiating influence or power depends on the extent of its trade. In a negotiation based around tariff reduction, bargaining power depends not only on how far you are willing to cut your tariff but also on the size of the trade flows to which the proffered tariff cut will apply. Small tariff cuts on big trade flows are worth much more as bargaining chips than big cuts on small flows. So even a country that knows where its interest lies may not be able to achieve it because of lack of negotiating influence.[52] This is very frustrating for countries with small trade sectors. However, it is *unjust* only if a country's trade sector is being deliberately kept small by others' denial of market access.[53] While true of some countries, the external trade of others, notably in Africa, is constrained not by lack of access to markets but by unresolved difficulties of supply. These do not involve global injustice, only misfortune. They cannot be helped by trade negotiations alone, however they are arranged. They need other remedies, including financial aid and technical assistance.

7. IMPLICATIONS FOR JUSTICE AND ORDER

How would the nineteenth century figures with whom I began have assessed the new WTO? Saint-Simon would have been gratified to see the international legists at work on the adjudication and enforcement of the rules of trade, now removed from the hurly-burly of diplomacy and political pressure and entrusted to the decisions of dispute panels, the Dispute Settlement Body and the Appellate Body of the WTO. He would have been disappointed that there are still no 'scientists' to direct the work of the legists, and wonder why a group of independent economists is not called in to rewrite the rules. To Bentham, too, it would have been self-evident that such an international judicial establishment, if capable of calculating the greatest happiness of the greatest number, would be the appropriate framework for achieving global prosperity. At the same time, he would have criticized roundly the host of particular WTO rules that do not derive from the utilitarian theory of justice.

---

[52] ' ... powerful countries have far more bargaining chips to use ... to leverage less powerful countries into "agreeing" on the preferred "consensus decision",' according to Sampson, 'The World Trade Organization after Seattle', 1101.

[53] This would breach norms of non-discrimination and universality.

If List had been present at Seattle, he would have recognized in the proceedings the arrogance of the hegemonic state in its insistence in pressing
ahead without an agreed agenda, its unwillingness to pursue any agenda of
procedure or substance but its own, and its abuse of its position as Chair of the
meeting to pander to its domestic interest groups. He might well have reflected
on the difficulties experienced by China in cutting a deal with the US on entry
into the World Trade Organization.[54] China has invested much in building up
its own national strategic industries, which are highly unlikely to withstand the
US and European competition that WTO entry would unleash.[55] So List would
have sympathized with China's repeated 'last minute' hesitations in clinching
the long-drawn-out membership deal.[56]

Nevertheless, US hegemony has produced a distinctly different trade system from that which evolved under British hegemony, whose ideal of justice
List first criticized. In response to concerns that free trade can cause social
instability within nations, the ideal of embedded liberalism is of a balance
between free trade and protection, rationalized by a mixture of different norms
of justice.[57] The political reality behind this is that the behaviour of the hegemonic nation in international trade, the US, is driven by the disparate interests of two groups of great domestic business corporations, which are united
only by their willingness to pay the bills of the major US political parties.
US corporations that export want other countries to liberalize and provide
them with more market access, while those which sell mainly into US domestic
markets want to block out foreign competition. For both their sakes, the US
government would like to have it both ways. The ideal of embedded liberalism, when constrained by US national interests, produces the asymmetric
liberalism of the hegemonic power.[58]

Some think that increased judicialization of international trade would be bad
because it would tilt the US political balance in favour of more protection.[59]

---

[54]   This is not so fanciful as it sounds. List used the case of China, along with Ireland, to illustrate the dangers to weak countries of participating in free trade; M. Yaffey, 'Friedrich List and
the Causes of Irish Hunger', in Helen B. O'Neill and John F. J. Toye (eds), *A World Without
Famine? New Approaches to Aid and Development* (Basingstoke: Macmillan, 1998), 87.

[55]   Peter Nolan, *China and the Global Economy* (Houndmills: Palgrave, 2001), 159–232.

[56]   As described in 'Prospect of WTO entry looks distant for China', *Financial Times*
(14 March 2001), 14.

[57]   Thus Krasner's 1976 argument that hegemony *as such* leads to an open structure of trade
seems to be too simple. See Charles Lipson, 'The Transformation of Trade: The Sources and
Effects of Regime Change', *International Organization*, 36/2 (1982), 453–4.

[58]   The idea of asymmetric liberalism is captured in the following remark of Alan Winters: 'The
1980s saw increased numbers of VERs, tighter MFA [Multi-Fibre Agreement] restrictions, and
more anti-dumping actions, but this did not prevent [liberal] opinion from covering trade policy
when [industrial] countries offered development policy advice.' L. Alan Winters, *Trade Policy as
Development Policy: Building on Fifty Years Experience* (Geneva: UNCTAD, 2000), 5.

[59]   Goldstein, 'International Institutions and Domestic Politics', 149–51.

That is valid up to a point, but their argument assumes that the DSM would be effective in striking down existing administered protection, whereas in fact it cannot touch abuse of the AD provisions.[60] I have argued that increased judicialization, or even the achievement of perfect formal justice, would not prevent a systemic bias of outcomes against developing countries. To me, it seems naïve to believe that mere judicialization, the streamlining of formal justice, can remove injustices in the world trade system so long as gross economic inequalities between nations remain.

I have argued further that the combination of the new rule on countervailing duties and judicialization will eventually outlaw performance-related industrial subsidies in the developing countries, striking down one of their most important policies for rapid development. Judging the WTO rules on subsidies as substantively unjust requires clarity about what resemblances and differences between nations are relevant to the treatment of like cases alike and different cases differently. I believe that the existing inequalities of economic and political power between developed and developing countries do constitute a relevant difference for the purpose of deciding the substantive justice of these rules. If any reneging of multilateralism is to be legitimized, it should be in favour of the economically weak, not the economically strong. The substantive injustice of disregarding a country's stage of development is actually worsened by an improvement in formal justice. Judicialization tightens the screws of unjust rules.

How then might List's 'true freedom of trade' be achieved in the twenty-first century? The Uruguay Round promises made to developing countries must be fulfilled. Then the overall process of trade liberalization on a multilateral and non-discriminatory basis must continue. Tariffs on industrial goods of special export interest to developing countries must be reduced. The failure of the Uruguay Round to eliminate administered protection in a wide range of intermediate industries must be rectified. The heavy protection of developed countries' agricultural sectors must be reduced. Neither developed nor developing countries should be contemplating a retreat into protectionism, rather the reverse. At the highest level of generality, it is not free trade but its absence that they should beware.

Nevertheless, if in the end both justice and order depend on the possibility of removing existing gross economic inequalities by the successful development of the developing countries, both goals will be ill-served by quasi-judicial attempts to block off the most promising—for some countries—fast track to development. I believe that there is a morally compelling case for developing countries to be given exceptional treatment on 'specific' industrial subsidies for

[60] Baldwin, 'Imposing Multilateral Discipline', 310–11; Das, *The World Trade Organization*, 425.

infant industry purposes, provided always that these are selective, temporary, and performance-related. The idea of 'special and differential treatment' of developing countries, which was added to GATT and survives in different forms in the WTO Agreements, needs to be revisited, simplified, and given greater precision.[61] It is in every nation's interest that late developers succeed in catching up, because that is the only route to a world of less poverty and conflict. If their path is blocked 'for legal reasons', the legitimacy of the present hegemonic ideal of embedded liberalism can only erode further, and then world trading arrangements are bound to become more disorderly.

[61] The present position where 'special and differential treatment' (SDT) consists of an arbitrary deadline for full compliance, unenforceable promises of technical assistance for transitional difficulties, and a wish to confine SDT to the 48 Least Developed Countries is highly unsatisfactory. See the discussion of SDT in Pangestu, 'Special and Differential Treatment'.

5

Order and Justice Beyond the Nation-State: Europe's Competing Paradigms

KALYPSO NICOLAIDIS AND JUSTINE LACROIX

Should global capitalism be tamed? Can we seek global justice in the absence of a global super-state and if so, would we risk shattering the existing world order? There is little doubt that the end of the Cold War has led to a re-framing of the tension between order and justice that is at the heart of international relations. While international order during the Cold War was classically seen as prior to justice, a goal in its own right, the end of the Cold War generated a new exploration of the order-justice relationship along more liberal lines.[1] In this view, these two imperatives are not independent or even contradictory. On the contrary, order would best be realized by meeting the demands of justice expressed around the world. Has a 'just world order' become attainable, we asked, and should the pursuit of global order and justice thus be seen as two sides of the same coin? A decade on, there is cause for scepticism. The realist view is alive and well among world elites, for whom order must prevail and is predicated on a stable inter-state system. At the same time, the idealist or cosmopolitan view that considerations of order are never value-free, and that the problem of justice cannot be assumed away, while it is not new, has certainly gained in relevance in a world where principles such as 'the duty to intervene' or 'the duty to provide global public goods' are increasingly sold on the basis of both order and justice imperatives. This book explores both the overall contours of this universal debate and the diversity of views among states, societal and institutional cultures.

What, if any, is the European Union's approach to the fundamental tension between the pursuit of an orderly and a just world, and how might this approach have changed in the last decade? Within the context of this book, the EU is, of course, a very special case. It is both an international institution

We would like to thank Ailish Johnson for research assistance, Vivien Collinwood for her editing work, and Rosemary Foot and Andrew Hurrell for their insightful comments.

[1] Rosemary Foot expands on this argument in her introduction to this volume.

with distinct norms, policy frameworks, and practices, and a collection of actors with heterogeneous traditions and views. These actors are, above all, member states, ranging from older nation-states like France and Britain, irremediably attached to the classical attributes of statehood, to northern 'liberal internationalists' and the southern populist states of the Mediterranean. Together the states speak for the EU as an institution, alternately in harmony or in conflict with its supranational components, namely, the Commission, the Parliament, and the European Court of Justice. Increasingly, however, it has become impossible to apprehend this Union without taking into account independent voices of transnational European actors—from trade unions to non-governmental organizations (NGOs) and business groups—whose distinct views and competing notions of order and justice undoubtedly influence intergovernmental policy-making. This chapter cannot do justice to the multiplicity of actors which comprise the Union. Its more modest aim is to analyse ideal-typical views and to indicate how EU practice can be assessed against such views.

How, then, has the EU confronted the balance between order and justice goals *as a Union*? At its origin after the Second World War, the European project was about creating a new regional order on the war-torn continent: one of perpetual peace sustained by orderly commerce and a stable Franco-German axis. A core question, recurring since the creation, has been whether the economic order thus engineered ought to be flanked by a security order and, if so, how. In this vision, the EU has been a modern echo of the Peace of Westphalia, a minimal set of norms and institutions to establish and sustain an enduring order between the sovereign nation-states of western Europe. One could argue that this 'equilibrium', negotiated and renegotiated throughout the seventeenth and eighteenth centuries, constituted the very origin of the political significance of the term 'Europe'. And yet the EU has become more than an advanced instance of international cooperation or a regional United Nations. With the acceptance of a majority of its population it has now ventured into the core areas of sovereignty of the nineteenth-century nation-state—army, police, and money—and, more reluctantly, and with much less support, into the core domain of the twentieth-century sovereign functions of the state, namely, the welfare state. As a result, it has become a polity in its own right—indeed, a polity now engaged in a fascinating process of self-definition, one aspect of which involves competing notions of social and political justice.[2] Whether characterized as a federation in the making, a federation

---

[2] In analysing notions of justice in the EU context we need to distinguish between national standards that may be convergent enough to be mutually recognized—welfare state provisions, administration of justice, civic rights—and harmonized or common standards, policies, or rights—from redistributive policies to the Charter of fundamental rights.

of nation-states, or simply a new kind of post-modern Union of peoples, the EU today is unquestionably more than an assembly of states.[3]

This evolution makes the EU unique in another way, which is the starting point for our argument. For any polity or political community, how are approaches to order and justice prevailing *within* the polity related to those practised *externally*? Is there continuity between the two or are there separate logics operating for 'us' and for 'the Other'? This question is pertinent for China, India, Russia, or the United States, as discussed elsewhere in this volume. The difference with the EU is that it is already a miniature world, an experiment in bringing together different peoples that have vowed to remain such. In this light, the tensions and dilemmas present in externalizing notions of justice from the realm of a single polity, where a sense of solidarity is taken as given, to a multi-polity setting are already at play *within* the EU itself. This internal EU experience has more grounds for being relevant to the international realm than, say, internal notions of justice in the US or China. In short, all the arguments about the feasibility and desirability of the pursuit of justice *beyond the state* or *beyond the nation-state* have been rehearsed inside the EU context among both scholars and policy-makers. To be sure, these two types of 'externalization', from the state to the EU and from the EU to the world, follow different logics and belong to different disciplines. Nevertheless, we believe that there are implicit assumptions that can be profitably extrapolated from one realm to the other. We seek to make these assumptions explicit and to draw out their implications for order and justice debates in international relations.

We argue that there exist two core paradigms in Europe, combining both positive and normative arguments regarding the kind of 'community' that the EU represents and the possibility for a 'just order' both within the EU and beyond it. These two paradigms—the 'national' and 'post-national' paradigms—constitute the focal points for debates in political theory, but also lie at the heart of much political discourse on European affairs. They underline fault-lines and party alignments in the domestic public sphere. Beyond their relevance to the *internal* EU debate, however, we argue more tentatively that they correspond to two different visions of the EU's external role. Should Europe exist globally through power-projection or attraction, as a 'hegemon' or as a 'beacon', as a 'superpower' or as a 'model'? In the first instance, enhancing order externally is an end in itself, while in the second, it may or may not be a precondition for enhancing the consistency between the internal and external pursuit of greater justice. In the former case, the international relations of the EU should be conducted on the assumptions of the classical realist state system, while in the latter, international institutions can, and

---

[3] This is true irrespective of the theoretical framework adopted to understand its decision-making dynamic, whether intergovernmental, neo-functional, institutionalist, or supranational.

should, play a key role in mediating relations between states. From a theoretical standpoint, therefore, we seek to relate the internal European debate over identity and justice beyond the state, to broader debates about justice and order in the realm of international relations. But our theoretical scope is modest and our approach bottom-up, that is, centred on intra-European debates. Links with ideal normative theory are therefore left mostly implicit.

This chapter is organized as follows. In the first section, we discuss the two paradigms and their implications. In the second section, we provide a brief historical overview of the EU's relative focus on justice and order in its international relations, and ask to what extent the end of the Cold War has led to a reframing of this balance. In doing so, we ask whether and to what extent the post-national paradigm has taken hold in the EU's recent external strategy, and argue that the key evidence here is whether consistency between internal and external EU policies has been sought and—at least partially—realized. In the third section, we fine-tune our argument by showing that, in practice, EU institutions and the member states they represent implicitly 'balance' imperatives of order and justice differently in different policy areas, but are usually far from achieving consistency between internal and external policies. We explore three issue-areas: human rights and citizenship; enlargement; and global governance.

1. JUSTICE BEYOND THE NATION-STATE?

The central goal of any polity, beyond mere survival, is the pursuit of some kind of a just order. In Western democracies, at least, this has for decades been based on principles of political freedom, equal participation, democratic self-determination, and social solidarity. Political theorists have long sought to tease out which is the 'we' that can legitimately proclaim and define applicable principles of justice among individuals with different notions of the good and right life.[4] What, however, of the attempt to arrive at a 'social contract' for international affairs? If such principles are meant to apply beyond bounded political communities—in Europe, say, or indeed universally—on what grounds can they be extrapolated? In his *Law of Peoples*, John Rawls argues that an ideal theory of justice, as put forth for the domestic level in *Principles of Justice*, could not be extended as such to the international level.[5] Only representatives of 'peoples' rather than individuals in the domestic context could be called to adopt principles of justice behind a 'veil of ignorance' at the global level, and, if they did, they would call for basic principles of

---

[4] For an overview of the relevant literature, see Chapter 1.
[5] J. Rawls, *The Law of Peoples* (London: Harvard University Press, 1999).

coexistence such as interdependence, equality, non-intervention, and the entitlement to defend oneself, short of waging war; in short, a 'morality of and for states'.[6] Thus, Rawls suggests that the potential for justice among 'peoples' cannot extend to considerations of individual claims vis-à-vis humanity as a whole, nor can it entail enforcing egalitarian principles meant to empower individuals vis-à-vis their community.[7] However, as even Rawls recognizes, and as his critics stress, there is always possibility for change. 'The relatively narrow circle of mutually caring peoples in the world may expand over time and must never be viewed as fixed.'[8]

Has the EU created the basis for one such circle of mutually caring people? Is it possible or even desirable to pursue a 'just order' in Europe without assuming away the plural nature of its polity and of its peoples? What of the horizon of justice beyond Europe? The debate within Europe has been framed by two broad types of responses to this question.

The Horizon of Justice in the Nation-centric Paradigm

The first response to the question of justice beyond the nation-state in Europe is that of self-styled 'national republicans' in France[9] and 'liberal nationalists' in Britain,[10] who consider the nation to be the ultimate horizon of political community. They stress how, in the last two centuries, various forms of nationalism, based on various degrees of 'constructed' historical consciousness, have moulded collective identities that, in turn, have functioned as the basis for civic responsibility and the building of the state. National consciousness then sustained solidarity based on shared citizenship, leading strangers in 'imagined communities' to feel responsible for one another and ready to make sacrifices for their political community, be it as taxpayers or as soldiers. Moreover,

---

[6] S. Hoffmann, *Ideal Worlds*, Working Paper 62 (Cambridge, MA: Centre for European Studies, Harvard University, 1995).

[7] For a forceful critique, see for instance contributions in T. Pogge (ed.), *Global Justice* (Oxford: Blackwell, 2001).

[8] Rawls, *The Law of Peoples*, 112–13; quoted in A. Hurrell, 'Global Inequality and International Institutions', *Metaphilosophy*, 32/1–2 (2001), 40.

[9] J.-M. Ferry and P. Thibaud, *Discussion sur l'Europe* (Paris: Calmann-Lévy, 1992); R. Debray, *Le Code et le glaive. Après l'Europe, la nation?* (Paris: Albin Michel, 1999); E. Todd, 'Gauche des dominés, gauche de la nation?', *Le Banquet*, 7 (1995); E. Todd, L'illusion Economique. *Essai sur la Stagnation des Sociétés Développées* (Paris: Gallimard, 1999); D. Schnapper, *La Communauté des Citoyens: Sur L'idée Moderne de Nation* (Paris: Gallimard, 1994). For a discussion of the French national republicans, see J. Lacroix, 'Les Nationaux-Républicains de Gauche et la Construction Européenne', *Le Banquet*, 15 (2000) and C. Laborde, 'The Culture(s) of the Republic. Nationalism and Multiculturalism in French Republican Thought', *Political Theory*, 29 (2001).

[10] D. Miller, *On Nationality* (Oxford: Clarendon Press, 1995); D. Miller, *Citizenship and National Identity* (Cambridge: Polity Press, 2000); A. D. Smith, *Nations and Nationalism in a Global Era* (Cambridge: Polity Press, 1998).

the welfare state as the systematic institutionalization of mutual economic sacrifices was created in this national context.

While this historical analysis is relatively uncontroversial, what does it imply today? For the nation-centric school, the nation-state remains the largest social construct compatible with redistributive sacrifices. Dissociating historical and cultural membership from political membership is mere utopia. Its proponents do acknowledge that modern democracy is defined by universal principles; but even then the nation is the only unit in which a 'limited form of universal'[11] has come to acquire practical significance. The *ethnos* can be turned into the *demos* only at the national level, as this is the only level where the values of liberty, civic responsibility, and political justice acquire true meaning. It is indeed this double-edged construct of *demos* and *ethnos* that led to the subjective internalization of the very idea of 'borders' and to people's notion of what it means to 'be in the world', as Hannah Arendt would say, through exclusionary belonging. But it is also this very same construct that has linked the notion *of universality of democratic right* with national belonging.

Thus, democracy and nation are linked, above all, because in our modern world only national identity has managed to foster the kind of identification with the common good which defines a true political citizenship: one founded not only on some abstract recognition of equal individual rights, but on a sense of responsibility for the public interest. How else could such a sense of responsibility develop if not through identification with the political community and its history? 'Where do we owe obligation without affiliation?'[12] Citizenship and nationality are intrinsically intertwined. Without citizenship, nationality would not lead to a future-oriented civic project. Without nationality, citizenship would lack the kind of substance that emanates from the sense of a shared world.

More importantly for the argument here, a shared national identity would be the only basis for substantiating aspirations towards greater social justice. To the extent that today the state is expected to provide 'positive freedoms' in the form of collective goods, what better framework than the nation-state? As Beveridge stressed in his famous 1942 report, social insurance requires 'a sense of national unity above and beyond any kind of class or sectional interests'.[13] If social justice cannot simply be based on the kind of low-key altruism one may feel for humanity as a whole, if it is the stuff of polity rather

[11] P. Rosanvallon, 'Les Conditions d'un Nouveau Contrat Social: La Citoyenneté et ses Différences', *Témoin*, 9 (Summer 1997), 43–4.

[12] A. Finkielkraut, *L'ingratitude. Conversation sur notre temps* (Paris: Gallimard, 1999), 112–13.

[13] A. Wolfe and J. Klausen, 'Identity Politics and Contemporary Liberalism', in K. Hinrichs, H. Kitschelt, and H. Wiesenthal (eds), *Kontingenz und Krise: Institutionspolitik in kapitalitischen und postsozialistischen Gesellschaften* (Frankfurt: Campus Verlag, 2000), 29.

than charity, and if it is to be consensual rather than coercive, it requires a level of mutual commitment compatible with the sharing at stake.[14] Only the kind of pan-German feelings elicited by the fall of the Berlin Wall could justify the sacrifices born by West Germans for their East German compatriots.

In this light, what does the national-sovereignist vision imply for the nature of the European construct and, at the same time, for Europe as an actor on the international scene? If the link between nation, democracy, and social justice is not only historically contingent but also conceptual, it follows that only a 'nation-like' EU could be the basis for the systematic pursuit of justice on the European continent. This could then lead us to two possible viewpoints.

First, one could argue, along with the majority in the national school, that, in spite of growing interdependence between civil societies in Europe, citizens continue to identify symbolically and politically with the national rather than the European level. As Renan put it a century ago, 'communities of interests create trade treaties, but a *Zollverein* does not make a nation'.[15] Thirty years ago, Raymond Aron similarly argued that the fundamental mistake of the founding fathers had been to ignore Hegel's distinction between members of civil society and citizens.[16] Since it is not a nation, the EU cannot aspire to the pursuit of justice. Its core function is the creation and maintenance of order both internally and externally. The difference between the two is one of method: internally, the order agenda needs to be shaped by consensus between sovereign member states—as is the case in the realm of the 'Third Pillar' of Justice and Home Affairs; externally, shaping world order is a function of power projection.

Alternatively, a number of national sovereignists do not exclude the possibility of a true political European order in the long term, most likely in the context of a general mobilization against a common enemy.[17] Nevertheless, if such a development were to occur, it would not imply the end of the national logic and form. If allegiances were to shift from the national to the European level, this would not mean that the EU had paradoxically replaced the nation-state, but 'that it has become itself a nation-state on a larger scale'.[18] This is the only outcome with which national-sovereignists would feel comfortable. It is worth stressing, then, that the national logic is not monopolized by the opponents of European integration. There is actually a clear intellectual convergence between nationalism and supranationalism, or between the most

---

[14] M. Canovan, *Nationhood and Political Theory* (Cheltenham: Edward Elgar, 1996), 30.

[15] J. E. Renan, *Qu'est ce qu'une Nation?* (Paris: Presses-Pocket, 1992), 52.

[16] R. Aron, 'Is a Multinational Citizenship Possible?', *Social Research*, 41 (1974).

[17] Canovan *Nationhood and Political Theory*, 79; Debray, *Le Code et le glaive*, 116. See also R. Debray, 'Des Européens et des Européistes', *Le Monde* (16 February 2001), 13, and Schnapper, *La Communauté des Citoyens*.

[18] Canovan, *Nationhood and Political Theory*, 119.

extreme anti-Europeans and the more radical pro-Europeans. They all consider the nation to be the ultimate horizon of democracy, either within the borders of existing nation-states or within those of a new 'European motherland'. Thus, they share Ernest Gellner's 'nationalist paradigm': 'a principle which states that the national unit and the political unit should be congruent.'[19] Suffice to stress how the symbolic terrain upon which European leaders and Eurocrats tried to construct the new Europe in the 1970s and 1980s—by resort to European myths, to European history, the introduction of a new flag, and a new anthem—was precisely that upon which the nation-state has traditionally been founded,[20] reproducing a century later the national 'invented traditions' of the nineteenth century.[21]

Most importantly for our purposes, this convergence is reproduced in the way in which the nation-centric and supranational schools both support the prospect of 'Europe as a superpower'—Debray's '*l'Europe puissance*'. At a minimum, the EU's international role lies in projecting or, even better, *magnifying* the power of individual member states in shaping international order; this is the Gaullist conception of the EU. Or, if it is to claim an international identity, or 'actorness',[22] it should do so in ways similar to those sought by national powers as seen through the traditional realist lens by opposing or at least balancing a common enemy or competing power. A widely shared assumption among both nation-centric and supranational views is indeed that, if the EU is to achieve international significance, it must challenge the US and eventually be assessed on similar terms to its rival across the Atlantic: as a shaper, not a taker, of 'world order', and through coercive means if necessary.

What does this imply for the prospect of justice beyond the European level? In short, if order can be projected 'outside', justice continues to belong 'inside'. The imperative of justice remains circumscribed by 'national' boundaries, be it within the traditional nation-state or possibly, in the long term, within a new European nation. This is, after all, the dichotomy that prevailed in Europe throughout the colonial era and beyond. We could label it the 'Tocquevillian model', with reference to the political philosopher's contrasting views on how European nations could perfect democracy *à l'Américaine* on the one hand, and how, on the other, France ought to implement a 'torched earth' policy of systematic repression against 'locals' to bring order to its

[19] E. Gellner, *Nations et Nationalismes* (Paris: Payot, 1989), 11.

[20] C. Shore, 'Inventing the People's Europe. Critical Approaches to European Community Cultural Policy', *Man*, 28/4 (1993), 791.

[21] E. Hobsbawm and T. Ranger (eds), *The Invention of Traditions* (Cambridge: Cambridge University Press, 1983).

[22] C. Hill, 'The Capacity-Expectations Gap, or Conceptualizing Europe's International Role', in S. Bulmer and A. Scott (eds.), *Economic and Political Integration in Europe: Internal Dynamics and Global Context* (Oxford: Blackwell, 1994).

Algerian colony.[23] All sides in Europe today may have moved beyond such a hierarchical and schizophrenic world view, but the essence of the tension remains the same.

In the end, under the nation-centric paradigm, the survival and promotion of the states system is not only the basic underlying condition of order but also of the pursuit of justice. If justice is attainable only inside state-like borders, then both international order and justice are predicated on the preservation of norms of sovereignty and non-intervention. To be sure, European or global action might be necessary to preserve states' capacity to act for the promotion of justice inside their borders: for example, preserving states' income-raising capacities or control of immigration. Hence, the so-called 'Chevenement group' of sovereignist parliamentarians from different EU member states has been pressurizing national parliaments into requesting ever more stringent compliance with EU-level rules of Justice and Home Affairs, especially in matters of asylum and immigration. This does not mean, however, that the nation-centric school has abdicated the global justice agenda. On the contrary, they argue, it is the very existence of circumscribed communities that makes it possible to envisage a universal approach to justice, not one so abstract and detached as to be unable to elicit significant solidarity and sharing of wealth. At best, such 'unrooted', 'decontextualized' cosmopolitan justice expresses itself through generalized guilt where 'one feels responsible at once for all of the world's misery and for no misery in particular'.[24] Is this a fair characterization of the alternative view of justice beyond the state?

The Post-national Paradigm: Justice Within and Justice Beyond

There is, indeed, a second, post-national response to the question of justice beyond the nation-state in the European context. Building on Habermas and, more generally, the universalist or cosmopolitan tradition of international political theory, it holds that European integration provides an opportunity for a profound renewal of the classical categories of political thought, thereby allowing for a dissociation between the juridical order of the political community and the cultural, historical, and geographical order of national identities.

Here, the nation-centric argument is turned on its head. It is precisely because we cannot deny the centrality of the nation-state to the European project that we need to move into another categorical realm at the European level.

---

[23] See A. de Tocqueville, 'Travail sur l'Algérie' and 'Rapports sur l'Algérie', in *Oeuvres Complètes* (Paris: Gallimard, Bibliothèque de la Pléiade, 1991). For a recent discussion, see O. Le Cour Grandmaison, 'Quand Tocqueville legitimait les boucheries', *Le Monde Diplomatique* (June 2001). See also T. Todorov, *De la Colonie en Algérie* (Brussels: Complexe, 1988) and *Nous et les Autres* (Paris: Seuil, 1989).

[24] Ferry and Thibaud, *Discussion sur l'Europe*. See also Miller, *On Nationality*, Ch. 3.

It is neither realistic nor desirable to suppose that the secular phenomenon of nation-building could take place at the European level and that the EU, divided as it is between many national and sub-national cultures, be associated with any mythic European 'motherland'. Indeed, under the national paradigm the 'natural' character of the nation is often opposed to the 'artificial' character of European integration, overlooking the fact that most European nations were built by the artifice of internal and external force; nations are not natural, organic entities, historical amalgamations of archaeological-like strata of deeds and memories. Whatever the primary material, they are constructed, both by visionary leaders and by social forces. Needless to say, no one would suggest at this point building a European nation by force. But those who defend a 'post-national' view are not satisfied with even a peaceful strategy of identity-building at the European level which would draw on the commonalities amongst European traditions and cultures. '[S]uch a chauvinism of European unity would mean duplicating the nationalist principle at the supranational level.'[25] Europe should have no ambition to replace national bonds.

This is because the initial fusion of nation with democracy and justice should not be granted *normative* significance. After all, the nation-state established only temporarily the close link between the *ethnos* and the *demos*.[26] What is at stake in European debates is precisely the need to radically question the contingent equation between the nation, social justice, and democracy. Post-national thinking does not deny the importance of local, national, and regional identities. It merely claims that neither cultural factors—namely, the reference to Judeo-Christian ethics, to Roman law, to Germanic freedom, and so on—nor communitarian impulses—membership of a historical community with shared values—are necessary or sufficient to underpin a modern polity dedicated to the pursuit of justice. Rather, such a community should serve to enhance the coexistence between diverse pre-political identities, and the *ultimate* motives for our attachment to it ought to be rooted in a common allegiance to shared principles of political and social justice flowing from a liberal political morality and a common set of political institutions through which these principles can be realized.[27] In the twenty-first century, this ought to be true regarding our national loyalty as well—a theme Habermas developed under the label of 'constitutional patriotism'.[28] Indeed, constitutional patriotism is not an oxymoron—combining the cold juridical with the warm emotional—because we live in an age where the love of justice can lead, and has

---

[25] J.-M. Ferry, 'Pertinence du Post-National', in J. Lenoble and N. Dewandre (eds), *L'Europe au Soir du Siècle. Identité et Démocratie* (Paris: Esprit, 1992), 53.

[26] J. Habermas, *L'Intégration Républicaine* (Paris: Fayard, 1998), 22.

[27] C. Laborde, 'From Constitutional to Civic Patriotism', *British Journal Of Politics and International Relations* (forthcoming).

[28] J. Habermas, *The New Conservatism. Cultural Criticism and the Historians' Debate* (Cambridge: Polity Press, 1989).

led, to extreme sacrifices. Constitutional patriotism differs from Nicolet's 'legal patriotism'—the attachment to the abstract principles of democracy and of the rule of law—in that it rests upon a relationship to one's history; and from Renan's 'historical patriotism' in that it rests on a *critical* relationship to one's history.[29] Its core imperative—that, after the holocaust, national histories and traditions could not be left unexamined—extends beyond Germany to all European nations.[30] Thus, at the European level, constitutional patriotism requires that states and the peoples of these states move away from their self-centred national memory and recognize the Other by recognizing the crimes committed against him or her.[31] European identity is not about forgetting, as Renan would have it, since, from the very beginning, it was founded on the permanent remembrance of its internal conflicts and thus on mutual responsibility. 'The Other' for Europe is Europe itself.

The tension between unity and diversity or universality and the respect for differences[32] is, then, at the core of the post-national paradigm. Solidarity in political contexts beyond the nation-state requires a double commitment: to a shared allegiance to universal values and to sharing diverse political cultures and institutions. It may be the case that the quasi-impossibility of sustaining the 'right' balance between these two requirements is responsible for the utopian character of much cosmopolitan political theory. In the European context, the implication of the post-national paradigm on this count seems to oscillate between two poles. For Habermas and his followers, the core of constitutional patriotism ought to be the same throughout Europe and can become the basis for a common political culture.[33] In another variant of post-national thinking, mutual identification ought not to be equated with a sense of common identity. Aside from communities of identity, there can be communities of interest and indeed communities of fate that borrow from, rather than merge with, participating political cultures to address common problems or pursue common dreams.[34] Thus, the European project requires the mutual recognition of the various political subcultures that constitute it, leading in time to a progressive opening of national public opinions to one another through political debate and confrontation.[35] Building a just order in Europe

[29] J.-M. Ferry, *La Question de l'État Européen* (Paris: Gallimard, 2000), 168.

[30] Habermas, *The New Conservatism*, 223.

[31] Ferry, *La Question de l'État Européen*, 177.

[32] Andrew Linklater, *The Transformation of Political Community: Ethical Foundations of the Post-Westphalian Era* (Cambridge: Polity Press, 1998).

[33] J. Habermas, 'Pas d'Europe sans Constitution Commune', *Le Point*, 1491 (13 April 2001), 102.

[34] R. Howse, 'Searching for a Plan A: National Unity and the Chretien Government's New Federalism', in H. Lazar (ed.), *Canada and the State of the Federation* (Toronto: Queen's Institute for Intergovernmental Relations, 1998).

[35] K. Nicolaidis, 'Conclusion: The Federal Vision beyond the Federal State', in K. Nicolaidis and R. Howse (eds), *The Federal Vision: Legitimacy and Levels of Governance in the United States and the European Union* (Oxford: Oxford University Press, 2001), 473.

does not call for the emergence of a homogeneous community where the solemnity of law is grounded in the will of a single *demos* but calls instead for instituting a discipline rooted in, and emanating from, a community of Others.[36] Critically, the post-national logic calls for a certain type of mutual recognition, very different indeed from that prevailing in classical international law where recognition is purely formal and which authorizes what can be seen as the kind of 'moral autarchy' that accompanies strict sovereignty rights. This more holistic form must include acknowledgement not only of the past violence inflicted by nations or groups on one another, but also of the mutual contributions made to each other's political, economic, and moral progress precisely by retaining an unassailable share of difference. In this light, pinning down through constitutional projects the trade-offs required by the pursuit of justice may not be desirable, whether in Europe or, even more so, as a means of strengthening international regimes.[37]

What does the post-national vision imply beyond Europe? Most fundamentally, it speaks against the reification of the European boundary, whatever it may be. If the core dynamic is one of *shared* political and cultural identities rather than *common* identity, there is bound to be a spillover effect from the transformation of regional to global community, from our relationship to the other European to our relationship with the non-European Other. To be sure, communities of interests do not have to be purely instrumental. Shared challenges and projects can create *communities of fate*. But these will be understood in a very different way from those who refer to fate as a link between a collective origin and a collective destination, a common journey based on the constant moulding of national consensus. Instead, a community of fate through a post-national lens refers to the common uncertainties that peoples may have to face together. Understood in this way, there is again no radical separation between a European community of fate and a universal community of fate, only a gradation in the amount and range of common uncertainties to be faced and managed, and therefore in the magnitude of calls for solidarity. This does not imply equating the EU's pursuit of justice within its borders with that beyond its borders, but it does imply that the *consistency* between them should be of paramount concern.[38]

---

[36] J. Weiler, 'Federalism and Constitutionalism: Europe's *Sonderweg*', in Howse and Nicolaidis (eds), *The Federal Vision*. See also J. Weiler, *The Constitution of Europe* (Cambridge: Cambridge University Press, 1999).

[37] Howse and Nicolaidis, *The Federal Vision*.

[38] This formulation does not in itself allow adjudication between different degrees of global solidarity and redistribution, which are related to the *substantive* criteria for universal or transnational justice. It is consistent with the cosmopolitan *minimal* claim that 'a domestic project of justice cannot be conceived without a conception of transnational justice' since 'internal justice cannot be established on the basis of external injustice' (R. Forst, 'A Critical Theory of Transnational Justice', in Pogge (ed.), *Global Justice*, but it may or may not encompass more extreme cosmopolitan views stressing the causal role played by the global economic order of

It is through this consistency requirement that the post-national view opens up a space for a new international discourse and practice for the EU. In many ways, the EU is still far from being the first 'post-Westphalian' international society as some cosmopolitan analysts argue.[39] But, exploring new forms of solidarity beyond the state, the EU can be seen as a beacon for the rest of the world, highlighting ways in which the pursuit of justice can break the bonds of the homogeneous community. In short, the EU becomes the potential means of externalizing a certain European tradition of justice. It can aspire to be more democratic and just than its nations of origin, working as it were from a blank slate or at least a slate where the weight of national designs may come to cancel each other. In this light power is based on influence not coercion, engagement rather than threats, economic rather than military might. It would be inconsistent for a project based on the peaceful pursuit of internal order to pursue international order mainly through military means. Under a post-national logic, hard power is not an end in itself, and the 'EC does not need and has not needed to acquire state-like qualities to exert an important influence in the world'.[40] Military power should be used, if at all, to bolster a global justice agenda under the flag of collective security rather than as part of alliance politics. Thus, at the global level, the post-national paradigm is consistent with a belief in strong international institutions and shared sovereignty. From a normative viewpoint , however, it does not assume that the EU's internal policies *actually* constitute an optimum of any sort. The EU may be a pioneer but not necessarily a model. And internal-external consistency may or may not serve alternative *substantive* conceptions of global justice. In short, if our two paradigms clearly differ regarding the *rationale* for pursuing justice (or not) beyond the nation-state, drawing out their respective implications in terms of *outcome* is a much more tentative enterprise.[41]

2. FROM THE NATION-STATE TO EUROPE, FROM EUROPE TO THE WORLD: EXPORTING ORDER? INSPIRING JUSTICE?

We now turn to the concrete political and policy implications of these two paradigms, with a brief overview of the EU's record on the order and justice

---

which Europe is part in the reproduction of poverty in the Third World. See for instance T. Pogge, 'Priorities of Global Justice', in Pogge (ed.), *Global Justice*.

[39] Linklater, *The Transformation of Political Community*.

[40] Hill, 'The Capacity-Expectations Gap'.

[41] In this vein, see for instance Rawls's discussion of the conceptual versus concrete difference between his 'duty of assistance' and a global egalitarian principle of redistribution. Rawls, *The Law of Peoples*, 115–20.

agenda and an assessment of how the end of the Cold War has affected this equation. We then ask which of the two paradigms more accurately describes the EU's trajectory and its current philosophy.

Europe During the Cold War: The Making of a 'Civilian' Power

Throughout its history, the very idea of Europe has fluctuated between a hegemonic notion, first promoted by the French monarchy, a Great Power system codified in the Congress of Vienna, and a more egalitarian view of Europe, both as a system of states and in terms of civilian rights, as promoted in the eighteenth century by the British and the Dutch. Hegemony or Great Power concert implied joint surveillance by powerful states of movements of population and minorities; the latter, in line with Kant's democratic and cosmopolitan ideal, corresponded to a more open vision of Europe as an integral part of a world federation of republics.[42] The European balance of power and the notion of popular national sovereignty were intrinsically linked to Europe's hegemonic position in the world throughout the colonial period. In the nineteenth century, political boundaries within the European space, self-conceived as the centre of the world, were also the basis for dividing the rest of the world. European nation-states exported the very form of the border—the geography of the European regional order—beyond Europe's boundaries as a means of creating a world order in their own image. Paradoxically, in the era of the EU the reverse dynamic has become true. Europe has, to a great extent, become a micro-cosmos, a reflection, on a regional scale and perhaps in more acute form, of global realities—from the projection of global diversity onto the European space to the regional management of the multi-faceted constraints and opportunities of globalization.

As noted earlier, the EU has since its inception carried connotations of regional order: bringing stability, security, and peaceful entanglement to the nations of Europe. This is the dimension of the EU project emphasized by realists, for whom 'it is clear that the notion of the EC/EU as an island of stability, and a piece in the jigsaw of the Cold War, is tied closely to the constitution of a geopolitical boundary between the Community/Union and the disorderly or threatening world outside'.[43] There is no denying that the EU has played a central part in establishing a presumption of order in the western part of the continent, including by sustaining the division of Europe— a role Joffe described as 'America's European pacifier'.[44] In short, the EC, at

---

[42] E. Balibar, *Nous Citoyens d'Europe: Les Frontières, l'État, la Peuple* (Paris: La Découverte et Syros, 2001).

[43] M. Smith, 'The European Union and a Changing Europe: Establishing the Boundaries of Order', *Journal of Common Market Studies*, 34/1 (1996), 14.

[44] J. Joffe, 'Europe's American Pacifier', *Foreign Policy*, 54 (1984).

the time, was the institutional anchor of regional order in the Cold War era, and it sustained this order both as an 'island of stability' and as the most prominent ally of the US in the bipolar contest. By channelling existing disagreement between member-states—often France vs the rest—over the extent to which Europe should rest content to play second fiddle to the US, the existence of the EC dampened potential transatlantic rifts and enhanced the predictability of its member states' foreign policies. This became even more the case after the first enlargement to include Britain, Denmark, and Ireland in 1973. Over time, successive French governments managed to rally more forces to their view, from the German left to the new members of the 'club med', to civil society groups demonstrating against US missiles. But the EC consistently provided not only the European but also the transatlantic 'glue'.

To the extent that the EC did exist internationally, it was as a civilian power focused on managing the external dimension of its internal market and its potentially negative externalities. Its own dedication to maximizing the wealth-creating effect of economic interdependence made it hard to ignore the demands for justice emanating from the rest of the world, especially from newly independent states. The EC both inherited the post-colonial guilt of its member states and provided an institutional 'venue' to assuage that guilt, a venue that would be less vulnerable to accusations of post-colonialism than individual member states' 'development' ministries. The EC Commission, in particular, sought early on to interpret its role as 'guardian of the Treaties' as including a commitment to export the benefits of 'managed trade' beyond its internal borders. As a result, and perhaps paradoxically, it started to shape a highly original and ambitious approach to development assistance, above all through the Lomé Conventions, which quickly became the most important source of aid in the Third World. It also engaged in the progressive and long-term institutionalization of its relationship with countries from the South, including with Mediterranean countries, ASEAN, Central America, and Mercosur. As a result, member states collectively and individually became by the late 1970s 'the rich countries most likely to win trust and exert influence in the South particularly Africa'.[45]

Nevertheless, the EC's contribution to global justice in these years should not be exaggerated. Aside from a handful of countries, most of the Asian, Caribbean, and Pacific states (ACPs) could not sustain growth simply on the basis of price-indexed aid for their primary commodities—their share of the budget devoted to such support was after all only 3 per cent of the overall EC budget—and, if EC protectionist lobbies happened to be offended, it was always clear what policy option would be chosen. Unsurprisingly, 'justice beyond' remained secondary at a time when the EC itself was operating under

---

[45] Hill, 'The Capacity-Expectations Gap'.

a mainly nation-centred paradigm, where its *raison d'être* was 'designed to maintain order between independent political communities rather than to realise shared normative commitments such as greater justice'.[46]

After the Cold War: Superpower as a Means to an End?

The end of the Cold War did not spell the end of the Union's order agenda; on the contrary. But it did affect the balance struck between order and justice imperatives both within Europe and in European foreign policy. The end of bipolarity, combined with post-cold war *disorder*, led to growing consensus over the Union's role as a potential exporter of order not only around Europe but also *beyond* Europe. But through what means, and to what ends? The tension became more acute and explicit between those who envisaged a truly 'Western' rather than US hegemony, based on the rule of law and the expanding jurisdiction of international institutions, and those intent on balancing 'the sole remaining superpower'.[47] Throughout the 1990s, European leaders explored ways of shifting the EU's focus from the maintenance of internal *political order* to the shaping of *geopolitical order*, while retaining consensus among member states. While it was clear that this could not be done short of endowing the EU with an autonomous military capacity, there was wide disagreement as to the ultimate function of an EU security apparatus independent of NATO. The theme, of course, was not new. In 1983, Hedley Bull reflected a widespread sentiment when he argued that the EU would never be a player in the world without its own defence.[48] A decade later, the alleged gap between the EU's *capacity* and the *expectations* it had created was still far from closing, since the EU was yet to gain 'dimensions of sovereignty to acquire a federal foreign policy ... which would give it the external quality of a state (and *ipso facto* superpower status)'.[49] Nationalist, anti-Atlanticist, and supranationalist pro-Europeans were joined in the late 1990s by pro-Atlanticist Britain in a bid to play a leading role in a new, albeit familiar, prospect of 'Europe as a superpower'. Thus, the 'capacity-expectation' gap was narrowed through the progressive formalization of a new Common Foreign and Security Policy incipient at Maastricht (1993) and confirmed at Amsterdam (1997), St Malo (1998), and Nice (2000). Ambiguities remained, however, as to what ought to happen in case of US-EU disagreement over the desirability of intervention.

---

[46] Linklater, *The Transformation of Political Community*, 207.
[47] R. Keohane, J. Nye, and S. Hoffmann (eds), *After the Cold War: International Institutions and States Strategies in Europe, 1989–1991* (Cambridge, MA: Harvard University Press, 1993).
[48] H. Bull, 'Civilian Power Europe: A Contradiction in Terms?', in L. Tsoukalis (ed.), *The European Community: Past, Present and Future* (Oxford: Blackwell, 1983).
[49] Hill, 'The Capacity-Expectations Gap', 316.

More fundamentally, critics on the left and within NGOs deplored the old-fashioned logic of a force-centred approach to power and the fact that it would detract from the core economic and social functions of the Union. In any case, since it would be impossible to match US levels of defence spending, why divert resources better deployed on aid, technical support, institution-building, and trade liberalization? Perhaps most fundamentally, how could a political entity so successful at creating order *within* through the logic of interdependence now turn to the old logic of coercive action externally? If it had to intervene through force, then the EU had better stick to areas of comparative advantage, such as conflict prevention, peacekeeping, and post-conflict management—a view dominant in the EU Commission and with Scandinavians. Moreover, they argued, the EU could aspire to be a 'superpower' externally only to the extent that its actions would reflect the hierarchy of states within the Union, a condominium of big member states. And that, in turn, would fundamentally betray 'the community spirit'. 'Civilian Power' thinking ought not to be abandoned as if it had been a second best all along, but reinvented to fit new international circumstances.

In spite of the controversy surrounding what kind of power it ought to be, there was a widespread sense in European capitals at the beginning of the 1990s that the EU was poised to become the *fer de lance* of a new international politics—a 'just' new world order. By the beginning of the twenty-first century this sense had been dampened but not obliterated. Three kinds of institutional/ideational arguments can be invoked here. First, by the early 1990s, Europe had become the most institutionally dense environment in the international system.[50] This meant that existing European habits of cooperation and institutional frameworks could be built upon in tackling global issues. Freed from Cold War strategic constraints, the EU now had the necessary room for manoeuvre to mould other regional organizations and international institutions in ways more congenial to its own vision of justice. The open question was, and still is, whether the rest of the world shares the EU's emphasis on institutionalism, and whether institutions can in and of themselves affect rather than reflect global imbalances of wealth and power.

Second, and more substantively, the unique political character of the EU gives it a significant comparative advantage in shaping challenges at the global level. While European nation-states in the colonial era exported their political models, economic structures, and internal conflicts, Europe has now become the place where many of the world's problems crystallize and get 'played out': refugee inflows and socio-ethnic tensions, transnational economic inequalities and calls for redistribution, the controversial balancing of social standards and trade liberalization, the two-edged sword of free movement of people, product,

[50] Keohane *et al.*, *After the Cold War*.

and capital—'goods' versus 'bads'—and the tension between liberal and conservative values in coordinating police and justice systems. So, European political systems have not only the institutional capital but also the substantive know-how to promote a shift in the global agenda. The reason for caution on this count is the lack of ambition of the EU's own internal justice agenda, including on economic redistribution, due to its nature as a regulatory state and the dismal size of its budget: 1.24 per cent of the EU's GDP.

Finally, the argument goes, the EU has the most credibility among powerful actors in the international system in playing such a leading role. In spite of its prospective military mantle, the EU still stands for civic statehood, peaceful coexistence, and the promotion of the rule of law in the realm of inter-state relations. Many still believe that precisely because of its origins and its essence as a civilian power it is this feature, more than military might, that enhances its potential for 'actorness' on the international scene. The EU is about politics, influence, and persuasion, not coercion. In this sense, the European version of Joseph Nye's soft power, of 'power without weapons', may lie precisely in its mastery of politics as a continuation of war by other means.[51] Opponents of its new security plans stress that the EU's reputation as a civilian power, rather than its potential military might, makes it a credible mediator and peacekeeper in conflict-prone regions around the world. Its claim to impartiality, if not always neutrality, is all the more credible given that EU states have often found themselves on different sides of a conflict on historical grounds. Such impartiality is bolstered by acting through the EU, an organization that has allegedly both incorporated and transcended these differences. Moreover, this reputation is strengthened by the rising prominence of, and access to decision-making by, NGOs in the EU and their insistence that internationally agreed norms must reflect ethical imperatives. Most prominently, the EU's main self-defined mission in the 1990s has been to promote these values of civic statehood and law across the European continent.

Indeed, since the late 1980s the EU has significantly increased its global presence on two counts: development assistance and peace-building. It has greatly increased its aid budget and scope of action—it now gives 55 per cent of world aid while progressively abandoning aid 'tied' to specific imports from the donor countries—and has been at the forefront of advocating 'sustainable development' strategies on the part of international organizations like the World Bank. To be sure, order and justice rationales are not easy to disentangle here. Part of the rationale for development assistance is the prevention of conflict, mass movement of people, and generalized unrest spreading beyond national boundaries. Regional order in Africa or Latin America affects world order and depends in turn on sustainable growth, which rests *inter alia* on enhancing the perception and reality of greater equity in the distribution of

---

[51] J. S. Nye, *Bound to Lead? The Changing Nature of American Power* (New York: Basic Books, 1990).

wealth. Similarly, the EU's increasingly assertive role as a mediator and peace-builder reflects the notion that the 'rights of people' and not only the 'rights of states' need to be protected at the level of international society. In the last decade, EU representatives have engineered new approaches to post-conflict nation-building in a number of war-torn societies, from the Balkans to Central America and the great lakes of Central Africa, through, *inter alia*, the funding of institution-building and NGO action on a previously unprecedented scale.

To some extent, therefore, both paradigms may sometimes inspire the same action, and the distinction between them is more one of emphasis in ends rather than in the means *per se*. But there remain numerous points of contrast and tension between the two foreign policy paradigms, ranging from defining the objectives, targets, and scope of interventionism abroad to the fundamental assessment of the character and meaning of borders. We can only indicate succinctly here how to tease out some of these differences.

3. THE EU'S SHIFTING JUSTICE AND ORDER AGENDA: HUMAN RIGHTS, ENLARGEMENT, AND GLOBAL GOVERNANCE

If a post-national agenda had taken hold in Europe, we would expect to see a significant degree of consistency between internal and external goals and policies. This final section examines how far this is in fact the case in relation to three important issue areas: human rights and citizenship rights; enlargement; and global governance.

Human Rights and Citizenship Rights Within and Without

Despite the fact that the original constituent Treaties did not refer to the protection of fundamental human rights, the European Court of Justice began in the late 1960s to rule that respect for such rights was part of the legal heritage of the Community. National actions incompatible with fundamental human rights were deemed to be incompatible with the Community legal order. It took a long time, however, for the EU to even start to match such legal prohibition with a proactive human rights policy in the face of resistance from a number of member states. To this date, it is not clear whether the Union possesses adequate legal competence in relation to a wide range of human rights issues, both internal and external.[52]

Nevertheless, the 1990s were a period of significant consolidation in this field, propelled by both internal and external sources. Internally, after completing the

---

[52] P. Alston and J. Weiler, *The European Union and Human Rights: Final Project Report on an Agenda for the Year 2000*, (Florence: European University Institute, 1998). This working paper contributed to the international report of 'wise men', *Leading by Example* (Florence: European University Institute, 2001).

internal market, leaders were realizing the need to move the Union into areas closer to their citizens' concerns. Externally, the end of the Cold War had removed the Soviet human rights bogeyman and turned the spotlight back onto the West. Thus, under the 1997 Amsterdam Treaty, any member state violating human rights in a 'serious and persistent' way can lose its rights under the Treaty; Austria came close in 1999. In the same period, EU lawmakers have taken notable initiatives in a wide range of fields, from gender equality to racism and xenophobia. Significantly, this heightened justice agenda has come in tandem with the enforcement of a much more systematic 'order' agenda for the Union, including through the coordination of police and control of movement of people in a borderless Europe. Under the heading of 'Justice and Home Affairs' introduced at Maastricht and revisited at Amsterdam, the goals of order and justice come together in the commitment to 'provide citizens with a high level of safety within an area of freedom, security and justice'. However, no specific mention is made of achieving these objectives within a framework that fully respects the human rights of all, including non-citizens, and EU institutions continue to be largely cut off from the administration of justice within member states.

On the external front, the EU has also considerably increased its emphasis on human rights in the last decade. Arguably, it has unique potential to spearhead a global human rights agenda, given its emphasis on positive forms of incentives in its foreign policy-making and its financial resources to back it up. The move, described in Chapter 2, towards greater emphasis and concerns with individual rights and democracy is certainly prominent in the evolving EU approach towards development aid, political cooperation, and the promotion of democracy. Close to home, it has insisted that states seeking accession must satisfy strict human rights requirements, including minority rights. Other governments wishing to enter into cooperation agreements with the Union or to receive aid or benefit from trade preferences must commit to respect human rights. Various types of human rights clauses are included in over 50 Community agreements, and are especially prominent in supporting countries in transition to democracy and in post-conflict peacemaking situations. But critics point out that the Union does not go far enough in this respect, in terms of the scant attention paid to home-grown monitoring institutions, to the lack of clear procedural rules for the suspension and termination of external agreements, and to the prevailing hands-off approach to regulating the practices of EU-based multinationals.

In this context, the Union's human rights policies, or lack thereof, have come under increasing scrutiny in the post-cold war era, culminating in particular in the events to mark the 50th anniversary of the Universal Declaration. Echoing many others, Alston and Weiler have argued:

The irony is that the Union has, by virtue of its emphasis upon human rights in its relations with other States and its ringing endorsements of the universality and indivisibility of human rights, highlighted the incongruity and indefensibility of combining an active external policy stance with what in some areas comes close to an abdication of internal responsibility. At the end of the day, the Union can only achieve the leadership role to which it aspires through the example it sets to its partners and other States. *Leading by example* should become the *leitmotiv* of a new EU human rights policy ... Our analysis thus makes no fundamental distinction between the internal and external dimensions of the Union's human rights policy. To use a metaphor, it is clear that both must be cut from a *single cloth*.[53]

In short, they conclude, 'as long as human rights remain a suspect preoccupation within, their status without will remain tenuous'.[54] There are numerous examples of such inconsistency. Thus, the EU provides funding and expertise to assist governments in third states to establish national human rights commissions, but such commissions have not been set up within most EU countries. EU policies are dominated by 'securitarian' or 'order' agendas, at the expense of the very human rights values promoted by its representatives in international fora.[55] Member states continue to apply widely differing interpretations in implementing common asylum measures, provide inadequate safeguards to protect the obligation to ensure *non-refoulement*, have applied widely differing interpretations of who constitutes a refugee, and have not always complied with common EU rules.

To be sure, the right of states to regulate or exclude immigrants or refugees is a source of intense ethical controversy among politicians and philosophers in Europe as in the US. National-sovereignists would argue that the law of peoples entails a conception not only of what the legitimate political units are but also who is entitled to become a citizen. But for the post-national critic an inclusive conception of European citizenship is needed, capable of bridging the gap between exclusionary and nation-centred concepts and a diffuse, but inconsequential, notion of universality. In the spirit of Hannah Arendt's 'right to rights',[56] the treatment of such extreme cases as those who suffer exclusion to the point of threat to their survival becomes the very test of universal justice. In the words of Etienne Balibar, representative of the most radical post-national view, today 'European citizenship is not conceived as a recognition of the rights and contributions of all the communities present in Europe, but as a post-colonial isolation between "autochtone" and "allogenes" populations, which in turn reinforces communitarian exclusionary patterns.'[57] Under this radical view, the Maastricht Treaty was significantly flawed in that it transformed the status of the foreigner in Europe by making European citizenship

[53] Alston and Weiler, *The European Union and Human Rights*, 21 and 23.
[54] Ibid., 21
[55] S. Lavenex, 'The Europeanization of Refugee Policies', *Journal of Common Market Studies*, 39 (2001).
[56] H. Arendt, *The Origins of Totalitarianism* (London: Allen & Unwin, 1958).
[57] Balibar, *Nous Citoyens d'Europe*, 307.

an addition of national citizenship. While within each country 'the Other' can still be considered as a member of another sovereign state, benefiting from mutual recognition, at the Union level he or she becomes excluded from within. Followed to its most radical conclusion, the post-national ethos has led various activists and intellectuals in Europe to argue that there is inside the EU a regime of quasi-apartheid which has led to replacing the traditional outside enemy with the figure of the enemy from within.[58] According to many human rights groups, exclusionary nation-centred constituencies are calling the shots, promoting an exclusionary logic in the EU, using borders as a means of police control, social exclusion, and exclusion of individuals from basic means of survival. They argue, without much success, that the EU should define itself as a community of *accession to citizenship*, albeit shared citizenship. In light of such demands, but even in light of the more moderate views expressed in *Leading By Example*,[59] if the status of the foreigner in Europe is to be used to gauge the consistency test, the nation-centric logic has not been superseded, be it as reflected in member states' or EU-level policies.

Managing Europe's Borders in the Context of Enlargement: The Politics of Inclusion and Exclusion

Shamefully, in the eyes of many, EU enlargement to the newly democratic countries of eastern and central Europe did not become an immediate imperative after 1989.[60] How could western Europe not want to share with great urgency the fruits of four decades of growth and freedom? How was it possible not to want to export east of Europe the benefits of enlightenment, reform, and democratization? Speedy accession and generous conditions were from the very beginning of the decade presented as a 'moral imperative' in most political and intellectual discourse. In practice, however, moral imperative gave way to other priorities on the EU's post-Maastricht agenda, from monetary union to creating a common judicial space and institutional reform. Geopolitical concerns about maintaining or restoring order in Europe's periphery continued to be paramount, albeit without granting a sense of historical urgency to the issue. This led in 1993 to the formal offer of membership to the first wave of candidate countries: Hungary, Poland, and the Czech Republic. Above all, the explosion of conflict in the Balkans greatly increased the awareness of risks of destabilization from lingering nationalism. Tellingly, the first concrete conditionality programmes put in place by the EU throughout eastern-central

[58] Balibar, *Nous Citoyens d'Europe*, 308.   [59] See n. 55.
[60] See for instance Timothy Garton Ash, *History of the Present* (London: Vintage paperback edn, 1991), 289 ff.; for an early discussion on the politics of enlargement see K. Nicolaidis, 'Eastern European Trade in the Aftermath of 1989: Did International Institutions Matter?', in Keohane *et al.*, *After the Cold War*.

Europe, the so-called 'stability pacts', were aimed at internal or cross-national tensions related to the treatment of ethnic minorities. A paramount concern on the part of the EU leadership at this point, and indeed to this day, was to fore-stall mass inflows of temporary or permanent migrants from the east. In short, even while the EU may have helped to create circumstances within these coun-tries that ultimately served the interests of the disenfranchised, the immediate rationale was certainly order on the European continent.

In this there was both continuity and change between pre- and post-1989. For much of its existence the EU was based on a 'politics of exclusion' and, in its current form, is still a 'daughter of the Cold War'. Once Gorbachev's 'com-mon European House' and other such continent-wide projects were buried in the immediate aftermath of 1989—and with them any real options to renegoti-ate borders and alliances on the continent—there was no possibility for the re-foundation of Europe on all-inclusive terms. EU decision-makers seem to have wanted to preserve for as long as possible the advantages of the existing division of labour between zones of unequal development, and furthermore to postpone any rethinking of European identity as emanating from the successive episodes of the 'European civil war'.[61] The new vision in the West, if it can be so called, was that of the 'real Europe' as opposed to the 'outside Europe' which would need to be 'Europeanized'. This notion of Europeanization only super-ficially echoed the slogan, so popular in the east in the early 1990s, of 'the return to Europe'. Europeanization as practised in the context of enlargement resembles 'internal colonialism'—to pick up on Timothy Garton Ash's expres-sion referring to the West German's attitude to their eastern compatriots[62]—and it goes along with a militarization of Europe to maintain the existing order both within and at its margins. Vaclav Havel's 'return to Europe' refers to a Europe whose culture, politics, and historical identity borrow from all sources, 'from the Atlantic to the Urals'—a striking end to 80 years of continental civil war. With policy firmly defined by the first view, the *reunification* of Europe has given way to *access* to the EU as the guiding imperative of the decade.

On what grounds, then, is accession conducted? Albeit under an assump-tion of fundamental asymmetry between the two sides of Europe, the EU has moved some distance in the post-cold war era towards a 'politics of inclusion'. Yet this evolution is far from unambiguous or complete.[63] Although it used to be clear what it meant to be inside and outside—a complex web of associ-ation agreements codified the hierarchy of relations between the EU and most of the outside world—that conceptual clarity has been lost. Moreover, the

---

[61] E. Hobsbawm, *The Age of Extremes: The Short Twentieth Century, 1914–1991* (London: Abacus, 1995).
[62] T. Garton Ash, *In Europe's Name: Germany and the Divided Continent* (London: Vintage, 1994).   [63] Smith, 'The European Union and a Changing Europe'.

geopolitical boundary of the EU has changed from the straightforward security blanket of the Cold War to a more multi-layered reality. Countries associated with the EU gain access to numerous types of status, following both the movement towards convergence and the distance left for achieving membership. With the EU a constantly moving target, the two are not necessarily correlated. In order to provide 'objective' criteria for establishing such degrees of accession, the EU Council has designed extensive conditions layering the path to membership.

But there is little attempt, it seems, to deal with accession conditionality in a way consistent with the internal dynamics of the EU. This is paradoxical given that accession is supposed to be first and foremost about economic and political convergence. In its forceful advice to the candidate countries' governments, the EU Commission has not applied the kind of arm's-length approach that has benefited member states, insisting on the application of 'accession economics' rather than development economics in countries that ought to concentrate on a development agenda.[64] Thus competition policy standards are often applied in more uncompromising ways than within the EU, even in environments which do not yet have fully functioning markets. Exigencies of compliance with the *acquis communautaire* far outstrip the kind of compliance expected from existing member states. Most paradoxically, convergence to an EU where mutual recognition of laws, regulations, and standards has become the norm, these countries are meant to converge to a 'European model' which, to some extent, is a utopia in the fertile minds of Brussels eurocrats.

It could be argued that the EU's enlargement strategy may at times contribute to *disorder* in the region. For one thing, its rating of actual or potential candidates creates signals for the rest of the world—from investors to neighbours and allies—making the implied link between non-EU status and disorder a self-fulfilling assessment; this is especially true for the second and third wave of applicants. Moreover, the unpredictability, inconsistency, and complexity of the EU's conditions is not conducive to the creation of a common political culture and policy forum, and the accession game has become a source of division as states in the periphery start to compete for inclusion. It may be the case that the EU's enlargement to the other half of Europe, along with the costs that it entails, testifies to the Union's ultimate commitment to creating, on the continent at least, a zone of greater justice. Yet the post-national critic would point out that the EU's lack of attention to the spillover effect of its own internal policies—from agriculture to justice and home affairs—and to the redistributive impact of the policies dictated to the candidate countries betrays a much more conservative agenda, at least in the short run.

[64] H. Grabbe and K. Nicolaidis, *Fostering Social Inclusion in Central and Eastern Europe: The Role of EU Accession Conditionality*. World Bank Working Paper, 39 (Washington, DC: World Bank, 2000).

Ultimately, the tensions and contradictions associated with EU enlargement are reflected in the most fundamental question of all: who ought to be included in the new European order? This question came to a head with the prospect of Turkish membership. Under the nation-centred or 'communitarian' logic, Turkey is not part of Europe historically and culturally defined, for example, by Roman law, Christianity, humanism, or liberalism. People in the EU cannot realistically envisage building a just order predicated on such an assumption. Here the exclusionary approach to defining 'who is us?' applies consistently to outsiders within and without. Hence, German Christian Democratic leaders consistently link their position on Turkey's membership with Turkish immigrants in Germany.[65] Similarly, in 1998 the left wing of the Social Democrats and, maybe more significantly, their Green allies brought to government an ideology of cosmopolitan inclusiveness and multicultural tolerance with implications on both the internal front—reform of the German nationality laws—and the external front—support for Turkish formal candidacy in the EU. More generally, the conflicts in the former Yugoslavia have led to the beginning of a questioning, if not redefinition, of the historical boundaries of Europe. The dominant cultural paradigm for European identity has lost its hegemony, and there is an increasing sense that European citizenship can be based on a commonality of *political* agendas. In short, there is an emerging definition of European citizenship that is much more inclusive and fluid than its previous, more implicit incarnation. As a result, the EU may come to focus less on the maintenance of boundaries and more on their continual redrawing and redefining.

The EU's Promotion of Global Governance

The shift from talk of 'a new world order' at the beginning of the 1990s to that of 'global governance' ten years later is symptomatic of the ascendancy of the justice agenda on the world stage. And the EU, through its bilateral relations and its representation in international institutions, has proclaimed itself to be the advanced guard in promoting many aspects of such an agenda, from economic redistribution to 'fair trade', sustainable development, democratization, and domestic institution-building. The term 'governance' and the *praxis* it represents is especially popular in the EU both because it offers an alternative model to classical party politics and because it seems to erase the divide between public and private management of collective affairs. On the one hand, 'governance' conveys the importance of including multiple stakeholders—which undoubtedly increases the prominence of justice claims, albeit often

---

[65] K. Nicolaidis, 'Europe's Tainted Mirror: Reflections on Turkey's Candidacy Status After Helsinki', in D. Keridis and D. Triandaphilou (eds), *Greek Turkish-Relations in the Era of Globalization* (Dulles: Bassey's, 2001).

inconsistent ones. On the other hand, critics contend that the term 'governance' is a bureaucratic, apolitical construct meant to convey the notion that all problems can be resolved through technical fixes without the need for addressing fundamental political conflicts and choices.

In a new version of Europe's 'narrative of projection', the European Commission and its supporters suggest that the EU has a particular role to play in fostering new more legitimate modes of world governance, in part by exporting its own institutional experience.[66] As a result, there is great emphasis on the creation or maintenance of international institutions as well as on the new flexible modes of cooperation EU leaders are currently experimenting with under the umbrella of 'open method of cooperation'. Indeed, short of a world state or a world government, a theory of international justice needs to address the *methods* states adopt in their relations, an issue that is lacking in theories of international justice expounded by political theorists. This does not mean, however, that such relations should necessarily be anchored in stronger institutions. Indeed, the EU experience itself could suggest otherwise, a model of 'global subsidiarity'.[67] But the nation-centred and post-national schools provide different readings of what global subsidiarity entails. For the former, the EU should not be bound irrevocably by international commitments; subsidiarity stands in as a rationale for sovereignty. For the latter, the notion of subsidiarity should be interpreted in a subtler manner, as calling for non-hierarchical modes of governance, an emphasis on process and checking power and on the mutual recognition of laws and regulations as well as of identities. In this view, interactions and cooperative endeavours may be intense, but they do not necessarily imply centralized coercive decision making and enforcement.

When it comes to applying such reasoning to the EU's policies on development, we are still a far cry from an ideal global theory of justice that could reach principles comparable to those of Rawls's *Theory of Justice*, including a global 'difference principle' dealing with the huge economic and social inequalities that exist in the world. Yet, even under a minimalist view, natural and historical contingencies have prevented 'the poorer and less technologically advanced societies of the world from attaining historical and social conditions that allow them to establish just and workable institutions' that would

---

[66] See for instance the 'Contribution of the EU to Global Governance' by the Commission working group on Global Governance, *White Paper on Governance* (Brussels: EU Commission, July 2001). For a discussion, see K. Nicolaidis (with R. Howse), ' " This is my Utopia"—The EU, the WTO, Global Governance and Global Justice: Synergies of Crisis, Narratives of Projection', in J. W. H. Weiler, J. Peterson, I. Begg (eds), Integration Expanding European Union: Researching the Fundamentals (Oxford and Malden, MA: Blackwell, 2003).

[67] Howse and Nicolaidis, *The Federal Vision*; R. Howse and K. Nicolaidis, 'Legitimacy and Global Governance: Why Constitutionalizing the WTO is a Step too Far', in R. Porter and R. Vernon. (eds), *Efficiency, Equity, Legitimacy: The Multilateral Trading System at the Millennium* (Washington: Brookings Institution Press, 2001).

in turn allow them to take advantage of global economic integration.[68] It is thus incumbent upon more favoured societies to help them counteract such contingencies by providing them with the incentives and means to set up such institutions at both the governmental and non-governmental levels. While international society has evolved in this direction in the last decade, the EU alone has moved decisively in this direction—in particular in Africa—doing away with tied aid and narrow macroeconomic conditionality. Aid policy may come to mirror, on a much more modest scale, redistributive policies to poorer regions in the EU. But the current bargains over the latter in the context of enlargement act as a stark reminder of the importance of the recipient country's bargaining power in shaping these policies.

In the trade realm, the agenda of the US and Europe in the GATT-WTO has consistently been to promote a liberal economic order in their image, with safeguards, exceptions, and exemptions shaped by their internal societal bargains, from the voluntary export restraints of the 1970s to the trade linkages of the 1990s. The blanket Third World opt-out of the 1960s and 1970s was followed by irresistible pressures to liberalize in the wake of the debt crisis, the Washington consensus, and the bargains of the Uruguay Round. Perhaps, most recently however, EU representatives have been more prone than the US to champion a Third World agenda, albeit with gaping exceptions, especially in agriculture. As the redistributive implications of the Uruguay Round agreements have become more obvious—for example, the creation of winners and losers between countries and not only within countries—EU negotiators have had to reconsider the 'justice' implications of their positions. In the post-Uruguay Round era, the EU's emphasis has been on seeking ways of shaping a more equal, or just, economic order, without paying much attention to requirements of procedural justice. While, as John Toye argues in Chapter 4, procedural justice will not make up for substantive justice because states do not enter into dispute settlement procedures similarly endowed, it is noteworthy that the EU has dismissed the demands of NGOs for transparency in dispute settlements even more readily than the US. Even on substantive grounds, the EU is loath to endow the WTO with 'constitutional authority' to adjudicate once and for all on fundamental political trade-offs. Hence, in its positions regarding trade disputes, in particular with the US, the EU Commission appears consistently to argue that the lack of converging national preferences points to the limits of international dispute resolution. There may be first-order conflicts[69] unamenable to compromises—for example, hormones in beef, the banana regime—that simply need to be left unresolved. When such conflicts arise reflecting differences in fundamental values regarding 'fairness', the distribution

---

[68] Rawls, *The Law of Peoples*, 52–3.
[69] A. Kojève, *Outline of a Phenomenology of Right* (Oxford: Rowman and Littlefield, 2000).

of risk, social needs, or the legitimacy of domestic contracts, EU lawyers have pursued a minimalist institutionalist line. Accordingly, we need to accept that conflict will go unresolved and that the system is about managing such sustained differences rather than creating 'order' at all costs. The coexistence of economic justice and political diversity is at that price.

4. CONCLUSION

Where does the EU stand, and where is it headed, on the order and justice agenda? Are justice concerns projected from the national to the EU levels now more systematically extrapolated to the global level? According to Balibar, 'we are now in an untenable in-between: *after the end* of classical national sovereignty (but not of national identities as echoes of history), *before the beginning* of a post-national sovereignty'.[70] But perhaps this 'in-between' is precisely what makes Europe so relevant to global debates on this issue.

We have discussed how, under the nation-centric paradigm, the EU can be seen as magnifying the logic of the inter-state system and should be used as such. On the alternative view, it helps transform and subvert this logic. In the first case, the Union is the forum in which European states negotiate continuously to maintain order among and around themselves, as sovereign states would in an 'anarchical society', simply more intensely. In the second view, the Union is a polity in which European peoples are inventing new norms of justice and solidarity beyond the state. In so doing, they constitute a laboratory not only for other regional endeavours but more importantly for global forms of cooperation.

The end of the Cold War has brought the tension between these two models to the fore. During the Cold War, the EU served as a mechanism by which European states managed the implications of bipolarity and systemic competition and thus focused on maintaining their internal version of world order. By the 1990s, however, the removal of the superpower overlay made it clear that 'the mosaic of "medieval Europe" with highly fragmented and often localized power sources would put into doubt the notion of an EU based on an identifiable power structure and consequent behavioural patterns'.[71] The EU that is emerging is a complex animal indeed. It aims to speak with a single voice on the world scene, but its internal dynamics increasingly contradict such ambition.[72] As

---

[70] Balibar, *Nous Citoyens d'Europe*, 293.

[71] Smith, 'The European Union and a Changing Europe', 8.

[72] S. Meunier and K. Nicolaidis, 'EU Trade Policy: The Exclusive versus Shared Competence Debate', in M. G. Cowles and M. Smith (eds), *The State of the European Union: Risks, Reform, Resistance and Revival*, vol. v (Oxford: Oxford University Press, 2001).

a result, the EU may have the capacity to shape an 'order and justice' agenda beyond its borders, but its members still need to agree on one. Moreover, they need to view the choices that they make internally as having a direct effect on their external standing. This implies addressing the 'unfortunate, although perhaps inevitable, element of schizophrenia that afflicts the Union between its internal and external policies'.[73] It is also a powerful argument against the transformation of the EU project into a state rather than into a truly transnational and decentralized federal construct with universal appeal.[74]

To be sure, while a majority of people and leaders in Europe still seem to think of pooling sovereignty as a concession made to the quest for regional order, a post-national paradigm is emerging in Europe that consists in part in laying the foundations for developing a 'justice' agenda beyond the state. Ultimately, this normative paradigm ought to point to the concrete channels and the practical ways by which such an agenda can be pursued. The role of institutions is crucial in this regard in that they can shape and not only reflect perceptions of a common interest in dealing with global justice claims,[75] thereby helping to create 'communities of interests' or 'communities of fate' at both the regional and the global levels. If it is partly a function of the strength of such communities and the institutions which shape them, the 'boundedness' of the quest for justice can be subject to change. But such a quest by political communities at any levels of aggregation cannot be based solely on institutions, procedures, and legal niceties; it needs a minimum degree of mutual identification.[76] This message, elaborated by the nation-centric school, has the merit of forcing the post-nationalists to come to grips with the moral and political underpinnings of their own advocacy of justice beyond the borders of the nation. There is indeed a middle ground between the straight dichotomous Tocquevillian logic underlying the first paradigm and the utopian cosmopolitanism model of a borderless world polity. The post-national school recognizes the power of collective identification but also the fact that there can be different grounds for creating a community of justice. Political communities may rest on bonds of solidarity in the face of harm and uncertainty without necessarily requiring bonds of common identities. They may rest on deep mutual recognition of identities—identification in a minimalist sense—rather than on their homogenization.

In the realm of *praxis*, many will argue that the EU needs to become a military superpower in order to support its ambitious justice aims. But if one takes a stricter consequentialist approach and adopts an outsider's view of the EU, then it is less relevant to ask what kind of entity it *is* than what it *does*.

---

[73] Alston and Weiler, 'The European Union'.
[74] Nicolaidis, 'Conclusion: The Federal Vision beyond the Federal State'.
[75] Hurrell, 'Global Inequality and International Institutions'.
[76] M. Telo, *Démocratie et Construction Européene* (Paris: Calmann-Lévy, 1996).

And on that count, it can be argued that since the early 1980s it has exercised a 'variable and multidimensional presence'[77] in international affairs that is less easily described in terms of power than in terms of presence and influence, be it in international organizations, in zones of conflict and mediation, or in the context of development. This influence has increased in the last decade, even short of a security arm, simply because non-military modes of intervention, including through economic incentives and political networking, often seem better suited than force to the post-cold war world. Whilst we have not discussed here the long-term impact of the events of September 11, we believe that, if anything, they are likely to increase the divergence between the roles of the EU and the US in international affairs and their respective attitudes to coercive diplomacy. In this light, the post-national school would argue, the EU can play a distinctive role, pertaining to a different logic altogether from the classical realist emphasis on competition and relative strength. As a civilian provider of international order, the EU is better poised at the beginning of the new millennium to adjudicate credibly between justice claims in different parts of the world and to project power as a means of bolstering this more neutral, mediatory role. In the end, however, who could deny that the tensions and contradictions of the past between the order and justice rationales in international policies are still with us today? Europeans, like their American counterparts, still find themselves choosing to promote unjust peace and are, perhaps less often, prepared to pay the price for disorderly justice.

---

[77] D. Allen and M. Smith, 'The European Community in the New Europe: Bearing the Burden of Change', *International Journal*, 47/1 (1990).

6

Order versus Justice: An American Foreign Policy Dilemma

John Lewis Gaddis

The city of Kishinev, once part of the Russian empire and then the Soviet Union, and currently the capital of Moldova, is only about 500 miles from the province of Kosovo, which was once part of Yugoslavia and is now officially still part of Serbia. Neither place can be said to have exactly riveted the attention of the United States during most of the twentieth century. And yet there is a curious connection between them, for in each location—Kishinev at the beginning of the century and Kosovo at its end—the question arose of what Americans should do when the government of another sovereign state brutalizes its own citizens. Despite sympathy for the victims, the presidents in power at the time, Theodore Roosevelt and William Jefferson Clinton, responded very differently to their plight. These differences reflect a persistent dilemma for US relations with the rest of the world during the past century, and what is likely to be an even greater one in the century to come.

Begin with the events in Kishinev in April 1903, when a pogrom resulted in the deaths of about 45 Jews, injury to another 4,000–6,000, and the destruction of the homes of about 10,000 more. No Americans were involved in this incident, but the American Jewish community, then only beginning to emerge as a significant force in domestic politics, did put pressure on the Roosevelt Administration to forward a petition of protest to the Russian government. This the president agreed to do, although with some reluctance; it was the first time that the US government had associated itself with a condemnation of Russian anti-Semitism solely on humanitarian grounds. The effect was minimal, for the Russian government rejected the petition and the pogroms continued. So too did the American protests, with growing misgivings on Roosevelt's part. 'For the Jews in Russia we were able to accomplish a little, a *very* little', he wrote. But he added that 'out in the West we always used to consider it a cardinal crime to draw a revolver and brandish it about unless the man meant to shoot.

Portions of this chapter have appeared in the *Hoover Digest*, 2 (2000).

And it is apt to turn out to be sheer cruelty to encourage men by words and then not to back them up by deeds'.[1]

Now fast-forward to the events of March 1999 when, in response to long-standing concerns about Serbia's treatment of its Kosovar minority, the US negotiated the Rambouillet Agreement in an effort to safeguard their rights, only to have the government of Slobodan Milosevic reject it just as peremp-torily as the Russian tsar had rejected the petition Roosevelt had forwarded 96 years earlier. This time, however, the US did a good deal more than just publicly protest. Together with its NATO allies, it began an immediate bomb-ing campaign against Serbia that produced, almost as immediately, as many as a million Kosovar refugees—about four times the number that had already fled to escape Serbian repression. It was two and a half months before Milosevic capitulated and agreed to withdraw his forces from what was still officially—though no longer in practice—Serbian territory. In contrast to what one might have expected of these two American presidents, it had been Roosevelt who spoke softly and Clinton who wielded a big stick.[2]

Nor was this the first such instance. The 1990s had seen a series of military interventions by the US, sometimes acting alone, sometimes with allies, in defence of human rights: examples included Kuwait in 1991, Somalia in 1992, Haiti in 1994, and Bosnia in 1995. By the time of the Kosovo operation, there-fore, there was beginning to be talk of a 'Clinton Doctrine': an implied prom-ise that the US would from now on come to the assistance of victims, not just of aggression, as the Truman Doctrine had pledged half a century earlier, but also of brutality, even if this occurred *within* the boundaries of sovereign states.[3] In short, Americans were now to encourage men and women by words *and* follow up with deeds. The century ended, as far as US foreign policy was concerned, very differently from the way in which it began.

1. WORDS VERSUS DEEDS

There was certainly nothing new in 1903 in an American policy of encourag-ing men by words and *failing* to back them up with deeds. The very first words of the Declaration of Independence provided as potent an encouragement as

---

[1] The incident is discussed in John Lewis Gaddis, *Russia, the Soviet Union, and the United States: An Interpretive History*, 2nd edn (New York: McGraw Hill, 1990), 41–3.

[2] For a succinct overview of the Kosovo operation, see the International Institute for Strategic Studies' *Strategic Survey 1999/2000* (London: Oxford University Press, 2000), 102–12.

[3] See, for example, Charles Krauthammer, 'The Clinton Doctrine', *Time* (5 April 1999), and Wolf Blitzer's CNN interview with President Clinton on 20 June 1999, *Public Papers of the Presidents of the United States: William J. Clinton, 1999*, i (Washington, DC: Government Printing Office, 2000), 542.

any government has ever offered—'all men are created equal'—but the deeds of the young American republic did little to enforce that principle. The fact that the man who wrote those words himself owned slaves suggests such a yawning gap between aspirations and accomplishments that we might well consider it a defining element of the American character.[4]

It showed up clearly in foreign policy. Having committed themselves to the pursuit of equality, the Founding Fathers immediately sought assistance from King Louis XVI of France, the most visible symbol of inequality around at that time, in pursuing American independence. Having attained it, Americans provided sympathy, but little support, for others who tried to follow their example: for the Latin Americans who declared their independence from Spain during the Napoleonic wars; for the Greeks hoping for liberation from the Ottoman Empire during the 1820s; for the Hungarians whose hero Louis Kossuth found applause but no assistance when he toured the US in the hope of reviving the failed European revolutions of 1848.

There were, to be sure, *some* instances during the nineteenth century in which Americans did intervene in the internal affairs of other states on behalf of oppressed minorities. However, these tended to coincide suspiciously with American interests, as when the US went to war with Mexico, ostensibly on behalf of beleaguered Texans, but wound up absorbing not just their territory but also what would later become New Mexico, Arizona, and California; or half a century later when it declared war on Spain, purportedly on behalf of oppressed Cubans, but wound up taking all of the Philippines. If humanitarian considerations were at work in these instances—and no doubt they were to some extent—then it was a selectively self-serving kind of humanitarianism.[5]

By the time of Roosevelt's Administration, the US had become a world power, but the last thing TR wanted to do was to reform world politics. Stability far more than equity was his goal. Indeed he won the Nobel Peace Prize, not for his role in protesting the Kishinev pogroms, but rather for mediating the Russo-Japanese War and thereby restoring order, not justice, in east Asia. It is pretty clear now that the only reason Roosevelt made his public protest against Russian anti-Semitism was that the Kishinev pogrom occurred prior to the 1904 election, in which he hoped for Jewish support. When even worse pogroms broke out in Russia after the election, Roosevelt refused even to go that far. '[W]e could do nothing', he told the financier Jacob Schiff, 'and where we can do nothing I have a horror of saying anything'.[6]

[4] Joseph J. Ellis, *American Sphinx: The Character of Thomas Jefferson* (New York: Vintage, 2001), makes the point particularly well.

[5] For a good recent discussion, see Anders Stephanson, *Manifest Destiny: American Expansionism and the Empire of Right* (New York: Hill and Wang, 1995).

[6] Gaddis, *Russia, the Soviet Union, and the United States*, 44.

2. CLOSING THE GAP

It would not be long, though, before the US had attained at least the *capacity* to do much more to right wrongs beyond its borders. The critical event here was the First World War, from which it remained aloof for almost three years while the great European powers bloodied themselves to the point of exhaustion. When the Americans did enter the war in April 1917 they did so from a position of great strength, so much so that their relatively brief intervention in that conflict may have done as much to shape its outcome as all the fighting they did in Europe in the Second World War. Sensing the power at his disposal, Woodrow Wilson took his country into the war with the greatest encouragement of men by *words* since 1776: the US would, he said, fight to make the world 'safe for democracy'.[7] His deeds, however, were far less impressive. Wilson sought self-determination within the old Austro-Hungarian and Turkish empires, knowing that this would weaken their ally, Germany. He hoped for it in Russia, calculating that it could only undermine the Bolsheviks, who had taken power six months after the US entered the war. He was not prepared to support it, though, for the peoples of the European colonial empires, many of whom sent representatives to the Paris Peace Conference but who came away empty-handed. Nor did he follow through on his own idea of extending American protection over the Armenians, survivors of the first great genocide—this one at the hands of the Turks—of the twentieth century.[8]

Despite his rhetoric, therefore, Wilson never placed the priorities of justice on a par with those of order. And it soon became clear that whatever Wilson was willing to do did not matter anyway, because the American people were not about to assume responsibilities beyond their borders. Instead they resorted during the 1920s and 1930s to a kind of moral anaesthesia in international affairs. Confronted with increasingly horrendous examples of brutal behaviour on the part of the Japanese, the Germans, and the Soviet Union, they simply averted their eyes, taking refuge in the belief that such behaviour was about the best you could expect from foreigners, but that nothing of what they did to one another could really affect Americans.

Franklin D. Roosevelt never shared that view. The US, he understood, could never wall itself off from what was happening elsewhere in the world, and

---

[7] Speech to Congress, 2 April 1917, quoted in Tony Smith, *America's Mission: The United States and the Worldwide Struggle for Democracy in the Twentieth Century* (Princeton: Princeton University Press, 1994), 84.

[8] N. Gordon Levin, *Woodrow Wilson and World Politics: America's Response to War and Revolution* (New York: Oxford University Press, 1968), This is still the best single-volume exploration of Wilsonian contradictions.

from the late 1930s on he did all he could to overcome isolationism and to bring American power to bear on behalf of the increasingly beleaguered Western democracies. It was partly in the effort to win public support for this policy, and also partly because he believed in them, that he resurrected Wilsonian *words* in two great pre-war pronouncements: the Atlantic Charter and the Four Freedoms. But Roosevelt was in no better position than Wilson to follow through with deeds. He knew that this new war could hardly make the world safe for democracy because it would require the assistance of an odious autocracy—Stalin's Soviet Union—in order to win it. FDR did his best to persuade Stalin to use his power in eastern and central Europe with restraint. But when one of Roosevelt's aides complained that the Yalta agreement on Poland was so soft that the Russians could stretch it all the way to Washington, the president replied: 'I know, Bill, I know. But that's the best I can do for Poland at this time.'[9] FDR's cousin TR, I think, would have understood.

And what of the Holocaust, the event that now looms largest in our minds when we think of the Second World War? The honest answer is that it did not then. Roosevelt and his advisers surely knew that the Nazis were killing Jews in large numbers, just as Wilson knew that the Turks were killing Armenians. But they did not know, or did not believe, the scale of the killing. And even if they had known and believed, it is not at all clear that they would have done much differently. Their single-minded priority was to win the war. Anything that distracted from that objective, as they thought the bombing of Auschwitz would, was to be rejected. Anything that advanced it, as they expected the atomic bomb to do, was to be embraced, whatever the cost.

Victory therefore required moral compromises: collaborating with Stalin, blinking at the Holocaust, building the bomb. But the sense at the time was that without victory there could be no justice for anyone; that with victory there might at least be justice for some. It was with that grim sense of determination—a determination resigned to the realities of an imperfect world in which the goal of 'justice for all' was still a long way off—that the Americans fought the second great war of the twentieth century.

3. COMPROMISES: EUROPE

The early Cold War was no more free from moral compromises than the Second World War had been. There were, to be sure, unprecedented international

---

[9] Quoted in John Lewis Gaddis, *The United States and the Origins of the Cold War, 1941–1947* (New York: Columbia University Press, 1972), 163. My discussion of Roosevelt here follows this volume, as well as Robert Dallek, *Franklin D. Roosevelt and American Foreign Policy, 1932–1945* (New York: Oxford University Press, 1979).

prosecutions of defeated enemies for crimes against humanity. But the Nuremberg trials were conducted jointly with the Soviet Union, whose own crimes were certainly comparable to those of the Nazis and, in terms of the number of victims, even worse. One of that country's prosecutors at Nuremberg was none other than Andrei Vyshinsky, who had led the legal lynching of Stalin's former associates during the Moscow purge trials of the late 1930s.[10] That was only one of many reminders that the Second World War had been won by means that left half of Europe under authoritarian control. Nor was it clear, given the economic conditions that existed in the rest of Europe, that authoritarian solutions would not take hold there as well. George Orwell's classic novel *Nineteen Eighty Four* captured the pessimistic sense of many Europeans at the time that post-war standards of justice might well be those of Vishinsky. If so, there didn't seem to be much hope.

We now know, of course, that Orwell's vision was too bleak: that the Marshall Plan did bring about economic recovery in Europe, and that on that basis democratic practices did take root in several places: West Germany, Italy, and—later—Spain, Portugal, and Greece, where they had not previously flourished. The peaceful climate in which this happened, though, was purchased only at a price: by learning to live in Europe with justice for some but not for all. This was most dramatically evident in the city of Berlin, divided right down the middle by a border separating those sectors where democratic principles applied from those in which they did not. But Berlin set the pattern for the division of an entire country along much the same lines. And Germany set the pattern for the division of a continent. The fact that we no longer spoke of 'Europe' during the Cold War but rather of 'western Europe and eastern Europe' reflects the extent to which, during this long conflict, the demands of justice were subordinated to the requirements of order.

Despite some talk of 'rollback' and 'liberation' during the late 1940s and early 1950s, and a few very ineffective covert operations, the US and its allies did little to challenge this post-war settlement. Whether it was riots in East Berlin in 1953, or the bloody suppression of a revolution in Hungary in 1956, or the construction of an actual wall in Berlin in 1961, they confined their protests to rhetoric: to words but not deeds. The reason, of course, was the fear of another great war, this time with the Soviet Union itself, this time fought with nuclear weapons. As President Eisenhower put it at the time of the Hungarian uprising, it was not clear 'how much we should poke the animal through the bars of the cage .... [T]he Soviets are scared and furious,

---

[10] Vyshinsky's role is discussed in detail in Robert Conquest, *The Great Terror: A Reassessment* (New York: Oxford University Press, 1990). Soviet crimes against humanity are most thoroughly documented in Stéphane Courtois *et al.* (eds), *The Black Book of Communism: Crimes, Terror, Repression*, trans. Jonathan Murphy and Mark Kramer (Cambridge, MA: Harvard University Press, 1999).

and there is nothing more dangerous than a dictatorship in this state of mind'.[11] What this meant, however, was that dictators would continue to have the right to stifle even the slightest pressures for self-determination within their sphere of influence. Very much as the promise of justice during the Second World War had had to wait for the attainment of total victory and even then was not wholly attained, so now the pursuit of justice during the Cold War came up against the more urgent need to prevent total war. When the alternative appeared to be the Bomb, blinking at brutality seemed the most prudent thing to do.

4. COMPROMISES: THE THIRD WORLD

The Cold War also privileged order over justice when it came to the Third World. Americans had felt little sympathy for European colonialism at the end of the Second World War, and yet concerns quickly arose in Washington that, if national liberation movements proceeded too fast or too far, they might bring Marxists to power who might then align themselves with the Soviet Union. The US sought, as a consequence, to slow such movements. Yet this often meant aligning with authoritarians on the right, a pattern familiar from its long relationship with Latin America that was now extended throughout much of south-east Asia, the Middle East, and Africa. Some of Washington's most questionable actions during the Cold War resulted from this fear that Third World nationalism might open the way for communism: CIA intervention in Iran and Guatemala, support for the Diem regime in South Vietnam, the alienation of Nasser in Egypt, the effort to overthrow Castro in Cuba, cooperation with the Mobutu dictatorship in the Congo, opposition to the freely elected Allende government in Chile, the abortive intervention in Angola during the mid-1970s.

There should be no romantic illusions here. Some Third World nationalists like Castro and Ho Chi Minh were also communists, prepared at least for a time to serve as Soviet surrogates and disinclined at any time to respect democratic principles. It is also worth noting that one particular nationalist who was also a communist and who was also the object of romantic illusions in the West—Mao Zedong—turned out to be the greatest practitioner of death by government in all of history, having allowed his Great Leap Forward to produce a famine that resulted in the starvation, between 1958 and 1961, of

---

[11] Quoted in John Lewis Gaddis, *We Now Know: Rethinking Cold War History* (New York: Oxford University Press, 1997), 236–7. I have drawn more generally on this book in the account of the early Cold War presented here.

some 30 million of his own citizens, another atrocity from which the world until recently averted its eyes.[12] So one can hardly say that Mao and the Third World Marxists were consistently agents of justice. What is clear, though, is that they were not consistently agents of a coordinated, revolutionary movement controlled from Moscow either, and that the US too often associated itself with agents of injustice in seeking to contain or suppress a conspiracy that for the most part did not exist.

5. HELSINKI: THE TURNING POINT

By the early 1970s, the Americans' preference for order, stability, and predictability in the Cold War had advanced to the stage that even their adversaries had begun to share certain aspects of it. The world revolution, it was clear, was nowhere on the horizon. Meanwhile the costs of the Cold War were taking their toll, and the danger of nuclear war was threatening everyone, without regard—as Khrushchev noted—for the class principle. It was also the case by then that the communists had fallen out with one another, so that both the Soviet Union and the People's Republic of China could now look to the US as at least a tacit ally.

We remember this development as 'détente', and most Americans welcomed it at the time for lowering the risk of war and the opportunities it gave them to exploit differences among their enemies. But here too there were moral compromises. Détente involved an American president flying all too gleefully to Beijing to shake the hand of Chairman Mao, whose country was still recovering from the horrors he had inflicted on it and who had only begun to moderate the purges of his own former associates during the Cultural Revolution. Détente required cooperating with a Soviet leadership that had just crushed all signs of independence in Czechoslovakia, had promised with the Brezhnev Doctrine to apply similar treatment to any other Soviet satellite that might seek to loosen Soviet controls, and was now planning to crack down on its own internal dissidents. And détente meant West Germany's acceptance, in the form of *Ostpolitik*, of the possibility that a third of the German people might always live under a repressive regime that had never subjected itself to free elections and in which as many as one out of every four citizens was working for the secret police.[13] So when the Conference on

---

[12] See Jasper Becker, *Hungry Ghosts: Mao's Secret Famine* (New York: Henry Holt, 1998).

[13] There is as yet no comprehensive international history of détente. Most of these issues are discussed, though, in Timothy Garton Ash, *In Europe's Name: Germany and the Divided Continent* (New York: Random House, 1993) and in Raymond L. Garthoff, *Détente and*

Security and Cooperation in Europe (CSCE), which the Soviet Union had long sought as a means of legitimizing the post-Second World War boundaries it had imposed there, produced the Helsinki Final Act on 1 August 1975, the event seemed on the surface the very institutionalization of moral compromise. The price of stability in Europe, it now appeared, was accepting its division as permanent. The urge for order had finally triumphed over the demands of justice.

But Helsinki turned out quite differently. Today we remember it the other way around, as the moment at which justice began to claim a status at least *equal* to that of order in Cold War politics. The CSCE process has yet to find its proper historian,[14] but it is clear enough that different people expected very different things from it. For the Soviet Union, the highly publicized Helsinki meeting was supposed to acknowledge formally its sphere of influence in eastern and central Europe. For the Americans, who went along with it reluctantly, the conference provided a way of obtaining concessions from Moscow on other issues at relatively little cost. For the West Europeans, Helsinki secured at least a paper commitment to the free movement of people across borders. For dissidents in eastern Europe and within the Soviet Union itself, Helsinki marked an internationally agreed limitation of sovereignty: the first official recognition by the Soviet Union that the manner in which a state treats its own citizens was a legitimate matter for international concern.

This last accomplishment was the most important one. For by suggesting that when it came to matters of justice sovereignty was not absolute, and by establishing that states were not free to treat their citizens, or those within their sphere of influence, in any way they liked, Helsinki broke new ground. It was, in one sense, the product of détente in that it could never have come about had there not been that lowering of Cold War tensions. But Helsinki also represented a lowering of the guard on the part of leaders in Washington, Moscow, and elsewhere who had assumed the indefinite sustainability of a single international system containing separate standards of behaviour with respect to human rights.

6. THE COLLAPSE OF THE SOVIET UNION

That it might not be sustainable first became clear within the context of American domestic politics, where support for détente was already eroding as the Helsinki conference was taking place. Whether for reasons of politics or

Confrontation: American-Soviet Relations from Nixon to Reagan, revised edn (Washington: Brookings Institution, 1994).

[14] But see Samuel F. Wells, Jr (ed.), *The Helsinki Process and the Future of Europe* (Washington: Wilson Center Press, 1990).

principles or both, Senator Henry Jackson had become a vocal and influential critic of the Nixon-Kissinger foreign policy for its alleged insensitivity to human rights and its acceptance of a status quo that, as he saw it, only benefited the Soviet Union. Kissinger's thoughtful efforts to justify détente, the most ambitious effort by an American statesman since Wilson to reconcile the requirements of order and justice, had met with total neglect, probably because no one took seriously what Kissinger said in public. If it wasn't classified, most people assumed, it couldn't be important.[15] And as the 1976 presidential campaign got under way, both Carter Democrats and Reagan Republicans began attacking détente for its alleged privileging of order over justice, so much so that President Ford felt obliged to forbid his own subordinates from publicly using the word.

Meanwhile, the crackdown on dissidents inside the Soviet Union and in eastern Europe had backfired. Brezhnev and his advisers had seen in détente a licence to suppress resistance: achieving order within the international system would make it easier to impose order at home. What they failed to see was that, by signing the Helsinki agreement, they were instead licensing the dissidents and their external allies to transform these domestic issues into foreign policy problems. Brezhnev 'thought this would not bring much trouble inside our country', the long-time Soviet ambassador to Washington Anatolii Dobrynin has recalled. 'But he was wrong.… [Helsinki] gradually became a manifesto of the dissident and liberal movement, a development totally beyond the imagination of the Soviet leadership.'[16]

We do not normally think of Jimmy Carter and Ronald Reagan as pursuing similar policies, but on the issue of order versus justice in Cold War politics they certainly did. Both were prepared to sacrifice at least some of the cooperation that had emerged in Soviet-American relations during the Nixon-Ford-Kissinger years; neither was willing to avert eyes, as previous administrations had done, when human rights abuses occurred within Moscow's sphere of influence. To be sure, there were differences. Carter's concerns about human rights were broader, applying to allies in Latin America as well as to adversaries in the Marxist-Leninist world; Reagan's tended to target the latter and neglect the former. From the Soviet perspective, though, there was not much difference: Moscow did not like what was happening in either administration, and détente suffered as a result.[17]

[15] See John Lewis Gaddis, *Strategies of Containment: A Critical Appraisal of Postwar American National Security Policy* (New York: Oxford University Press, 1982), 342–3.

[16] Anatolii Dobrynin, *In Confidence: Moscow's Ambassador to Six Cold War Presidents* (Seattle: University of Washington Press, 2001), 346.

[17] Garthoff, *Détente and Confrontation*, and *The Great Transition: American-Soviet Relations and the End of the Cold War* (Washington: Brookings Institution, 1994) provide a full, if still provisional, account.

However, it was not until Reagan's 'evil empire' speech in March 1983 that it really became clear to what extent the US was prepared, in the interests of human rights, to 'poke at the animal inside its cage'. For in that address, an American president actually said what many of his predecessors had thought but not felt able to say because it seemed to be too dangerous: that the denial of justice within the Soviet sphere was indeed evil, and that nothing, not even the requirements of maintaining order in the Cold War, could excuse it. We now know that there was indeed danger during this period: that precisely because of Reagan's rhetoric, the Soviet leadership became convinced that the Americans were about to launch a nuclear first strike, and went on a risky and extended military alert, arguably the second most perilous moment of the Cold War.[18]

But this did not last. What was remarkable about the Soviet reaction to the 'evil empire' speech is that, as time went on, the Russians themselves gradually came around to acknowledging that theirs had indeed been an evil empire, and they began to change their policies. As they did so, Reagan began to change his rhetoric. And so it happened that on that memorable spring day in 1988 when Reagan and Gorbachev walked amicably through Red Square, greeting bystanders and bouncing babies, the Soviet leader came close to admitting that Reagan had been right in what he had said five years earlier. Reagan, for his part, admitted that the Soviet Union under its new leadership was evil no longer.[19]

I am sure that Reagan and Gorbachev hoped, in their own respective ways, to bring the Cold War to an end. But I am almost as sure that they did not have in mind doing so by altering the bipolar configuration of world politics that had existed since 1945. They envisaged a world in which the US and the Soviet Union would remain superpowers but their antagonism would simply fade away. This was what Gorbachev's advisers meant when they spoke of depriving the US of an adversary. The Soviet Union would replace the Brezhnev Doctrine with the Sinatra Doctrine: the east Europeans could do it 'their way'.[20] And within the Soviet Union *glasnost* and *perestroika* would produce a new kind of communist state, one whose survival and prospering would depend upon securing justice for its citizens, not upon denying it as had been the case during the more than seven decades in which that system had existed.

George Bush probably had such an outcome in mind when he resisted the temptation to 'dance on the Berlin Wall' as it was coming down in

---

[18] The 1983 war scare is recounted from the American side in Beth A. Fischer, *The Reagan Reversal: Foreign Policy and the End of the Cold War* (Columbia: University of Missouri Press, 1997), 122–40; and, from the Soviet side, in Christopher Andrew and Vasili Mitrokhin, *The Mitrokhin Archive: The KGB in Europe and the West* (London: Penguin, 1999), 278–9.

[19] Gaddis, *Russia, the Soviet Union, and the United States*, 336.

[20] David Reynolds, *One World Divisible: A Global History Since 1945* (London: Penguin, 2000), 556.

November 1989 and when, as late as the summer of 1991, he advised unreceptive Ukrainians that their best interests lay in remaining a part of the Soviet Union. It is true that he pushed the Russians hard on German reunification. Here the policy was 'like it or lump it', based on the assumption, which proved to be correct, that Moscow would have no choice but to embrace the liking over the lumping. Even so, though, Bush and German Chancellor Helmut Kohl kept the Russians carefully informed at every step of the way, allowing them to salvage at least some dignity in what was, for them, an increasingly difficult situation. These efforts paid off when war broke out in the Persian Gulf early in 1991 and Moscow did not come to the assistance of its former ally, Saddam Hussein. And when Gorbachev's government and ultimately the Soviet Union itself disintegrated in the wake of the August 1991 coup, there was more of a sense of loss than of triumph in Washington and other Western capitals, for the 'evil empire' had reformed itself, and it was not at all clear what was to replace it.[21]

7. KUWAIT, KOSOVO, AND THE POST-COLD WAR WORLD

When President Clinton came into office in 1993, therefore, he inherited a situation in which, for the first time in the twentieth century, the requirements of international order and justice seemed close to coinciding. It was one in which all of the great powers could agree on the virtues of market capitalism, in which most—China being the exception—could accept democratic principles, and in which none was any longer committed to seeking the overthrow or the annihilation of any other. The fact that the United Nations had sanctioned military action to secure justice for Kuwait with no objection from any permanent member of the Security Council seemed to suggest what President Bush had called a 'new world order', one in which the old Cold War dilemma of having to choose between order and justice had disappeared. One could have it both ways, or so it appeared.

It quickly became apparent, though, that things were not that simple. Part of the explanation had to do with the unpleasant fact that some people, if allowed the right of self-determination, will use it to oppress or even kill other people. Experiences like those in Somalia, Rwanda, the Balkans, and the Israeli-Palestinian conflict show that, while the world had come *closer* than

---

[21] See, on these issues, Philip Zelikow and Condoleeza Rice, *Germany United and Europe Transformed: A Study in Statecraft* (Cambridge, MA: Harvard University Press, 1995); Charles S. Maier, *Dissolution: The Crisis of Communism and the End of East Germany* (Princeton: Princeton University Press, 1997); and Don Oberdorfer, *From the Cold War to a New Era: The United States and the Soviet Union, 1983–1991*, revised edn (Baltimore: Johns Hopkins University Press, 1998).

ever before to a universal standard of justice by the end of the twentieth century, it had by no means reached that goal. There were still plenty of places where what one group of people might perceive as 'justice' could come across to others as its wholesale, even violent, denial. In such situations, the imposition of order—preferably by external mediation but possibly by external force—might be the only remedy.[22]

But that raised a second problem, which had to do with the source of such order: there was as yet no supranational authority capable of providing it. Kuwait turned out to be the exception, not the rule, for the 1990s; elsewhere the UN was less successful in securing justice, whether because of mismanagement as in Somalia and Bosnia, neglect as in Rwanda, or paralysis owing to the inability of its most powerful members to agree on the need for such action in the first place, as in Kosovo. The alternative was regional authority, a solution the Clinton Administration embraced by persuading NATO to undertake more successful humanitarian interventions in Bosnia and Kosovo. It did so, however, only at the price of alienating the Russians and the Chinese, who worried about precedents set for their own discontented minorities as well as the prospect that it would henceforth be left to Washington alone to determine what 'justice' was in the first place.[23] As a result, the consensus on the requirements for order and justice towards which the great powers had seemed to be moving as the decade began was nowhere in sight as it ended.

Meanwhile, the Kosovo operation caused yet another problem, anticipated almost a century ago by Theodore Roosevelt: it raised false hopes. These were most apparent among the Kosovars themselves, many of whom assumed that NATO's intervention on their behalf meant that Washington and its allies now favoured Kosovo's independence from Serbia. This was never the case, though, a fact that became all the more awkward when the Serbs themselves overthrew Milosevic and began embracing democracy, even as the Kosovo Liberation Army—no bastion of either democratic procedures or humanitarian sensibilities—began seeking not just independence but a Greater Kosovo carved out at the expense of Macedonia. Finally, there was the question of consistency. If the Clinton Doctrine required aiding the victims of brutality in Kosovo, why did it not in Rwanda, Chechnya, Tibet, Iraq, the Sudan, or Sierra Leone? The application of universal principles on so selective a basis could not help but raise questions about what the standards for selection were to be and whether expediency as much as morality determined them.[24]

---

[22] Such is the argument in Robert D. Kaplan, *The Coming Anarchy: Shattering the Dreams of the Post Cold War* (New York: Random House, 2000). See also, for an account of how this was done in Bosnia, Richard Holbrooke, *To End a War* (New York: Modern Library, 1998).

[23] Ian Clark, *The Post-Cold War Order: The Spoils of Peace* (New York: Oxford University Press, 2001), 50.

[24] Henry Kissinger makes the point strongly in *Does America Need a Foreign Policy? Towards a Diplomacy for the 21st Century* (New York: Simon and Schuster, 2001), 257–8.

8. THE LESSONS OF KOSOVO

So did Kosovo establish a precedent? The answer, at first glance, would appear
to be 'no'. There is now a general sense that the NATO intervention there was
ill-conceived, badly executed, and, in the light of these deficiencies, extraordinarily fortunate in its outcome, a pattern that can hardly be expected to repeat
itself often.[25] It was with these considerations in mind that two eminent
Americans—Henry Kissinger, former National Security Adviser and Secretary
of State in the Nixon and Ford administrations and still the most prominent American 'realist', and Joseph S. Nye, Jr, Dean of the John F. Kennedy
School at Harvard University, high-ranking veteran of the Carter and Clinton
Administrations and co-founder of the 'neo-liberal' school of international relations theory—proposed post-Kosovo criteria for when humanitarian intervention should violate sovereignty in the future. Despite the fact that they come
from opposite ends of the political and theoretical spectrum, Kissinger and Nye
agree that the standards should be tough ones: so tough, indeed, that it is hard
to conceive of situations in which all of them might apply.

Kissinger's standards include: (1) *consistency*, by which he means that the
intervention must reflect what the rest of the world will understand to be a universally applicable policy, otherwise it will appear 'as an arbitrary exercise of
American dominance and, in time, as an act of selfish hypocrisy'; (2) *sustainability*, the requirement that the policy command support from both American
public opinion and the international community; and finally (3) *contextuality*:
'if America's actions do not take account of the historical context, they will
sooner or later be defeated by growing local obstacles or require a mobilization
of power incompatible with the domestic American consensus.'[26]

Nye goes even further. He would insist on: (1) *proportionality*—the use of
violence only in the most egregious cases, where the case is compelling, the
actions involved will not unduly punish the innocent, and the prospects for success are strong; (2) *complementarity*—the presence of convincing national and
international interests apart from humanitarian concerns; (3) *collaboration*—
regional actors must be willing to participate; (4) *clarity* regarding the meaning of 'genocide', with intervention only where there can be little question
that it is indeed taking place; and (5) *restraint* with respect to intervention in
civil wars over 'self-determination', which Nye regards as a 'dangerously

---

For a devastating assessment of the Clinton Administration's handling of genocide in Rwanda,
see Samantha Power, 'Bystanders to Genocide', *The Atlantic*, 288 (September 2001).

[25] See, for example, the assessment of General Wesley K. Clark, who commanded the NATO
operation against Serbia, in his memoir *Waging Modern War: Bosnia, Kosovo, and the Future
of Conflict* (New York: Perseus, 2001), especially 417–61.

[26] Kissinger, *Does America Need a Foreign Policy?*, 256–7.

ambiguous' principle too often used by activists on both sides to justify atrocities.[27]

Neither Kissinger nor Nye regards the Kosovo campaign as having met their criteria. And yet both acknowledge having publicly supported NATO's bombing of Serbia once it began. 'The scale and ferocity of Milosevic's ethnic cleansing could not be ignored', Nye explains:

European allies such as the United Kingdom, France, and even Germany joined the United States in calling for NATO action. If the United States had then pulled the rug out from under its pro-interventionist allies, it would have produced a NATO crisis on the scale of Suez in 1956. The humanitarian impact had grown immensely and was now reinforced by a strategic interest in the future of the American alliance with Europe ... It does no good to lament the more prudent paths not taken at an earlier stage.[28]

Kissinger's reasons are similar: 'Despite many reservations, I supported the Kosovo operation after it began in many television appearances because I felt that failure of such a major NATO enterprise would have been the worst possible outcome.'[29]

There are echoes here of an earlier time and another place: the cause is questionable; the process has been anything but thoughtful; we should have taken earlier opportunities to bail out; but now that we're in, there's no choice but to support the president's policy. 'Time and time again in these critical weeks', one historian notes, the most important critics 'showed themselves unwilling to state publicly what they believed privately, to challenge the administration's interpretation of the stakes, of the risks, of the costs.'[30] That war, though, was the one in Vietnam, and the historian is Frederik Logevall, whose careful new history of how the US got involved attaches almost as much responsibility to the role of dissenters, who knew better but went along, as it does to that of the Kennedy and Johnson Administrations themselves.

Kosovo, very fortunately, was not Vietnam. Milosevic caved in under the pressure of two and a half months of bombing, just as Ho Chi Minh had been expected to do three and a half decades earlier. Force did prove effective as an instrument of humanitarian intervention, even within the boundaries of what everyone recognized to be a sovereign state and at remarkably little cost to the nations that wielded it. One can't help but wonder, though, whether standards defined ahead of time for when this should happen again will bear any relevance to the actual situations confronted. For, as both Kissinger and Nye would acknowledge, statecraft, like warfare, is an unpredictable business. One can go

---

[27] Joseph S. Nye, Jr, 'Redefining the National Interest', *Foreign Affairs*, 78 (July–August 1999), 32–3.

[28] ibid., 34.

[29] Kissinger, *Does America Need a Foreign Policy?*, 263.

[30] Frederik Logevall, *Choosing War: The Lost Chance for Peace and the Escalation of the War in Vietnam* (Berkeley: University of California Press, 1999), 336.

only so far in stating the principles according to which one *should* act. How one *will* act when it comes to the crunch still remains to be seen.

9. SEPTEMBER 11TH

That fact became obvious on September 11 2001, when the most devastating terrorist attacks in modern history reversed the equations Americans had used to balance the requirements of order and justice throughout most of the twentieth century. The question no longer was how far the US should go in challenging other states' sovereignty in defence of human rights. Rather, the palls of smoke that hung over New York and Washington on that bright clear morning represented an actual violation of *American* sovereignty, as well as an implicit challenge to *all* sovereignty as traditionally conceived, at the hands of an anti-sovereignty for whom 'justice' sanctioned mass murder. The human rights of everyone were now at stake and, since the attack had in every sense 'hit home', it left no opportunity to blink, or to avert eyes, or to anaesthetize.

Prior to September 11, the new administration of George W. Bush had shown considerably less interest than its predecessor in defending the rights of oppressed minorities and somewhat more interest in repairing Washington's strained relationship with Moscow and Beijing. The terrorist assaults reinforced these tendencies, as it suddenly became vital to recruit all the help the US could get in rooting out Osama bin Laden and al-Qaeda wherever they operated. Knowing their own states' vulnerability to this kind of terrorism, Russian and Chinese leaders immediately lent their support, as did the self-appointed president of Pakistan, a country both the Clinton and Bush Administrations had treated as a pariah until that point because of its undemocratic government and its recent acquisition of nuclear weapons. So too did several central Asian successor states to the Soviet Union, Uzbekistan chief among them, which now shared an *interest* with the US in fighting terrorism, though hardly a commitment to its *values*.

Such support, of course, carried a price. It was difficult, under these circumstances, to imagine another Kosovo-like operation carried out against the wishes of Moscow, Beijing, or even Islamabad. Expressions of concern for embattled Chechens and Tibetans virtually disappeared. The old Cold War habit of determining allies solely by their effectiveness in fighting a common threat seemed likely to replace the more recent post-Cold War standard of common principles. The world was again a dangerous place and, as a consequence, the demands of stability appeared, once again, to have trumped those of equity.[31]

[31] John Lewis Gaddis, 'And Now This: Lessons from the Old Era for the New One', in Strobe Talbott and Nayan Chanda (eds), *The Age of Terror: America and the World After September 11* (New York: Basic Books, 2001).

And yet, even in the stark clarity of the September 11 aftermath, there were unexpected ambiguities. One of these had to do with pursuing the perpetrators, for was that not also the pursuit of justice? No grievances, no matter how widely spread or deeply held, could have justified what they had done. Did it not follow, then, that no restraints, apart from the obvious ones of avoiding injury to the innocent, should restrict the retaliation that was bound to follow? Certainly respect for sovereignty, when the sovereignty in question was that of the odious Taliban, carried little weight: when the Americans invaded Afghanistan there were no complaints at all among the great powers, and few from anyone else.

Another ambiguity arose out of the enthusiasm with which the Afghans themselves responded to this development. No nation had more successfully resisted invasion in the past, as the British and the Russians had painful reasons to remember. In this instance, though, most Afghans appeared to welcome the Americans, gleefully shaving their beards, discarding their *birka*s, and reopening their schools. A military operation designed to restore order—and to seek revenge—became an instrument of justice. The last thing the Bush Administration had intended to do in occupying Afghanistan was to reform it, but that is what it wound up doing. Here too order and justice were by no means polar opposites.

Nor were they in one other sense that became clear after September 11. It turned out that al-Qaeda's principal recruiting ground lay, not in Afghanistan, but in Egypt and Saudi Arabia, precisely the states in which the US had *not* pushed hard for democratization and the defence of human rights during the 1990s, for fear of destabilizing the pro-American regimes that operated there.[32] A preference for order over justice in that part of the world had generated powerful resentments that Osama bin Laden had exploited, with devastating results for the US. So what did September 11 mean for the old American dilemma of how to weigh the respective claims of order and justice? It meant most obviously, as had Kosovo, that the dilemma remained.

10. STRATEGIES FOR THE FUTURE

Since Americans have never resolved this issue at home—their domestic history has seen many precarious balances struck between the demands of order and justice—it is unrealistic to expect them ever to settle the matter once and for all in their dealings with the outside world. Still, it might be helpful to pose the problem in terms of alternative strategies and to compare their respective

---

[32] See, on this point, Bernard Lewis, 'The Revolt of Islam', *The New Yorker* (19 November 2001), 57; and Michael Ignatieff, 'Is The Human Rights Era Ending?', *New York Times* (5 February 2002).

results. Call them the 'inside-out' and the 'outside-in' approaches to the problem of reconciling order with justice. Both would accept that there are going to be, for the foreseeable future, disparities of power, wealth, and influence: that there will continue to be big and small states; that there will be majorities and minorities within them. But there the similarities end.

The *inside-out strategy* would work *with* the powerful to discipline their use of power. It would seek to convince those who possess authority that it is in their own interest to treat those without it in ways that they themselves might wish to be treated if the roles were reversed. Whether through the use of international legal norms, or the lure of economic rewards, or threatening the isolation that comes with sanctions, or simply withdrawing the acknowledgment of legitimacy—something never to be underestimated in dealing with authoritarian regimes—the idea would be to encourage a long-term evolutionary process by which dictators would become democrats.

Can this work? In some ways it already has. It has done so within NATO, where regimes like those in Portugal, Greece, and Turkey gradually abandoned authoritarianism and subjected themselves to constitutional checks and balances. Spain's admission to NATO in 1982 took place only after it had made an equivalent transition. The whole premise of *Ostpolitik* was to work with the East German and other east European regimes to make them more humane; and while the results are still debated they were by no means totally negative. Similar approaches have produced similar results outside of NATO, in countries like South Korea, Taiwan, the Philippines, Mexico, and in much of the rest of Latin America. The biggest success story for the inside-out strategy, though, was the Soviet Union itself, where during the late 1980s a formidably powerful autocracy concluded that it could not continue to live that way, and proceeded to change its character profoundly from within.

Such inside-out strategies are, of course, subject to criticism. It is hard to avoid complicity, especially at the beginning of the process, in the distasteful character of the regime one is seeking to transform. For there is no effort here to challenge that state's sovereignty or even to question its authority; there are no immediate attempts to rescue its victims, who are told only that they must be patient and that things will gradually improve. It is often necessary to defer to, and even flatter, whatever despot is in charge: you cannot expect to convince by condemning. As a consequence, it is easy to look as if you are consorting with dictators instead of subverting them. But such subversion has, in the end, taken place under the inside-out strategy: not everywhere all the time, but more often than one might think.

The alternative method of seeking order and justice would be the *outside-in strategy*. Here one would champion the cause of a small state, or of a group within a state, without regard to the interests, concerns, or prestige of the regime that is oppressing them. The point would be to stick to principle: if confrontation results, so be it; if sovereignty is compromised, well, many people think that it is an outdated concept anyway. Where the inside-out strategy sought justice by transforming those who had denied it, the outside-in strategy directly challenges deniers of justice in the expectation that, since they are in the wrong, they can only surrender. The inside-out approach assumes the possibility of redemption. The outside-in approach regards that prospect as naive and those who entertain it as morally compromised.

Can this strategy work? There are surely some situations where dictators are not redeemable: where an outside-in confrontation is the only option. One thinks, first of all, of Hitler, and what the practitioners of an inside-out strategy—we remember them as the appeasers—had to learn about him. It is not at all clear that Stalin could ever have been persuaded to change his methods, even though several of his successors were persuadable. The same is probably true of Saddam Hussein. We will never know whether the Cambodian genocide, the Rwandan horrors, or the Bosnian atrocities could have been prevented by challenging those that perpetrated them; it is clear enough, though, that appealing to their better natures, as the inside-out strategy would recommend, did not work. Those precedents weighed heavily on American and NATO planners when they confronted, and successfully ended, Milosevic's ethnic cleansing in Kosovo. The Bush Administration did not even try reasoning with Osama bin Laden and his Taliban sidekick, Mullah Omar: its persuaders came in the form of bombs, missiles, and ground forces. And they too were successful.

11. SUSTAINABILITY

How, though, do we know when to apply which strategy? So much depends upon the circumstances and on the quality of leadership available that it is difficult to answer this question in advance. A good test to keep in mind, though, is that of *sustainability*: how might one best preserve whatever settlement one is able to achieve? That in turn requires linking hegemony with legitimacy. A stable international order depends not just upon the authority of the victors but also upon the willingness of the vanquished as well as everyone else to regard the settlement imposed on them as legitimate. It has to appear just as well as irresistible, otherwise ways will be found to resist it and ultimately to subvert it.[33] The great power settlements of 1815 and 1945, which met that

---

[33] The point was made long ago by the young Henry Kissinger in *A World Restored* (New York: Houghton Mifflin, 1957), 1–3. For a strong post-Cold War reiteration of the principle, see Clark, *The Post-Cold War Order*, especially 12, 195–6.

standard, lasted for decades. The settlement of 1918–19 did not, with
disastrous results. The Cold War's outcome left the US in a position of
power unmatched since the Roman Empire, and the events of September 11
paradoxically reinforced it. But does the rest of the world regard this new
global settlement as just and therefore legitimate? The US has paid remarkably little attention to this question.

It is clear now that there was, throughout the 1990s, a progressive *hardening*
of the terms that made the post-Cold War system, in the words of its most careful chronicler, Ian Clark, 'too much of an enterprise of political imposition, and
too little of genuine consent'.[34] There were various explanations for this: the
decisiveness of the West's victory; the absence of any clear alternative to which
the defeated might defect; a growing tendency within the US to return to the
unilateralism that was, for so long, so prominent a feature of that country's
approach to the rest of the world. None of it reflected a deliberate strategy.

What was particularly striking, though, was the extent to which an American
commitment to justice contributed to this hardening of terms. This happened
first with the Clinton Administration's determination to bring Poland,
Hungary, and the Czech Republic into NATO, against strong objections from
Moscow.[35] The objective here was to right old wrongs; but the effect was
to pile a new humiliation upon a Cold War settlement that the Russians
already regarded as painfully humiliating. Meanwhile, and however well-
intentioned its motives, the Kosovo campaign gave leaders in both Russia and
China reason to worry that American policy had shifted from efforts to work
with them to achieve reforms to a campaign aimed, even though in the name
of reform, at splitting away portions of what they regarded as their territory.
There was, again, no desire on Washington's part to humiliate or alarm. But
the Clinton Doctrine did that, nonetheless.

These fears waned in the wake of September 11, but new ones arose when
President Bush reserved the right to fight terrorism collectively where possible but unilaterally where necessary. The Bush Doctrine set off alarm bells
throughout the coalition that had rallied against al-Qaeda because it seemed
to suggest that the US alone would determine who future terrorists were and
what was to be done to contain them. Washington would not wait, understandably enough, for terrorists to announce their existence through attacks
like those on September 11. Washington's allies, also understandably, worried
about what such a unilateral pursuit of order and justice might mean.[36]

[34] Clark, *The Post-Cold War Order*, 253.
[35] The best account is James M. Goldgeier, *Not Whether But When: The U.S. Decision to
Enlarge NATO* (Washington: Brookings Institution, 1999).
[36] For one example, see Jonathan Freedland, 'Patten Lays Into Bush's America', *The
Guardian* (9 February 2002), reporting on an interview with European Union External Relations
Commissioner Chris Patten.

So what is the most *sustainable* method of achieving both order and justice in an age of both American hegemony and American vulnerability? Should it be the inside-out strategy, or the outside-in strategy, or some combination of both? Should the effort be multilateral, or unilateral, or some compromise between the two? There is no way to answer such questions without knowing the specific situations that give rise to them, but there are a few general principles worth keeping in mind: that authority relies on legitimacy, that hegemony rests upon a foundation of consent, that it is possible to lead while still listening, that modesty breeds less resistance than arrogance, and that the pursuit of justice can undermine order even as the pursuit of order can compromise justice. Or, to put it another way, the objective of American leadership should always be to ensure that there are worse things, and that in its absence it would be missed.

7

Russian Perspectives on Order and Justice

S. NEIL MACFARLANE

To Drink Tea Is Not to Cut Wood
—*Russian proverb*[1]

This chapter reviews Russian perspectives on the nature of, and potential trade-offs between, order and justice. The international behaviour of states reflects not only the demands imposed on them by the international system or processes of domestic political contestation, but also the distinctive perspectives their elites bring to policy-making. National perspectives on order and justice in international relations are rooted in history and the cultural interpretation of history.[2] The examination of history and culture as formative elements of identity is, therefore, a necessary elements of the analysis of state behaviour.[3]

Following Hedley Bull, I take order to mean a pattern 'in relations of human individuals or groups that leads to a particular result ... an arrangement of social life such that it promotes certain goals or values'. These goals include preservation of the system and society of states, maintaining the external sovereignty of states, and the limitation of violence.[4] Justice, as used here, refers basically to equality of treatment and to notions of fairness and reciprocity.[5] The principal issues arising in recent discussions of international justice have

---

[1] Noted by James Billington in *The Icon and the Axe: An Interpretive History of Russian Culture* (New York: Vintage, 1970), 27.

[2] William Zimmerman, *Soviet Perspectives on International Relations, 1956–67* (Princeton, NJ: Princeton University Press, 1969), 6.

[3] For a similar point, see Peter J. Katzenstein, *The Culture of National Security* (New York: Columbia University Press, 1996), 23–4.

[4] Hedley Bull, *The Anarchical Society: A Study of Order in World Politics* (New York: Columbia University Press, 1977), 18–19. Typical Russian definitions of order clearly reflect what Bull refers to as the 'Augustinian' approach to order in that the concept is held to have an intrinsic moral content. The leading dictionary of the Soviet period defines it as 'a regulated well-organised, and correct (right) situation'. Akademia Nauk SSSR-Institut Russkogo Yazyka, *Slovar' Russkogo Yazyka*, III (Moscow: *Gosudarstvennoe Izdatel'stvo Innostranykh i Natsional'nykh Slovarei*, 1959), 423.   [5] Bull, *The Anarchical Society*, 78–9.

been national self-determination, the redistribution of wealth, and the place of human rights in world politics. The solidarist tradition seems to presume that these notions pertain in an essential sense to individual human beings or to groups. However, as will become clear in the following, the claim for justice can equally well be made by states seeking equal treatment in what they perceive to be an unequal system of states.

Russian conceptions of order played an important role in the development of international society through the nineteenth and twentieth centuries. In the 1990s, the global significance of Russian perspectives on international relations diminished as Russia faced the implosion of its economy and the atrophy of the central state and its military capabilities. Even in this moment of weakness, however, Russian views on this topic, and in particular the Russian pursuit of a hegemonic hierarchy within the borders of the former USSR, were critically important to Russia's closest and weaker neighbours. More broadly, the Western relationship with Russia remained a central issue of regional order in Europe[6] and in coping with global weapons proliferation. This relationship was troubled by serious tension between Russian and Western conceptions of both order and justice.

In the context of the US-led campaign against terrorism, Russian views on order and justice have regained some of their earlier importance. Western states seek Russia's cooperation in the campaign against terror, since this campaign targets states and movements in proximity to the former USSR and which the Russians know well. In addition, Russia is the pre-eminent power in the Caspian basin and central Asia, a region of growing significance in global energy production, which is deemed particularly vulnerable to the spread of terrorism and access to which has proved necessary in addressing strategic objectives vis-à-vis Afghanistan.

Teasing out Russian perspectives on these issues is not an easy task. In the first place, international relations discourse on order and justice is largely Western. Russia had no developed tradition of scholarship on international politics prior to the Russian Revolution. The success of that revolution meant that Russian conceptualization of international relations evolved along lines very different from those of the West during much of the twentieth century.[7]

---

[6] See S. Neil MacFarlane, 'NATO in Russia's Relations with the West', *Security Dialogue*, 32/3 (2001).

[7] For an extremely useful discussion of the evolution of Soviet perspectives on international relations in the Khrushchev and early Brezhnev periods, when a sub-discipline of international relations finally emerged in the USSR, see Zimmerman, *Soviet Perspectives on International Relations*. See also Allen Lynch, *The Soviet Study of International Relations* (Cambridge: Cambridge University Press, 1987), which takes the discussion through the Brezhnev period. The changes in Soviet perspectives during the Gorbachev period are well summarized in Steven Kull, *Burying Lenin: The Revolution in Soviet Ideology and Foreign Policy* (Boulder, CO: Westview, 1992). Margot Light, in *The Soviet Theory of International Relations* (Brighton: Harvester

The ideological rigidity of the Soviet state imposed severe limits on the social sciences in general and, more specifically, on the capacity of Russian specialists to participate systematically and fruitfully in the evolution of scholarly approaches to order and justice.

The Gorbachev years saw a dramatic opening of communication and cooperation between Soviet and Western scholarly communities in international relations and a flowering of a Soviet perspective on order and justice that strongly reflected Western liberal perspectives on international politics. But that opening was brief and was aborted by the collapse of the USSR, its disintegration into 15 successor states, and the substantial obstacles to scholarly activity associated with economic crisis, political instability, and the substantial atrophy of academic infrastructure in Russia. The corpus of serious Russian thinking on this topic is, consequently, very thin. The conclusions one might draw on Russian perspectives are likely, therefore, to be inferential and tentative rather than being grounded in a substantial historically rooted tradition of scholarship on the subject.

In addressing Russian perspectives on order and justice, and recognizing these shortcomings, I attempt to answer several questions:

1. What are Russian perspectives on order and justice and how have they evolved over time?
2. Are these perspectives distinct from other traditions of thinking about order and justice, and, if so, how? In particular, how do Russians react to the incipient solidarism in international society's hesitant embrace of global environmental protection, human rights, humanitarian intervention, national self-determination, and the attendant re-conceptualization of sovereignty and the place of the state in international politics?
3. What are the implications of how Russians think about order and justice for Russia's participation in international society?

In emphasizing the importance of unit-level experiential and cognitive factors in the definition of national perspectives on international politics, one must also recognize that, in Russia as elsewhere, there is a plurality of views on international relations and the state's place therein. Nonetheless, one can identify certain enduring patterns that have reasserted themselves rather strongly in the contemporary period. It is these commonalities that I focus on. Although Russians might agree that order is a pattern of activity and behaviour that sustains certain elementary or primary goals, their conception of this pattern focuses heavily on control and the specific values of the Russian state as opposed to those values that may or may not be shared by a wider constellation

Wheatsheaf, 1988) provides an illuminating overview of the entire period of Soviet theorizing about international relations from the revolution to the mid-Gorbachev period. It is striking that there is no reference to international order or justice in the indexes of any of these studies.

of international actors. In many respects, Russian conceptions of regional and international order have been projections of the effort to establish and maintain order within the Russian state.

There is, to my knowledge, no substantial Russian tradition of thought about individual or group rights as matters of importance in international politics.[8] Arguments about justice in Russian discourse about international politics have tended to focus on justice for the Russian state in the international system. Reflecting a deep sense of exclusion and unequal treatment, justice for Russia has tended to mean the achievement of the status and rights that Russians perceive to be their due. That is to say, to the extent that there is a Russian conception of international justice, it has been egoistic rather than solidarist.

It would be incorrect, however, to suggest for these reasons that the institutions of international society have been irrelevant to Russia. Participation in these institutions is a means of securing recognition and status: consider Russia's intense pressure during and after the Gorbachev period to be admitted to the G-7. These institutions may also play some role in constraining other powers in the system: consider Russia's use of the veto in the Security Council and its recourse to customary legal principles and the Charter of the United Nations to forestall external interference in matters of domestic jurisdiction. And they may be useful instruments in power-political struggle: consider the Soviet role in marshalling opinion in the UN in opposition to colonialism and in support of 'national liberation' and the 'new international economic order'. But these examples merely serve to reinforce the point that principles of order and justice are both subordinate to a rather traditional statist power-political agenda.

1. THE DEVELOPMENT OF RUSSIAN PERSPECTIVES ON ORDER AND JUSTICE IN THE PRE-SOVIET PERIOD

As suggested above, an understanding of Russia's history is fundamental to the study of contemporary Russian perspectives on the issues to hand. In the first place, the Putin Administration is only three years old. Its views on order and justice in international politics are still in the process of formation and have not been fully articulated. The period prior to Putin's assumption of the presidency was one of considerable chaos and indecision in Russian foreign

---

[8] A 1991–2000 survey of the leading journal of the Russian international relations fraternity, *Mirovaya Ekonomika i Mezhdunarodnye Otnoshenia* (World Economy and International Relations), indicates that no article has been published on this subject over the period in question.

policy-making and of considerable contestation regarding Russian identity
and Russia's relations with other countries. Analysis of the historical development of Russian perspectives on international relations may give us clues
concerning what is likely to emerge.

Second, awareness of history—and myth—is a fundamental characteristic
of Russian culture. The country is in the midst of defining its identity. This
process has involved a rediscovery of history. Many current Russian perspectives on their role in world politics are deeply embedded in this history. The
recent discussion of Russian identity in terms of Eurasianism—and distinct-
ness from the West—draws heavily on the Russian understanding of their
experience on the borderland between the two continents and three cultural
complexes. The current Russian perception that their state is on the front line
in the defence of Europe against Islam (*sic*) is rooted in the long-standing
view that Russia's historical role has been one of defending the front lines of
Christian civilization against threats from Asia.[9] Much of the recent Russian
disquiet with the penetration of Western ideas, including ideas about rights
and justice, reflects a historically deep fear of the erosion of Russian culture
by Western imports and of the corrosive effect of such ideas on the state's
capacity to retain control over its territory and people.

The first identifiable Russian polity was the constellation of Kievan Rus'
and the associated states of Novgorod, Suzdal, and others. This grouping grew
out of the struggle between settled peoples on the forest-steppe fringe and the
nomadic tribes moving back and forth through the expansive grasslands
between Asia and southern Europe.[10] It largely disappeared under Mongol
pressure in the early thirteenth century. In contrast to the later development of
Russian political culture, the political systems of these city states were, for the
most part, quite democratic, with political power residing largely in the hands
of assemblies of citizens—the *veche*—and princes serving in considerable
measure at the pleasure of these assemblies. Land was held privately and there
existed a substantial rural and urban middle class.

With the destruction of Kiev, the locus of Russian identity shifted north-
wards into the forest. The formative period of modern Russia was one of considerable violence at the hands of external forces from both east and west.
Russia was a vast country, it lacked natural boundaries, and its infrastructure
was rudimentary. These challenges placed a premium on order and hierarchy

[9] This view is not limited to Russians. One American historian of Russia noted that 'the cultural accomplishments of the high medieval West ... might not have been possible without the
existence of a militant Christian civilisation in Eastern Europe to absorb much of the shock of
invasions by less civilised steppe peoples'. Billington, *The Icon and the Axe*, 4.
[10] For a summary, see George Vernadsky, *A History of Russia*, 6th edn (New Haven: Yale
University Press, 1969), 20–30.

as forms of control.[11] The challenges of state consolidation left little space for the development of domestic pluralism or individual rights.[12]

The experience of defeat by the Mongols favoured an emphasis on absolute centralized power, since an effective response to this threat had been impeded by the partial disintegration of the Kievan polity into a constellation of city-states. The ideological basis for reconsolidation was Russia's role as the 'Third Rome', the defender of Orthodox Christianity after the fall of Constantinople.[13] The history of thinking about Russia's place in world affairs in both the tsarist and the Soviet periods is animated by a deeply rooted sense of mission.[14] Periodic profound internal crises[15] enhanced Russian cultural sensitivity to disorder and suspicion of individualism, and reinforced wide-spread acceptance of the strengthening of the state at the expense of the individual and of the emphasis on rigid social order. Popular acquiescence in the concentration of power was strengthened further by the close links between state and religion and the cult of the tsar that provided religious justification for autocracy.

A second theme characteristic of the periods of Mongol dominance and Muscovite assertion was isolation. The Mongol invasion, the later fall of Constantinople, and the emergence of hostile polities—the Baltic Germans, Lithuania, Poland, and Sweden—in the West distanced Russia from the high medieval flowering of European culture and from the Renaissance and later Enlightenment. Russian isolation was the product not only of circumstances but, to some extent, of choice. There is a strong strain in Russian historical thought that isolation had its advantages:

The withdrawal of the Russian nation into the remote north-east was important because it enabled the Russian state to grow strong far from Western influences. We see that

---

[11] Geography itself had important implications for Russian views of the international system. As Henry Kissinger once put it, 'Russian history has led to a very understandable concern for security because Russia has lived in a geography that set no natural boundaries'. Henry Kissinger, 'Russian and American Interests after the Cold War', in Stephen Sestanovich (ed.), *Rethinking Russia's National Interests* (Washington, DC: Center for Strategic and International Studies, 1994), 3. Sergei Medvedev wrote in this context that 'statecraft in Russia can thus be interpreted as authority's permanent quest for compromise with territory': 'Power, Space and Russian Foreign Policy', in Ted Hopf (ed.), *Understandings of Russian Foreign Policy* (University Park: Pennsylvania State University Press, 1999), 21.

[12] As Billington, *The Icon and the Axe*, 19, put it: 'The individual had to subordinate himself to group interests to accomplish his daily tasks.'

[13] Iver Neumann, *Russia and the Idea of Europe* (London: Routledge, 1996), 6–7.

[14] On this point, see, for example, Paul Goble, 'Russia as a Eurasian Power', in Sestanovich, *Rethinking Russia's National Interest*, 42–3.

[15] That is, from the Time of Troubles between 1598 and 1613 through to the massive rebellion against Catherine II—the Pugachevshchina—in 1773–4, the Decembrist revolt in 1825, the terrorism of *Narodnaya Volya* in the late nineteenth century, the 1905 revolution, and the Russian Revolution of 1917.

those Slav nations that have come prematurely into contact with the West strong in its civilisation and in its Roman heritage, have lost their independence and some have even lost their nationhood.[16]

Only one Russian prince had ventured beyond the borders of Russia before Peter I set off on his 'Great Embassy' to the West in the seventeenth century. Russian subjects were forbidden to travel abroad. Perhaps uncharitably, one French observer noted in 1672 that this prohibition resulted from fear that exposure to the outside might threaten the 'chains of slavery' binding the Russian people. Peter's intention to travel abroad to build alliances and to learn from the West was greeted with consternation by the boyars and the clergy.[17]

The theme of isolation blends with that of victimhood.[18] Many Russians believed that the above-mentioned developments of European civilization were made possible, at least in the early stages, by the role of the eastern Slavs as the shield of Europe against invasion from Asia. As Billington notes, the proverb cited at the beginning of this chapter reflects 'a certain suppressed bitterness toward more sheltered people' whose capacity to lead more refined lives rested on Russia's guarding of the gate.[19]

As the Russian state matured and expanded westwards at the expense of Poland and Sweden, physical isolation was reduced. Russia became a significant great power in the European system. It was recognized as an equal by Austria-Hungary by virtue of the two states' cooperation against the Ottoman Empire. Its links to Europe were consolidated by the dismemberment of Poland in 1792–1815 and by Russia's participation in the Napoleonic wars. Its arrival was recognized in the central role that Russia played at the Congress of Vienna and in the Concert of Europe.

But Russia's approach to the West was deeply ambivalent. The roots of this ambivalence lay in the rupture between eastern and western Christianity. The formative period of the Russian state was characterized by a sense of cultural superiority with respect to the West and fear that contact would weaken the state and pollute Russian culture. The abrupt end of Catherine II's abortive flirtation with Enlightenment liberalism in the Radishchev affair is illustrative. In 1790, Alexander Radishchev, a member of the nobility educated at government expense at the University of Leipzig, published an anonymous travelogue,

---

[16] Sergei M. Soloviev, *Sobranie Sochinenii* (St Petersburg: Obshchestvennaia pol'za, n.d.), 3, cited in Adam Ulam, 'Nationalism, Panslavism, Communism', in Ivo Lederer (ed.), *Russian Foreign Policy* (New Haven: Yale University Press, 1962), 42.

[17] In 1075, Grand Duke Iziaslav of Kiev visited the Holy Roman Emperor at Mainz. The quotation is from Mgr de Carlisle and is cited in Henri Troyat, *Peter the Great* (New York: E. P. Dutton, 1987), 89.

[18] See also Chinese conceptions of victimhood in Chapter 8.

[19] Billington, *The Icon and the Axe*, 27.

A Journey from St. Petersburg to Moscow, in which he initiated a discussion of the rights of man and advocated equality of rights between Russia's estates, praising Cromwell's regicide along the way. He was condemned to death, and then, when the sentence was commuted, dispatched to Siberia in chains. Catherine commented that his book suffered from 'the French infection: an aversion to authority'. Subsequent to his exile, all Russians studying in France were recalled.[20]

Several later tsars presided over, and sometimes encouraged, openings that addressed liberal concerns of justice and rights: for example, Alexander I's grant of a constitution to Poland and Alexander II's establishment of partially representative organs of local government and emancipation of the serfs. However, these moments were generally followed by severe conservative and order-based reactions.[21] The domestic political development of Russia in the nineteenth century reflected a strong preoccupation with order and left little place for the emergence of concern for justice. In the meantime, the continuing expansion of the Russian Empire into the Caucasus and then central Asia dramatically increased the already significant ethnic diversity of the Empire. The contemporaneous rise of nationalist consciousness amongst Baltic, western Slavic, and—to some extent, Caucasian—minorities provided yet another impulse to illiberality in the Russian state, evident in the gradually increasing effort at russification of non-Russian peoples and the ruthless suppression of the Polish rebellion of 1863 under, ironically, Alexander II.[22]

Russian foreign policy during the nineteenth century was in some respects an external projection of these internal preoccupations of the state. In the first half of the century, it was dominated by the effort to address the implications for international society of the liberal strivings within member states of the Concert of Europe. Russia's conception of international order at this stage implied not merely the regulation of the international behaviour of states but the preservation of their internal structures against challenges from below.[23] This preference was betrayed in the external reflection of Alexander I's domestic retreat from reform: the effort to transform the Concert of Europe into a Holy Alliance to 'intervene in other countries against revolutionary

---

[20] This summary and the quotations are taken from John Alexander, *Catherine the Great* (Oxford: Oxford University Press, 1989), 282–4.

[21] Neumann comments in this context that: 'Periods ... when the Russian Westernisers have the upper hand in the debate, have in the past been superseded by a turn away from the concurrent political life of Europe.' *Russia and the Idea of Europe*, 2.

[22] Hajo Holborn, 'Russia and the European Political System', in Lederer, *Russian Foreign Policy*, 390.

[23] In this respect, the early and mid-nineteenth century Russian conception resembles, in form if not content, the Burkean view of international society, membership of which was predicated not merely on acceptance of international structures and rules but on respect for a certain kind of domestic normative structure. I am indebted to Jennifer Welsh for this insight.

upheavals',[24] an impulse strengthened further for his successor by the Decembrist uprising. The results were evident in the 1820s, when Russia supported Austrian intervention to suppress revolutionary movements in Naples and the Piedmont against possible French counter-intervention, and in 1849, when Nicholas I dispatched an army of 120,000 men into Hungary to crush the Hungarian revolution.

In a somewhat contradictory vein, Russia also became involved in a number of interventions ostensibly to protect the rights of oppressed minorities in other states. In 1821, Alexander I strongly urged intervention by the Concert powers in the Greek War of Independence on behalf of the Orthodox Greeks. He was restrained only by the persuasive power of Prince Metternich and Castlereagh.[25] However, it is necessary to situate this episode in the context of a long-standing politico-military rivalry between Russians and Turks and the Russian interest in weakening their principal rival in the Black Sea basin. Moreover, Alexander focused on the defence of orthodoxy rather than human rights per se. His diplomacy reflected his somewhat mystical image of Russia as the defender of true Christianity in the face of godlessness. Later in the century, Russia became involved in the support of southern Slavic challenges to the Ottoman and Austro-Hungarian Empires in the Balkans. Superficially, the Russian embrace of the Slavic cause in southern Europe suggested some concern with matters of justice, at least as they related to self-determination. But, again, this concern was geographically limited to an area of long-standing power-political interest, and directed at Russia's main competitors for influence in the region. That this line of Russian policy did not extend to a general endorsement of the self-determination of peoples was evident in Russia's reaction to the emergent nationalism of non-Russian peoples within the borders of the empire.

In short, Russia's imperial history displays little evidence of the embedding of liberalism at home. For much of the post-Kievan period, Russia was insulated and isolated from the evolution of liberal thought in Europe. When Russian leaders concluded that, to survive, they had to absorb elements of Western culture, they quite deliberately sought to exclude the normative elements of Western imports. Western ideas concerning justice and rights had limited resonance in this period of Russian history.

The internal preoccupation with order and the concentration of power was in part a product of having to cope with severe and chronic external challenges to the Russian state. In turn, Russian foreign policy and thinking about international society strongly reflected the concern to preserve Russia's own domestic structure of power. In the face of expressions of revolutionary activity in

---

[24] Holborn, 'Russia and the European Political System', 383.
[25] Henry Kissinger, *A World Restored: Metternich, Castlereagh and the Problems of Peace 1812–1822* (Boston: Houghton Mifflin, 1954), 288–9, 295.

nineteenth century western and central Europe, Russia's focus became increasingly conservative and statist.[26] To the extent that concerns of 'justice' impinged on Russian foreign policy, they concerned the claim to equality of the Russian state in the emerging European international society. This they achieved not by persuasiveness of argument but by force of arms. In the limited number of instances where Russia displayed concern for the aspirations of other peoples to justice, these concerns closely followed the power-political interests of the Russian state.

2. PERSPECTIVES ON ORDER AND JUSTICE DURING THE SOVIET PERIOD

The rejection of autocracy in the 1917 Russian Revolution ushered into power a movement committed to the ultimate solidarist goal: socialist revolution at home and the overthrow of the states system and reordering of societies abroad. This revolution was to involve a radical redistribution of power and wealth from capitalist elites to the proletariat. The revolutionaries also had a number of perspectives that bear rather directly on matters of international justice and especially the norm of self-determination. Lenin's limited writings on colonialism displayed a declaratory commitment to the liberation of the oppressed peoples of the European empires. This extended to an embrace of the principle of national self-determination for the non-Russian peoples of the former Russian Empire.

However, it is useful to examine this commitment in greater detail. For Lenin, the nation was epiphenomenal, while fragmentation of large economic units into smaller—national—ones was retrograde.[27] Why then would he support self-determination? In the Russian Empire, Lenin took the view that extension of the right of self-determination would defang minority nationalism.[28] He also noted that the decision to exercise the right to self-determination rested with the proletariat, the group that, in his view, would be least likely to make the choice in the face of successful socialist revolution in Russia itself.[29] There is in this account no sense of the intrinsic value of national

[26] On this point, see Adam Ulam, 'Nationalism, Pan-Slavism, Communism', in Lederer, *Russian Foreign Policy*, 41.

[27] V. Lenin, 'On the Question of National Policy' (1914), in *Collected Works*, XX (Moscow: Progress Publishers), 223; at http:www.marxists.org/archives/lenin/works/cw/

[28] V. Lenin, 'The Socialist Revolution and the Right of Nations to Self-determination' (1916), in *Collected Works*, XXII, 147.

[29] V. Lenin, 'The Right of Nations to Self-determination' (1914), in *Collected Works*, XX, 428; 'The National Question in Our Programme' (1903), in Collected Works, VI, 454–6.

self-determination. National self-determination was of value to the extent that it furthered socialist revolution.

Outside Russia, the instrumental dimension of advocacy of self-determination was even clearer. The national self-determination of oppressed peoples in Europe would weaken the conservative multinational empires of central Europe that stood in the way of socialist revolution. The emergence of smaller—and weaker—new states in eastern Europe established a buffer between the new Russia and traditional threats in central and western Europe. The challenge from colonial peoples would promote revolutionary change in the metropolises while diminishing the capacity of the imperialist states to engage Soviet Russia.

To say that the advocacy of national self-determination was instrumental is not to say that solidarist concerns were irrelevant to Lenin. Lenin was suggesting after all that national self-determination had instrumental value in the pursuit of a more ambitious universalist end: world proletarian revolution. On the face of it, this universalist commitment remained a fundamental justice-based challenge to international order. However, this universalism differed substantially from what later became liberal solidarism in its emphasis on classes rather than individuals and its devaluation of political as compared with social and economic rights.

Moreover, Lenin and his colleagues inherited a state with real security concerns, not least the harsh settlement imposed on Russia by Germany at Brest-Litovsk in early 1918 and the subsequent Entente interventions in the civil war. The early development of Soviet foreign policy reflected a strong tension between the universalist revolutionary impetus of communism and the particularist, statist, and conservative pursuit of power in order that the state—and the leader—survive. This tension was embodied in the combination of support for revolution and the quest for recognition and stabilization of relations with neighbouring states in 1920–3. Under Stalin, and to judge from Soviet engagement with social revolution in Germany,[30] the civil war in China,[31] the more general evolution of Comintern involvement in anti-colonial struggle in the 1920s and 1930s, and, finally, the Spanish Civil War,[32] the revolutionary strand of foreign policy rather rapidly took a back seat to considerations of power politics and also domestic political consolidation against the remnants of Trotskyism.[33] At the same time, however, the USSR strengthened the

---

[30] On Soviet involvement in the revolutionary process in Germany, see Franz Borkenau, *The Communist International* (London: Faber and Faber, 1938).

[31] See Conrad Brandt, *Stalin's Failure in China* (New York: Norton, 1958).

[32] For an account of Soviet policy towards the Spanish civil war, see Fernando Claudin, *The Communist Movement from Comintern to Cominform* (Harmondsworth: Penguin, 1975), 211–42.

[33] One analyst goes so far as to say that 'Trotsky, and all that Trotsky represented, was Stalin's real fear; Hitler was largely his excuse for fear'. George Kennan, *Russia and the West under Lenin and Stalin* (New York: Mentor, 1961), 238.

balance of power logic of its European diplomacy, joining the League of Nations and strenuously advocating its principles of collective security in the attempt to shore up the western democracies in the face of the growing challenge from Hitler. The power-political essence of Stalin's foreign policy was underlined yet again in his post-Munich abandonment of the policy of containment of Germany and his alliance with his principal external threat in the hope of diverting it elsewhere.[34]

In short, in Stalin's pre-war foreign policy there is little evidence of a desire on the part of the Soviet leadership to explore opportunities for a durable cooperative structure of international order such as that envisaged in the League. Instead, Stalin's approach to the other great powers was strongly informed by an effort to ensure that no anti-Soviet combination emerged among them and to buy time to strengthen both his internal hold on power and the industrial and military capacity of the Soviet state. The revolutionary commitments of Soviet leaders waned with the passage of time and were clearly subordinated to the perceived dictates of the state's and the leader's foreign policy. Bodies such as the Comintern ostensibly devoted to the pursuit of revolution across the globe became instruments in a limited statist foreign policy as well as in Stalin's domestic consolidation of power. The more independent non-Soviet members of the organization, and those exposed to external influences, were thoroughly purged out of a fear that they might contaminate the Soviet party itself or threaten Stalin's own leadership of the movement.

However, this is not to say that Marxism-Leninism was insignificant as a factor influencing Soviet thinking about international relations. As a cognitive framework, it had important implications for Soviet perspectives on international order. The Manichaean vision of struggle between new and old, the associated assumption of the fundamental hostility of the capitalist states to the USSR, and the belief that the adversary was doomed by history created significant limits on the possibility of 'societal' cooperation between states. Cooperation would be tactical, temporary, and subject to sudden reversal in changing circumstances. The possibility of a shared normative framework was equally limited. Although the USSR participated in many of the institutions of international society—for example, the balance of power, international law, diplomacy—and vigorously sought to establish and then defended its status as a great power, on the whole these were matters of necessity and had little intrinsic normative value.

---

[34] Indeed, even during the period when the USSR was seeking to balance against Germany, Soviet diplomats continued to explore the possibility of accommodation with Germany in the hope that the imperialist powers would fight each other, leaving Stalin alone to consolidate his hold on power at home. On this point, see Vojtech Mastny, *Russia's Road to the Cold War* (New York: Columbia University Press, 1979), 19.

3. POST-1945 SOVIET PERSPECTIVES ON
ORDER AND JUSTICE

The dictates of the war against Germany to some extent reversed the USSR's isolation, as relatively large numbers of Westerners were posted to the USSR and as the Red Army advanced into central Europe. However, victory brought a renewal of obscurantism in the anti-cosmopolitan campaign, an assault on liberal thinking and foreign influence reminiscent of the clerical hierarchy's campaign against the 'judaizers' under Ivan III. Russian soldiers returning from the west were deported in large numbers to Siberia. Many returning prisoners of war were shot. The more prominent beneficiaries of the limited cultural and intellectual thaw during the war years were purged. Those who had developed associations with Western personnel in Moscow were ruthlessly harassed.

Several elements of post-war Soviet foreign policy pertain to the theme of this chapter. One is the consolidation of a sphere of influence in eastern Europe and the evolution of the structure of power in Europe and at the global strategic level. Between 1945 and 1950, Soviet diplomacy became increasingly preoccupied with the defence of the state's security through thoroughgoing suppression of the states and societies under the USSR's control to provide a buffer, if not a launching point, against its adversaries in western Europe. Here again, Russia displayed the view that obedience of states in its sphere of influence was an insufficient guarantee of security. As with Novgorod in the fifteenth century and as with Alexander I's conception of a holy alliance, regional order was perceived to be predicated on the homogeneity of the internal arrangements of states. This conception endured beyond the death of Stalin and informed the Soviet suppression of liberalization in Hungary in 1956, Czechoslovakia in 1968, and—indirectly—Poland in 1980–2.

The record of systematic Soviet intervention in eastern Europe illustrates a peculiar duality in Soviet thinking about equal sovereignty as a constitutive principle of international order. On the one hand, the Soviet leadership was adamant in its assertion of the USSR's sovereign rights; on the other, it systematically abused the analogous rights of its eastern European neighbours. Soviet interference in the domestic jurisdictions of eastern European states was accompanied by a normative justification—the Brezhnev Doctrine—similar in implications, if not in content, to Alexander I's view of the Holy Alliance. The argument was essentially that, although each communist party had a right to apply socialist principles, it did not have a right to abandon them. A retreat from socialism in any particular state threatened the viability of the socialist enterprise as a whole. As such, the other members of the socialist community had not only a right but a responsibility to resist any abandonment of socialist orientation.[35] Although the doctrine was applied principally to eastern Europe, Soviet spokesmen hinted at its applicability to Mao's China. The Soviet intervention in Afghanistan also suggested its broader applicability.

In the larger European context, Soviet perspectives on international order gradually settled into a bipolar balance of power framework. Initially, order was perceived to rest on the possession and deployment of sufficient force to control the buffer and discourage Western attempts to challenge the Soviet position in eastern Europe. With the passage of time, the stabilization of the situation in both eastern and western Europe, and the gradual emergence of a nuclear balance, the USSR began to explore options for the cooperative management of the region, seeking legal recognition of the division of Europe and legitimization of the territorial status quo.

This regional process was paralleled at the global level by efforts to develop concepts and structures to manage the Soviet-American relationship. The competitive essence of international relations remained. However, given that 'the atomic bomb does not observe the class principle',[36] Soviet leaders sought to develop mutual understandings and structures that limited prospects for direct confrontation. The result was a strategy of 'collaborative competition'. [37] The agreements of the 1960s on nuclear testing, the hot line, and nuclear non-proliferation reduced the downside risks of bipolarity while sustaining the pre-eminence of the two superpowers in the international system. The process culminated in the 1970s with Brezhnev's embrace of détente, both in Europe—viz. the Soviet-German Treaty, the Four-Power Agreement on Berlin, and the Conference on Security and Cooperation in Europe (CSCE)—and in Soviet-American relations.

Détente floundered in the late 1970s, in part as a result of differing conceptions of what it implied with regard to international order.[38] Kissinger apparently saw détente as a means of tempering the USSR's revisionist agenda in international relations and bringing it into a pluralist status quo at a time when American power was in relative decline.[39] Soviet leaders, in contrast, saw it in transformative terms as a way of pursuing the global competition between socialism and capitalism while lowering the risks of competitive

[35] See Sergei Kovalev, 'Mezhdunarodnye Ob'yazannosti Sotsialisticheskikh Stran', *Pravda* (26 September, 1968), 4.

[36] *Pravda* (14 July 1963). This remark appeared in the Soviet exchange with the Chinese over peaceful coexistence.

[37] George Breslauer, 'Why Détente Failed', in Alexander George (ed.), *Managing U.S.-Soviet Rivalry* (Boulder, CO: Westview, 1983), 320.

[38] As Ted Hopf remarked, 'The death of détente began with its birth, particularly with the unrequited expectations of both sides': 'Introduction: Russian Identity and Foreign Policy after the Cold War', in Hopf (ed.), *Understanding Russian Foreign Policy*, 3.

[39] See Henry Kissinger, *Diplomacy* (New York: Touchstone, 1994), 703–4, 714–60.

behaviour,[40] establishing the USSR's status of equality with the US, and reaping the advantages of cooperation in areas of mutual benefit. They also sought to slow trends that were perceived to be threatening to the USSR, such as the Sino-American rapprochement.[41]

The evolution of Soviet policy towards the UN also illuminates the Soviet understanding of order during the Cold War. Membership in an international institution of this type and in a prominent role highlighted the tensions between the revolutionary and statist aspects of the Soviet approach to international relations. The UN was established primarily as a structure for the cooperative management of international security. However, a glance at its Charter suggests that issues related to justice—for example, human rights and economic and social development—were also central to the conception of the organization. Soviet approaches to the formation of the UN indicated little interest in concerns of international justice and a strong focus on preservation of its sovereign rights and the prerogatives of great- power-hood. In this context, Soviet diplomacy betrayed a strong statist and pluralist conception of order organized on the basis of power and the privileged status of the great powers.[42]

At various points in its history, the USSR strongly resisted efforts to shift the attention of the organization from political and security issues to those of development and culture.[43] The focus on the international security role of the UN was accompanied by a strong emphasis on the broadest possible interpretation of the sovereignty of the great powers and the strictest possible limitation on the capacity of the UN to restrict its exercise. Soviet representatives therefore argued strongly and successfully for the grant of the veto to the great powers on matters before the Security Council. It appeared that the Soviet interest in membership in the UN lay not in the desire to create a viable multilateral structure for the management of international security but in the quest for recognition as a great power, for a forum in which to articulate its

---

[40] For example, Alexander George explains Soviet pursuit of the Basic Principles Agreement (1972) as follows: 'For the Soviets, the virtue of the agreements consisted in making it safer for them to engage in low-level, controlled efforts to advance their influence in third areas.' Alexander George, 'The Basic Principles Agreement of 1972', in George, *Managing U.S.-Soviet Rivalry*, 82.

[41] On the nature and significance of differences between Soviet and American conceptions of détente, see Raymond Garthoff, *Détente and Confrontation: American-Soviet Relations from Nixon to Reagan* (Washington: Brookings Institution, 1985), 24–68.

[42] See V. M. Molotov, 'Statement to the Committee on Political and Territorial Questions of the Peace Treaty with Italy of the Paris Peace Conference' (14 September 1946). Foreign Minister Molotov's statement is striking for its defence of special rights and obligations of great powers.

[43] A. Dallin, *The Soviet Union at the United Nations* (New York: Praeger, 1962), 22. This position proved to be quite enduring. In 1970, Soviet concern over the diluting effect of multiplication of institutions and functions was forcefully restated. See V. Israelyan, 'International Security and the United Nations', *International Affairs*, 11 (1970).

opposition to the West in the context of the Cold War, and in the belief that membership—and, *a fortiori*, the veto—would prevent or constrain the use of the organization for anti-Soviet purposes. In short, the organization was not, in Soviet eyes, a vehicle for the promotion of concerns of justice in international relations, but was a means of pursuing self-interested policy objectives: strengthening the norm of sovereignty and the principle of non-intervention at least amongst the great powers, institutionalizing Soviet status within the latter group, and impeding the development of coalitions hostile to Soviet objectives in an organization in which the USSR and its allies were a distinct minority. The pattern of Soviet behaviour in the Security Council during the UN's first 45 years suggested deep scepticism regarding the multilateralization of problems of international security, and even greater antipathy to the development of UN roles in the management of internal conflict and the expansion of the secretary-general's autonomy in international politics.[44] Underlying this pattern was a deeper point. The UN was a product of a treaty amongst equal states. Its position, therefore, was derivative and not separate from the member states.[45]

During the same period, the membership of the UN expanded to include increasing numbers of recently independent Third World and non-aligned states. The balance in the General Assembly shifted in a potentially anti-Western direction, and the USSR came to see it as a means of pursuing the bipolar struggle in a different form. This brings me to a third theme: Soviet perspectives on decolonization. The USSR displayed little interest in this issue—and the broader question of influence among nationalist movements and governments in the Third World—during Stalin's last years. The acceleration of the process of decolonization in the 1950s, evidence of increasing assertion against Western influence in key regions such as the Middle East, and the arrival of Nikita Khrushchev to the Soviet leadership all contributed to a substantial growth in Soviet engagement on the question of national self-determination.

In the UN, the USSR transformed itself into an ardent advocate of decolonization. It was a key sponsor of the General Assembly's Declaration on the Granting of Independence to Colonial Countries and Peoples (Assembly Resolution 1514–1960) and of the Committee of 24 established to monitor progress in implementation of the declaration. In the 1960s and 1970s, it

---

[44] Soviet scepticism regarding multilateral military engagements in international crises was evident in their reaction to the emergence of peacekeeping under Secretary General Dag Hammarskjöld. In particular, the gradual extension of the ONUC mission in the then Republic of the Congo encountered an adamant Soviet insistence that UN peacekeeping engagements not exceed the shared objectives of permanent members. The Soviet proposal for reform of the position of Secretary General was a transparent attempt to extend the veto principle to the operations of the Secretariat.   [45] Dallin, *The Soviet Union at the United Nations*, 157.

forcefully supported the efforts of national liberation movements to receive a hearing at the UN and to be recognized as the sole legitimate representatives of their peoples. Soviet representatives also strongly supported the movement at the UN to condemn apartheid and to assist South Africa's—and Namibia's—liberation movements to assert the rights of these countries' majority populations.

Once again, however, it is necessary to qualify this apparent embrace of national self-determination as an aspect of international justice. In the first place, the Soviet embrace of the principle was highly selective. The USSR strongly held to the view that self-determination should be territorial rather than reflect the identities of peoples. There is, for example, a striking lack of support for sub-state self-determination claims in Soviet diplomacy throughout the 1950s, 1960s, and 1970s.[46] Several factors explained this selectivity. First, the USSR itself was a multi-ethnic state that could be subject to sub-state claims for national self-determination. Second, the overwhelming majority of Third World states were viscerally hostile to the claims of minorities within those states to self-determination; embracing such claims would yield few advantages in the contest for influence in the Third World.

The power-political motivations of the Soviet embrace of decolonization and the national liberation revolution were clear. The cause of national liberation was a means whereby the USSR could undermine Western and in particular American influence and position in the Third World and secure the support of the non-aligned movement in the global bipolar competition. As the Sino-Soviet conflict developed, support for national liberation was also a means to limit the expansion of Chinese influence in Afro-Asian states. In other words, although one would not want to discount completely the normative commitment of many in the USSR to the anti-imperialist cause, Soviet approaches to decolonization appear to have had far more to do with the competitive pursuit of power and relative gain than they did with principles of justice.

Similar conclusions may be drawn from Soviet approaches to the issue of global redistribution of wealth from North to South. The Soviet leadership went on record very early in the Khrushchev period to the effect that the elimination of economic dependence was an essential element of achieving 'genuine freedom' in the Third World.[47] From there, it was a short step to support of ideas regarding a 'new international economic order', the purpose of which was to eliminate the system of 'neo-colonialist' exploitation embodied

---

[46] The one exception was the eventual Soviet support of the self-determination claim of Bangladesh.

[47] Nikita Khrushchev, 'Speech at Rangoon University' (1955), as reprinted in *International Affairs* (Moscow), 1 (1956), 235.

in unequal trade, foreign investment, and 'enslaving aid'.[48] There is, however, a slight difference between Southern and Soviet formulations of the question of redistribution. Soviet commentary appeared to focus on dissociation of Third World economies from the developed Western economic system. Third World formulations seemed to focus more on the restructuring of existing economic relations. The difference may be explained in terms of the political objective of weakening the West through detaching its Southern hinterland. And, although the USSR supported the movement for a new international economic order within the UN during the early and mid-1970s, it rejected any notion that the USSR had any share of the redistributive responsibility. The imperialist powers were the cause of underdevelopment; they were responsible for rectifying it.

The last issue for consideration here is that of human rights. The record of Soviet Cold War diplomacy betrays a fundamental antipathy to this aspect of international justice. Soviet resistance to the notion that human—and particularly civil and political—rights constituted matters of legitimate international concern dated back to the effort to draft the Universal Declaration of Human Rights in the last half of the 1940s. When the Declaration was submitted to the General Assembly in December 1948, a Soviet representative commented that 'a number of articles completely ignore the sovereign rights of democratic governments' and that the question of national sovereignty 'is a matter of the greatest importance'.[49] The Soviet delegation attempted unsuccessfully to defer consideration until the following year and then abstained from the vote, along with Ukraine and Byelorussia.

The USSR then launched a prolonged rearguard action, impeding the development of follow-on covenants to operationalize the objectives outlined in the Declaration. In this effort they emphasized the importance of economic and social, as opposed to political and civil, rights.[50] Soviet discomfort with the internationalization of human rights issues was one reason among many for the 18-year gap between adoption of the declaration and adoption of the covenants and for the weakness of compliance instruments associated with the two covenants when they were adopted.

Soviet scepticism regarding the internationalization of human rights extended beyond the UN to regional fora. During the early and mid-1970s, the

[48] See, for example, Karen Brutents, *National Liberation Revolutions Today*, I (Moscow: Progress Publishers, 1977), 9, 29, 45, 47, *inter alia*.
[49] As cited in Tom J. Farer and Felice Gaer, 'The UN and Human Rights', in Adam Roberts and Benedict Kingsbury (eds), *United Nations, Divided World: The UN's Roles in International Relations*, 2nd edn (Oxford: Oxford University Press, 1993), 248. Several years later, a Soviet scholar warned that the draft covenant on civil and political rights was structured in such a way as to give the West a 'basis in theory ... for the policy of interference in the domestic affairs of other states'. V. V. Evgenev, 'Pravosub'ektnost': suverenitet i nevmeshatel'tsvo', *Sovetskoe Gosudarstvo i Pravo*, 2 (1955), 75.   [50] Farer and Gaer, 'The UN and Human Rights', 250.

USSR was enthusiastic about the process of negotiation leading to the Helsinki Agreements of 1975. Its principal objective in these negotiations was to secure acceptance of the post-Second World War territorial status quo in Europe. It also sought to reduce barriers to economic exchange between East and West, and hoped that the conclusion of the agreements would further the general process of détente in Europe. In pursuit of these objectives, Moscow ran into strong pressure from NATO and neutral states to include a basket of provisions concerning individual human rights and freedom of movement for people and information within the CSCE space. These provisions encountered substantial resistance from the USSR. The Soviets accepted Basket III only because they believed that the language was vague enough to protect their interests.[51]

The root of Soviet resistance to the internationalization of human rights lay in an unwillingness to contemplate meaningful external assessment of and engagement in human rights issues within the USSR and its allied states and, more profoundly, in the recognition that the liberal conception of political and civil rights contained in the Declaration and Covenants was antithetical to the Soviet perspective on domestic order. As at many points in Russia's past, concerns over domestic order had a significant impact on the Soviet approach to international justice.

In general, therefore, although the USSR was engaged in many aspects of the agenda of international justice during the Cold War, this engagement would appear to reflect less a commitment to justice per se than a perception that the process of decolonization and the campaign for the redistribution of economic power were useful instruments in power-political competition. Where justice concerns had no obvious impact on this central struggle, they were largely ignored. Where they carried potential threats to Soviet sovereignty or to Soviet domestic arrangements, they were actively resisted.

4. THE GORBACHEV PERIOD

By the late Brezhnev period, the Soviet economy and polity were stagnating, in part because of the rigidities of the command economy and in part owing to the demands of sustaining the bipolar competition with the US. In 1985, Mikhail Gorbachev took office as general secretary of the Communist Party and embarked on a radical process of domestic reform revolving around the concepts of *perestroika* (restructuring), *glasnost'* (openness with regard to the flow of information and opinion), and *demokratizatsia* (the democratization of

---

[51] Garthoff, *Détente and Confrontation*, 475.

political structures). These reforms had important implications for the rights of citizens as they involved a substantial relaxation of the previous fixation on the problem of order with its associated inattentiveness to matters of justice.

Soviet foreign policy also came to be dominated by new political thinking. The most fundamental revision in this body of thought was a questioning of the previous interpretation of international politics primarily in terms of class struggle. The thought of Gorbachev and his colleagues strongly reflected the awareness of global identity and solidarity[52] that is a key theme in this book. Russian spokespersons emphasized the rising importance of global concerns—disarmament, environmental degradation, and underdevelopment—and called for a 'deideologization' of international relations in the effort to cope with these problems cooperatively on the basis of shared interests that transcended the divisions of world politics. As Gorbachev once put it: 'The nations of the world resemble today a pack of mountaineers tied together by a climbing rope. They can either climb on together to the mountain peak or fall together into an abyss.'[53]

One possible abyss was that of nuclear war.[54] Security came to be seen not so much as an issue of relative gain but as a mutually constituted good. The USSR was secure to the extent that others perceived themselves not to be threatened by the USSR. This suggested a military posture based on 'reasonable sufficiency'—sufficient resources to defend but insufficient to raise fears of impending attack. These reformulations produced a string of arms-control agreements, beginning in December 1987 with the INF Treaty, the moves towards partial unilateral disarmament, and the quite deliberate effort to resolve the conflicts in the Third World that divided the superpowers while drawing down limited Soviet resources.

This effort involved substantial change in the Soviet approach to the UN. The organization came to be seen not so much as a forum in which to sustain Soviet sovereignty and status as a great power, to undercut Western influence over the non-aligned states, and to constrain the US and its allies, but as a promising vehicle for the cooperative management of international security. The competitive vetoes of the Cold War gave way to consultation among and joint action by the permanent members in addressing the lingering wars in Angola, Namibia, Cambodia, and Central America. Despite the long-standing relations between the USSR and Iraq, when the latter invaded Kuwait in 1990

---

[52] As Kull, *Burying Lenin*, 1, puts it: 'contradicting the Marxist-Leninist view of social reality as most fundamentally conflictual, new thinking claims that the most fundamental reality is the underlying unity of the world.'

[53] Mikhail Gorbachev, *Perestroika: New Thinking for Our Country and the World* (New York: Harper and Row, 1987), 140. See also Light, *The Soviet Theory of International Relations*, 297.

[54] Mikhail Gorbachev, 'Address to Warsaw Treaty Anniversary Meeting', TASS (26 April 1985).

the USSR signed on to the raft of resolutions mandating coalition action against aggression.

One important aspect of the re-conceptualization of security in the USSR was the changing significance of the eastern European allies in Soviet foreign policy. The Soviet military presence there enhanced Western threat perceptions. Meanwhile, maintenance of the buffer was costly at a time when the USSR had few resources to spare. The Soviet leadership therefore accepted meaningful self-determination on the part of these states and, more importantly, their peoples. When allied regimes found themselves under imminent threat, the Soviet leadership chose not to interfere with the popular will to determine their own futures.[55]

In parallel with efforts to enhance respect for human rights within the USSR—for example, freedom of speech and the press, and the recognition of the right to emigrate of the country's Jewish population—the USSR reversed its traditional position on the relationship between human rights and sovereignty, enthusiastically embracing the promotion of human rights as matters of legitimate international concern. The USSR also accepted that states had *international* obligations regarding the treatment of their own citizens, and that international society should develop means not only to monitor human rights but also to prevent their violation.[56] The emergence of the human dimension of the CSCE/OSCE in 1990–1 owed much to the active diplomacy of the USSR, culminating in the meeting in the USSR's capital that produced the Moscow Mechanism. Here members agreed that 'the commitments in the field of the Human Dimension of the CSCE, are matters of direct and legitimate concern to all participating states and do not belong exclusively to the internal affairs of states'.[57]

The emergence of new thinking may be seen in some respects as a repetition of attempts by Russian leaders to redress a decaying situation by wholesale import of Western ideas and/or practices. Recognizing an increasing gap in power and power potential between the USSR and the West, Soviet leaders sought to reduce spending on the military and divert resources to the civilian economy. This required a reduction in Western pressure and enlisting the West in assisting Russian recovery. As Foreign Minister Shevardnadze put it in 1987:

The main thing is that the country does not incur additional expenses in connection with the need to maintain its defence capacity and protect its legitimate foreign policy

---

[55] For an extremely useful account of change in Soviet policy in eastern Europe, see Jacques Lévesque, *1989: La Fin d'un Empire: l'URSS et la libération de l'Europe de l'Est* (Paris: Presses de Sciences Po, 1995).

[56] 'Shevardnadze Outlines Arms Cuts', Moscow TASS (5 June 1990); cited in *Foreign Broadcast Information Service: Soviet Union* (6 June 1990), 8.

[57] CSCE, 'Document of the Moscow Meeting of the Conference on the Human Dimension of the CSCE' (1991); at http://www.osce.org/docs/english/1990–1999/hd/mosc91e.htm

interests. This means that we must seek ways to limit and reduce military rivalry, eliminate confrontational features in relations with other states, and suppress conflict and crisis situations.

In this respect, one might conclude that these revisions in Russian thinking on order and justice, internally and externally, were, once again, instrumental in character. After all, as Gorbachev explained to his colleagues in 1995, the real question of the last part of the twentieth century and the beginning of the next one was whether Russia would remain a great power.

On the other hand, there is good reason to believe that the changes discussed here reflected a more fundamental learning process. The ideas informing change in Soviet domestic foreign policy were the product of a group of intellectuals that had matured in the Khrushchev and Brezhnev periods. They reflected a deepening awareness that command socialism had produced stagnation at home, while the state's 'socialist internationalist' foreign policy had produced isolation and crippling levels of military spending. The combination was potentially fatal to the Soviet state.

In the context of this volume, what is striking about the evolution of Soviet perspectives on international relations in the late 1980s is the strong influence therein of Western liberal solidarism in the areas of development, human rights, and security. However, as with past episodes of liberalization and Westernisation, this one too produced a reaction, this time in the form of a conservative *coup d'état* in August 1991. The coup was reversed not by Gorbachev loyalists, of whom by this time there were few, but by Russian President Boris Yeltsin. The failure of the coup, the discrediting of the party and the Soviet state, and the radical shift of power from the centre to republican institutions rapidly produced the collapse of the USSR into its 15 constituent republics and the re-emergence of a specifically Russian polity at the centre of the former Union.

5. RUSSIAN VIEWS OF ORDER AND JUSTICE IN THE POST-COLD WAR PERIOD

The dissolution of the USSR in 1991 reduced Russia to its seventeenth-century borders. A new line of buffer states divided it from Europe. Its economy collapsed. Much of the Russian population descended into a poverty from which it has yet to re-emerge. Criminality and corruption became rampant as influential entrepreneurs sought to 'steal the state' in the context of a haphazard and ill-conceived privatization. Russia's military strength largely evaporated in the face of the crisis in the defence budget and failures in the logistics chain. The first (1994–6) and second (1999–) Chechen wars eloquently displayed the hollowing out of Russian military capability. Central authority over the country was imperilled by the self-assertion of subjects of the Russian Federation and the consequent 'war of laws' between the centre and the regions as the latter attempted to assert the primacy of their own legislation in areas that, constitutionally, lay in federal jurisdiction. In the early 1990s, speculation concerning the likelihood of collapse of the Russian Federation was common.[58] In the meantime, the former Soviet republics lining Russia's southern border descended into profound instability and, frequently, civil war.

In many of these respects, the crisis of the early and mid-1990s was reminiscent of many other historical examples of implosion in the Russian Empire. In turn, as in the past, it had profound implications for how Russians thought about international order. Given their abrupt demotion from superpower status, the profound changes in their immediate neighbourhood, and their sudden recovery of *national* sovereignty, Russians had little idea of who they were in their new international circumstances[59] and little firm idea of what that meant for their foreign policy.

The development of a coherent view of international relations was significantly hampered by the disappearance of the centralizing discipline of the Soviet era and the profound competition both within and between agencies with foreign policy responsibilities. The first two years after the collapse witnessed a significant contestation in Russian foreign policy between the residual liberal internationalism of the Gorbachev era, a revanchist radical nationalism, and an incipient pragmatic realism.[60] Over time, amidst considerable confusion and ambiguity, opinion gradually coalesced around the latter perspective. Several dimensions of this view deserve mention. First, and contra the extremes of Gorbachevian new thinking and the perceived kowtowing of Russian foreign policy to the West in the first year of independence, it was widely held in both the academic and policy-making communities that Russia was in fact not part of the West and could not be, lying as it did geographically and culturally at the intersection of European and Asian civilizations and drawing its identity from both.[61]

Second, and more practically, Russia had interests that were distinct from, and sometimes in tension with, those of the West and notably the US. It could

---

[58] Jean Radvanyi, 'And What If Russia Breaks Up: Towards New Regional Divisions', *Post-Soviet Geography*, 33/2 (1992).

[59] For a useful account of the problem of identity in post-Cold War Russian foreign policy, see Hopf, 'Russian Identity and Foreign Policy after the Cold War', 1–14.

[60] For accounts of these contending perspectives, see S. Neil MacFarlane, 'Russian Conceptions of Europe', *Post-Soviet Affairs*, 10/3 (1994); Aleksei Arbatov, 'Russia's Foreign Policy Alternatives', *International* Security, 18/2 (1993); and Alex Pravda, 'The Politics of Foreign Policy', in Stephen White *et al.* (eds), *Developments in Russian and Post-Soviet Politics*, 3rd edn (Basingstoke: Macmillan, 1994).

[61] See MacFarlane, 'Russian Conceptions of Europe' and also Bobo Lo, 'A Study in Ambivalence: Russian Attitudes towards the West', unpublished paper, 1.

not afford to subordinate its interests to the preferences of outsiders. The evolving discussion shed considerable light on the evolution of Russian perspectives on both order and justice. Three themes are discussed here: Russia's views of actors in international relations and the structure of international order; the structure of regional order; and the place of human rights in international relations with particular reference to the evolving discussion of humanitarian intervention.

Whereas in the Gorbachev era there was some limited consideration of actors other than states, this largely disappeared after the Soviet collapse. Russian discourse returned to a more or less exclusively statist position. International relations was about interactions between states. This re-emphasis was an external reflection of the crisis of the Russian state and the effort to stabilize and restore it in the face of fissiparous pressures from below. The Russian focus was not just on the state but also on the distribution of power. The Russian view of contemporary international order betrayed considerable unhappiness with the 'unipolar' and hegemonic distribution of power in the 1990s. The effort of the US to enlarge NATO, for example, was perceived to be a unilateral effort to take advantage of the weakness of others to consolidate the hegemonic position of the US in the European and international systems. Russians also displayed considerable unhappiness with NATO out-of-area operations. Securing Russian compliance and cooperation in the IFOR/SFOR operation in Bosnia was an extremely difficult process. NATO's unmandated intervention in the Federal Republic of Yugoslavia in 1999 was greeted with outrage as a violation of international law (see below).

Unhappiness with the prevalent distribution of power was accompanied by a strong advocacy of multipolarity and a persistent investigation of third-party arrangements that might carry some potential for balancing America's preponderance.[62] For some in Russia this meant an alliance of the have-nots. In the early years after the Soviet collapse some Russians warned, for example, that a failure on the part of the West to treat Russia equitably would drive Russia into the hands of those actually or potentially hostile to the West. In this context, but also for economic and security reasons, Russia made significant efforts to sustain and to strengthen relations with Iran (arms transfers and the sale of nuclear technologies), India (arms transfers including missile propulsion technologies), and China (arms transfers, the signing of a treaty of friendship and cooperation in 2001), and the agreement on a regional cooperation organization joining China and Russia with four central Asian republics in 2001.

---

[62] See, for example, the position of former Prime Minister Evgenii Primakov as described in Oksana Antonenko, 'Russia, NATO, and European Security after Kosovo', *Survival*, 41/4 (1999–2000), 128.

Given Russian concern over balancing the US, it was unsurprising that the planned enlargement of the EU and the deepening of the Union to include a meaningful presence and policy in foreign and security affairs drew little criticism in Russian analyses.[63] The Russian interest in multipolarity as an answer to American hegemony in international politics betrayed a traditional competitive understanding of international order based on the maintenance of a balance of power, as did Russian resistance to NATO engagement in southeastern Europe and the Alliance's enlargement in central and northern Europe.

Despite its opposition to NATO's two interventions in the former Yugoslavia, when faced with the choice of being inside or outside the game Russia ultimately contributed to both. This reflected several factors. The one that concerns us here is the Russian desire to be seen as a key player in European security. The one thing worse than having NATO play a leading role in the management of regional conflict with Russia co-opted into the process was to have NATO play this role with Russia left outside. Aside from the wider negative consequences of isolation, the latter outcome would have limited Russia's capacity to constrain the North Atlantic community as the Western alliance proceeded with its effort to restructure European security.

Russian participation in the Bosnian and Kosovo operations also displays their deep concern to retain status as first among equals in Europe. Negotiations over the chain of command governing relations between NATO and the Russian contingent in Bosnia, the unilateral Russian occupation of the Pristina airport by Russian forces in mid-1999, and the Russians' campaign to obtain their own zone of occupation in Kosovo—alongside the British, the German, and the American ones—all suggest sensitivity to considerations of prestige. There were no obvious strategic reasons for such actions. One is therefore driven to the conclusion that the key issue here was status, the desire for recognition of Russia's claim to play a central role in decisions on security matters.

One senses a similar concern in the Russian approach to national missile defence and the ABM Treaty in 2000–1, in the priority that Russia placed on the role of the Security Council as the principal locus of decision-making on matters of international security,[64] and in the Russian quest for membership of the G-7. The first two indicate a strong desire to retain positions achieved during the Cold War. The third highlights Russian efforts to obtain recognition as a co-equal member of newer selective institutions of governance in international society.

Although the discussion thus far has emphasized the Russian conception of international order and its place in that order, one senses an element of

[63] See Vladimir Baranovsky, 'Russia: A Part of Europe or Apart from Europe?' *International Affairs*, 76 (2000), 452–3.
[64] See 'The Foreign Policy Concept of the Russian Federation' (28 June 2000), 4. Posted at http://www.mid.ru/eng/concept.htm

concern over justice—for Russia—in many of the positions discussed above. Russian discourse and diplomacy on the UN, the G-7 (G-8), and NATO and European security reflected not only a calculus of interest, but also a claim for equality and equal treatment as a matter of right. Indeed, given the decline in Russian power, recognition of their justice-based claim was perhaps all they could hope for.

Rights-based reasoning extended into Russian consideration of sub-regional order within the Commonwealth of Independent States. For most of the period after the USSR's collapse, the Russian conception of sub-regional order was hegemonic. It was to be an order centred on and largely determined by Russia, in which the roles of external powers and external institutions were limited.[65] This order reflected not only a calculus of power and threat, but also an argument about rights encountered at previous points in this chapter. Russia asserted rights as a sovereign great power *vis-à-vis* the international system as a whole and justified the attentuation of the sovereignty of neighbouring, weaker states. Russian officials, foreign policy documents, and non-governmental elites have repeatedly stressed that Russia has special rights and obligations in the 'near abroad'. In making this point, they draw the obvious parallel with the Monroe Doctrine that, ironically, appears to have evolved from an illegitimate manifestation of imperialist imposition to a justification for Russian behaviour.[66]

If the historical pattern holds, the decade of domestic disorder is likely to be followed by a re-emphasis on the primacy of order over rights within the country and the sacrifice of the latter to the former where these are perceived to be in conflict. The assault on the independent media and related violations of the rights of liberal opponents in 2000–1 suggest that the pattern is repeating itself, although in a somewhat attenuated fashion given the unprecedented level of Russian interdependence with the West and the priority that the Putin Administration appears to place on the positive development of relations with the West.

And, again to judge from historical precedent, the process of domestic consolidation is likely to be accompanied by resistance to the emergence of international norms that might constrain Russia's capacity to order its own house. This resistance was evident in Russian perspectives on the renewal of

[65] See 'Foreign Policy Concept of the Russian Federation' (25 January 1993), as translated in FBIS-USR-93–037 (25 March 1993), 6; Sovet po Vneshnei i Oboronnoi Politike, 'Vozroditsya li Soyuz?' *Nezavisimaya Gazeta* (23 May 1996).

[66] Yevgenii Ambartsumov, then Chairman of the Supreme Soviet's International Affairs Committee, called in 1992 for a foreign policy doctrine proclaiming 'the entire geopolitical space of the former Union a sphere of vital interests (following the example of the US Monroe Doctrine)'. He stressed further that Russia should obtain international recognition of its role as the guarantor of stability in the former USSR. *Izvestia* (7 August 1992).

the campaign against Chechnya by the Putin Administration in 1999. Russian behaviour in Chechnya was difficult to reconcile with a number of undertakings of the Russian government. Russian military activities in 1999 and 2000 appeared to be inconsistent with the state's commitments under international humanitarian law, and notably Protocol II Additional to the Geneva Convention of 1949.[67] Russian official conduct was equally difficult to square with the political obligations under the Human Dimension of the OSCE.[68]

This brings the analysis squarely to contemporary Russian perspectives on justice in international relations. The Russian government unequivocally rejects criticism along these lines, arguing that the affair in Chechnya is a domestic matter. However, it grudgingly permitted the return of the OSCE Mission to Chechnya and the secondment of Council of Europe personnel to the office of the Russian human rights monitor in Chechnya. This concession reflected Russian sensitivity to the potential political costs of ignoring Western views on the question rather than any obvious internalization of a solidarist normative framework. More positively, the Russian government took steps to prosecute Russian military personnel accused of violations of human rights, but reasonably clearly viewed this as a matter of domestic rather than international law. The prosecutions themselves have been pursued in a selective and dilatory fashion.

This background, coupled with Russia's historical sensitivity to challenges to the doctrine of sovereignty and non-intervention, at least as it concerns actions targeted on Russia, explains a very consistent Russian rejection of the notion that there was an emergent norm of international justice regarding humanitarian intervention. A review of Russian positions in the Security Council on this matter since 1991 indicates a careful and consistent effort to ensure that individual cases had no cumulative effect as precedents. Russia clearly expressed its agreement with China and the bulk of the non-aligned movement to the effect that there was neither a right nor a duty of intervention for humanitarian, or broader rights-based, reasons and criticizing the notion as a challenge to the formation of a 'fair and rational' international order.[69]

Russian academic analysis of humanitarian intervention, like that concerning international justice more broadly, is very thin on the ground, particularly when contrasted to the discourse on the state, power, and the distribution of power. To the extent that such a discourse exists, it focuses on discrediting the

---

[67] This protocol extends Geneva Convention protections of civilians in war to internal conflict. Apparent Russian violations relate to Article 4 (para. 2) concerning fundamental guarantees, Article 5 (paras 1 and 2) concerning treatment of detainees, and notably Article 13 concerning protection of the civilian population.

[68] See S. Neil MacFarlane, 'What the International Community Can Do to Settle the Conflict [in Chechnya]', *Central Asia and the Caucasus*, 4 (2000).

[69] 'Moscow Joint Statement of the Heads of State of Russia and China' (18 July 2001–1347-18-07-2001), section 7.

concept rather than elaborating or defending it.[70] The main lines of the Russian academic critique of humanitarian intervention focus on the threat that the concept poses to sovereignty.[71] In addition, the notion of rights subsumed in the concept is deemed to be Western rather than reflecting a universal understanding. The articulation of a 'right of humanitarian intervention' is instrumental, justifying the pursuit of political objectives at the expense of other states. Russian discussion highlights the lack of effective criteria governing humanitarian intervention and its arbitrary application in practice. The potentially destabilizing domestic consequences of the doctrine for countries facing internal insurgencies are also emphasized.

Perhaps most telling is the Russian perspective on mandates. Although Russians do not exclude the possibility of the use of force in the face of truly compelling humanitarian emergency, legitimate authority to mandate such force rests with the Security Council. Western and particularly British arguments to the effect that, in the event of Security Council incapacity to act, general international law provides a basis for action outside the Council framework are rejected.[72] As Baranovsky puts it:

> Even if human rights are becoming a more weighty factor of the international life, they should be inscribed into the existing UN-based legal framework and by no means prioritized at the expenses [*sic*] of the Westphalian principle of states' primacy—this logic seems predominant even in the circles recognizing the importance of 'humanitarian' rationales in the world politics.[73]

6. SEPTEMBER 11 2001 AND RUSSIAN VIEWS ON ORDER AND JUSTICE

The events of September 11 2001 resulted in a substantial reorientation of Russian foreign policy along a number of lines. Russia acquiesced in the

---

[70] On this point, see Vladimir Baranovsky, 'Humanitarian Intervention: Russia's Approaches', paper presented at the Second Pugwash Workshop on Intervention, Sovereignty and International Security (Como, Italy, 28–30 September 2000), 4. The following description draws on this work.

[71] Putin is reported to have stated as early as February 2000 that 'it is inadmissible, under the slogan of so-called humanitarian intervention, to override such basic principles of international law as sovereignty and the territorial integrity of states'. See Evgenii Petrov, 'Doktrina Putina?' *Nezavisimaya Gazeta* (2 February, 2000, electronic version).

[72] The December 1997 draft National Security Concept identified efforts to weaken the UN and the OSCE or to mount interventions without a UN mandate as a major threat to Russian national security interests. See *Krasnaya Zvezda* (9 October 1999), 4–5. See also 'The Foreign Policy Concept of the Russian Federation' (28 June 2000), 5. Posted at http://www.mid.ru/mid/eng/concept.htm   [73] Baranovsky, 'Humanitarian Intervention', 10.

deployment of substantial US and allied forces in a region in which the Russian Federation had previously resisted external military engagement. President Putin enthusiastically embraced the West's war on terrorism and clearly articulated the view that this was a common struggle of the 'civilized world' against the forces of evil. He made clear in the face of the choice posed by the US that he perceived Russia's lot to lie with the West.[74]

The result was a dramatic turn for the better in Russia's relations with the West and with NATO. Russia came to be seen as a central player in a Western endeavour of global proportions. Criticism of Russia's policy in Chechnya largely disappeared and key leaders recognized the war as a 'struggle against terrorism'. Whether this constituted a fundamental turn towards a Western, liberal orientation in Russian foreign policy was another matter: 'In a short while, when the euphoria of joint participation in the anti-terrorist coalition subsides, the tough reality will take the upper hand and Russia and America will part ways again, since there exist many reasons for them to part ways.'[75] Among these were policy differences—for example: on missile defence and the desirability of a formal treaty framework for future arms control arrangements—enlargement of NATO to the Baltics, the potential use of bases in central Asia and the Caucasus for attacks on targets such as Iraq, geopolitical tensions: for example, whether the current American deployment in central Asia, to which Russians have agreed, is transformed into a deeper, more permanent American military engagement in the region, which Russians may oppose, and, most fundamentally: differences in political systems. In the latter context, differences of view on the fate of independent media and on the implications of Russia's prosecution of the war in Chechnya for human rights re-emerged in January 2002.[76]

What does this mean in terms of the balance between order and justice in international relations? The embrace of the American anti-terrorist agenda suits the current Russian government's perception of national interest. Cooperation with the American-led agenda in Afghanistan serves the Russian objective of the elimination of 'radical Islamism' both in the Russian Federation and in central Asia. The Russian government is also taking advantage of American interest in its cooperation in this joint endeavour in order to re-balance its relationship with NATO. Its success thus far is indicated in

[74] Indeed, at the level of identity Putin has made this clear ever since he emerged at the top of Russia's political hierarchy. See Vladimir Putin, *Ot pervogo litsa* (Moscow: Vagrius, 2000), 156, as cited in Lo, 'A Study in Ambivalence', 1. The crisis in Afghanistan makes it possible to pursue Putin's self-identification as a European and a Westernizer.

[75] These citations are taken from Igor Torbakov, 'Good Bush-Putin Rapport Can't Hide Obstacles to Long-Term US-Russian Cooperation', *Eurasianet* (20 November 2001); at http://www.eurasianet.org/departments/insight/articles/eav111901.shtml, posted 19 November 2001.

[76] See Peter Baker, 'New Criticism Signals Tension between U.S. and Russia', *International Herald Tribune* (16 January 2002), 4.

Lord Robertson's indication that NATO is considering ways of giving Russian real decision-making power in the Alliance.[77] In this respect, the move corresponds to Russian status concerns as well.

Finally, Russian cooperation in this endeavour is a way of purchasing Western acquiescence in its campaign in Chechnya. The connection between elements of the Chechen resistance and the al-Qaeda network is reasonably well-established. Both American and British spokesmen have accepted the Russian 're-branding' of the war in Chechnya as a counter-terrorist operation. There is no evidence of any Russian adjustment in a liberal direction of its positions on sovereignty, order, justice, and rights in this context. The American and British shift on Chechnya suggests the reverse: an increasing Western willingness to tolerate, if not to approve of, Russian dissent from the purported emergence of a societal consensus on the rights-based attenuation of principles of sovereignty. Increasing pressure on neighbours such as Georgia, related to the campaign in Chechnya but also reflecting broader Russian strategic designs in the southern Caucasus, has met with little Western criticism. To recall the proverb that begins this chapter, the Russians have not been persuaded to drink tea; their Western colleagues have apparently been convinced of the merits of chopping wood.

7. CONCLUSION

This volume asks whether the evidence in the post-Cold War era of an evolving solidarist consensus indicated the possibility that concerns of justice might be more effectively promoted in international society. The extent to which this outcome might emerge depends on the degree to which these normative concerns are shared by the major actors and groups in world politics. Examination of the history of Russian perspectives on international order and justice suggests little receptivity in Russian discourse to the attenuation of the rights of states, and particularly the great powers, by the promotion or defence of individual or group—for example, self-determination—rights. Nor does Russian behaviour over the country's history display any particular commitment to international redistributive justice, although at times Russian governments have recognized instrumental value in advocating international economic justice.

Russian perspectives on order and justice are deeply rooted in the geographical situation of the country and Russia's historical difficulty in consolidating the state and in defending it against external threat. The Russian answer to these

---

[77] Michael Wines, 'Russia Could Get Veto Power in New NATO', *International Herald Tribune* (23 November 2001), 1, 3.

challenges has been to insist on the primacy of order over justice domestically. Its privileging of order over justice at the international level is in many respects an external projection of this internal preoccupation. The Russian conception of order is profoundly state-centric and has focused on the rights and sovereignty of great powers. Successive Russian governments, whatever their ideological stripe, have displayed little sympathy for arguments that weaken these prerogatives. There is a component of justice evident in this insistence; Russia has argued for equality as a matter of right and continues to do so. But this is an argument regarding justice for the state rather than being evidence of solidarism.

Whereas at the international level Russia has focused on the establishment and preservation of its equality with other great powers, its perspective on its immediate region has been hierarchical, hegemonic, and interventionist. Its logic of hegemony has remained focused on the security and power of the Russian state. To the extent that norms have been projected within this space by Russia or beyond it, this projection has tended to reflect Russian concerns over domestic order—as with Russian perspectives on the Holy Alliance—or regional security—as with the communization of eastern Europe. Despite considerable political, economic, and social change, Russia's view of order and justice in international relations remains statist, traditional, and conservative. There is no obvious evidence from this case to support the general proposition debated in this volume that there is an emergent solidarist consensus on matters of justice in international relations.

8

An Uneasy Engagement: Chinese Ideas of Global Order and Justice in Historical Perspective

RANA MITTER

'When China has contact with foreigners', warned the Chinese official Li Hongzhang in 1863, 'we should first understand their ambitions, be aware of their desires, and thoroughly know their points of strength and weakness, honesty and dishonesty, before we can expect to secure just treatment.'[1] In the modern era, China has always found engagement with the international system a frustrating experience. In the dying decades of the imperial era and the Republican period of the early twentieth century, China struggled to be seen as an equal in a structure that seemed designed to deny the value of the political culture that had sustained China for centuries, if not millennia. During the high period of Maoist rule, China was keen to project itself as a revisionist power, at war with the complacent and stagnant Western-dominated order. Even in the contemporary era, the strong adherence of Chinese foreign policy-makers to the classical international legal norms of respect for sovereignty and non-interference in the domestic affairs of other states has left China seeming inadequate in the face of increasingly dominant solidarist approaches to international questions of order and justice in international society, approaches driven by concern for issues such as human rights and the environment.

Yet the issues arising from the relationship between order and justice in international society are highly relevant to China. It is notable that the debate on the link between concepts of order and justice in international society is

I am most grateful for the comments of contributors to the seminar series on 'Order and Justice in International Relations' in 2000 and to the associated colloquium in 2001, in particular those of Rosemary Foot and Andrew Hurrell, which greatly improved my original text.

[1] 'Li Hung-chang's Support of Western Studies, 1863,' in Ssu-yu Teng and John K. Fairbank, *China's Response to the West: A Documentary Survey, 1839–1923* (Cambridge, MA: Harvard University Press, 1979), 74.

generated, in large part, by countries that have a high degree of control over the definition and operation of those concepts. Steve Chan has observed that 'it is perhaps difficult for Americans and Britons to appreciate how the traumas of national setback have shaped other countries' worldviews'.[2] This is certainly true in the case of China, where imperialism and invasion over the last 150 years have profoundly shaped the way in which contemporary China treats the notions of order and justice in international society. Furthermore, most of the terminology in which the debate is conducted is of relatively recent vintage in Chinese thinking, going back no later than the late nineteenth century. Yet China is an active participant in the post-Cold War order, and makes no secret of its conviction that the West's behaviour in the past means that China deserves special treatment in the present.

This chapter starts with a brief consideration of the ways in which concepts of order and justice between states were conceptualized in pre-modern China; goes on to explore the response to the arrival of Western thought and imperialism in the late nineteenth and early twentieth centuries; analyses the importance of revolutionary thought in Mao Zedong's revision of world order in the early Cold War era; and concludes by examining the new pragmatism which underlies contemporary Chinese conceptions of what a just world order might be. It will be suggested that China has felt itself to be an outsider in the international community for most of the last 150 years, adapting its behaviour to fit global norms only to see those norms metamorphose and once again deny China what it perceives as its rightful place. China does engage with the new norms of international society, sometimes productively, but usually uncomfortably.

1. CHINA IN THE PRE-MODERN WORLD

For many Western observers, notably Marx, Chinese society before the opium wars of the nineteenth century was a somnolent and static society that had followed 'traditional' paths for centuries before the impact of the West. Historians have long since reassessed this view, showing that Qing China (1644–1911) was not an insular society refusing to acknowledge the outside world but rather one of the world's great empires, with significant influence on other states in the region.[3] There has been a shorthand understanding of pre-modern Chinese foreign relations that argues that China's relations with the non-Chinese

[2] Steve Chan, 'Chinese Perspectives on World Order', in T. V. Paul and John A. Hall (eds), *International Order and the Future of World Politics* (Cambridge: Cambridge University Press, 1999), 201.

[3] See, for instance, Susan Naquin and Evelyn S. Rawski, *Chinese Society in the Eighteenth Century* (New Haven: Yale University Press, 1987), 27–32.

world were deeply hierarchical. The spectacle of foreign leaders coming to bring 'tribute' to the capital in Beijing was widely known and remarked upon, and the idea that China was at the centre of the civilized world was clearly a cultural given for the elites.[4] Yet this interpretation risks confusing form with substance. There is a great deal of evidence which shows that the pre-modern Chinese in reality regarded themselves as being part of a much flatter hierarchical system than their own rhetoric would suggest. The 'tribute' system was, after all, frequently a way for the Chinese court to retain nominal control over remote areas while suzerain rulers were in fact virtually autonomous: a tacit acceptance that Chinese authority could not stretch beyond the empire's military capabilities. In the eighteenth century, the Qing dynasty demanded 'tribute' from various peoples, notably the Koreans, in exchange for permission to trade in China; but in terms of its practicalities the system might just as usefully be termed a tariff system in which a tax was paid to obtain trading rights. Nor, when they proved useful, was the Qing inflexible about relations with other states. Very early in its rule, the dynasty's increasing fear of Russian expansion prompted its pragmatic decision to sign the Treaty of Nerchinsk in 1689, which defined borders between the two states and in which Russia's equality was tacitly accepted.[5]

Instead, the establishment of norms such as those embedded in the language of tribute should be seen as a natural part of a world-view in which the concepts of order and ritual were closely interlinked. If ideology is the cement that binds modern societies, then pre-modern China used *li*, generally translated as 'rituals', to very much the same effect.[6] The relationships between the various parts of human society were tied into a religio-philosophical system in which the establishment of 'correct order' was crucial. Yet these norms could also be used pragmatically. Constantly, we see that the *nominal* acceptance of these ritual norms was acceptable within the system of order expected. The Qing dynasty demonstrated this effectively when the Manchu rulers, who had overthrown the ethnic Chinese Ming dynasty in 1644, went on to launch a campaign to woo the elites by setting forth a Confucian programme for rule. And in practice the tributary ritual requirements made of many suzerain states were nominal rather than real; the form of a world dominated by the Son of Heaven hid the reality of a sophisticated understanding of inter-state relations. Perhaps most striking is the phenomenon analysed by David Bello, in which Kokand, a central Asian state which was officially a tributary of the Qing, traded opium into the western borderlands of China in a way that demonstrates

[4] See Mark Elvin, 'The Inner World of 1830', in Tu Wei-ming (ed.), *The Living Tree: The Changing Meaning of Being Chinese Today* (Stanford: Stanford University Press, 1994), 44.
[5] Naquin and Rawski, *Chinese Society*, 29–31.
[6] See Myron L. Cohen, 'Being Chinese: The Peripheralization of Traditional Identity', in Tu, *The Living Tree*.

that the relationship between the two was not one of equals but rather one in which Kokand was in control.[7]

The idea of 'justice' in these inter-state relations is more difficult to identify. But it is worth remembering that the traditional Confucian world-view had a moral concept which was supposed to temper the undoubted dominance of 'order': the idea of *ren*, often translated as 'benevolence'. In other words, those who were privileged to be at the top of the hierarchy were not permitted to abuse that superior position with impunity but were required to exercise reasonable, in effect *just*, control over the ruled. This applied at all levels of society: husband to wife, master to servant, and so on, and certainly the relationship of the Qing court to its suzerain and tributary territories fitted this description.

This understanding of *ren*, of course, has to be squared with the facts. The reality of Qing foreign policy was brutal war where they felt their rule was being challenged, and the campaigns in central Asia during the eighteenth century were bloody. But just as the reality of pragmatism in state-to-state relations does not discount the importance of following the conventions of ritual norms, the reality of bloody combat does not discount the importance of the concept of *ren* in dealing with other states. Benevolence, of course, is not justice. It does not rest on the assumption that the inferiors in society had a *right* to expect such treatment; it was more akin to the concept of *noblesse oblige*. But it is worth noting that, in that concept, there was a safety-valve in the world-view operating in Qing China which stopped the pure exercise of power as the dominant requirement of the system. 'The distant barbarians come here attracted by our culture', noted the Yongzheng emperor in 1726, 'we must treat them with generosity and virtue'.[8]

Qing conceptions of international order were also undeveloped because rulers were not that interested in other countries. Even if they were prepared to act within Chinese cultural norms, countries at the border were peripheral and therefore barbarian. China kept up a healthy trade with the outside world, but it was heavily regulated; and the Chinese did little research to find out more about foreign lands. The concept of international relations, which suggests a world system, as opposed to a pragmatically run, case-by-case system of inter-state relations was alien to the Qing. These norms, however, only remained workable during a period when the Qing could for the most part choose for themselves how to deploy their strategies of inter-state order and benevolence. The arrival of the Western imperial powers reoriented China's

---

[7] David Bello, 'Opium in Xinjiang and Beyond', in Timothy Brook and Bob Tadashi Wakabayashi (eds), *Opium Regimes: China, Britain, and Japan, 1839–1952* (Berkeley: University of California Press, 2000).

[8] Jonathan D. Spence, *The Search for Modern China*, 2nd edn (New York: W. W. Norton, 1999), 90.

sense of its place in the world in two important ways. First, it moved China from a broadly autonomous position to one which was submissive and subordinate. Then, it provided an influx of Western-derived concepts that provided new tools for China's foreign policy-makers to rethink China's position in the world order. The encounter with the Enlightenment-driven schema of modernity would be sudden and wrenching.

2. MODERNITY AND MODELS OF ORDER AND JUSTICE

From the mid-nineteenth century to the mid-twentieth, China lost control of its position in the international system. This point is well-known but has to be kept constantly in mind when one tries to understand how the dominant discourse of the time, a Western-derived language of international order, was received and interpreted in China. The Opium War of 1839–42 confronted the Chinese court for the first time with an opponent whom they could neither defeat nor appease. It was clear early on that the war was not necessarily about opium per se but about the determination of the Western powers to use their technological superiority to impose a world-view shaped by the idea of an imperial, globalized international society. The parallel experiences of the Chinese and the Japanese are instructive here. The Meiji Restoration of 1868 saw a new elite emerge in Japan who adopted a centralized modernization programme. In China, many of the intellectual elites also felt that the country must come to terms with the political language and concepts espoused by the newly arrived Western powers. There was also, between the 1910s and the 1940s, an alternative 'authoritarian' model of order and justice, influenced by the challenges to democracy in the West and Japan, which had significant although not majority support for much of that period in China.

In writing about the engagement between China and the global human rights community in the 1990s, Rosemary Foot observes that 'norms are expressed through language and the process of argumentation and debate can shape what is said subsequently in both domestic and international venues'.[9] This is just as true, perhaps more so, for China in the late nineteenth century. For the now dominant global discourse into which China had been thrust unwillingly was shaped by concepts expressed in the vocabulary of Western political thought. This discourse depended on ideas shaped by the European experience of modernity and, when first introduced to China, was alien enough to be translated by transliterations from English or, much more frequently,

[9] Rosemary Foot, *Rights Beyond Borders: The Global Community and the Struggle over Human Rights in China* (Oxford: Oxford University Press, 2000), 9.

by imports from Japan, where the Meiji reforms had made necessary the creation of hundreds of neologisms to translate previously alien concepts such as 'nation', 'autonomy', 'republic', and the essential suffix '-ism' to coin names for political doctrines.[10] Throughout the period from the late Qing onwards, terms such as 'order', 'justice', and 'international relations' were translated into Chinese using lexemes which were themselves invented or adapted only a few generations ago. This is not to argue by any means that such terms could not therefore be internalized; the experiences of Taiwan and Japan, to name but two east Asian countries that have created an effective hybrid between Western discourse and autonomous practice, show that clearly. However, terms such as 'order' and 'justice' have never necessarily translated into terms that have immediate resonance in societies in which they did not originate, just as 'benevolence' is a poor approximation of all the implications that lie behind *ren*, and 'rituals' is shorthand for a massive cultural repertoire that is encapsulated in *li*.[11] Although there were some creative attempts to combine Chinese thinking with Western ideas, such as the late Qing philosopher Kang Youwei's theory of *datong*, or 'great harmony', the strongly anti-Confucian, pro-Western 'new culture' or 'May Fourth' intellectual movement of the 1910s and 1920s pushed these ideas to the sidelines of Chinese political thought.

Along with the development of the concept of the nation came other new strands of thought, including constitutionalism, liberalism, and socialism. Among the most powerful of these strands, however, was Social Darwinism. It is no exaggeration to say that China's modernizing elites from the late Qing through the Republic, and even into the present day, have had their ideas both of order and of justice significantly shaped by the assumptions of Social Darwinism.[12] In China, the influence of Social Darwinism continued even into the inter-war period at a time when the experience of the First World War had made its nostrums less popular in much of the West.

In 1911 the Chinese imperial dynasty was finally overthrown and a Chinese Republic set up, which lasted until the establishment of the People's Republic of China (PRC) in 1949. The Republic broadly coincided with the period in

[10] For an analysis of this type of 'translated modernity', see Lydia H. Liu, *Translingual Practice: Literature, National Culture, and Translated Modernity–China, 1900–1937* (Stanford: Stanford University Press, 1995), particularly Appendices A to G.

[11] It is after all historical circumstance, not inherent universality, that has meant that it is order and justice, not *ren* and *li*, in international relations, which has become the overarching model and the subject of this volume.

[12] See, for instance, Benjamin Schwartz, *In Search of Wealth and Power: Yen Fu and the West* (Cambridge, MA: Harvard University Press, 1964). For contemporary examples of this phenomenon, see Edward Friedman, 'Preventing War Between China and Japan', in Edward Friedman and Barrett L. McCormick (eds), *What if China Doesn't Democratise? Implications for War and Peace* (Armonk: M. E. Sharpe, 2000); and Geremie Barme, 'To Screw Foreigners is Patriotic: China's Avant-Garde Nationalists', in Jonathan Unger (ed.), *Chinese Nationalism* (Armonk: M. E. Sharpe, 1996).

which the debate over the acceptance or rejection of Wilsonian norms dominated international relations globally and when order and justice were discussed at an international level far more frequently than had been previously possible. The Wilsonian model was clearly violated many times over during the inter-war period, but it became firmly established as a standard against which events were judged. In its international behaviour, China appeared to be gradually socialized into the Wilsonian international order. However, this socialization only hid a deeper anger, as Chinese at all levels of society *always* found talk of self-determination and the restoration of China's sovereignty much less convincing than did the West. After all, during the Republican period, China was in a curious position. It had representation at the League of Nations, a status it desired as it indicated its entry into the dominant international system. The large number of colonies which still existed meant that relatively few non-European nations were eligible for full membership at the time, something which made China's membership that much more significant. Yet China was clearly not a fully sovereign nation either. In addition to areas that were outright colonies, such as Hong Kong and the International Settlement and French Concession of Shanghai, there were plenty of other indications that China's status within the international community was highly anomalous. Most powerfully felt was the principle of 'extraterritoriality', which allowed foreign citizens of various countries to avoid being subject to Chinese law, and the preferential tax rates that were given to foreign businesses. All this caused great resentment, at both the elite and the popular levels, as shown, for example, in the explosions of anger such as the May Fourth student demonstrations of 1919 and the May Thirtieth anti-imperialist demonstrations of 1925, which were followed by extensive boycotts of foreign companies.

The reality that China could no longer define its own position in the international system contributed in part to the continued power of Social Darwinism as an explanatory world-view for the Chinese *and* the Japanese. Both saw themselves as victims in a world order where conflict was as prevalent as consensus. The Washington Treaties give a good example of how actions perceived by the Western powers as integrating China and Japan into the international system in fact fuelled further resentment. Thus, a significant portion of domestic Japanese opinion was angry at the agreement made to limit the size of their navy; and measures put forward to stabilize the Chinese Republic were undermined heavily by the French refusal to implement their terms because of a financial dispute over reparations for the Boxer uprising of 1900.[13] The conflict that existed between the Chinese and the Japanese

[13] Arthur Waldron, *From War to Nationalism: China's Turning Point, 1924–1925* (Cambridge: Cambridge University Press, 1995), 32–3.

through much of the early twentieth century obscures the fact that the two countries were operating with a very similar view of the way that international order worked, and consequently had a similar concept of justice, or rather the lack of it, within that order.

The idea that underpinned the League, that force alone was no longer a viable way to organize international society, was strongly supported among many policy-makers in China and Japan, not least because there was so much intellectual traffic between the two. However, its acceptance was pragmatic rather than born of conviction. Between the death of president Yuan Shikai and the ascendancy of Chiang Kai-shek—the period from 1916 to 1928— Chinese foreign policy was not driven by any ideologically complex conception of the country's role in the international system. Although there were exceptions, most foreign ministers were undistinguished and their conception of national interest consisted of little more than subscribing to the tenets of late Qing anti-foreignism and nationalism. Since China was divided between competing contenders for power at this time, it was also hard for the country to speak with one voice.

Chiang Kai-shek's Nationalist government (1928–49) was significantly different.[14] The fact that Chiang's government was ultimately unsuccessful in establishing stable rule in China obscures the importance of his ideological vision of China's place in the world. His record has also been misrepresented by careless characterizations of him as 'conservative' or 'pro-Western' in his thought. This hides the reality that Chiang's aims for China were as revisionist as those of the Communists: in foreign policy terms there was little to choose between their ultimate goals. This can be seen in the policy of 'revolutionary diplomacy' that operated in the early years of the Chiang government and which demanded wholesale revisions of extraterritoriality and tariff rights in China.[15] As Youli Sun argues, the occupation of Manchuria in 1931 created an immediate crisis that forced the Nationalists to back-pedal on 'revolutionary diplomacy' in favour of a pragmatic policy which would allow them to play off the Western powers against Japan.[16] For the time being, Chiang felt, opposition had to be concentrated on Japanese imperialism alone. But this pragmatic change of tack does not indicate any fundamental shift in the Nationalists' view that imperialism as a whole was the primary source of

[14] I have used the standard pinyin romanization system for all Chinese names, with the exception of two that are better known to Western readers in the traditional form: thus Chiang Kai-shek, rather than Jiang Jieshi in pinyin, and Sun Yatsen rather than Sun Zhongshan.

[15] See Donald A. Jordan, *Chinese Boycotts versus Japanese Bombs: The Failure of China's 'Revolutionary Diplomacy'* (Ann Arbor: University of Michigan Press, 1991), and William C. Kirby, 'The Internationalisation of China: Foreign Relations at Home and Abroad in the Republican Era', *The China Quarterly*, 150 (1997).

[16] Youli Sun, *China and the Origins of the Pacific War, 1931–1941* (New York: St Martin's Press, 1993), 5–6.

China's problems and that the Wilsonian order and the League of Nations were little more than a sham. It was the enthusiasm of Chinese liberals for Western ideas of 'democracy' and 'liberalism' during the May Fourth Movement, according to Chiang—or, rather, his ghost writer Tao Xisheng—that 'caused the decay and ruin of Chinese civilization, and made it easy for the imperialists to carry on cultural aggression'.[17] Furthermore, his government's attempts to renegotiate the unequal treaties with the Western powers fell victim to those powers' 'policy of watchful waiting', hoping that the civil wars of the late 1920s and early 1930s would prevent them having to give up their extraterritorial privileges.[18] Dai Jitao, one of Chiang Kai-shek's chief ideological strategists, also noted in 1931, during the Manchurian crisis, that the League was the tool of Western powers trying to prevent another war in Europe and that China could hope for little from it: 'Each [League Council] country's main policy is absolutely to avoid war with Japan ... For this reason, the League cannot apply any effective sanctions ... the League is simply an international body which was spawned by the European war.'[19]

Republican China also had a significant public sphere, capable of influencing the state without being dependent upon it. This was in part a product of the relative freedom of speech available in enclaves of imperialism such as the International Settlement in Shanghai, as well as the inability of Chiang to exercise full political control over areas outside China's central seaboard provinces. In this period, public opinion acted as a more autonomous influence on the shaping of foreign policy via the press, demonstrations, and so on than it does in China today. Mainstream non-governmental public voices, as seen in the press, shared a common disillusionment with Wilsonianism.[20] Typical is Yan Cheng, a pseudonymous political columnist, who wrote in 1932: 'The League of Nations is an organization that is a body of all the imperialists, a tool to oppress colonies and to divide up weak and small nations.'[21] The Manchurian crisis of 1931 was powerful evidence to all those in China who believed that survival of the fittest rather than the justice of League inquiries and commissions was the way in which order was to be created. Consequently, some political writers looked to Mussolini and later Hitler as

[17] Chiang Kai-shek, *China's Destiny*, trans. Philip Jaffe (London: Dennis Dobson, 1947), 100.

[18] Chiang Kai-shek, *China's Destiny*, 132.

[19] Dai Jitao, 'Tezhong waijiao weiyuanhui dui Ri zhengce baogaoshu' [Report of the foreign relations special committee on policy toward Japan], in Li Yunhan (ed.), *Jiu-yi-ba shibian shiliao* [Materials on the September Eighteenth Incident] (Taipei: Zhengzhong, 1977), 325.

[20] It is worth noting briefly that the concept of public opinion is a very difficult one to define in the context of China. In the pre-1949 period, it is generally considered to reflect the views of the 5–10% or so of the population who lived in cities and had access to the press. See, for example, Parks M. Coble, *Facing Japan: Chinese Politics and Japanese Imperialism, 1931–1937* (Cambridge, MA: Council on East Asian Studies, Harvard, 1991), 76.

[21] *Jiuguo xunkan* [Salvation journal], 23 (10 October 1932), 4.

powerful revisionist figures in the international order; and for some it even seemed that compromise with Japan's pan-Asianist idea was preferable.[22] Indeed, the perceived tendency of the Chinese public to be seduced by pan-Asian blandishments led Du Zhongyuan, a leftist writer and one of the single most prominent journalists of the time, to use his weekly editorial column to warn repeatedly: 'Pan-Asianism is Japanese imperialism, nothing more, and nothing less.'[23]

The nature of the Japanese alternative to the League has significance in the context of our own time, as well as during the Republic. Both Chiang's and later Mao's regimes would use China's history, and particularly its encounter with imperialism, as the basis for their revisionist claims within the world order. However, the centralizing, nationalist, and broadly 'progressive' version of history espoused by both the Nationalists and the Communists was by no means the only one under consideration during the Republican period. Ideas of formalized federalism were widespread in the 1910s and 1920s, and in fact Nationalist China was a de facto federation because of Chiang's ultimate lack of control outside his central China heartland.[24] Similarly, post-war considerations of pan-Asianism have tended to dismiss it as a cover for Japanese imperial ambitions in east Asia—as indeed it became. However, the original tenets of pan-Asianism, an ideology which posited Asian regional cooperation in opposition to European imperialism, was a powerful influence on many Chinese thinkers at the time, not least Sun Yatsen and the prominent Nationalist politician Wang Jingwei. Wang Jingwei's acceptance of the role of collaborationist president in Japanese-occupied Nanjing from 1940 to 1944 has meant that he is now generally regarded as merely an opportunist quisling. Yet, while Wang was clearly motivated in large part by self-pitying resentment at being sidelined by Chiang Kai-shek during the 1930s, he also collaborated in part because he had in mind the long, and now often forgotten, legacy of Sino-Japanese cooperation in the early twentieth century in cultural, educational, and even military matters. Wang was bitterly disappointed as it became clear that the Japanese regime in China was little more than an exploitative imperialist government. However, it remains worth considering whether there was the *potential* for an east Asian regionally-based cooperative order that would right the perceived injustices of Western domination, an order which was lost through Japanese arrogance and insincerity.

---

[22] For instance, *Jiuguo xunkan*, 43 (30 April 1933), 2.

[23] 'Dayaxiyazhuyi' [Pan-Asianism], in Du Zhongyuan, *Yuzhong zagan* [Various thoughts in prison] (Shanghai: n.p., 1936), 68.

[24] The most comprehensive deconstruction of the dominant narratives of modern Chinese history is Prasenjit Duara, *Rescuing History from the Nation: Questioning Narratives of Modern China* (Chicago: University of Chicago Press, 1995).

In short, we should ask *which* of the 'modern' models of order and justice in international society had most influence in China during the inter-war period. This was the last time that there was a powerful inter-state discourse on order and justice that consciously rejected Enlightenment norms of rationality, democracy, and equality.[25] While the Cold War also saw polarization between two ideologies, *both* of those thought-systems sought to define themselves in the language of democracy and political progressivism. The fascist project—to use an unsatisfactory blanket term for Japanese militarism, Italian fascism, and Nazism—consciously embraced hierarchy, authoritarianism, and anti-democratic norms, and it was unclear until some time into the early 1940s whether or not the authoritarian model would triumph over the democratic one.[26] Even Chiang Kai-shek was among those who drew on fascist ideology during the 1930s, and the ideas of order and justice put forward by some important Japanese political thinkers during this period provided an alternative model that could not be dismissed out of hand. The continuing residue of Social Darwinist assumptions in east Asia also fuelled the anti-progressive ideal. Colonel Ishiwara Kanji, one of the two architects of the Manchurian invasion of 1931, believed that his military coup was the first stage of planning for a racial war between the Western powers and the east Asian ones, and saw the invasion as a means of forcing the Chinese to take up their rightful place as part of a wider Asian alliance that would expel white imperialists from Asia.[27] Although later experience showed how Wang Jingwei and other collaborators with the Japanese were cruelly deceived by the reality of Japanese rule in China, there was no particular reason that they should have *automatically* considered an authoritarian, race-based idea of a just order in east Asia to be less attractive than a supposedly democratic and progressive one sponsored by powers which maintained imperial rights and attitudes on Chinese territory. However, the dominance of nationalist historiography after Japan's defeat in 1945 meant that this consideration of two opposing ideologies, each potentially viable, had to be recast as an 'inevitable' victory for the forces of democratic nationalism over anomalous and venal collaborators.[28]

---

[25] However, it should be noted that there are non-state manifestations of radical Islam which provide a theologically informed response, varying between complement and counterpoint, to those norms in our own day.

[26] This case has been powerfully made in the context of Europe in Mark Mazower, *Dark Continent: Europe's Twentieth Century* (London: Allen Lane, 1998).

[27] Ishiwara Kanji, the architect of the Manchurian crisis, is one of the more notable Japanese pan-Asianists to have later been deeply troubled at the exploitative and brutal nature of wartime Japanese imperialism in China. He advocated a more cooperative partnership between China and Japan against the West all the way through the Pacific war. See Mark Peattie, *Ishiwara Kanji and Japan's Confrontation with the West* (Princeton: Princeton University Press, 1975).

[28] See David P. Barrett and Larry N. Shyu (eds), *Chinese Collaboration with Japan: The Limits of Accommodation, 1932–1945* (Stanford: Stanford University Press, 2001).

3. ORDER AND JUSTICE IN THE MAO ERA

The Sino-Japanese War ended with China on the victors' side, but it was immediately followed by the devastating civil war and the eventual victory of the Chinese Communist Party (CCP) in 1949. The first quarter-century of the PRC, inevitably associated with the rule of Mao Zedong, shows both continuities with and changes from Republican understandings of order and justice in the international community. The PRC was not the first Chinese government to have openly advocated 'revolutionary diplomacy'—this had, after all, been the aim of the Nationalists before the forced reorientation of their agenda in 1931—but it was the first to be in a strong enough position to act on the intention and furthermore, to do so beyond China's traditional geographical reach. The PRC marks a high point in the modern Chinese ability and desire to act as a revisionist power in the international order. Furthermore, Mao's own convictions as a romantic revolutionary leader who wanted to carve a distinct place for China in the international community gave additional impetus to the formulation of a new order.[29] Even before the Sino-Soviet split of 1960, China's attempts to set its own international agenda were made clear.

Since 1949, the CCP has portrayed itself in a variety of guises, sometimes simultaneously. Even while trying to work out the nature of its relationship as the USSR's Cold War ally in the 1950s, the PRC used fora such as the 1955 Bandung Conference to try to position China as a potential Third World leader. During the Mao era, the official rhetoric was largely anti-imperialist and in favour of freedom and liberation for colonized peoples. This seemed only natural: having liberated themselves from a century of Western oppression, the Chinese were in a good position to feel sympathy for other peoples in the same position. Mao's rhetoric during this period was powerful. In 1960, for instance, he made public statements that 'expressed full sympathy and support for the heroic struggle of the African people against imperialism and colonialism ... [and] the patriotic and just struggles of the South Korean people and the Turkish people against U. S. imperialism and its running dogs'.[30] The most important document in this context was Lin Biao's 1965 article, 'Long Live the Victory of the People's War!', which declared that Mao's revolutionary strategy was a blueprint for wars of national liberation around the globe.[31] During this period, China was the most prominent global advocate of

---

[29] See, for instance, John Lewis Gaddis, *We Now Know: Rethinking Cold War History* (Oxford: Oxford University Press, 1997), Ch. 3.

[30] Mao Zedong in *Hongqi*, 10 (1960), cited in Stuart R. Schram, *The Political Thought of Mao Tse-tung* (Harmondsworth: Pelican, 1969), 380.

[31] Thomas W. Robinson, 'Chinese Foreign Policy from the 1940s to the 1990s', in Thomas W. Robinson and David Shambaugh (eds), *Chinese Foreign Policy: Theory and Practice*

what Hedley Bull characterized as a revolutionary view of justice in international society, which gave priority to justice, however defined, even if it led to the destruction of international order.[32] In Beijing's terms, justice in the high Cold War era was tied strongly to anti-imperialist, Marxist-led nationalist movements, that is, movements whose experience was similar to that of the CCP itself.

China's interventions in various disputes show that the rhetoric was sometimes matched by policy decisions. Before sending People's Liberation Army 'volunteers' into Korea, Mao enjoined them to remember that they were fighting 'in order to support the Korean people's war of liberation and to resist the attacks of US imperialism'.[33] Mao also actively supported the Vietnamese communist movement, and had frequent meetings with leaders of the National Liberation Front (NLF); after a souring of relations with the Vietnamese, his radical urges in south-east Asia were turned towards Pol Pot and the Khmer Rouge in Cambodia. Particularly notable was Beijing's support for the PKI, the Indonesian Communist Party, in the early 1960s, which led to the coup attempt of 1965 by an Indonesian military, unhappy at the increasing influence of a Chinese-backed party in their domestic politics.[34] Both the US and the USSR noted the virulence of Beijing's revolutionary language and used examples such as Korea and Indonesia to argue that China could not easily be socialized into the international community.

However, the rhetoric and sometimes the reality of the PRC acting as an agent of anti-imperialism contrasts with the less confrontational Five Principles of Peaceful Coexistence, first articulated at Bandung in 1955 and periodically revived at times when China wishes to turn a cooperative face toward the international community. The combination of these approaches has, in Samuel Kim's phrase, allowed China 'to be all things to all nations on global issues'.[35] In Korea and south-east Asia, the revolutionary agenda had real bite. Elsewhere, relatively little of China's active rhetoric of liberation during the Mao era was translated into practical attempts to upset the established international order.[36] Even at a time when it appeared that China was implacably

---

(Oxford: Oxford University Press, 1994), 558; Peter Van Ness, *Revolution and Chinese Foreign Policy: Peking's Support for Wars of National Liberation* (Berkeley: University of California Press, 1970), 69.

[32] Hedley Bull, *The Anarchical Society: A Study of Order in World Politics*, 2nd edn (Basingstoke: Macmillan, 1995), 90.

[33] Mao Tse-tung (Mao Zedong), *Selected Works*, v (Beijing: Foreign Languages Press, 1977), 43.

[34] See Van Ness, *Revolution and Chinese Foreign Policy*, 101–10.

[35] Samuel S. Kim, 'China's International Organizational Behaviour', in Robinson and Shambaugh, *Chinese Foreign Policy*, 403.

[36] For an account of how Chinese liberationist rhetoric mostly coexisted with acceptance of the status quo in post-war Africa, see Philip Snow, 'China and Africa: Consensus and Camouflage', in Robinson and Shambaugh, *Chinese Foreign Policy*.

opposed to the dominant order, there were also signs that it was prepared to compromise as well as confront.

The rhetoric of revolution also hides another complication that comes to light particularly in the Chinese intervention in Vietnam. Mao's statement of support for the NLF in 1967 is well-known: 'The fraternal people of southern Vietnam and the entire fraternal Vietnamese people can rest assured that your struggle is our struggle.'[37] However, through the official CCP rhetoric and into the present day, one can see a very powerful and much older mind-set that defines a just international order not only in terms of anti-imperialism but in terms of a strong China first and foremost. The rhetoric of equality between nations has been valuable at times when it is China that is being disadvantaged, but when China wishes to impose its strength such ideas go by the board. Just as Soviet foreign policy cannot be honestly assessed without understanding the importance of pan-Slavism and great Russian chauvinism, so the Chinese sense of their own place in a just international order must take ideas of Chinese regional hegemony into account. One clear and rather poignant example of this came to light in the conversations between Mao and Vietnamese leaders who came to Beijing during the Vietnam war.[38] Statements such as Mao's comment to Nguyen Thi Binh in 1972, 'We belong to the same family. The North (Vietnam), the South (Vietnam), Indochina and Korea, we belong to the same family and support one another' and the request of Mao that a Vietnamese name be 'translated' into Chinese hint, not too subtly, at China's continuing desire to be the 'elder brother' in the revolutionary order.[39] While this factor does not erase the reality of 'fraternal assistance' under Mao, it certainly complicates it.

4. ORDER AND JUSTICE IN THE CONTEMPORARY ERA: THE NATURE OF THE DEBATE

Gei Zhongguo yige jihui—Give China a chance!—was a much-heard slogan in the run-up to the September 1993 decision by the International Olympic Committee (IOC) on where the 2000 Olympics would be held. The Chinese authorities were confident that Beijing would be the chosen city. This confidence led to Tian'anmen Square being decorated with hundreds of 'Beijing 2000' banners in the run-up to the decision, banners which mysteriously

---

[37] Mao Zedong, in *Renmin Ribao* [People's Daily] (19 December 1967), in Schram, *Political Thought*.

[38] These conversations have been translated and edited in Odd Arne Westad *et al.* (eds), *77 Conversations between Chinese And Foreign Leaders on the Wars in Indochina, 1964–1977*, Cold War International History Project Working Paper 22 (Washington, DC: Woodrow Wilson International Center for Scholars, 1998).   [39] Westad *et al.*, *Conversations*, 185, 186, 18.

disappeared immediately after the announcement of Sydney's victory.[40] But the memory of that snub did not, and it was felt by Chinese at all levels to be a continuing sign that the US-dominated world order was attempting to shut China out, with the IOC being held up as representative of the wider international community. The phrase 'give China a chance' summed up the issue that many felt was at stake: China was attempting to obtain its rightful place in the international community, and if it were denied that place, as with the Olympics, it was not just a shame but symbolic of a wider systemic injustice. The award in 2001 of the 2008 summer Games to Beijing did not change the underlying suspicions in Chinese minds. For, even in the contemporary era, China does not regard the international order as a neutral forum. Rather, it sees itself as a victim deserving compensation for the slights of history. Although post-Mao foreign policy has been marked by a new pragmatism, its dealings with the wider world are still shot through with classical Marxist thinking—using terms such as 'hegemonism'—and the Beijing government is in foreign affairs the inheritor of the historical baggage of its Qing and Republican forbears. Yet at other times it projects itself as a 'great power' (*daguo*). This mixture of victimology and aggrandizement is a potent one.

When one considers the nature of current Chinese debates on the relationship between order and justice in international society, it is notable that the discourse is still largely controlled by agencies of the state. Since the ascent of Deng Xiaoping in 1978, China can no longer be termed a totalitarian state, and the level of free expression is incomparably greater than it was, say, during the Cultural Revolution. However, there are still significant boundaries on what can be said or published, particularly on sensitive subjects such as China's national security. Gerald Chan, in his comprehensive survey of contemporary Chinese thinking on international relations, notes that even in academic discussions of international relations, where varying views and debates are clearly to be heard, 'the official views inevitably seep through academic writing'.[41] Similarly, in his pioneering work on China's 'America Watchers', David Shambaugh notes that 'Chinese intellectuals have long had a symbiotic relationship with the state'.[42] This is not to argue that there are therefore no differences of view expressed in China on these issues but to emphasize that the debates take place within defined limits and that the differences between governmental and academic sources used below should not be exaggerated.

What, then, does the CCP and the government it controls see as a just world order in the post-Mao, post-Cold War era? It is clear that the idea of 'national

[40] Geremie Barme, 'To Screw Foreigners is Patriotic', 188.

[41] Gerald Chan, *Chinese Perspectives on International Relations: A Framework for Analysis* (Basingstoke: Macmillan, 1999), xii.

[42] David Shambaugh, *Beautiful Imperialist: China Perceives America, 1972–1990* (Princeton: Princeton University Press, 1991), 289.

sovereignty' based on territorial definitions has become paramount for the
Chinese in the post-Mao era as the rhetoric of exporting revolution has been
abandoned. While it has had to come to terms with the solidarist agenda that
has superseded the strictly territorially bounded interpretation of sovereignty
in global discourse, China remains wary of agendas which cross borders. It is
understandable why sovereignty looms so large; after all, almost every incur-
sion onto Chinese soil between 1839 and 1945 was based on some interpretation of international law, however dubious: the opium wars, the refusal to
return German colonies to Chinese sovereignty at the Paris peace conference,
the Japanese occupation of Manchuria. It is therefore unsurprising that after
the death of Mao, the more pragmatic successor Chinese leadership found the
international order which had dominated the world during most of the post-
Second World War era to be in fact fairly congenial to them. This order was
largely based on a doctrine of non-interference in the domestic affairs of other
countries, and marked an era during which Hedley Bull could write that 'the
framework of international order is quite inhospitable to projects for the realization of cosmopolitan or world justice'.[43]

However, as Foot has argued, the Chinese leadership rejoined the world
order just as its values were changing, moving on significantly from the
Bullian formulation and allowing 'common values and some notion of the
common good' to be given priority.[44] This change seemed, once again, to
many Chinese policy-makers to be a means of wrong-footing the Chinese
within the international order. As will be seen below, events such as the 1999
Kosovo war in particular made the Chinese government very worried. The
scenario in which a government attempting to put down ethnic conflict on
its own territory could then be subjected to attack by NATO was deeply troub-
ling for the Beijing leadership, which has separatist problems of its own in
Xinjiang and Tibet. The human rights debate that regularly comes into play
when China's place in the world is discussed also worries Beijing, which
takes issue in many ways with Western definitions of 'human rights'.[45] One
significant point of conflict is that the Chinese leadership sees justice in the
international community as being *primarily* a collective issue for a country
rather than for individuals within those countries. However, the Chinese leadership also knows that there are no longer realistic alternatives to participation in the new global order, and therefore its strategy has been participation
within that order's structures while lobbying to preserve its own viewpoints
and interests.

[43] Bull, *The Anarchical Society*, 83.

[44] Rosemary Foot, 'Chinese Power and the Idea of a Responsible State', *The China Journal*,
45 (January 2001), 2.

[45] For an account of the issues surrounding China's engagement with international human
rights debates, Foot, *Rights Beyond Borders*, is the most comprehensive discussion.

Chinese foreign policy after Mao switched rather suddenly from supporting a revolutionary ideology to preferring a system-maintaining one. The high level of control that a small central leadership has been able to exercise in communist China explains the speed of the transformation. The change in orientation is also explicable in the context of the goals of the leadership group dominated by Deng Xiaoping, the paramount leader from 1978. Domestically, the need to recover from the social and economic chaos of the Cultural Revolution meant that trade and expertise from abroad were actively embraced, and this meant engagement, not confrontation, with the Western-dominated global order. Domestic necessity forced the revolutionary state to follow international norms. Furthermore, as discussed above, even at its most rhetorically menacing, the Chinese leadership had held back from large-scale active fomentation of international disorder, and events such as the opening to the US in 1971–2 showed that détente was possible even under Mao. Since 1978, the primary paradigm has, with some exceptions, been pragmatic, policy-driven realism expressed in idealist language. In an analysis of Dengist foreign policy, Li Xiangqian, a researcher from the Central Party Historical Research Institute, characterized the massive demobilization of China's armed forces in 1985 as 'a crucial action' which 'shook the world'. In Deng's own words, 'Now that we are establishing that we are a peaceful power, it is absolutely essential that we remove the appearance of being a warlike power, and [show] that we really want to take on this role'.[46] No more would China stalk the world stage calling for revolution.

Yet, beyond generalities, it is hard to characterize just what China's new position was. Chinese international relations scholars have been trapped in what Samuel Kim has characterized as an imbalance between 'right-based theory and might-based practice': 'far from theory being a guide to action, Chinese scholars seem to be seeking to capture an ever-shifting Chinese policy as a guide to theoretical formulation.'[47] Yong Deng notes that 'the emerging consensus among Chinese authors is that national interests in international relations can be understood *sui generis* and are to be separated from domestic politics'.[48] This overwhelming desire to separate the domestic and international spheres, and to commodify the 'national interest' so that it cannot be unpicked further into separate or, worse, individual interests, is central to Chinese approaches to questions of order and justice in international society.

[46] Li Xiangqian, 'Deng Xiaoping dui dangdai Zhongguo waijiao xingxiang de zhanlue sikao' [Reflections on Deng Xiaoping's policy on the shape of contemporary Chinese foreign relations], in Gong Li (ed.), *Deng Xiaoping de waijiao sixiang yu shijian* [Deng Xiaoping's foreign policy thought and practice] (Harbin: Heilongjiang jiaoyu chubanshe, 1996), 40.

[47] Kim, 'Chinese International Organizational Behaviour', 402–3.

[48] Yong Deng, 'The Chinese Conception of National Interests in International Relations', *The China Quarterly*, 154 (June 1998), 313. See also Yongjin Zhang, 'International Relations Theory in China Today: The State of the Field', *The China Journal*, 47 (January 2002).

One crucial issue is language, just as it was during the late nineteenth century. For the most part, the analysis of order and justice in Chinese policy circles is still tied to the linguistic and philosophical repertoire introduced via Japan during the late Qing; and the Westernized and Marxist bias of Chinese social sciences, particularly since 1949, has meant that elements from non-Western analytic traditions, even China's own, are very hard to find. The active hostility to Chinese traditional thought during the height of the May Fourth 'new culture' movement of the 1920s and the whole of Mao's period in power, culminating in the policy to smash 'old thinking' during the Cultural Revolution, further withered enthusiasm to work creatively on an engagement between classical Chinese thought and Western social science and philosophy. For that reason, it has become far less fruitful to try to contrast Western and non-Western elements—and their hybrids—in Chinese international behaviour than has been the case with the Islamic states, India under its Hindu ultra-nationalist government, or even perhaps post-communist Russia. In the 1990s, as the CCP begins to legitimize some aspects of Chinese traditional culture as part of its new nation-building project, there are some analysts who are attempting to use classical Chinese thinking to develop a new interpretation of international relations, but they are still relatively few in number.[49]

5. HUMAN RIGHTS AND SOVEREIGNTY

Nonetheless, the fact that concepts are relative neologisms does not rob them of their power, and communist China's rejection of the pre-modern past until very recently has forced Chinese thinkers into dealing with the pack of political cards dealt by the Western-dominated order. The compatibility or conflict between notions of order and justice in international society is as important a topic in current Chinese thinking as it is in the West. However, the *terms* in which these ideas are understood are significantly different. It is especially notable that the dominant discourse in Chinese international relations attempts to coordinate two strands that are somewhat at odds. On the one hand, there is a strong desire to define an avowedly Chinese, or non-Western, position on issues such as human rights, humanitarian interventions, the primacy of national sovereignty, and so forth. On the other, the arguments are all made within the linguistic and conceptual constraints of international

[49] Song Xinning, 'Building International Relations Theory with Chinese Characteristics', *Journal of Contemporary China*, 10/26 (2001), 70. For an example of one discussion along these lines, see Chen Lai, 'Shei zhi zeren? Shei zhong lunli?: Cong rujia lunli kan shijie lunli xuanyan' [Whose responsibility? Whose ethics? Looking at a world declaration of ethics from a Confucian ethical point of view], *Dushu* [Readings], 10 (1998), 8–12.

relations as defined in the West, and quite often use and adapt solidarist terms. Rather than any indigenous concepts, most of the terms of discussion are set up as adaptations of existing Western-derived concepts: thus the Chinese alternative to 'human rights' is 'socialist human rights' and a response to calls for 'justice' is a demand for 'global social justice'.[50] The Chinese position is less to deny the validity of the terminology in which the debate on the new world order takes place than to appropriate its terms and redefine them according to its own agenda.

China's willingness to use and appropriate solidarist language stems from a wider tendency since 1978 to operate within the norms of international order. Most Chinese writing on foreign policy serves to explain or justify China's role as a 'responsible state' in the new order.[51] Many aspects of China's behaviour support the argument that, broadly speaking, the country follows international norms and adapts its actions so as not to violate those norms where it can avoid doing so. Nonetheless, Chinese writings do not tend to stress the importance of new global issues and values at the expense of national sovereignty. There are a few scholars who argue that national sovereignty has become a more fissile concept because of the new importance of globalization and non-state actors, but they are still very much in a minority.[52] The arguments analysed below represent the mainstream of thinking, which maintains a pluralist reality while trying to adopt the language of solidarism.

In the following sections, the views of analysts attached to the Institute for International Relations in Beijing, recently renamed the Foreign Affairs College, are used as a microcosm of wider thinking in the Chinese leadership about the nature of order and justice in the post-Cold War world. The Institute is affiliated to the Ministry of Foreign Affairs, and Gerald Chan describes it as one of the major think tanks which is 'more concerned with policy studies and the analysis of current events ... than IR as an academic discipline'. Certainly the reflection of official positions is very clear in the writings published in the Institute's main publication, *Guoji guanxi xueyuan xuebao* (*GGXX*: 'Journal of the Institute of International Relations').[53]

In one typical piece dealing with the sovereignty issue in the context of a more transnational global society, the analyst Ji Xiaogong writes: 'Any country,

---

[50] The wider issue of how far post-colonial nations derive their discourses from colonial models is discussed in Partha Chatterjee, *Nationalist Thought and the Colonial World: A Derivative Discourse?* (London: Zed Books, 1986).

[51] Foot, 'Chinese Power', 15–17. See also Xia Liping, 'China: A Responsible Great Power', *Journal of Contemporary China*, 10/26 (2001).   [52] Chan, *Chinese Perspectives*, 79.

[53] Chan, *Chinese Perspectives*, 96. I am grateful to Professor Song Xinning of Renmin University for giving me further information about the College of Foreign Affairs, formerly the Institute of International Relations. The College's website is http://www.fac.edu.cn (in Chinese, with some English text).

nation, and people which strives for development and progress, and is moving toward civilization and a system of law, will positively seize and maintain the implementation of human rights.'[54] However, he then states that 'human rights is a socio-historical categorization' and goes on to pursue the argument that the concept is not universal but contingent on historical development and circumstances. Ji offers a sophisticated Marxist argument that human rights are a product of the capitalist system's need to combat the influence of religion in Europe, but makes an uncompromising conclusion on this basis: 'human rights are a "specialized product" of the advanced countries of Europe and America, but they do not have any connection with the majority of countries and peoples in Asia, Africa, and Latin America.'[55]

This conclusion shows another tendency: once again, as in the age of Bandung, China puts itself forward as a voice for the developing world and against perceived Western, particularly American, hegemonism (*baquanzhuyi*). Ji argues that countries in the developing world have historically had their human rights denied by colonialism, and their poverty means that they have given priority to their 'right to survival'. Now that these countries are no longer formally colonized, he argues, the discourse of human rights and freedom is used to further the interests of capitalism: for instance, Western 'freedom' means the 'freedom to own property privately'.[56] Thus the Western concern with human rights is not, in this conception, primarily concerned with increasing justice but rather with hindering the redistribution of power and wealth between states. Ji states that developing countries believe human rights to be economic, not just social, and that such rights are not just individual but collective.

Ji's stress on collectivism is essential to the most dominant thread of argument running through Chinese writing on this topic: the primacy of a Westphalian definition of national sovereignty. Stressing China's role as a voice for the Third World, Ji notes that almost all human rights resolutions at the UN are aimed at developing countries, and praises China's role in actively fighting back against such resolutions. 'There is a mistaken international view', he states of the West, 'that all western countries' human rights situations are just fine, and that all developing countries' human rights situations are wrong.'[57] However, as will be seen below, China's objections are in fact relatively rarely turned into actual vetoes at the UN. Furthermore, China has taken part in various international human rights treaties and bodies, for instance in 1998 signing—although not, at the time of writing, ratifying—the International Covenant on Civil and Political

---

[54] Ji Xiaogong, 'Guoji renquan wenti jiqi zai fazhanzhong guojia de shixian' [The international human rights problem and its implementation in developing countries], *Guoji guanxi xueyuan xuebao* [Journal of the Institute of International Relations: Beijing], *GGXX*, 2 (1998), 1.

[55] Ji Xiaogong, 'Guoji renquan wenti jiqi zai fazhanzhong guojia de shixian', 2.

[56] Ji Xiaogong, 'Guoji renquan wenti jiqi zai fazhanzhong guojia de shixian', 4.

[57] Ji Xiaogong, 'Guoji renquan wenti jiqi zai fazhanzhong guojia de shixian', 5.

Rights and in 1982 becoming a member of the UN Commission on Human Rights.[58] Since there are no immediate penalties for not joining these bodies, China's behaviour seems to show it torn between criticisms of an international order that seems unfriendly to some aspects of China's domestic policy, and participation in a system of which it wishes to become a respected part so as to fulfil its aim of being a 'great power'. Engagement with the system also allows China to adapt it to its own purposes, as with the UN conference on racism held in Durban, South Africa, in 2001, where Beijing's pressure prevented the issue of Tibet being given more than a cursory mention and stopped at least one hostile NGO from being invited to attend.[59]

As has been repeatedly stressed above, despite Chinese mistrust of the transnational solidarist agenda of the new order, Chinese official policy has been to sign up to parts of it and broadly to follow norms that allow it to present itself as a 'responsible power'. This restraint is shown in the language of officially sponsored sources such as those cited above. However, despite the lack of what would be characterized in the West as a truly autonomous public sphere, there are significant voices who are published in other officially permitted journals but whose agenda is less constrained by the specific demands of government foreign policy. These writers give an insight into how issues of what China is owed by the international community—but rarely what the international community might demand from China—are discussed amongst those intellectuals who are not directly involved in policy-making but who can be regarded as opinion-formers in the rarefied world of Chinese intellectual elites.

Geremie Barme, writing in the mid-1990s, characterized the dominant Chinese discourse among Chinese intellectuals as 'a crude pre-World War I positivism' which has been fuelled by media hype about the Asian miracle.[60] Powerful among them was a form of conservative thought which had been stimulated in particular by Samuel Huntington's famous article and then book *The Clash of Civilizations*, which was translated in China and received great attention there. Huntington's conservative Chinese critics engaged with his work while critiquing it strongly. In the journal *Zhanlue yu guanli* ('Strategy and Management') in 1994, the critic Wang Xiaodong rebuffed Huntington's model that the new world order would circulate around culture. Wang did not accept the idea that China could now be called a Confucian civilization in any

---

[58] Foot, *Rights Beyond Borders*, 3.

[59] 'Race Concessions Fail to Appease US', *The Guardian* (27 August 2001), 9. On the hesitant nature of Chinese responses to international regimes, see Elizabeth Economy, 'The Impact of International Regimes in Chinese Foreign Policy-Making: Broadening Perspectives and Policies … But Only to a Point', in David M. Lampton (ed.), *The Making of Chinese Foreign and Security Policy in the Era of Reform, 1978–2000* (Stanford: Stanford University Press, 2001).

[60] Barme, 'To Screw Foreigners is Patriotic', 189.

meaningful sense, and noted that China did not aim to Confucianize the rest of the world. In effect, Wang said that conflicts which may be termed 'cultural' or 'ideological' are really only a new way of masking traditional national interest, a position, in effect, in which order is subordinated to power, not justice. In this world-view, justice as an issue in international relations can been seen only as a chimera: there is *only* power.[61] This is at odds with the official position, which tends to talk idealist while acting realist. There are other readings that dissent from this view, of course. *Dushu* ('Readings') is one of the more venerable 'liberal' journals, and it frequently presents views that do not posit a necessary opposition to the West. However, scholars have used it as a forum to argue that discussions about cultural relativism, orientalism, and so on are merely examples of how the ways in which various countries which have been hard done by in the world order buy into a patronizing Western discourse which deigns to include them. This is hardly a liberal position as recognized in the West, but is nonetheless a powerful one, reflecting disillusionment with the more uncritical pro-Western strands of thought that characterized some of the classically 'liberal' May Fourth generation of the 1920s.[62]

Domestic mass audiences also receive a more confrontational account of the issue of justice for past wrongs done to China, particularly in the presentation of the relationship with Japan. Edward Friedman has astutely observed that the Tokyo-Beijing relationship filters into areas of domestic discussion where it does not immediately seem relevant, again including the Kosovo bombing.[63] It is easier to understand how the perception of a threat from Japan has become widespread in Chinese society when one notes the immense financial and ideological investment that has been made by the PRC government since the mid-1980s in a wholesale recasting of popular memory of imperialism and the 1937–45 Sino-Japanese war: broadly speaking, before that date the war period was heavily underplayed in CCP historiography, whereas it now forms part of an educational and popular culture that rekindles popular memory of Japanese atrocities in China. This creates a widespread feeling that Japan must be made to pay for its past crimes, a feeling which can then be leveraged by the Beijing government to seek economic and diplomatic concessions from Japan.[64] Again, it should be stressed that these more confrontational views do not dominate China's international behaviour, which remains constrained by norms. However, it is not sufficient simply to ignore their significance in the mental maps of the policy-making classes in

[61] Barme, 'To Screw Foreigners is Patriotic', 190–2.
[62] Barme, 'To Screw Foreigners is Patriotic', 193.
[63] Friedman, 'Preventing War Between China and Japan', 99–100.
[64] See Rana Mitter, 'Behind the Scenes at the Museum: History, Memory and Nationalism in the Beijing War of Resistance Museum, 1987–1997', *The China Quarterly*, 161 (March 2000).

Beijing.[65] Furthermore, domestic public opinion, once galvanized, is not entirely under the control of the state. While it is always in control of the foreign policy agenda, Beijing still needs to find ways to explain that policy that will please the differing demands of its domestic as well as its foreign audiences.[66]

6. KOSOVO AND THE LIMITS OF HUMANITARIAN INTERVENTION

National sovereignty is essential to the Chinese definition of a just world order. It should be emphasized that, as part of its engagement with the international order, China became reconciled to enterprises such as peacekeeping operations, agreeing to pay towards some of them and even, from 1990, taking part as an observer.[67] Furthermore, in 1994 China abstained from, rather than vetoing, UN Security Council (UNSC) resolutions to set up international presences in Rwanda and Haiti, and voted in favour of a multinational force in Bosnia and the possibility of such a force in Zaire between 1995 and 1997.[68] It also took part in UN operations in Cambodia and East Timor.[69]

However, Chinese policy-makers rarely seem very enthusiastic to their domestic audience about such actions in the international arena. Much more prominent for this audience is the influence of an educational system and media that repeatedly stress the need to resist violations of Chinese sovereignty in the present because of the crises of the past. Ji Xiaogong states flatly and definitively: 'One cannot use the question of human rights to interfere in other countries' internal politics.'[70] Writing in the 1970s, Walzer's example of a justified humanitarian intervention was the case of the Indian army in the

---

[65] On occasion, the Chinese leadership can call up popular anti-Japanese anger when it feels that it needs leverage with Tokyo. For example, since the 1980s Chinese calls for reparations for the Rape of Nanjing have been used to put pressure on the Japanese government to supply more generous aid to China. See Mark Eykholt, 'Aggression, Victimization, and Chinese Historiography of the Nanjing Massacre', in Joshua A. Fogel (ed.), *The Nanjing Massacre in History and Historiography* (Berkeley: University of California Press, 2000), 51.

[66] For a wide-ranging account of domestic factors in the shaping of Chinese foreign policy, see Joseph Fewsmith and Stanley Rosen, 'The Domestic Context of Chinese Foreign Policy: Does "Public Opinion" Matter?' in Lampton, *Making of Chinese Foreign and Security Policy*.

[67] Sally Morphet, 'China as a Permanent Member of the Security Council, October 1971–December 1999', *Security Dialogue*, 31/2 (2000), 160.

[68] Morphet, 'China as a Permanent Member', 161.

[69] However this participation has been somewhat hesitant. See Samuel Kim, 'China and the United Nations,' in Elizabeth Economy and Michel Oksenberg (ed.), *China Joins the World: Progress and Prospects* (New York: Council on Foreign Relations Press, 1999), 55.

[70] Ji 'Guoji renquan', 5.

East Pakistan war of 1971.[71] At the turn of the twenty-first century, a prominent case has been the bombing of Serbia during the 1999 Kosovo war. This example is, if anything, even more important for the Chinese because of the destruction of the Chinese embassy in Belgrade in a NATO bombing raid. Discussions of the morality of the bombing of Belgrade in China have not tended to weigh up issues of sovereignty versus humanitarian imperatives, but have painted the issue firmly as one of egregious NATO, and particularly US, hegemonism. They show the limits of Chinese adaptation to solidarist concepts. One piece written in the wake of the Kosovo war by two philosophers from Fudan University in Shanghai, Tang Jianbo and Chen Jiandong, again shows the way in which Western-derived discursive models are shaped to fit a Chinese agenda. The article argues that the new world order needs a new global ethics, and it starts in a way that echoes much Western discussion, suggesting that the old world order had no effective way to deal with global problems and acknowledging that a state's domestic problems can sometimes become matters of international concern, particularly when internal disturbances harm the stability of neighbouring states. However, the authors then argue that a strengthened international law is needed to prevent 'hegemonism in international society', and go on: 'The international intervention caused by the Kosovo problem made us develop doubts about the existing international law.'[72]

Once again, it becomes clear that the 'global ethics' which is advocated here does not reflect solidarist values of justice, but is still based on the irreducible core of the inviolability of national sovereignty. Moving away from Kosovo, the authors condemn US and British air raids on Iraq on the grounds that they did not have UN approval—which China, it is implied, would not give. They stress at length the need for 'global social justice'—again, referring mainly to economic development—and argue that the new global ethics should transcend national boundaries to develop a 'greater feeling of global responsibility'. Yet they are at pains to stress that the 'so-called spreading of human rights' is the propagation of a Western set of values that are not truly global.[73] At no point in this discussion of 'global ethics' are the issues such as ethnic cleansing which prompted NATO intervention in Kosovo discussed on their own merits: instead, the Kosovo case is used to argue an agenda which speaks to interests of China, expressed through its role as a representative of the Third World as a whole. Wu Xinbo, also of Fudan University, writing in a Western journal, observes that 'the Chinese media has never presented a comprehensive and balanced picture about the situation in Kosovo, nor did it criticize

---

[71] Michael Walzer, *Just and Unjust Wars: A Moral Argument with Historical Illustrations* (New York: Basic Books, 1977), 105–7.

[72] Tang Jianbo and Chen Jiandong, 'Quanqiu lunli yu guoji xin zhixu de jianli' [The establishment of global ethics and a new international order], *GGXX*, 3 (2000), 9–10.

[73] Tang and Chen, 'Quanqiu lunli yu guoji xin zhixu de jianli', 12–13.

Milosevic's policy toward the ethnic Albanians', as their greatest concern was to prevent the break-up of Yugoslavia's territorial integrity.[74]

Similar in its premises is an article by Wu Hui on 'Undertaking international responsibilities', which also uses Kosovo as a starting point. Again, the premise appears to be solidarist at first but turns out to be a more complex argument for pluralism. Here, the international responsibilities which are under discussion are those of the US—no pretence is made that it is NATO rather than the US which is the target—to pay compensation for its 'clear violation of international law' which 'inflamed the anger of the Chinese masses'.[75] An international court needs to be established, argues Wu, so that the 'private legal structures of the superpowers' do not dominate international behaviour. The position is made even clearer in Wang Hui's analysis of US democratization projects in former communist states in eastern Europe, condemned as 'hegemonism' aimed at setting up a 'Pax Americana', which by implication will take on China next. Economic and political hegemonism are combined, he argues, when countries such as Kenya and China are made to sign up to American definitions of 'democracy' and 'human rights' before they are permitted to receive foreign aid or enter the World Trade Organization (WTO). At one point, Wang refers to American expansion as *yexin*; the term literally means 'wild ambition' but is particularly significant because it became a staple of Chinese political discourse in the 1930s when reference was made to Japanese expansion on the Chinese mainland.[76] 'National sovereignty is still what the majority of countries prize most', concludes Wang.

Yet sometimes one does encounter discussion of other issues in international society where it serves China's interests to contradict its normal position on sovereignty and outside involvement in domestic conflicts. In 1981–2, for example, China reversed its previous opposition to the use of UN peacekeeping forces, and approved and even paid a contribution towards UNFICYP, the force sent to Cyprus.[77] In this case, there was no direct benefit to China to doing so, and its action helped to reposition China as a responsible member of the world community, reinforcing Foot's argument that China is seeking to accommodate itself to the new global norms even when there is no direct sanction or penalty associated with not doing so.[78]

China is not always entirely disinterested on the question of humanitarian intervention, however. The issue has in the past come a little closer to home

---

[74] Wu Xinbo, 'Four Contradictions Constraining China's Foreign Policy Behaviour', *Journal of Contemporary China*, 10/27 (2001), 295.

[75] Wu Hui, 'Lun guoji zeren de chengdan' [Undertaking international responsibilities], *GGXX*, 4 (1999), 8.

[76] Wang Hui, 'Meiguo duiwai ganyu de xin quxiang' [America's new tendency to intervene in foreign affairs], *GGXX*, 1 (2000), 17–19.

[77] Kim, 'China's International Organizational Behaviour', 422.

[78] Foot, *Rights Beyond Borders*, 258. See also Morphet, 'China as a Permanent Member', 160.

on one of the most pressing transnational issues, that of refugees. Wu Hui has written about the position of refugees in international law, noting that China has signed up to international declarations on the protection of refugees. The two cases where China has accepted people fleeing conflict under these protocols were in 1978–9 and in 1981–2, where refugees, mostly ethnic Chinese, from Vietnam were taken in: 286,000 in the first case and around 2,500 in the second. Yet, as Bonnie Glaser has observed, China's behaviour during the Sino-Vietnamese war of 1979 contradicted what would become its position during the Kosovo conflict in two fundamental ways: first and most obviously by the violation of Vietnamese sovereignty, and second by accepting the expelled ethnic Chinese minority onto Chinese soil as genuine refugee victims, in effect, of 'ethnic cleansing'.[79] However, it is hard to conceive of active Chinese involvement in such a case which did not directly affect the interests of China. Elsewhere, inactive neutrality seems to be China's preferred position.

In sum, the Chinese position allows it to observe many of the norms of the new world order without necessarily welcoming them wholeheartedly. Despite its self-positioning as a champion of Third World sovereignty against Western hegemonism in the UN, China's veto in the UNSC has in practice been used only quite rarely. It voted for 91.5 per cent of 625 resolutions passed between 1990 and 1999.[80] Furthermore, China has signed up to international covenants on human rights, suggesting at least a nominal acceptance of the idea of the international recognition of such rights. Nor has China shown any great enthusiasm for reform of the UNSC to allow more Third World countries to join it; although it has supported this position, it has hardly been active in pushing the issue to the top of the agenda. China signs up to the current consensus in large part on an instrumentalist basis, calculating that there are concrete and symbolic benefits to be gained from doing so, rather than from any widespread conversion to solidarist values within the policy-making classes. As long as the maintenance of a party state is paramount, there will always be a significant barrier in the way of internalization of those values.

7. NEO-IMPERIALISM AND INTERNATIONAL JUSTICE

One more immediately practical consequence of China's partial willingness to engage with solidarist values is the possibility of international structures

---

[79] Bonnie S. Glaser, 'Discussion of "Four Contradictions Constraining China's Foreign Policy Behaviour"', *Journal of Contemporary China*, 10/27 (2001), 305–6.
[80] Morphet, 'China as a Permanent Member', 160.

being used to right injustices in the international system when those injustices are perceived as collective ones. China's strategic use of the politics of victim-hood also emerges in its quest for what it sees as global justice on issues such as trade or the environment. On this interpretation, Chinese policy-makers tend to characterize China as a weak state defined, as Bates Gill has suggested, by what '*others do to China*', which conflicts with its desire to project itself as a great power.[81] Therefore, there are considerable advantages both domestically and internationally to China's projection of itself as a victimized country.

From the late 1990s onwards, China's desire to enter the WTO was a clear indication of its desire to integrate into international society and reap the advantages that come from subscribing to its norms.[82] Liu He, the executive vice-president of China's State Information Centre, made it clear that China expected tangible benefits from joining.[83] Liu acknowledged that there would be a short-term negative impact on employment and deflation but 'in general, the gain in social welfare will compensate the loss caused by the partial adverse impact of WTO'.[84] For the Chinese, the WTO issue is closely tied up with longer-standing historical memories of unfair trade, particularly the 'unequal treaties' and extraterritoriality forced on China in the late Qing era. Having decided to use victimhood as an important means of projecting its grievances and demands on the world stage, the Chinese government is in a good position to claim to be a victim once more if the new trade order fails to measure up to expectations.

Nor is China waiting to see what the results of WTO membership will be before securing its position, but has already staked a claim in areas where it perceives the global trading order to be unjust. An example of such an issue is 'environmental colonialism' (*huanjing zhiminzhuyi*). This term covers two separate but related issues: the use by developed countries of domestic environmental legislation to throw up barriers against imports from developing countries, and the dumping of polluted waste in developing countries; as China's own domestic priorities are focused more on economic growth than on environmental controls, it is perhaps unsurprising that it is the former that gains more attention. In the *GGXX*, Tao Yinliang addresses the fear that an 'environmental superpower'—again, the US—will 'unjustly' (*bugongzheng*) use environmentalist concerns as an excuse to set up neo-protectionist tariffs,

---

[81] Bates Gill, 'Discussion of "China: A Responsible Great Power"', *Journal of Contemporary China*, 10/26 (2001), 29.

[82] See Chapter 4. On the ambivalence in China's position on the WTO, see Margaret M. Pearson, 'The Case of China's Accession to the GATT/WTO', in Lampton, *Making of Chinese Foreign and Security Policy*.

[83] Liu He, 'Systematic Changes and New Institutional Arrangement After China's Accession to WTO', in Ippei Yamazawa and Ken-ichi Imai (eds), *China Enters WTO: Pursuing Symbiosis with the Global Economy* (Chiba, Japan: Institute of Developing Economies, Japan External Trade Organization, 2001), 8.   [84] Liu He, 'Systematic Changes', 10.

and cites Malaysian prime minister Mahathir Mohammed's warning in 1995
that Western concerns about the environment were another means of controlling growth in developing economies.[85] Tao's argument is framed in terms of
redistributive economic justice: among the issues he cites are that the US uses
25 per cent of the world's resources with only 5 per cent of its population, and
that Third World countries' intellectual property and patent rights on their own
natural products are being violated by First World multinationals. On the issue
of dumping Tao's language is extremely strong, referring to it as 'a pollution
invasion', the word 'invasion' (*ruqin*) once again being closely related to the
terms used for the Japanese invasion of China during the 1930s. Environmental
colonialism, in Tao's analysis, is simply an updated version of traditional
imperialist and hegemonist manoeuvres by developed countries, showing the
need again for an international order which will offer more justice to countries
such as China.

8. CONCLUSION

China is an active participant in the world order, but one somewhat ill at ease
with its own status and position. This is reflected in its changing self-projection
as a great power, wishing to play a dominant role in the new order, and as victim of history, seeking justice from an international community which it feels
served it ill over the last 150 years. The Chinese policy-making elite uses the
language of international engagement to define its place in the world order of
today; it talks in terms of human rights, international trade, and peaceful coexistence, while appropriating the meaning of those terms for its own purposes.
But we should beware of examining only those parts of the Chinese world-
view which fit with liberal Western perspectives—which, of course, are perceived in China not as liberal but hegemonist. The government of Chiang
Kai-shek also paid court to the values of international society in the inter-war
period through its membership of the League of Nations, participation in
international law conferences, and so on. However, that did not imply that
Chiang and his allies therefore internalized those values. The international
order was on trial then, and was perceived by most Chinese to have failed. It
is on trial again today, and the Chinese agenda encompasses ideas of justice
and of order, but on Chinese terms.

The contradictions in China's position are magnified by the challenge that
its half-desired, half-resented sister-state Taiwan presents. Taiwan's quest for

[85] Tao Yinliang, 'Luelun dangdai guoji guanxi zhongde huanjing zhiminzhuyi' [A discussion
of environmental colonialism in contemporary international relations], *GGXX*, 3 (1996), 9.

a new sense of national identity which combines Taiwanese and Chinese elements is regarded by Beijing as part of a hegemonist plot by outside powers to deprive China of territory that is 'rightfully' its: to cite an official PRC publication, 'in recent years, the movement for Taiwan independence on the island of Taiwan has become more strident, casting a shadow over cross-Straits relations and peaceful national reunification' because of the influence of 'foreign forces'.[86] The fact that Taiwanese former President Lee Teng-hui has made such play of his Japanese connections and upbringing merely adds to that suspicion; in a China which primarily sees issues through a realist lens of national interest. Taiwanese identity cannot easily be accommodated outside a Chinese sovereign context. However, the story is ambiguous, and if one looks for it there is also evidence that in this case the linear straitjacket of history has loosened a little. The same policy statement claims that Taiwan has been offered near-autonomy if it just accepts nominal sovereignty from Beijing, with specifically no interference in Taiwan's way of life, autonomy including in military affairs—something emphatically not granted to Hong Kong—and no mainland administrators on the island, although Taiwan would send representatives to Beijing.[87] Clearly Taiwan's government has the twin problems of deciding how far Beijing is sincere and dealing with the fact that a considerable part of Taiwan's population has reconfigured its sense of identity in a direction that does not accept even the slightest of connections with the Beijing regime. However, the Chinese position, on the face of it, sounds not dissimilar to the suzerainty agreements of the high Qing. It would be intriguing if a combination of the new global concepts of transnational justice and a precedent from the last glory days of the Chinese imperial order enabled China to solve its most pressing territorial question.

[86] *Taiwan wenti yu Zhongguo de tongyi* [The Taiwan problem and Chinese unity] (Beijing: Guowuyuan Taiwan shiwu bangongshe, 1993), 19–20.   [87] *Taiwan wenti*, 16.

9

Indian Conceptions of Order and Justice: Nehruvian, Gandhian, *Hindutva*, and Neo-Liberal

KANTI BAJPAI

As world politics becomes increasingly globalized, and hitherto marginal voices begin to be heard, it is time to ask: how do different peoples and societies think about order and justice in world politics? What is the relationship between order and justice in non-Western traditions of thought? The tragic events of 11 September 2001 and the ensuing war in Afghanistan underscore different notions of order and justice in world politics and suggest that we ignore these at our peril. Mapping these different conceptions, bringing contesting idioms and arguments into a truly worldwide conversation over appropriate notions of order and justice, and, at a minimum, understanding more clearly the areas of agreement and the nature of differences are more urgent than ever.

This chapter argues that in the Indian discourse on world politics it is possible to discern multiple Indian conceptions of order and justice. Historically, three perspectives have dominated Indian thinking. The first and still dominant perspective is that of Nehruvian internationalism or Nehruvianism. The second is Gandhian cosmopolitanism or Gandhianism; the third is political Hinduism or *Hindutva*. A fourth, more recent, view may be called neo-liberal globalism or, more simply, neo-liberalism.[1] These four conceptions can be counter posed to the dominant Westphalian conception. Nehruvians have a 'Westphalian plus' view of order, while Gandhians argue that it is necessary to transform the current Westphalian international order into a genuine world order. Proponents of political Hinduism hold that it is India's destiny to build a *dharmic* world

---

[1] The terms 'Nehruvianism', 'Gandhianism', and '*Hindutva*' are well known in India. They have not been used in relation to different streams of Indian *international thought* as much as they have been used to describe broad political philosophical currents in India. The term 'neo-liberal globalism' is my own invention.

order. Neo-liberalism sees order primarily in terms of market logic. The tension between these four views and the traditional Westphalian model constitutes the order-justice problematic in Indian international thought.[2]

1. ORDER AND JUSTICE IN WORLD POLITICS

What is order in world politics? How have we come to think about order at this juncture in world history? Arguably the most authoritative discussion of the problem of order and its relationship to justice is to be found in the late Hedley Bull's classic work, *The Anarchical Society*.[3] In this text, Bull argues that order and justice are often in conflict with each other. In particular, human justice and cosmopolitan justice challenge the Westphalian international order based on the primacy of states that dominates world politics. This chapter argues that order and justice are not so clearly demarcated from each other. Conceptions of order seem to have notions of justice embedded within them; and it is hard to conceive of justice without simultaneously conceiving of a commensurate order. Order and justice may be better represented as order/justice, and the order versus justice problem can more realistically be thought of as the contest between various conceptions of order/justice.

The Westphalian conception of order/justice rendered by Bull will be compared and contrasted with the four Indian perspectives outlined at the start of this chapter. Three of these emerged from the nationalist struggle: Nehruvianism, Gandhianism, and political Hinduism. The fourth, neo-liberalism, has roots in the colonial and immediate post-colonial periods, but has gained greater currency since the end of the Cold War. Adherents and partisans of the four viewpoints are to be found among the various political parties, the bureaucracy, the armed forces, intellectuals and scientists, and the public at large. Those who articulate these positions do not necessarily do so as self-conscious 'representatives' of contending 'schools of thought'. However, if one abstracts from the plethora of writings on international affairs, these different tendencies are clearly visible. It should be said that Gandhianism is the least visible

[2] There is a fifth Indian tradition of international thought, namely, Marxism. I exclude it from this chapter principally because it is neither particularly Indian nor influential. Neo-liberal globalism is not Indian in its antecedents, but it is of growing importance in the Indian discourse on international relations. Gandhianism is of declining influence, like Marxism, but it is Indian and therefore merits inclusion.

[3] Hedley Bull, *The Anarchical Society* (New York: Columbia University Press, 1977). On a more prescriptive approach, see the various contributions of the authors of the World Orders Model Project (WOMP). Among others these include Rajni Kothari, *Footsteps Into the Future* (Nairobi: East African Literature Bureau, 1974) and Saul Mendlowitz (ed.), *On the Creation of a Just World Order* (New York: Free Press, 1975).

in contemporary Indian public life, but it has a following amongst the intelligentsia and therefore is not without influence.

Before I proceed to deal with these four conceptions, it should first of all be emphasized that this is necessarily a rather preliminary exploration of the order/justice problematic in Indian international thought. Indian writings, of the kind that developed historically in the West, are absent.[4] Reliance must be placed on the texts of a mere handful of modern figures such as Jawaharlal Nehru, Mahatma Gandhi, M. S. Golwalker, and, more recently, a group of strategic commentators and analysts. Second, what follows is a schematized presentation of the four sets of views rather than detailed textual analyses. Finally, since 'order/justice' is an awkward terminology, reference will be made, for the most part, simply to 'order'. At other times, it may be necessary to use the terminology 'order/justice' or 'just order'.

2. NEHRUVIANISM

Fifty years after Independence, and almost a decade after the end of the Cold War, Nehruvian internationalism continues to inform Indian thinking about the nature of war, peace, and international order. While increasing numbers of Indians at the elite level claim that Nehruvianism is irrelevant in both domestic and foreign affairs, the fact is that it still permeates Indian international thinking and continues to influence Indian policy-makers.[5]

The Nehruvian view of world politics takes for granted an international system constituted primarily by more or less sovereign nation states operating in an anarchic order in which the 'state of war' is a constant shadow.[6] This is a system regulated by the cultivation and use of power, in which states pursue their national interests with vigour and single-mindedness and are responsible

---

[4] Academic writings on Indian conceptions of order include: Jayantanuja Bandyopadhyaya, *North Over South: A Non-Western Perspective of International Relations* (New Delhi: South Asian Publishers, 1984); Rajni Kothari, *Transformation and Survival: In Search of Humane World Order* (Delhi: Ajanta, 1988), whose chapter 'Justice and World Order' is especially relevant; Gopal Krishna, 'India and the International Order: Retreat from Idealism', in Hedley Bull and Adam Watson (eds), *The Expansion of International Society* (Oxford: Clarendon Press, 1984); M. S. Rajan, 'Reforming the Sovereign States System: A Non-Aligned Perspective', in Kanti P. Bajpai and Harish C. Shukul (eds), *Interpreting World Politics* (New Delhi: Sage, 1995); and A. P. Rana, *The Imperatives of Non-Alignment* (Delhi: Macmillan, 1976). The ancient Indian writings of Kautilya constitute another Indian conception of order. See Kautilya's *Arthashastra*, ed. L. N. Rangarajan (New Delhi: Penguin, 1987).

[5] This is admitted even by critics of Nehru such as Jaswant Singh, India's Foreign Minister in the BJP-led government. See Jaswant Singh, *Defending India* (New Delhi: Macmillan, 1999), 58.

[6] See Krishna, 'India and the International Order', 270–1, on the Nehruvian use of the term 'anarchy'.

for defending themselves.[7] That said, it is also a realm in which states perceive and pursue common interests and find ways of resolving their disputes; conflict and war can be transcended.[8] Nehruvian internationalism accepts the central assumptions and concepts of a realist view of international politics but posits that, under certain conditions, states can overcome the rigours of anarchy and fashion at least seasons and locales of peace and cooperation.[9]

What is the Nehruvian view of world order? It is, essentially, Westphalian. States are the primary form of political organization in the world, and all peoples are entitled to live under their own freely chosen governors. States are the acting subjects of the international system.[10] As the acting subjects of world politics, they bear both rights and responsibilities. One of those rights is the use of force. Nehruvians are ambivalent about force: in their view, violence is both destructive and productive of order. On the one hand, Nehruvians argue that force and power cannot be the basis for enduring peace. Violence can only breed violence; and the untrammelled pursuit of power can only bring forth countervailing power.[11] Furthermore, in the long run, no balance of power can be stable, as attested to by the history of western Europe and the two world wars. On the other hand, Nehruvians recognize that states will, and sometimes must, use violence in their relations with each other. They therefore cannot ignore the role of force.[12] Ideally, states must have enough force to defend themselves, but no more. Any excess of armaments beyond a minimal defensive force should be eliminated by mutual agreement.[13]

Behind this faith in regulating interstate relations is the Nehruvian belief in human reason and the ability of individuals and collectives to forge common rules and work common institutions. Nehru and his successors set great store by the principles of *Panchashila*—mutual respect for one another's territorial integrity and sovereignty, mutual non-aggression, mutual non-interference in one another's internal affairs, equality and mutual benefit, and peaceful coexistence—all of which are compatible with Westphalian conceptions of order.[14] Nehru often referred to the inevitability of 'world government' and 'world

[7] Jawaharlal Nehru, *India's Foreign Policy: Selected Speeches, September 1946–April 1961* (New Delhi: The Publications Division, Ministry of Information and Broadcasting, [1961] 1983), 45–6.   [8] Nehru, *India's Foreign Policy*, 46.

[9] Nehru, *India's Foreign Policy*, 50–5. On India's acceptance of realism, see Jawaharlal Nehru, *Discovery of India* (New Delhi: Jawaharlal Nehru Memorial Fund with Oxford University Press, [1981] 1994), 539.

[10] Nalin Anadkat, *International Political Thought of Gandhi, Nehru and Lohia* (Delhi: Bharatiya Kala Prakashan, 2000), 116.   [11] Nehru, *Discovery of India*, 536–40.

[12] Krishna, 'India and the International Order', 272, and Nehru, *India's Foreign Policy*, 185.

[13] Nehru, *India's Foreign Policy*, 35, 45–6, on minimal defence. On India's considerable efforts on disarmament, see Nehru, *India's Foreign Policy*, 182–236.

[14] See Nehru's insistence on *Panchashila* as the basis for international order, particularly as a means of regulating relations amongst the newly emerging countries of the Third World. See Krishna, 'India and the International Order', 274.

federation'.[15] However, these references should not be read too literally. He was probably suggesting that states would increasingly collaborate in propagating international law and organizations and that the resulting edifice would be tantamount to world government or federation. While Nehruvians are supportive of rules and institutions, they are not naive. They recognize that the great powers in particular will try to bend the rules of the game in their favour. Law and organization might well serve rather than constrain power politics.[16] It is therefore vital for the weaker states to combine in resisting great power hegemony and ensure that rules and institutions reflect universal interests.

If the Nehruvian view of order is essentially Westphalian, it contains an additional element, namely, non-alignment. Non-alignment grew out of Nehru's understanding of post-1945 world politics and the challenges of expanding Westphalia beyond the Western society of states. The first of these challenges was the peaceful liberation of all Asian and African peoples from colonial and racial domination and achieving some degree of reconciliation between colonizers and colonized. The second, and more severe, challenge was the Cold War. By the early 1960s, most former colonies had joined the comity of nations as full and equal participants, at least in a juridical sense. Reconciliation with the colonial powers was achieved by the expansion of institutions such as the Commonwealth. The Cold War, on the other hand, grew more intense and threatened to destroy the newly won independence of Asia and Africa.

The Cold War bipolar distribution of power, Nehru reasoned, left little room for national autonomy.[17] The danger was that Asia and Africa would escape colonialism only to fall into a neo-colonial relationship with different and more powerful masters. This bipolar world had a further characteristic which posed a special problem, namely, that it was increasingly marked by the presence of nuclear weapons and the possibility of a third world war in which no one would be immune from devastation. Nehru predicted that the distribution of power would be totalizing; under the threat of global annihilation, there would be enormous pressures on virtually every country to side with one superpower or another. Furthermore, Nehru feared that the superpowers would squander global resources on war and conflict when those resources were sorely needed to rid the world of economic backwardness.[18]

Out of this realization came Nehru's and Nehruvianism's major contribution to the conception of international order, namely, non-alignment. Non-alignment was not one thing but many. At its core were four components. The

---

[15] Nehru, *Discovery of India*, 539–40, and Nehru, *India's Foreign Policy*, 182–3, for his argument that some form of world government was inescapable.

[16] See Nehru, *India's Foreign Policy*, 192–3, on Nehru's concerns about the great powers' domination of an international agency to be created for the control of atomic energy.

[17] Nehru, *Discovery of India*, 539–40.

[18] Krishna, 'India and the International Order', 271.

first and most important was rejection of bloc membership. Non-alignment, as Nehru and his followers repeatedly emphasized, did not mean neutrality. It meant that a country refused to be permanently attached to any one power or bloc. States had an obligation to pursue their national interests, and allying with a particular power, in certain circumstances, was a legitimate choice. States might also support one or other great power on a given issue.[19] What was unacceptable was to give up the *right* to choose and to blindly follow the dictates of a bloc. Those who affirmed non-alignment had the right, even the responsibility, to make their voices heard on international matters and to criticize or side with whomsoever they chose consistent with their interests, as well as the demands of international peace and stability.[20]

The second element of non-alignment was a belief in the utility of international rules and institutions as checks against great power domination and coercion. Nehruvians understood that the great powers could manipulate or flout international rules and procedures should they choose to do so.[21] However, even a rampant great power might be hemmed in by the lattice-work of norms and procedure. At the very least, that lattice-work might slow down the great powers and give the international community a chance to influence their thinking.

The third component of non-alignment was an alliance of the weak against the strong. There was, as some observers have noted, a balance of power element to non-alignment. Nehruvians set great store by the coming together of the weak states to resist the more powerful. While Nehru himself scorned the trade unionism of the weak countries, he was not entirely averse to this function of non-alignment. Clearly, his successors in India encouraged the idea of a coalition of Southern states against the dominant Northern powers. Nehruvians are not so untutored as to imagine that a Third World coalition could confront the great powers in any real military or balance of power sense; but they argued that an alliance of non-aligned countries could bolster the determination of each member to maintain an independent foreign policy and

[19] Nehru, *India's Foreign Policy*, 36.

[20] Nehru, *India's Foreign Policy*, 79 and Krishna, 'India and the International Order', 272. The freedom to choose was vital if India was to be truly free in the post-colonial period. As Nehru famously remarked, 'What does independence consist of? It consists fundamentally and basically of foreign relations. That is the test of independence. All else is local autonomy'. See *Jawaharlal Nehru's Speeches. Volume 1, September 1946–May 1949* (New Delhi: Ministry of Information and Broadcasting, 1983), 241.

[21] Nehru was a great supporter of the UN and of multilateral initiatives, but he feared that the great powers would use the organization and other fora for their own ends. Thus, Nehru was vehemently opposed to the idea of an international atomic energy commission as proposed by the US, which would have had extraordinary powers to regulate atomic energy worldwide. See Krishna, 'India and the International Order', 284, and Nehru, *India's Foreign Policy*, 192–3. Nehru also feared that the UN could become an interventionist body in the hands of the great powers. See Krishna, 'India and the International Order', 282.

to voice its views publicly, even if those views went against the wishes of the great powers.[22]

Non-alignment's fourth element was mediation and suasion. The non-aligned countries, resolutely aloof from permanent attachment to one bloc or the other, occupied a vantage point that might allow them to play a mediating role between the two sides. In a nuclear age, mediation between the two blocs was not just an investment in tension-reduction between two disputants; it was also a vital investment in the future of the human race. Non-alignment entailed commitment to pursue a dialogue with the great powers. The great powers, their leaders, and their people were not above reason, and they could be persuaded to follow more enlightened, peaceful policies if they were relentlessly engaged.[23]

Nehru's 'Westphalia plus' notion of order—Westphalia plus non-alignment—on the whole is compatible with traditional Westphalia.[24] What is in tension with Westphalian notions, however, is non-alignment's insistence on freedom of strategic choice and the ability of the non-aligned countries to play a constructive role in order building. In effect, Nehruvians call into question the notion that order can be built around some sort of exceptional role for the great powers and that these powers represent a stabilizing element in international order. Nehruvians do not doubt that the great powers can and will seek to dominate the international system and portray their domination in terms of order-building, but they question the efficacy of the great powers in maintaining peace and stability. In the Nehruvian perspective, it is not the great powers but rather the non-aligned that are positioned to play a positive and exceptional role in world affairs.

A second challenge to traditional Westphalian notions is the Nehruvian insistence on economic equality as the basis for international political equality. In the Nehruvian view, formal independence is only one aspect of the fight for international equality. Economic weakness means vulnerability to various forms of pressure and can compromise freedom of decision-making.[25] Nehruvians argue that the Northern and the Southern countries have to combine to rid the world of poverty, destitution, and economic backwardness in the post-colonial world. There are both moral and pragmatic reasons for doing so. The norm of international equality, if it means anything, requires that a country possess more than

---

[22] Nehru, *India's Foreign Policy*, 77–9, for Nehru's scepticism regarding a 'Third Force' and how it would be futile to attempt to balance against the great powers.

[23] See Krishna, 'India and the International Order', 272–3, and Nehru, *India's Foreign Policy*, 39–40, 47.

[24] Thus, the noted Nehru scholar, A. P. Rana, argues that Nehruvian non-alignment can be seen as an attempt to expand 'Western' Westphalia by constructing an 'Eastern Westphalia' of the liberated colonial countries in Asia and Africa. Rana is quoted in Anadkat, *International Political Thought*, 96–7.

[25] Nehru, *India's Foreign Policy*, 257, on the dangers of economic domination.

formal independence: it has to have the wherewithal to be truly free.[26] The former colonial powers in any case owe something to their erstwhile possessions and should make restitution for over a century of exploitation and domination. Nehruvians also argue that the global economy allows rich countries to exploit the post-colonial economies and deepen the misery of millions of people worldwide.[27] Apart from these moral considerations, there is a pragmatic consideration, namely, the preservation of international order. Unless poverty and underdevelopment are dramatically reduced, if not eliminated, there can be no order in the long term.[28] Misery and destitution cannot be the basis for an orderly world. Rich and poor have to combine to redistribute global resources and to regulate the international economic system to prevent the market-based global economy from ruining the weaker countries.[29]

In the Westphalian order of the post-1945 period there was little room for such radical schemes. The advanced states set up the IMF and World Bank to regulate the global financial system and to make available funding for economic development. However, contributions to these institutions were purely voluntary. In addition, the policies of the Bretton Woods institutions were designed to encourage the gradual freeing up of the world economy, not its regulation. The Non-Aligned Movement and the Group of 77 that grew out of it, on the other hand, wanted a global compact on economic redistribution and regulation.[30]

How serious is the Nehruvian challenge to traditional Westphalia? In the end, Nehruvians have had little choice but to accept post-war rules and institutions. This is clear from India's policies on the role of the great powers in the United Nations (UN) and on global economic redistribution. While non-alignment signified that much of the world rejected the idea of an exceptional role for the great powers, India, as an original participant in the setting up of the UN, and in pursuit of international order, had in fact accepted great power exceptionalism in terms of the veto of the Permanent Five. Nehruvian India ultimately chose to go along with this unequal structure, even though New Delhi has always made the point that the world body should eventually be made more equitable and accountable.[31] Similarly, the Nehruvian demand for international collaboration in regulating the global economy and reducing

[26] *Jawaharlal Nehru's Speeches*, I, 104–5, 202, and B. N. Pandey, *Nehru* (New Delhi: Rupa, 1976), 320, notes Nehru's insistence that foreign aid created obligations on the recipient; and also pp. 321–2 on how a country's economic policy determined its foreign policy.

[27] See *Jawaharlal Nehru's Speeches*, I, 365, and Anadkat, *International Political Thought*, 101–3, on Nehru's suspicion of capitalism.   [28] Nehru, *India's Foreign Policy*, 255.

[29] Anadkat, *International Political Thought*, 96.

[30] On North-South relations, see Roger D. Hansen, *Beyond the North-South Stalemate* (New York: McGraw Hill, 1979).

[31] Nehru, *India's Foreign Policy*, 32–3, 179–81, and Krishna, 'India and the International Order', 279–80, on India's UN policy in this period.

economic inequality was made within the constraints of a Westphalian order. India did not adopt a radical leftist position demanding the overthrow of global capitalism, nor did it opt for a dependency-like position of disengagement from the world economy. Instead, it chose to work within the UN to foster a North-South 'dialogue'; not destruction or disengagement but dialogue with the centres of global capitalism within the apex institution of international society. In this sense, Nehruvians, in Bull's terminology, have ultimately accepted the claims of order over justice.

3. GANDHIANISM

Five decades after India became free, there are vestiges of the legacy of Mahatma Gandhi. Gandhi died within months of Independence and did not play a direct role in fashioning Indian thinking about international life. However, a central concern throughout his life and teachings was how to overcome violence between individuals, communities, and states. Gandhian thought has coloured and conditioned virtually all aspects of Indian conceptions of social and political life.[32] Nehru was influenced by it, even though the first prime minister of India rejected or ignored much of the Gandhian approach on the grounds that it was utopian. For a new nation state, struggling to be sovereign and secure in a turbulent domestic and international environment, to follow Gandhi's precepts was, in the Nehruvian view, to court danger if not disaster.[33]

Gandhian cosmopolitanism is ambivalent about the nation state, the basic building bloc of the Westphalian system. On the one hand, Gandhians recognize that nationalism is a powerful liberating force at a particular stage in history and that it represents the possibility of a people's rise to self-consciousness, emancipation, and freedom.[34] In affirming nationalism and therefore the inevitability of a nation state, Gandhianism accepts the fact of an international system and everything that is implied by it: anarchy, sovereignty, conflict, war, and so forth. On the other hand, for Gandhi and his followers humanity must, and will, go beyond the nation state. For Gandhians, individuals are the irreducible subjects

---

[32] The writings of some other prominent Gandhians are Jayaprakash Narayan, *Nation Building in India*, ed. Brahmanand (Varanasi: Navachetna Prakashan, n.d.), *Jayaprakash Narayan: Selected Works*, I, ed. Bimal Prasad (New Delhi: Nehru Memorial Museum and Manohar Publishers, 2000), Vinoba Bhave, *Democratic Values: The Practice of Citizenship* (Kashi: Sarva Seva Sangh, 1962), and Vinoba Bhave, *Third Power*, trans. Marjorie Sykes and K. S. Acharlu (Varanasi: Sarva Seva Sangh Prakashan, 1972).

[33] Nehru, *India's Foreign Policy*, 45–6.

[34] See the discussion on 'swaraj' in *The Selected Works of Mahatma Gandhi. Volume 6: The Voice of Truth* (Ahmedabad: Navjivan Trust, 1968), 440–6 (hereafter *Selected Works*) and Anadkat, *International Political Thought*, 57.

of social and political life: they are moral and ethical agents who in the end are obliged to treat others with dignity and tolerance regardless of their class, caste, religion, or nationality.[35] The nation state will survive as a formal entity, but in order for it to contribute to the moral and ethical life of its citizens, it must be a radically decentralized institution that devolves decision-making power to small community governments or *panchayats*. The international system, in this vision, is important only in the transition to a world order which may formally comprise nation states but in which social and political affairs are ineluctably local. Order will result from the interactions within and between small, economically self-sufficient, face-to-face communities—the real, acting units of world politics. The key characteristic of those interactions must be *ahimsa* ('non-violence'), *satyagraha* ('truth power'), and economic equity.[36]

Gandhians affirm simultaneously the importance of nationalism, respect for the rights of individuals, and the necessity of a world community or world federation. They argue that Gandhi's conception of nationalism is inclusive and not exclusive, one that does not depend on fostering hatred and rivalry with peoples of other nations.[37] Instead, inclusive nationalisms form the basis for a stable world order. A people that has emancipated itself from colonial rule and is confident in its culture and traditions can understand and respect the emancipation, culture, and traditions of others and live in harmony with them.[38] Gandhi understood, however, that the new states that resulted from the nationalist struggle would not be perfect. They would fall prey to the temptation to constitute themselves as centralized states on the model of the colonial powers and could well become repressive, tyrannical, and unjust. If so, individuals being moral agents would have a responsibility ultimately to other individuals regardless of nationality, and this could mean that in certain circumstances they must oppose their own governments.[39]

Individual rights are not, however, sacrosanct. Individuals are part of and nurtured by communities, nation states, and indeed the world as a whole, and they should be prepared to sacrifice themselves for the greater good if that is required. Gandhi argued that, analogously, communities might have to sacrifice their rights, perhaps even their very existence for the nation, and so also the nation for the world community.[40] States that are truly free and confident

---

[35] 'The Individual is Supreme', *Selected Works*, VI, 438–40.

[36] 'What is Satyagraha', *Selected Works*, VI, 178–203, and 'The World of Tomorrow', *Selected* Works, VI, 201, on 'equal distribution' as the 'second great law of tomorrow's world'.

[37] 'Nationalism and Internationalism', *Selected Works*, VI, 246–8.

[38] 'Civilization and Culture', *Selected Works*, VI, 284–5.

[39] 'Non-Cooperation', *Selected Works*, VI, 205, and 'The Individual is Supreme', *Selected Works*, VI, 438.

[40] 'The Individual is Supreme', *Selected Works*, VI, 438–40, and 'Nationalism and Internationalism', *Selected Works*, VI, 246–8.

would undoubtedly enter into relations of interdependence and cooperation with other states. Gandhi felt that, ultimately, some form of world confederation—in which states, of their own free will, cooperated with others—was both desirable and inescapable.[41]

In the Gandhian view of world order, the internal structure of the nation state is a vital issue. That it should be democratic, with full adult franchise, is certain.[42] Beyond this, every country will evolve its own system of governance.[43] Above all, though, the state must be a moral community based on religious values. In saying this, Gandhi did not mean that the values of any particular religion should inform public policy and dominate social life. He meant instead that morality should inform statecraft, for politics without morality was an abomination. At the core of all religious teachings is the necessity of moral behaviour in personal and collective life, and most religions converged in their basic moral teachings and injunctions. This true inner essence of religiosity—ethical conduct, generosity, and tolerance—should be the basis of state policy.[44]

Gandhi also insisted that government should be limited: the government that governs least governs best.[45] Small, face-to-face communities, which produce their own goods and services and govern themselves with the minimum of interference from the national government, are the most democratic and peaceful. However, they are not selfishly self-regarding but rather are part of both a national and world community.[46] Their frugal, simple, democratic, and non-violent practices contribute to the stability of world order.

For Gandhians, the key to the functioning of these decentralized communities is non-violence and truth. Tolerance of others and moral behaviour flourish in such an environment. Countries made up of such communities require virtually no police force and military force.[47] They pose no threat to their neighbours. If attacked, they offer nothing but non-violent resistance. Thousands, even millions might die in resisting an attack non-violently, but, as Gandhi argued, this would in aggregate amount to fewer deaths than if there were armed resistance.[48] Eventually, the attacker would be sickened by its

---

[41] 'World Federation', *Selected Works*, VI, 258–9.

[42] 'Franchise and Voters', *Selected Works*, VI, 455–6.

[43] 'Swaraj', *Selected Works*, VI, 444.

[44] 'Politics and Religion', *Selected Works*, VI, 435.

[45] 'The State of Enlightened Anarchy', *Selected Works*, VI, 436–7.

[46] 'Decentralization', *Selected Works*, VI, 449–52.

[47] 'Disarmament', *Selected Works*, VI, 255–6, on the need for complete disarmament. According to Gandhi, the great powers were best placed to begin the disarmament process. As great powers, they were the most important part of any disarmament campaign.

[48] 'How to Combat Hitlerism', 411; 'India and Militarism', 439; and 'Non-Violent Defence', 444; all in V. V. Ramana Murthi (ed.), *Gandhi: Essential Writings* (New Delhi: Gandhi Peace Foundations, 1970).

own attacks against unarmed resisters and in time would be transformed by its encounter with non-violent resistance. Non-violence and truth force are very difficult strategies to live by, but Gandhi deemed them the most effective and enduring forms of political action and conflict resolution.[49]

The Gandhian view of order clearly differs from the Westphalian or even the 'Westphalian plus' Nehruvian model. In the Westphalian model, the sovereign nation state is at the heart of any conception of order. Order is conceived in terms of the relations, rights, and responsibilities of nation states vis-à-vis each other.[50] For Gandhians, the nation state is one mechanism of world order. Order consists of the totality of relations, rights, and responsibilities, as between individuals, communities, states, and other agents.

Second, Gandhians argue that economic equality is vital to the persistence of any order and that frugality and voluntary redistribution are the chief means by which equity can be achieved. Coercion in the service of economic justice is both ethically unacceptable and counter-productive. Gandhians argue that entrepreneurs and businesses have rights and responsibilities in any proper social order. Wealthy industrialists have essential talents and are an integral part of social order. They should properly be regarded as 'trustees' who would deploy their wealth for the benefit of their societies. In a proper national and world order, they could be persuaded to play a responsible role whereby they treated their employees well, produced socially necessary goods, and used their wealth to contribute to the economic uplift of those who were the most disadvantaged.[51] Class hatred is futile and can lead only to divisiveness and violence. Radical redistribution based on the destruction of the capitalist class or forced redistribution from the capitalist to the working classes is against the tenets of non-violence. Persuasion and self-regulation, more than coercion, will build a lasting and just order.[52]

A third difference between the Gandhian and the Westphalian notion of order, therefore, is that, while the latter upholds the role of violence, Gandhians see no place for violence. While Gandhi acknowledged that violence is better than cowardice, and that violence for self-protection and in the fight against oppression is better than amoral pacifism, he was convinced that non-violence is better than violence.[53] Non-violence makes greater demands

---

[49] 'If I Were a Czech', 391; 'Non-Violent Defence', 444; 'The Jews', 397; 'Jews and Non-Violence', 399; 'China's Travails', 404; and 'Non-Violence Resistance', 451; all in Murthi, *Gandhi*.

[50] Anadkat, *International Political Thought*, 53–4, on how Gandhi sees the state and mankind as a whole as the two elements of world order. Clearly, Gandhi was not so 'utopian' as to think that the nation state did not have a role in providing order.

[51] 'World of Tomorrow', *Selected Works*, VI, 261.

[52] 'World of Tomorrow', *Selected Works*, VI, 261–2, and 'Is Class War Inevitable?', *Selected Works*, VI, 426–34.   [53] 'Non-Violence and Cowardice', *Selected Works*, VI, 175–7.

on human endurance and integrity but, in the service of moral truth, it is infinitely preferable to violence. Complete and total disarmament is vital in this regard, for without the instruments of violence *ahimsa* would be made easier.

Fourth, Westphalian conceptions of order regards violence, a common set of basic rules, and the various regulatory institutions that have been made by states through mutual agreement as being at the core of any order. Gandhians not only reject violence, but they are also ambivalent about rules and institutions. What is problematic in their view is that behind these laws and organizations there must be a centralizing authority which monitors and enforces the protocols of social conduct. A world body or concert of great powers might constitute that central authority, but either way it is coercion that ultimately gives effect to the rules and institutions.[54] For Gandhi and his followers, morality and self-regulation rather than centralized political authority, power, and violence are the basis for order. Each individual, community, and state must exercise self-discipline and ensure that its behaviour is consistent with the tenets of non-violence and ethical truth.

In sum, the Gandhian challenge to Westphalia is to replace an international order built on states and the regulated use of violence with a world order comprising relations among individuals, groups, communities, and states based on non-violence and economic equality. The rights and responsibilities of individuals must be balanced against the rights and responsibilities of collectivities—groups, communities, states, and the world as a whole. In Bull's terms, Gandhians can be said to favour the claims of individual and cosmopolitan justice over international order.

4. POLITICAL HINDUISM

Political Hinduism or *Hindutva* is the third Indian conception of world politics. M. S. Golwalkar, who took over from K. S. Hegdewar, the founder of the right-wing Hindu organization Rashtriya Swayamsevak Sangh (RSS), is the prophet and principal voice of the view that India is not just a nation state but also a civilization, and, more fundamentally, a Hindu civilization. Religious writers, political party propagandists, and the publicly propagated views of

---

[54] Anadkat, *International Political Thought*, 62, notes that, for Gandhi, 'customs, conventions, agreements or treaties' were mere 'patchworks for survival'. Gandhi also argued that laws and treaties reflected the wishes of the most powerful and favoured the status quo. Hence, he was not particularly enamoured of the League of Nations or the UN. See Anadkat, *International Political Thought*, 73–4. Rules and institutions such as the various world organizations could at best postpone the moment of war, not eliminate war altogether.

various Hindu organizations make up the *Hindutva* view.[55] *Hindutva* proponents argue that Hindu civilization fell on hard times in the competition with other civilizations and, that to recover its vitality and integrity, it must be supreme in the Indian land mass and undergo the rigours of internal spiritual and organizational regeneration.[56] An India restored to Hindu domination will then help to shape a lasting and better world order.

In the *Hindutva* view, world politics is marked by struggle between civilizations and states. The struggle is primarily cultural but may become militarized as well. As against the Nehruvians and Gandhians, *Hindutva* proponents see violence more positively: violence can galvanize and emancipate a suppressed or colonized people.[57] In the *Hindutva* cosmology, peace results either from a balance of cultural and military power between civilizations and states or, in the end, by acceptance of the Hindu way of life.[58] Either way, Hindus must fortify themselves. In the *Hindutva* view, violence and war are unavoidable, even functional. There is little to suggest that *Hindutva* is either supportive of or hostile to Westphalian rules regarding the uses and limits of violence. Hindus must equip and organize themselves for the military struggle; and they must also go back to the basic principles, precepts, and practices of their culture in order to carry forward the civilizing role of Hinduism.

At one level, the *Hindutva* view of order is compatible with traditional Westphalia. Its proponents do not reject the basic rules and institutions of Westphalian order, including the notion of state sovereignty. The *Hindutva* view accepts the importance of institutions such as the balance of power and the exceptionalism of great powers. With time, when Indians rehabilitate themselves and acknowledge their essential Hindu identity, India will be in a position to join the great power oligarchy at the top of international order. India's claims will be based not simply on its power but also on its civilizational greatness and cultural contributions to the world.[59] *Hindutva* proponents offer little commentary on international law and organization, although,

---

[55] A group of organizations make up the so-called Sangh Parivar: the RSS, the Vishwa Hindu Parishad (VHP), the Bajrang Dal, and, of course, the Bharatiya Janata Party (BJP).

[56] M.S. Golwalker, *We or Our Nationhood Defined* (Nagpur: Bharat Publications, 1939), 2–15.

[57] On the attractions of violence, the need for national strength built around the revitalization of Hinduism, and the folly of non-violence, see M. S. Golwalker, *Bunch of Thoughts*, 3rd edn (Bangalore: Sahitya Sindhu Prakashan, 1996), 257–77, 326. Golwalker also notes, 'strength begets friends' (p. 313).

[58] Chapter 1 of Golwalker, *Bunch of Thoughts*, is entitled 'Our World Mission' and is a paean to Hinduism. Golwalker insists that India must be strong materially and culturally so that it is in a position to propagate Hindu values, which he portrays as the most universalistic.

[59] Golwalker, *Bunch of Thoughts*, 8–9, argues that power and civilizational greatness are mutually related. No one will take Hindu precepts seriously until Hindus become confident and powerful.

like the Nehruvians and Gandhians, they fear that the rules and institutions of international society may be captive to great-power interests.[60]

The most subversive notion harboured by *Hindutva* proponents is the superiority of the Hindu way of life and the destiny of Hindus to lead the world.[61] The West's individualism, materialism, and utilitarianism may have made it powerful, rich, and efficient, but these qualities have also rendered it selfish, self-centred, and exclusivist. The result is divisiveness, conflict, and domination.[62] Hindus, by contrast, believe that individualism must be tempered by self-restraint, materialism must be leavened by a spirituality that is dedicated to the search for truth, and utilitarianism—the greatest good for the greatest number—is inferior to an all-embracing inclusiveness based on the welfare of each and every individual.[63] Hindus are ecumenical, generous, tolerant, and life-affirming, and believe in the essential unity of all things and all peoples.[64] The genius of Hinduism is the insistence that unity and diversity can be reconciled. Thus, Hindus conceive of a world state in which individual distinctiveness can be reconciled with the collective good. 'This world state will be a federation of autonomous and culturally distinctive nations under a common centre linking them all'.[65] Regulating this unity will be rules of behaviour in consonance with *dharma* whereby each individual, community, and nation will have its own place and role in the totality and will coexist in harmony.[66]

This last element of order merits some comment. *Hindutva* thought is, at base, a form of conservatism. Ultimately, as in all conservative thinking, there is an insistence that there exists an elite in human affairs and that this elite is good for society, whether domestic or international society.[67] In effect, the *Hindutva* argument is that India is part of a cultural elite—indeed, that it may be the greatest culture of all—and that as a great civilization it will help build a more harmonious world order.[68] This order, as all orders, will necessarily be unequal and cannot be based on the wishes of lesser groups. Benign hierarchy, rather than strict equity, is the basis of order. Juridical, legal equality in international order is an idea that is acceptable to *Hindutva* proponents as long as India is struggling to secure its place as a sovereign entity; but

---

[60] Golwalker, *Bunch of Thoughts*, 3–4, on how the UN is a tool of the great powers.

[61] Golwalker, *We or Our Nationhood Defined*, 65–9, on how Hinduism is suited to leading the world spiritually.   [62] Golwalker, *Bunch of Thoughts*, 2–5.

[63] Golwalker, *Bunch of Thoughts*, 2.   [64] Golwalker, *We or Our Nationhood Defined*, 41.

[65] Golwalker, *Bunch of Thoughts*, 5–6.   [66] Golwalker, *Bunch of Thoughts*, 5–6, 16.

[67] Like most conservatives, Golwalker believes that society was a corporate entity, with different groups performing different functions. If so, in international society, too, different entities—states, in this case—must play different roles, with some leading and others following. See *Bunch of Thoughts*, 11, on society as a corporate entity.

[68] Golwalker, *We or Our Nationhood Defined*, 41–2, 65–7, on the superiority of Hinduism and its manifest destiny.

egalitarianism carried to extremes would prevent India from taking its place among the civilizational elites of the world.[69]

How will this Hindu-led world order come about? First, *Hindutva* proponents argue that Hindus must liberate themselves and bring into being an ideal Hindu state in India. India is a civilization-state in the sense that Hindu civilization originated, evolved, and attained its highest expression in the space now more or less occupied by the modern Indian state.[70] Unless Hindu civilization once again dominates the Indian land mass, it cannot play its world historical role. Foreign conquest, Muslim and British, capitalized on Hindu military and political weakness, causing Hindus to lose control of the state and to some degree their cultural pride. With the departure of colonial rule, Hindus have a chance to regain state power and restore their confidence in their religion and way of life. European colonial rule came at a time when Hindus were on the verge of liberating themselves from Muslim domination.[71] After independence, it is the rule of Hindu secularists that stands in the way of a second opportunity at liberation. Hindu civilization may once again be prevented from attaining its legitimate pre-eminence within India and its rightful place in the world.[72] Nehru and Nehruvians foisted secularism on the Indian people and used this to appease the minorities of India, particularly the Muslims.[73] In its foreign relations, independent India likewise failed to comprehend that national strength and interest were pivotal. Under Nehru, India allowed itself to be bested strategically by Pakistan and China and failed to assert itself with its smaller neighbours.[74] Sooner or later, *Hindutva* proponents argue, India will rid itself of the rule of the Hindu secularists led by Nehru and the Congress Party and achieve its final emancipation. A truly

[69] Golwalker, *Bunch of Thoughts*, 24–6, on how inequality is an inescapable feature of social life.

[70] V. D. Savarkar, *Hindutva: Who is a Hindu?* (Mumbai: Swatantryaveer Savarkar Rashtriya Smarak, 1999), 85. Savarkar notes that only China, 'Arabia', and 'Palestine' qualify as civilization-states. The latter two do not compare with India in terms of their size and power. Only China compares with India in terms of being a *great* civilization-state. See also Golwalker, *We or Our Nationhood Defined*, 4–9, and Deendayal Upadhyaya's views in C. P. Bishikar, *Pandit Deendayal Upadhyaya, Ideology and Perception. Part V, Concept of the Rashtra* (New Delhi: Suruchi Prakashan, 1991), 70–1.

[71] V. D. Savarkar, 'Hindu-Pad-Padashahi', in Verinder Grover (ed.), *V. D. Savarkar, Political Thinkers of Modern India*, XIV (New Delhi: Deep and Deep Publications, 1993), for an account of how the Hindus under Shivaji had nearly freed India from 'foreign' rule only to fall to the British. See also Golwalker, *We or Our Nationhood Defined*, 10–15, 59.

[72] Bishikar, *Pandit Deendayal Upadhyaya*, 70–1, and Golwalker, *Bunch of Thoughts*, 106–7, on the Congress government's anti-Hindu policies.

[73] Bishikar, *Pandit Deendayal Upadhyaya*, 155, on how post-independence India under Nehru and the Congress 'appeased' the religious minorities. Also see Golwalker, *We or Our Nationhood Defined*, 14–15, on the iniquities of the Congress Party.

[74] Golwalker, *Bunch of Thoughts*, 93–4, 268–9, 289–301.

emancipated India can then embark on its world historical role of constructing an order based on Hindu principles and precepts.

The second step in the construction of a Hinduized world order will be for
India to take its place as one of the leading powers. Unlike the Nehruvians
and Gandhians, *Hindutva* proponents are not averse to making India into
a military and economic power. As long as India is weak, it cannot hope to
advance Hindu ideals and practices. Who, after all, will listen to or be inspired
by a second-rate power that cannot defend itself and its interests?[75] As Hindu
India's power grows, would it press for changes in the present international
order in the transition to a Hinduized world order? *Hindutva* writings have
virtually nothing to say on this subject. However, one can imagine at least two
possible demands: first, a formalized, 'hard' spheres-of-influence role for
great civilizations whereby great civilization-states make their areas of influence virtually impermeable to outside influences[76]; and second, the giving of
cultural vetoes to the great civilization-states. Great civilization-states, in this
view, may be entitled to ask for changes in cultural practices and policies that
they do not like, primarily in their spheres of influence but also in other parts
of the world.[77]

Finally, over the long term Hindu principles, precepts, and practices will
come to dominate world politics not so much because India will, as a great
power, insist on dominating others, but rather because the superiority of the
Hindu way of life will become increasingly self-evident to the world at
large.[78] *Hindutva* proponents are confident that as in the past Hindu civilization will spread and hold sway without the use of violence. The efflorescence
of Hindu culture in India will dazzle the world, and India's example will persuade others to accept the leadership of Hindu civilization.[79] Westphalia will
give way peacefully to a Hinduized order.

In what way is the *Hindutva* view of order in conflict with Westphalia? At
one level, as noted earlier, it is not in any real conflict at all: a decentralized
order based on national sovereignty will afford Hindu nationalists the space
within which to take power domestically and convert India from a secular
democracy into a Hindu republic. The *Hindutva* ambition for India—attaining great power status—does not violate the basic rules of Westphalia either,

[75] Golwalker, *Bunch of Thoughts*, 8–9.

[76] *Hindutva* proponents argue that Indian civilization spread its influence not just to what is
now south, south-east, and east Asia, but also the Americas 'long before Columbus "discovered"
America', as well as Mongolia and Siberia. See Golwalker, *Bunch of Thoughts*, 7.

[77] The controversy in India recently over revisions in school history textbooks is instructive
here. BJP spokespersons have suggested that in future all textbooks will be vetted by religious
figures representing the major religions in India and that these figures will, in effect, have a veto
on what is written in these texts.

[78] Bishikar, *Pandit Deendayal Upadhyaya*, 134–5, 142, 147; Golwalker, *We or Our
Nationhood Defined*, 55–6, 67.   [79] Golwalker, *Bunch of Thoughts*, 17.

although clearly it would change the structure of world power. However, if an ascendant Hindu India demands either a 'hard' sphere of influence for itself or cultural vetoes for the great civilizations, it will be in conflict with Westphalian norms. To give great civilization-states spheres of influence is tantamount to reorganizing the international system on imperial lines, whereas Westphalia is based on the supremacy of the nation state. To grant them transnational cultural vetoes goes against the principle of sovereignty, which allows a people the right to its cultural practices as long as those practices do not violate the basic human rights charter of the world community. The *Hindutva* notion of a federal 'world state', with its component societies playing their different parts in harmony as defined by *dharmic* rules of behaviour, is also clearly not in consonance with Westphalia, which represents a decentralized order bound together by the most minimal rules and institutions.

In sum, the *Hindutva* notion of order would seem to go well beyond a mere international order. It would appear instead to describe what Bull calls a 'world order', with rules, rights, and responsibilities applicable not only to states but to the whole of humankind that would be governed ultimately by an all-embracing *dharmic* code of reciprocal obligations. This would be a highly differentiated order in the sense that rules, rights, and responsibilities would vary between individuals, groups, and states depending on their capabilities and roles. It might well be a hierarchical order in which, ultimately, individual rights as well as the rights of states would be subordinated to the cause of harmony in the world state. To put it in Bull's terms, *Hindutva* seems to favour a Hindu notion of cosmopolitan justice in which humanity's desire for harmony must be upheld against the rights of individuals and states to pursue their own selfish interests.

5. NEO-LIBERAL GLOBALISM

While the Nehruvian, Gandhian, and *Hindutva* schools of thought have long been at the centre of Indian discussions of international order, in the aftermath of the Cold War a fourth school has emerged: one that might be called neo-liberal globalism.[80] Neo-liberal globalists, like Nehruvians and *Hindutva* proponents, see an anarchic interstate system as the fundamental basis of international

---

[80] Neo-liberal globalism has no prophet-voices like Nehru, Gandhi, or Golwalker. However, it is possible to put together the outlines of this view from the writings of various commentators, mostly younger, emerging voices such as the strategic analyst, C. Raja Mohan; Sanjaya Baru, editor of the *Financial Express*; the Congress Party politician, Jairam Ramesh; and Shekhar Gupta, editor of the *Indian Express*. India's Foreign Minister, Jaswant Singh, also writes in the style of a neo-liberal globalist. See his *Defending India*, Ch. 5.

life, with sovereign states pursuing the national interest as the basic unit of international relations.[81] Without supranational authority, the international system is a self-help system, conflict, war, and rivalry are a constant possibility, and states cannot escape the responsibility for defence.[82] Having said that, neo-liberals argue that relations between states can go beyond the Hobbesian state of nature in a globalized world. States are not always in conflict. There exists a division of labour and resources between societies, and therefore states can improve their well-being through exchange or trade. Put another way, the international system is marked by anarchy but also by economic interdependence. Interdependence gives states a stake in each other's welfare and makes war a self-defeating possibility.[83]

Neo-liberals in India argue that, after the Cold War and the collapse of bipolarity, states are no longer polarized along the geopolitical fault-lines drawn after 1945. The ideological quarrel between the market and the command economy no longer exists. The market having won, virtually all states are reconciled to liberal economic policies at home and abroad as well as 'pragmatism' in interstate relations.[84] Trade, investment, and technology, far more than control of territory or war-making, are at the centre of international politics.[85] For the most part, rivalries between states have become commercial and peaceful, and economic strength increasingly serves as an instrument of external influence.[86] As trade, investment, and technology flow across national boundaries and as finance and commerce are freed from government control, states live in a globalized world in which their relative influence has declined. Corporations and banks and investment houses dispose of enormous power, and states have to deal with them in their search for investment and technology.[87] Narrow Old-World nationalism has declined. At the same time, other non-state actors have grown in importance. Some violently resist globalization and the democratization that often accompanies economic change. Ethnic strife, religious fundamentalism, anti-globalization protests, and economic dislocation, all these are the main sources of violence rather than the

[81] Jaswant Singh, *Defending India*, 278.
[82] See Sanjaya Baru, *National Security in An Open Economy*, a report of the Indian Council for Research on International Economic Relations (ICRIER), on the importance of defence, at http://www.icrier.com, 46. Also Sanjaya Baru, 'The Economic Dimension of India's Foreign Policy', *World Affairs*, 2/2 (1998), 49.   [83] See Baru, *National Security*, 13–14.
[84] C. Raja Mohan, 'India's Security Challenges', in Nancy Jetly (ed.), *India's Foreign Policy: Challenges and Prospects* (New Delhi: Vikas Publishing House, 1999), 82; Sanjaya Baru, 'Economic Diplomacy', *Seminar*, 461 (January 1998), 67; and Baru, 'The Economic Dimension', 90–1.
[85] Singh, *Defending India*, 274; Baru, *National Security*, 18; and Baru, 'Economic Diplomacy', 67, 69.
[86] Baru, 'Economic Diplomacy', 67; Baru, 'The Economic Dimension', 89; and Baru, *National Security*, 14–17.   [87] Baru, 'Economic Diplomacy', 67.

anarchy of states.[88] The world is growing wealthier, with major Asian powers in particular joining the Western industrialized countries at the pinnacle of economic well-being, and so a multi-polarization of the world must sooner or later follow.[89]

This neo-liberal view of order is not particularly antagonistic to Westphalian conceptions of order. An order based on the primacy of states is quite acceptable to neo-liberals. While they see the market as the motor of historical change, the state, in their view, will continue to remain the supreme form of political organization. Violence and war will continue to exist and states will continue to worry about national security in traditional terms.[90] In the neo-liberal view, the market and non-state actors will increasingly take over the economic and welfare functions of the state. The state's role will be to guarantee that the market can play its efficient allocative, productive, and distributive role.[91] As societies build on their comparative advantages, they will increase the flow of trade, investment, and technology between themselves. Everyone will be better off as a result. The incidence of major-power war should, in this interdependent world, gradually decline because the powerful states will be in the forefront of globalization. International law and organizations will play a role not so much in regulating war as in ensuring that a worldwide system of economic exchange is established and protected. Regionalism and multilateralism in economic affairs will increase. War will decline, but global violence may well increase as some non-state actors resist this globalizing world economy and as parochial forces, such as ethnic and religious extremists, resort to violence.[92] States therefore will also increasingly be focused on how to deal with non-state actors.

Significantly, however, neo-liberal globalists in India are less sympathetic to cooperative and collective methods of dealing with violence than counterparts in the West. They remain suspicious that the great powers, primarily the Western great powers, will use this as an excuse to intervene in the affairs of the rest of the world. That said, they reason that India as a great economic and military power and, as a liberal multi-ethnic society, should combine with the Western powers to ensure peace and stability.[93]

---

[88] K. Subrahmanyam, 'Asia's Security Concerns in the 21st Century', in Jasjit Singh (ed.), *Asian Security Concerns in the 21st Century* (New Delhi: Knowledge World, 1999), 19–20.

[89] On the growth of multi-polarity or 'polycentricism'—a term that some Indian analysts prefer to 'multi-polarity'—see Singh, *Defending India*, 277; Baru, 'The Economic Dimension', 96–9; and Subrahmanyam, 'Asia's Security Concerns', 11–12. For Subrahmanyam, multi-polarity is a function not just of economic change but also of the diffusion of military power.

[90] Baru, *National Security*, 5.

[91] On the continuing role of the state in buttressing the market, see A. N. Ram, 'Challenges to Economic Diplomacy', in Jetly, *India's Foreign Policy*, 117.

[92] On the rise of ethnic and religious extremism and the disruptive role of non-state actors, see Subrahmanyam, 'Asia's Security Concerns', 20.

[93] On the growth of cooperation between the major and lesser powers and the increase in multilateralism, see Baru, 'Economic Diplomacy', 68–9. Also see Subrahmanyam, 'Asia's Security

One of the key implications of the neo-liberal vision of order is that, though states will continue to be the primary form of political organization, conceptions of sovereignty and security will slowly change. A world in which the market comes to dominate must be a world in which hard notions of sovereignty will give way to softer ones. In a globalized world, state control over the economy and trade must perforce decline. A global regime of rules, evolved through negotiations amongst states, will lay down universal standards for the national economy and most likely for domestic politics and society as well.[94] Once such standards have been agreed upon, states will have to uphold these global norms and rules if they wish to benefit from the workings of the global economy. If the right to go to war is one of the marks of sovereignty, this also will in effect be abridged by globalization: war will remain an option of statecraft but will be seen increasingly as dysfunctional for the workings of the global economy.[95] Security conceptions also will change. National security will remain a concern, whether it is threatened by other states or by non-state actors. However, human security—the well-being and freedom of individuals and groups—will become more important, for, if individuals are not satisfied with their lot, there can be no political stability, and without political stability there can be no true national security. In a globalized world where ideas and information will flow more freely, international standards of human security will come to be defined, and states will be made accountable in the international community as never before.[96]

In the neo-liberal view, then, the existence of an interstate system based on free economic exchange is fundamental to order. Tensions between states, at least between the major trading states, will decline, but conflict between states and non-state actors will likely grow. Peace and stability will be threatened by extremisms of various kinds. A key element of international order-building must be the strengthening of Western enlightenment notions of rationality and democracy and the increasingly free movement of ideas, capital, goods, and people, for these, more than force, are ultimately the bulwark against disruption and subversion.[97]

The tension between Westphalia and the neo-liberal globalist vision of order can be described in four areas: economic and social norms, security,

Concerns', 19–22, on the growth of cooperation amongst states. Raja Mohan is a great champion of the argument that India and the US, as two plural democracies, should work together for order.

[94] Singh, *Defending India*, 275, recognizes the constraints on sovereignty in an economically interdependent world.

[95] Subrahmanyam, 'Asia's Security Concerns', 12, on globalization and interdependence and the avoidance of violence. Subrahmanyam argues that in addition the spread of nuclear weapons, global ecological problems, and the costs of modern war will restrain states from fighting.

[96] Baru, *National Security*, 4–5, notes that there is agreement on the 'minimal acceptable level of well-being' that defines human security.

[97] Baru, *National Security*, 48, argues that 'A free and prosperous people are the ultimate guarantee of national security'.

politics, and transnational flows. In each case, what is at issue is the status of sovereignty. Order-building in a globalizing world entails, first of all, the evolution of universal standards governing economic and social practices. This goes against the grain of the harder notion of sovereignty in Westphalia in which national economic and social policies are matters of domestic jurisdiction. The second tension emerges from the relative shift from national to human security. Here again the neo-liberal suggestion that global standards of individual well-being and freedom exist or will evolve and that states cannot avoid some degree of international accountability goes against the assumption that state security is primary and that standards of well-being and freedom are internal matters. Third, the neo-liberal suggestion that liberal values and democracy are at the heart of a stable order reverses the Westphalian sense that domestic values and institutions are autonomous from, and indeed prior to, the demands of international order and that international order should reflect the diversity and difference of domestic orders which are its constituent and constituting parts. Neo-liberals imply in effect that domestic politics must serve the cause of international order, not the other way round. Fourth, neo-liberal globalism and Westphalia are in tension over neo-liberalism's sense that the free flow of ideas, capital, and goods outside the control of governments is not only unavoidable but also desirable and that a proper order should positively enable these flows.

Neo-liberal globalists in India insist that they set great store by sovereignty and that they are 'realists'; but the trajectory of their thought leads them in directions that question sovereignty and the billiard-ball view of international order. The economistic logic of their view of world politics leads them to support the imperatives of order-building in a globalized world. Essentially, this means a shift to global norms and rules over the sovereign rights of states in respect of economics, security, domestic politics, and transnational flows. Neo-liberals see no *necessary* contradiction, though, between global standards and state rights. States, in a globalizing world, will come to recognize that their own welfare and therefore security are bound up with the spread of global standards which confer rights on individuals as well as other non-state actors, especially business enterprises. This then is the liberal/progressivist position on order and justice, as described by Bull, in which there is no irresolvable contradiction between the rules and institutions of Westphalian order and various alternative systems of rules and institutions.

6. CONCLUSION

What can we say about Indian conceptions of order/justice in light of these four reconstructions? Our review suggests that there are four dimensions along which we can compare the Indian order/justice discourse: the role of the state and sovereignty; the status of violence/war; the importance and/or utility of rules and institutions or, put slightly differently, law and organization; and the importance of the value of equality or equity.

All four conceptions of world politics and order concede or affirm that the nation state has a vital role, but there are differences with the role the state is accorded. States have come into existence historically and play an emancipatory role. Nationalism galvanizes an oppressed people and helps lead them to freedom and self-confidence. Sovereignty is an essential attribute of a free people. Nehruvians are perhaps the most sanguine about the long-term viability and necessity of states and sovereignty, although we should note that Nehru, in particular, did envisage some form of what he called world government or federation. Gandhians are probably the most radical in viewing the state as just one level or form of political organization. For them, local community government, the *panchayat*, is the true and best political unit for society. State sovereignty is important, but the rights and responsibilities of individuals and communities, as well as the welfare of humankind as a whole, also count. *Hindutva* proponents accept the state and sovereignty as being essential for the protection and advancement of cultural distinctiveness. However, in the long run world harmony demands something that transcends narrow state interests. A *dharmic* system of beliefs and practices must exist to reconcile parochial interests with the demands of global harmony. Neo-liberals insist on state sovereignty, yet the logic of globalization suggests that states must willingly accept global standards in areas that are regulated by national governments. All four conceptions seem to see the state and sovereignty in a much more contingent way than in the modern Westphalian conception as rendered by Bull.

What is the status of violence/war in Indian conceptions of order/justice? Here again there are differences. For Nehruvians, violence and war are a last resort in international life. States must be prepared for war but only in a defensive sense. Gandhians, once again, stand out as being the most opposed to a fundamental feature of Westphalia, namely, acceptance of large-scale organized violence. Gandhi and his followers almost absolutely reject violence and war as a means of regulating human relations. *Hindutva* proponents are the most accepting of violence. Violence, for them, can be emancipatory, even cathartic, for a repressed people. Neo-liberals also accept that violence is a part of social existence, but modern interstate warfare, especially among the big industrial powers in a globalizing world, must decline. War disrupts trade and capital flows and, in an increasingly interdependent world, is dysfunctional. Violence is much more likely between states and non-state actors. Non-state actors that resist modernity and globalization, from ethnic and religious fundamentalist groups to anti-globalization radicals, are the real threat to peace. States will have to use force to deal with these groups when necessary.

The one area in which Indians are most in agreement is in respect of international rules and institutions. All four conceptions accept that the existing corpus of international rules and institutions can serve to regulate world politics. However, all four are also suspicious about the prevailing Westphalian regime of rules and institutions. Interestingly, it is not the essentially Western provenance of Westphalian rules and institutions that is problematic; it is, rather, the fear that the powerful, mostly Western states will themselves flout Westphalian restrictions and injunctions and will use international law and organization to intervene in the internal and external policies of weaker states. In short, Indians fear that power politics and narrow national interest will trump the sanctity of norms and procedures. Once again, the Gandhians may have the most radical difference with Westphalia. Gandhians are sceptical of the utility of virtually *any* global rules and institutions because, in their view, behind these must reside some centralized structure of force and coercion, which they reject.

What, finally, do Indian conceptions of order/justice have to say about the importance of equality? Any notion of justice must in the end have something to say about this social value, particularly economic equality. All four conceptions support the juridical equality of states: all peoples must be free and sovereign, with no qualifications. Beyond this, there is disagreement, between Nehruvians and Gandhians on the one hand, and *Hindutva* proponents and neoliberals on the other. Thus, Nehruvians argue that formal equality amongst states is not enough; the post-colonial countries need to become economically strong before they can be truly equal. Progressive national policies and also an international commitment to redistribute resources are crucial to the prospects of economic equality. For Gandhians, economic equality is a crucial value. No society, domestic or international, can be just if it is marked by economic inequality. Economic equality cannot be achieved by the revolutionary redistribution of wealth; it can come only from the voluntary actions of the rich and the socially advantaged.

Hindutva proponents and neo-liberals, by contrast, are much more accepting of inequality. Supporters of *Hindutva* views argue that inequality is a social reality that cannot be wished away. Indeed, inequality and hierarchy are the basis of a harmonious order. In any society, some are more talented than others. Those who are more talented are best suited to shape and lead society and ensure its stability and harmony; the less talented must accept that this is for their good. On the global stage, there is cultural inequality. Some civilizations and cultures are better than others. Hinduism in particular has an exceptional, world-historical role because of its ecumenical and spiritual qualities. In a Platonic sense, this is just: those who are best equipped to perform a certain social role are endowed with that function for the good of society.

Neo-liberals have little to say explicitly about the issue of inequality. One can imagine neo-liberals arguing, though, that inequality arises from different talents and skill endowments. State interference in the market to redress inequality is counter-productive because it chokes off growth. The state's role is therefore to ensure that the market can do its job and that talents and endowments can be systematically improved for the population at large. Equality means equality of opportunity. At home, this means state support for education and health. Internationally, neo-liberals demand only a level playing field so that there are no special economic privileges for the more advanced economic powers. Aid and international compacts on redistributing wealth would interfere with market principles, and self-abnegation by the rich, as in the Gandhian scheme, would only cause market inefficiencies. Both strategies would stifle the rapid economic growth that is the surest way of generating the necessary surplus for vital social welfare programmes.

Clearly, there is great variety in Indian international thought and its corresponding notions of order/justice. One way of summarizing our findings is to ask: what would a just order look like in these four conceptions? For Nehruvians, a just order consists of truly sovereign nation states that are economically developed and autonomous in respect of their foreign policies; that use violence only in the last resort to settle differences; that operate rules and institutions democratically, without great power manipulation; and that, when necessary, are helped economically by those better off than themselves. For Gandhians, a just order is one where the rights and responsibilities of individuals and of communities, states, and humankind as a whole are in balance and where power is devolved to small, local governments; where violence is abolished; where self-restraint and frugality replace rules and institutions backed by power and coercion; and where economic inequality and, indeed, other forms of inequality give way to equality through non-violent struggle. For *Hindutva* supporters, a just order implies state sovereignty and cultural nationalism for all peoples within the overarching, harmonizing framework of a global *dharmic* regime; violence, when necessary, to protect cultural independence and political emancipation; rules and institutions that are free of great power domination but that will eventually conform to the superior values of Hinduism; and an acceptance of inequality for the sake of social harmony. Finally, for neo-liberals, a just order is one in which sovereign states in a globalizing world increasingly abide by global standards in areas of domestic governance; in which states use force when necessary to subdue ethnic, religious, and ideological extremism to preserve democratic, secular values and practices; in which rules and institutions work primarily to allow market forces to operate efficiently to produce wealth; and in which the surplus generated by a fast-growing economy is used to provide for equal opportunity rather than strict economic equality.

Of these four conceptions of a just order, the Nehruvian is closest to the Westphalian conception. The neo-liberal vision is perhaps next in terms of its compatibility with Westphalia. Gandhian and *Hindutva* ideas are the furthest from Westphalian notions. Indians no longer set much store by Gandhian ideas; and there are few *Hindutva* proponents who go as far as the prophet voices such as Golwalker and Savarker. Internal political and economic change as well as global geopolitical changes have taken their toll on Nehruvianism, which for so long dominated Indian thinking. For now, a three-way conversation between vestiges of Nehruvianism, political Hinduism on the rise, and a nascent neo-liberalism looks set to continue.

10

Order, Justice, and Global Islam

JAMES PISCATORI

Islam's place in the wider world has been subject to periodic and fierce controversy. In the mid-nineteenth century, Palmerston, in a back-handed compliment, spoke of the then 'dormant fanaticism of the Musulman race'.[1] Only some 20 years later Thomas Carlyle, who is often credited with a sympathetic depiction of the Prophet Muhammad, juxtaposed the 'unspeakable Turk' with the 'honest European'.[2] The supposed fanaticism of Muslims became more apparent from the 1880s as nationalist movements stirred in Egypt and Mahdism appeared in the Sudan. The agitation in India in the twentieth century compounded anxieties over Muslim hostility to the British Empire. The rise of Third World claims to distributive justice in the 1970s set the stage for more recent doubts about non-Western compliance with the norms of international order. The advent of the Iranian revolution engendered lively debates in the early 1980s over whether Islam was naturally revolutionary and subversive of interstate norms. To some extent, this mirrored mid-century Cold War fears of secular Arab nationalism in the Middle East, but Islam was thought to be an especially inflexible and demanding ideology precisely because of its religious core. At the demise of the Cold War, the debate was built on these earlier precedents and unabashedly conducted in terms of culturally induced international conduct. Some now saw Islam itself or its politicized sub-category, Islamism, as hostile to the West—'the West versus the Rest', in Samuel Huntington's formulation[3]—or at least to Western-dominated globalization— 'Jihad vs McWorld', in Benjamin Barber's evocative terminology.[4]

---

[1] Palmerston's letter to Lord Aberdeen, 1 November 1853, reproduced in Evelyn Ashley, *The Life of Henry John Temple, Viscount Palmerston, 1846–1865, with Selections from His Speeches and Correspondence*, II, 2nd edn. (London: Richard Bentley, 1876), 47.

[2] Quoted in *The Political Life of the Right Hon. W. E. Gladstone*, II (London: Bradbury Agnew & Co., n.d.), 12. Carlyle had included Muhammad as one of his heroes in *Lectures on Heroes, Hero-Worship and the Heroic in History* (Oxford: Clarendon Press, 1925).

[3] Samuel P. Huntington, 'The Clash of Civilizations?', *Foreign Affairs*, 72/3 (1993), 39.

[4] Benjamin R. Barber, *Jihad vs. McWorld* (New York: Times Books/Random House, 1995).

Although many commentators in both the West and Muslim world called into question such apparent determinism,[5] events were to raise urgent concerns. The attacks on New York and Washington in late 2001 and the subsequent launch of the war on the Taliban in Afghanistan and on 'global terrorism' revived ideas of an Islamic revolt against modernity and international order. Civilizational conflict seemed inevitable after all, and 'September 11th' became a powerful metaphor for the Islamic inflexibility and 'rage'[6] that many had long predicted. Margaret Thatcher, while exempting Islam as a 'religion', found nevertheless a characteristically sweeping parallel with Communist ideology: 'Islamic extremism today, like bolshevism in the past, is an armed doctrine. It is an aggressive ideology promoted by fanatical, well-armed devotees. And, like communism, it requires an all-embracing long-term strategy to defeat it.'[7] Bernard Lewis, an important historian of the Islamic world, wrote: 'If the people of the Middle East continue on their present path, the suicide bomber may become a metaphor for the whole region, and there will no be escape from a downward spiral of hate and spite, rage and self-pity, poverty and oppression.'[8]

A major problem with such analyses is that 'Islam' often appears as a uniform force, operating everywhere in the same way, exercising similar pulls on identity and affiliation. Throughout this chapter, in contrast, it is used to stand for a complex set of factors, and the 'Muslim world', likewise, refers to a large number of different societies. Although they are thus convenient shorthand expressions, it should not be assumed that they inevitably refer to a doctrinally defined agenda. As we shall see, Muslims invoke textual authority to substantiate their arguments but their identities and practices are also shaped by a number of other considerations such as nationalism, economics, social position, and ethnicity.

The argument that follows unfolds in four parts. It looks, first, at conventional debates about the compatibility of the Westphalian international order and prevailing Muslim norms and practices. It questions the assumption that they are inevitably pitched against each other. This assumption, it will be argued, rests on a simplistic reading of history, an exaggerated sense of the role of doctrine, and an underestimation of the flexibility that Muslim states have shown in adapting to the norms of international society. Second, the argument turns to a consideration of whether this conclusion may still be said to hold given the perceived challenges of globalization. We will see that Muslim responses are ambivalent. On the one hand, there is already a well-defined

---

[5] See, for example, Roy Mottahedeh, 'The Clash of Civilizations: An Islamicist's Critique', *Harvard Middle Eastern and Islamic Review*, 2/1 (1995).

[6] See, for example, Bernard Lewis, 'The Roots of Muslim Rage', *The Atlantic Monthly* (September 1990).

[7] Margaret Thatcher, 'Islamism is the New Bolshevism', *The Guardian* (12 February 2002).

[8] Bernard Lewis, 'What Went Wrong?', *The Atlantic Monthly* (January 2002), 45.

sense of victimhood and a belief that Muslim rights are being violated in an imperialistic global order. On the other hand, there is a double appreciation among some Muslims that globalization provides opportunities, and that, in order to utilise them, Muslims must still play within accepted, if slightly revised, rules of the game. Third, the chapter asks whether we are witnessing a radical revolt in Islamism whereby a powerfully revisionist approach to liberal international order is being articulated. Resentment at an American-dominated system is a forceful part of this criticism, but it takes its place alongside reproaches directed at Muslim rulers who are accused of benefiting from, and being manipulated by, Western hegemony. Finally, the linkage between external and internal challenges in modern Muslim societies will be explored. The discussion considers both the extent to which the search for justice is directed inwards, thus allowing for a tacit acceptance of the external international order, and the degree to which compelling claims to justice have also discernibly shifted perceptions of international society.

1. DEBATES ABOUT ISLAM AND INTERNATIONAL RELATIONS

Much of the academic and policy discussion of Islam and international relations focused until the 1990s on the question of Islam's compatibility with nationalism and the traditional norms of international relations. The conventional view was propounded by a curiously coexisting but potent combination of Orientalist and Muslim devout writers, who pointed to the inherent universalism of Islam and to the need and desirability in some circumstances for Muslims to combat unbelievers in morally sanctified struggle or jihad. Muslims constituted one community of faith—the *umma*—and were hostile to those who, at least for the moment, stood outside of it. A great deal was made of the medieval juridical division of the world into two rival, conflict-ridden realms, *dar al-Islam*—the realm of peace—and *dar al-harb*—the realm of war; the former would eventually expand and prevail over the latter. Among Western writers, Bernard Lewis argued that 'foreign policy is a European concept' and is alien to the Muslim world.[9] Elie Kedourie maintained that modern nation-states could not really emerge among Muslims since their political tradition of 'passivity and resignation' was as 'impracticable' now as it had been in the past.[10] Adda Bozeman argued that the modern idea of the territorial state conflicts with the borderless idea of a community of faith. She suggested that in so far as Islam is relevant to diplomacy, it is as a spur to

---

[9] Bernard Lewis, *The Middle East and the West* (New York: Harper Row, 1964), 115.
[10] Elie Kedourie, 'Islam and Nationalism: A Recipe for Tension', *The Times Higher Education Supplement* (14 November 1980).

anti-Westernism: 'The West now pays a heavy price'[11] for failing to understand that Arab Muslim states do not operate as Western states do, and therefore they will not resolve their dispute with Israel in the same manner as disputes are settled in the West. Moreover, it was inevitable that a state like Iran would descend into revolutionary turmoil, torn between its conflicting cultural legacies of Persian monarchy and Islam.

In simple terms, such views, abetted by a pious Muslim interpretation, appeared both to simplify Islamic history and to over-determine the role of culture. The assumption of inherent conflict between the Muslim and non-Muslim worlds ignored a variegated pattern of war and alliance, competition and cooperation across the Islamic centuries. Although they may not have conceded that Western states were equal to them, Muslim states regularly entered into territorial agreements and concluded peace treaties. In the sixteenth century, for example, Muslim practice closed the earlier debates among Muslim jurists as to the length of a truce between Muslims and non-Muslims. Invoking the seventh century Hudaybiyya treaty, jurists of at least two legal schools had argued that such agreements could last no more than ten years. But the treaty of 1535 between the Ottoman ruler Suleiman the Magnificent and Francis I of France endorsed the idea of 'valid and sure peace' between them in their lifetimes,[12] and from this point historical experience redefined the theoretical approach. In addition to maintaining regular diplomatic relations with non-Muslims, Muslims came to accept the realities of separate sources of power *within* the *umma* itself, as numerous Ottoman-Persian interactions and mutual concessions indicated.[13]

Flexibility existed in practice, then, but there was flexibility in thought as well. The texts of various schools of law accepted territorial division to which the law must bend, and medieval thinkers such as al-Ghazali, Ibn Taymiyya, and Ibn Khaldun came to accept that there was pluralism within the Islamic realm as well as between it and the non-Islamic realm. It is true that many modern Muslims, such as the influential South Asian thinker Abu'l A'la Mawdudi (1903–79), rejected the institution of the nation-state and many diplomatic conventions as alien and destructive of pan-Islamic union.[14]

---

[11] Adda Bozeman, 'Decline of the West? Spengler Reconsidered', *The Virginia Quarterly Review*, 59 (Spring 1983), 192–3; see also 'Iran: US Foreign Policy and the Tradition of Persian Statecraft', *Orbis*, 23 (Summer 1979).

[12] The treaty is reproduced in J. C. Hurewitz (ed.), *Middle East and North Africa in World Politics: A Documentary Record*, I, 2nd edn (New Haven and London: Yale University Press, 1975), 2.

[13] For a summary of inter-Muslim relations, see my *Islam in a World of Nation-States* (Cambridge: Cambridge University Press, 1986), 62–74.

[14] See, among others, his *Nationalism and India*, 2nd edn (Pathankot: Maktabat-e-Jama'at-e Islami, 1947), 9–10, 28–31, and *Unity of the Muslim World*, ed. Khurshid Ahmad (Lahore: Islamic Publications, Ltd, 1967), 11–14.

Ayatullah Khomeini (1902–89) was perhaps the most notable late twentieth century exponent of this view, and Principle 11 of revolutionary Iran's constitution commits the government to promoting Islamic unity.[15] Yet, for all his wider aspirations, Khomeini accepted the legitimacy of the territorial state of Iran when it was under attack by the Iraqis during the Iran-Iraq war (1980–8). By the same token, the validity of the Iraqi state was affirmed: 'Our nation ...will resist until it achieves its legitimate demands ... We are brothers of the Iraqi nation and regard its soil as sacred...'[16] In effect, Iran was validated as the vanguard of the Islamic revolution. The demands of political and economic intercourse, the development of an intellectual and pragmatic consensus, even if unenthusiastically developed, and the pervasive influence of modern, nationalized educational systems combined to make the nation-state and systemic norms a powerful presence on the modern Muslim landscape.

Given this background, the answers to two questions that Hedley Bull posed seemed clear: (1) how did the western international order expand to non-western areas? (2) what competing priorities were given to the values of order and justice in an expanded international society?[17] To the first question, utilitarian and normative factors combined in the Islamic world over the centuries to endorse international relations roughly as we have known it in the modern age. Pragmatic self-interest—or, in the cynical view, the inability to impose dogma on recalcitrant realities—unsurprisingly asserted itself. Moreover, Muslim understandings adapted to this pragmatism so that an 'Islamic international relations' came to look remarkably like 'Western international relations'. Political and intellectual elites endorsed, in Bozeman's formulation, four key principles: the sovereignty of territorially demarcated states; the equality of governments; the inviolability of solemnly concluded agreements; and the precedence of peace over conflict.[18]

The answer to the second question naturally followed. Order was not only a value but also a priority. In so far as the debate figured in Muslim writings, conservatism was dominant. In a way perhaps similar to the Soviet experience, the building of a strong state in the Muslim world was viewed as the indispensable precondition to a sustainable international order. What mattered

---

[15] Constitution of the Islamic Republic of Iran, 24 October 1979 as amended to 28 July 1989, in Albert P. Blaustein and Gisbert H. Flanz (eds), *Constitutions of the Countries of the World: Islamic Republic of Iran* (Dobbs Ferry, New York: Oceana Publications, Inc., 1992), 21.

[16] Khomeini's speech to Bangladeshi Muslim leaders, as reported by Tehran home service, 8 September 1982, in BBC, *Summary of World Broadcasts*, ME/7127/A/7 (10 September 1982).

[17] 'Justice in International Relations: The 1983 Hagey Lectures (1984)', in Kai Alderson and Andrew Hurrell (eds), *Hedley Bull on International Society* (Basingstoke: Macmillan, 2000); *The Anarchical Society: A Study of Order in World Politics* (Basingstoke: Macmillan, 1977), Ch. 4; Hedley Bull and Adam Watson (eds), *The Expansion of International Society* (Oxford: Clarendon Press, 1984), Introduction and Conclusion.

[18] Bozeman enumerated these concepts in her *The Future of Law in a Multicultural World* (Princeton: Princeton University Press, 1971).

was acceptance of the international game built around states and, to the extent that the sovereignty of Muslim states was sanctioned, a proximate form of justice was seen to be done. The impulse was instrumental, but it was in accord with a resonant Muslim tradition that held that 60 years of tyranny was better than a single night of anarchy. Muslim 'Third Worldist'-type demands for a new international economic order were tellingly framed in the discourse of sovereign rights and negotiated contractual arrangements.

From this schematic overview one can discern three embedded assumptions. First, culture—the ensemble of traditions, norms, and symbols of a people or community—is constructed. If essentialism is to be avoided, even a religious code such as Islam must be accepted as variable and evolving with changing circumstances. Second, historical practice carries weight in the process of moulding conceptual and normative understandings. Normative consensus is often the consequence rather than the source of historical experience. Third, the operational level, the domain in which this adaptation plays itself out, is that of political or state elites.

Because the overall picture of Islamic interaction with the international system was one of accommodation and pliancy, Bull's relatively rueful conclusions about the expansion of international order appear overstated. The expansion of international society, though clearly opportunistic and utilitarian in origin, seemed a less shallow phenomenon than he envisaged; the principles were being internalized over time. Moreover, Third World calls for distributive justice were not as potentially destabilizing as he assumed them to be. Nor were Muslim states merely passive bystanders in the formulation of new normative regimes such as that covering human rights. However much they may have disagreed with particular provisions, such as the right to change religion, they were not only fully participating in international fora, they were subtly reformulating their notions of human rights in terms of the dominant international idiom. Pakistan, Iran, and Egypt, for example, moved in various ways to accord women greater personal status and civil rights, and even conservative Saudi Arabia deferred to the discursive framework of human rights, thereby creating a future standard by which to judge the legitimacy of the regime. In sum, where Bull saw revolt against the West, one could instead see a modus vivendi. Where Bozeman saw a superficial Muslim adaptation to the dominant international system, others were able to detect more substantial and skilful conformity.

One Muslim writer has accurately pointed out, however, that, after years of debate over Islam's place in the international system, the score card remains mixed. On the one side, he thought the Arab and Muslim state condemnation of the Iraqi invasion of Kuwait largely bore out the thesis that the principles of the game were being accepted. Yet, on the other, loomed the flouting of diplomatic conventions in the taking of American hostages in Iran and the general rise of religious fundamentalism or Islamism.[19] Many would point out, for instance, that the more liberal provisions for women's rights have come under sustained Islamist pressure.

2. GLOBALIZATION

A new set of challenges, which can be summarized as globalization, has also arisen. These are so powerful that we are left wondering whether, in the global age, we are talking about new rules of the game. There is no doubt that Muslim societies, like all others, are inexorably being pulled in the direction of globalization: economic interdependence, cultural exchanges, intimate political interactions. On one level, there is nothing new about such interrelationships in the case of Islam, and it may be argued that 'Islam' is naturally transnational and cosmopolitan. The bedrock tenet of belief, *tawhid* (oneness), endorses the ultimate goal of one community of faith; the *hajj* is the great convocation of Muslims, indistinguishable in principle by national or sectarian identity; early and medieval Islamic history is replete with examples of networks of traders who significantly helped to advance the word of Islam; travelling elites such as students, scholars, judges, and political officials sought knowledge (*rihla*) far from their home societies or went on minor pilgrimages (*ziyarat*); Sufi orders rapidly spread from their spiritual centres and created expansive 'brotherhoods'; and the Ottoman empire constituted a multi-ethnic, far-flung political organization.

But today, it is argued, a new political geography may be emerging: (1) once primarily focused on relatively fixed frontiers and the control of territories, geopolitics now increasingly involves mobile groups and social movements with competing claims and counter-claims; (2) de-territorialization, to some extent, has taken place with large-scale migration under way and with new emphases on race and ethnicity as markers of identity; and (3) concepts of space and distance have been redefined: connections and disconnections, distance and proximity are notional. Through television, images of political and religious authority as well as community are daily projected into domestic space; and 'virtual Islam' takes Muslims into some ethereal neighbourhood that understates the physical, even perhaps to some extent the cultural, distances.[20] It is of course another matter, which we will later consider, whether

---

[19] Farhang Rajaee, *Globalization on Trial: The Human Condition and the Information Civilization* (Ottawa: International Development Research Center, 2000), 118–19.

[20] See Gary R. Bunt, *Virtually Islamic: Computer-Mediated Communication and Cyber Islamic Environments* (Cardiff: University of Wales Press, 2000).

such a changing political geography creates new space for opposition and protest.

If the French fear the cultural invasion of a successful United States, one can imagine the resentments in the Muslim world at what can only be seen to be waves of unwelcome Westernisation. The overwhelming Muslim and Islamist response is thus undeniably negative. However, very importantly, their reaction overlaps substantially with both Western and local secular criticisms. A number of interconnected objections are heard.

First, although globalization is historically rooted, dating from the crises that hit the developed capitalist economies in the 1970s, it has acquired the force of a pernicious ideology, a 'theology' according to Barber, whose genealogy is obvious. In the words of the Moroccan writer, Muhammad 'Abid al-Jabari: 'In addition to being an economic system, globalisation is an ideology that serves this system. Americanisation and globalisation [*al-'awlama*] are highly interconnected.'[21] In such an ideology, globalization becomes a finality, the logical conclusion of market forces that are regarded as largely beneficial; multinational corporations and international banks are the primary agents of development; and the state and the interstate system are the guarantors of the working of the market logic. Along with many others, Muslims doubt whether this trajectory is benign.

Second, polarisation is enhanced both among countries and within them. Rich states grow richer while poor states sink lower. Internally in both rich and poor countries, a hierarchy emerges whereby people at the top are integrated into the global economy—the 'symbolic analysts' of Robert Reich[22]—and those in the middle and at the bottom are in precarious or superfluous labour. Small segments of poor-country populations are integrated into the world economy, while rich countries are generating their own internal Third Worlds. The Malaysian writer Chandra Muzaffar argues that the kind of capital flight and currency speculation that adversely affected the 'tiger' economies of southeast Asia from mid-1997 led to sharply delineated stratification. Millions lost their jobs in the region, but Northern economies were also put at risk because of the outflow of capital to low-cost production centres. There could be no clearer evidence of the 'immoral character of the global economy' and no more 'damning indictment of globalisation itself'.[23]

[21] Muhammad 'Abid al-Jabari, 'al-Awlama: Nizam wa Idiyulijiyya' in *al-'Arab wa Tahadiyyat al-'Awlama* (Rabat: al-Majlis al-Qawmi li'l-Thaqafa al-'Arabiyya, 1997), 15.
[22] Robert Reich, *The Work of Nations: Preparing Ourselves for 21st Century Capitalism* (London: Simon & Schuster, 1993), 177–80.
[23] Chandra Muzaffar, 'Globalisation and Religion: Some Reflections', in Joseph A. Camilleri and Chandra Muzaffar (eds), *Globalisation: The Perspectives and Experiences of the Religious Traditions of Asia Pacific* (Petaling Jaya: International Movement for a Just World, 1998), 183–4.

Third, the autonomous regulatory power of the state—in spite of what some ideologues might have hoped—is decreasing. States and intergovernmental organizations have naturally played a role in enforcing the rules of the global economy and in enhancing national competitiveness, but their powers of shielding domestic economies from the negative effects of globalization have declined. As Susan Strange reminded us, the coordination of exchange rates is but one area of uncertainty over which no one exercises real power. Power is thus diffused in the international political economy and the state is in relative 'retreat'.[24] None of this offers any comfort to Muslim critics of globalization who evince at times an almost archaic trust in the protective power of national independence. Mahathir Mohammed, Prime Minister of Malaysia, opposes the 'absolute' capitalism that globalization 'theologians' advocate and argues for respect for 'the boundaries of our national jurisdictions'. Precisely because it imposed currency controls in 1998, he emphasises, Malaysia was able to protect itself from the regional economic downturn and to emerge a stronger, more confident trading partner.

Fourth, political authoritarianism and social fragmentation within societies are enhanced. Politicians are both corrupt and incompetent, lining their own pockets by the opportunities globalization at the top provides, but unable to overcome increasing segmentation by class, gender, and ethnicity or to provide effective social services. Moreover, globalization requires deployment of repressive police and military force in order to prevent disruption to the world economy by inconvenient outbursts of protest. In the words of Ibrahim Abu-Rabi': 'Th[e] fundamental power differential [between the Muslim world and the West] is having a deep impact on the internal functioning of Muslim societies and is leading to wider gaps between rich and poor within the Muslim world. The accompanying international shift in power is also solidifying Muslim military and political elites.'[26]

Finally, and most importantly, cultural homogenization—read, of course, Westernization—threatens people's indigenous identities. Echoing Ernest Gellner who argued that 'genuine cultural pluralism ceases to be viable' in tightly interdependent circumstances,[27] Muslim intellectuals have feared an erosion of cultural autonomy, a subversion of distinctive and cherished values as the communications revolution spreads. As Mahdi El Mandjra has put it, 'Post-colonialism is a weapon that aims at destroying cultural diversity' and

[24] Susan Strange, *The Retreat of the State: The Diffusion of Power in the World Economy* (Cambridge: Cambridge University Press, 1995), Chs 1, 5, 13.

[25] Mahathir's speech is exerpted in Chakravarthi Raghavan, 'No New Round Before Settling Implementation Issues, Mahathir' at http://www.twnside.org.sg/title/settling.htm (4th June 2002).

[26] Ibrahim M. Abu-Rabi', 'Globalization: A Contemporary Response', *The American Journal of Islamic Social Sciences*, 15/3 (1998), 26.

[27] Ernest Gellner, *Nations and Nationalism* (Ithaca: Cornell University Press, 1983), 55.

instilling one purportedly universal but specifically Western culture.[28] Although communication is more widely available and disseminated, it becomes increasingly disconnected from what Zygmunt Bauman calls the 'human condition'.[29] Rather, materialistic ideas and pornographic images mislead and debase the believer. This particular criticism of globalization builds on well-established Islamic criticisms of the materialism of modern culture. For instance, members of the Tablighi Jama'at, a transnational movement devoted to encouraging Muslims to greater faithfulness, speak of the 'apparent glitter' of the capitalist West that leads only to a 'mindless life' and 'social bondage'.[30]

This final and most prevalent objection is framed in the language of cultural aggression, but there is no doubt that culture and politics are seen as intimately interconnected. The consequence of globalized communications, it is affirmed, is that the marginal are further marginalized, and the only ones empowered are those who control the levers of information and entertainment—pre-eminently, of course, the news, music, and cinematic industries of the West, especially the US. In the words of Ali Mazrui, the complement of homogenization is inescapably 'hegemonization'.[31] In this sense, Muslim critics of globalization would not dissent from E. H. Carr's coolly analytical conclusion that values depend on hegemony, but would regret his seeming approval of the dependence.

A recurrent theme throughout all of this is an acute resentment at both the power and the intervention of the US. America has become a sign of the West generally and is widely thought to exercise an especially negative influence. Several criticisms are voiced. One is that the US exploits its dominance to marginalize the Muslim world. According to this view, economic interdependence inevitably rebounds to the advantage of the sole superpower: Although a new 'liberal' order of privatization and free trade is promoted, it does not treat all as equals; in fact, it is predicated on a system of inequality perpetuated by such institutions as the International Monetary Fund (IMF) and the World Trade Organisation (WTO), themselves utterly dependent on American power. 'Intrusive institutionalisation', to use Janna Thompson's phrase,[32] contributes to neither manageable order nor justice. Many Muslim

---

[28] Mahdi El Manajra, *La Décolonisation culturelle: Défi majeur du 21ème siècle* (Marrakech: Editions Walili, 1996), 215; see also his *Nord/Sud: Prélude à l'ère postcoloniale*, 2nd edn (Casablanca: Les Editions Toubkal, 1994), 148–56, 286–300.

[29] Zygmunt Bauman, *Globalization: The Human Consequences* (Cambridge: Polity Press, 1998), 3.

[30] See, for example, the letter of the Tablighi 'Shuja'at' from Flint, Michigan, 2 September 1971, translated in Muhammad Khalid Masud (ed.), *Travellers in Faith: Studies of the Tablighi Jama'at as a Transnational Islamic Movement for Faith Renewal* (Leiden: Brill, 2000), 113–14.

[31] Ali A. Mazrui, 'Globalization: Homogenization or Hegemonization', *The American Journal of Islamic Social Sciences*, 15/3 (1998), 2–4.

[32] Janna Thompson, *Justice and World Order: A Philosophical Enquiry* (London: Routledge, 1992).

writers echo the main argument, if not the exact terminology, of the Marxist Samir Amin, who speaks of globalization as the 'new imperialism', the latest development in a world capitalist system controlled from the imperial centres of the West.[33] Others would add a second charge against American power: its policies of support for Israel and its opposition to Palestinian rights, sanctions against Iraq, and assistance to narrowly based regimes in Egypt, the Maghreb, the Gulf, and elsewhere are all designed to insure its hegemony over the Muslim world. These policies perpetuate regional orders that are subservient to American grand designs. Finally, others see in American cultural aggressiveness the intent to create, at its best, a secular, pragmatic order devoid of moral considerations and, at its worst, a controllable, toothless Islam that will defer to American power rather than resist it. Although Ayatullah Khomeini did not specifically speak in terms of globalization, this last point is what he had in mind when he scathingly referred to a de-politicized and compliant 'American Islam'.[34]

If we stand back from these specific points, we can see a larger pattern of criticism emerging, with three constituent and implicitly interrelated elements. First, globalization has changed the rules of the game, for the worse. Second, the rights—economic, social, cultural, and political—of Muslims have been violated. Third, justice would be served by the redistribution of power both among and within countries. With regard to this last point, no clear idea about redistribution is proposed. But what unambiguously emerges is the sense that the prevailing regional sub-systems are skewed in favour of a US-dominated, interconnected political and economic order, which relies crucially on the assistance of local regimes. In this regard, the conservative discourse which we outlined in the previous section of this chapter has given way, in some quarters, to a rights-based, victimization-conscious discourse that is not dissimilar to leftist/secular and liberal/pluralist criticisms of globalization.

Yet the picture, again, is complicated. It may appear that a broad intellectual consensus has come into existence. This would move the Muslim position from accommodation to confrontation with the status quo; from the defence of order to the advocacy of justice. Although suggestive, this interpretation is not entirely

---

[33] For Amin's views, see, for example, *al-'Awlama: wa'l-Tahawullat al-Mujtama'iyya fi'l-Watan al-'Arabi*, publication of the Markaz al-Buhuth al-'Arabiyya (Cairo: Maktabat Madbuli, 1999), 17–70. Also see Mustafa al-Sharif, *al-Islam wa'l-Hadatha: Hal Yakun Ghadan 'Alam 'Arabi?* (Cairo: Dar al-Shuruq, 1999), 309–44.

[34] Ayatullah Muhammad Yazdi, head of the Iranian judiciary, invoked this point of view when he said: 'One should be very careful [because] the danger of an American-style Islam, that is, one that says the government has nothing to do with Islam, is far greater than that of weapons': BBC, *Summary of World Broadcasts*, ME/1106/A1–2, 24 June 1991. For similar criticisms, see, for example, the various authors represented in Muhammad Ibrahim Mabruk (ed.), *al-Islam wa'l-'Awlama*, 2nd edn (Cairo: al-Dar al-Qawmiyya al-'Arabiyya, n.d.).

convincing. Two factors need to be taken into account. First, not all Muslims are opponents of globalization, and even some critics see in it enriching possibilities for Muslim societies. Ali Mazrui, for example, moves effortlessly from criticizing the homogenizing and hegemonizing effects of globalization to considering the opportunities it may present. There is no doubt that the Muslim world is currently on the losing end, but portentous forces are at work. Even as 'cultural westernization of the Muslim world' has been occurring, the 'demographic Islamization of the western world' is taking place owing to the large and permanently settled Muslim minorities now living in Europe, North America, and Australia. Muslims may find the Western cultural offensive hard to resist, and their faith may accordingly be severely tested. But, on the positive side, Islamic ideas of tolerance, devotion, and family, for example, may enter into, and reinforce, Western societies. He does not explicitly say that Muslims may also be positively socialized by the experience of living in pluralist and participatory political societies. But, overall, this theorist of culture in international relations holds out hope that a creative energy will flow as values 'mix' and perspectives 'intermingle'.[35]

Anwar Ibrahim, former deputy prime minister of Malaysia, concedes that globalization can be oppressive and interfering, and Muslims must be on guard lest they fall victim to new forms of colonialism. But, warily approached and properly appreciated, globalization can be an invaluable 'ally'. Since the technology on which it is based is neutral, it can be used to advance not only economic development but also 'cultural re-empowerment'. Although he speaks principally in terms of Asian values, he includes Islam in this globalization-driven reawakening.[36] Muzaffar also finds positive elements in globalization. Foreign direct investment has functioned to reduce absolute poverty in a number of countries, particularly in the Muslim world; globalized trade has enhanced social mobility; and modern communications have stimulated learning and helped distant societies to know more of each other.[37] 'Ali al-Ha'il, a consultant to the Qatari state media, endorses the last point, seeing in global communications a means by which Muslims can revitalize their educational system and disseminate their ideas. In this way, they will be able to confront the 'media imperialists'.[38]

Second, apart from the diverse intellectual responses, Muslim political elites have not necessarily seen globalization as a threat to their entrenched

---

[35] Mazrui, 'Globalization: Homogenization or Hegemonization', 10–12.

[36] Anwar Ibrahim, 'Globalisation and the Cultural Re-Empowerment of Asia', in Camilleri and Muzaffar (eds), *Globalisation*, 1–4. Also see Ibrahim's *The Asian Renaissance* (Singapore and Kuala Lumpur: Times Books International, 1996), 17–32, 136–8.

[37] Muzaffar, 'Globalisation and Religion: Some Reflections', in Camilleri and Muzaffar (eds.), *Globalisation*, 180–1.

[38] 'Ali al-Ha'il, 'Islamization of Aspects of Globalization', at http://www.islamweb.net/english/new/week1/ok%205%20Globalization.htm (17 February 2002).

power. 'Quantitative globalisation'[39] is manifesting itself in different ways but does not inevitably lead to a diminution of state power. Moreover, integration into the world economy has been less than expected. As the World Bank pointed out, the economic situation of Middle East and North Africa (MENA) countries until the late 1990s was considerably bleaker than might have been anticipated. Compared with other regions, they lagged behind in exports, labour productivity, private investment, and management of natural resources precisely because their policies were out of tune with the demands of a globalizing economy. A 1995 study argued that these countries were less integrated with the world economy than they had been 30 years earlier, with the decline in trade particularly noticeable. Despite decades of diversification and industrialization policies, oil remained the fundamental point of integration. Internal reform was lagging behind other countries, notably in terms of ease of communication, trade liberalization, competitive labour practices, a reassuring investment regime, reduction in poverty, and sustainable exploitation of natural resources. In fact, if oil was taken out of the equation, the only region worse off was sub-Saharan Africa.[40] The enmeshment of a large part of the Muslim world was thus a matter of contention.

Yet there is no doubt that Muslim societies are unable to resist the pull of economic interdependence and are responding to the lack of integration for which the guardians of the international political economy have criticized them. Many of the Muslim states, including recently Saudi Arabia, have adapted their legislation to allow foreign ownership of businesses and property and to ease entry into the WTO. The Saudi Minister of Commerce has even hinted that *shari'a* courts are not flexible enough to handle complex disputes over trade and foreign investment.[41] It is clear that some states— self-evidently, weak ones—may lose autonomy as a result of globalization, and post-Westphalian notions of sovereignty may accordingly suffer erosion. But it is also the case that, in the short term at least, state powers may be strengthened. As Keith Griffin, Rodney Wilson, and others have pointed out with regard to Central Asia and the Middle East,[42] economic policy is still largely made within the national context. Saskia Sassen suggests that interdependence may lead to a privatization of governmental functions, in which

[39] Ngaire Woods, 'The Political Economy of Globalization', in Ngaire Woods (ed.), *The Political Economy of Globalization* (Basingstoke: Macmillan, 2000), 1.
[40] World Bank, *Claiming the Future: Choosing Prosperity in the Middle East and North Africa* (Washington, DC: World Bank, 1995), especially 15–31.
[41] He appointed a committee to investigate the establishment of special commercial courts: AME Info: Middle East Finance and Economy, at http://www.ameinfo.com/cgi-bin/fndaily/lisdtnews.cgi? (20 January 2002).
[42] For example, see Keith Griffin and Azur Rahman Khan, *Globalization and the Developing World: An Essay on the International Dimensions of Development in the Post-Cold War Era*, HDRO Occasional Paper No. 2 (New York: UNDP Human Development Report Office,

banks and financial enterprises take on the kinds of regulatory and legislative powers formerly reserved for the state. It is unlikely that this has yet occurred in most Muslim countries, and, even to the extent that it may, she argues that it would lead to new equilibria between the global and national, not the displacement of national authority.[43]

In the realm of globalized communications as well, states have found opportunities to reaffirm their authority. As always, there are pulls in each direction. The proliferation of newspapers, journals, satellite broadcasting, fax machines, CD-Roms, mobile telephones, and web sites has provided Muslims with an understanding of the problems and achievements of their fellow believers.[44] The distances across the Muslim world have seemingly shrunk, making, for example, the situation of Muslims in Kosovo or Somalia tantamount to a 'local' concern for Muslims elsewhere. The idea that technological advances would lead inevitably to new political and cultural openings is deterministic and should not be read into the communications revolution.[45] On the one hand, in so far as a new, broadening awareness does emerge, *umma*-consciousness may be said to be raised and a push thereby given to trans-state communal identification. On the other, some national governments, with one eye on their domestic publics and the other on rival states, seek to serve as patrons of new publications and media. In effect, they hope to cultivate new constituencies by which to enhance their own influence or to persuade old constituencies that their right to rule remains valid. Access to and control of means of communications—Qur'an and other book publishing, television and radio programming—are crucial to this plan. The Saudis, for example, not only have distributed millions of copies of the Qur'an in various languages but also regularly reach out to various groups throughout the world through their ownership of periodicals such as *al-Majalla* and *al-Watan* and

February 1992); and Keith Griffin and Terry McKinley, *Towards a Human Development Strategy*, HDRO Occasional Paper No. 6 (New York: UNDP Human Development Report Office, December 1992), 9 and *passim*. Also see Rodney Wilson, 'Introduction', Tim Niblock and Rodney Wilson (eds), *The Political Economy of the Middle East, Volume 2: International Economic Relations* (Cheltenham: Edward Elgar Publishing, 1999), xi–xvii, and Rodney Wilson, *Economic Development in the Middle East* (London: Routledge, 1995).

[43] Saskia Sassen, 'A New Cross-Border Field for Public and Private Actors: De-Nationalized State Agendas and Privatised Norm-Making', *Zeitschrift für Entwicklungspolitik* [Austrian Journal of Development Studies], 16/4 (2000); see also her 'The Spatial Organization of Information Industries: Implications for the Role of the State', in James H. Mittelman (ed.), *Globalization: Critical Reflections* (Boulder and London: Lynne Rienner Publishers, 1996), 46–8.

[44] For the argument that new forms of communications are helping to reshape identities and notions of authority, see Dale F. Eickelman and Jon W. Anderson (eds), *New Media in the Muslim World: The Emerging Public Sphere* (Bloomington: Indiana University Press, 1999), especially Chs 1–4.

[45] Mamoun Fandy, 'Information Technology, Trust, and Social change in the Arab World', *The Middle East Journal*, 54/3 (2000).

such newspapers as *al-Sharq al-Awsat* and *al-Hayat*. Although legal ownership of these may be in private hands, links with the royal family are substantial: The family of Prince Salman, the governor of Riyadh and brother of
the king, in the case of Saudi Research and Marketing controlling *al-Sharq
al-Awsat* and *al-Majalla*; Prince Khalid Bin Sultan, the Saudi commander
during the Gulf war of 1991, in the case of the influential and widely read
al-Hayat. In addition, there is Saudi ownership of the Middle East Broadcasting
Centre (MBC) and the United Press International.

The Qatari government's relationship to the al-Jazira channel is illustrative
of the way in which states may solidify their power by allowing the media
relative freedom. The television network's remarkably fresh openness of discussion, not to mention its special relationship with various radicals like
Osama Bin Laden, reflects favourably on a regime that, unusually for the
area, has taken a chance on non-intervention. Its vigorous and frank discussions of politics have intensely irritated Qatar's neighbours but, at the very
same time, have magnified the voice of the tiny shaykhdom—some refer
to it as the second superpower—and enhanced the legitimacy of its *amir*,
who notably came to power via a *coup d'état*. The government acquires a
kind of persuasive authority.[46] The communications revolution may not,
therefore, be respectful of territorial borders, but it enables governments to
bolster and project their legitimacy as well as to censor and control. Elites are
still largely able to harness the 'power of technology' in order to reconfirm the
'technology of power'.[47]

Both factors—an intellectual recognition that globalization may induce
positive results and a political recognition that regimes may enhance their
power—point, then, to ambivalence on the part of various Muslim elites.
Globalization doubtless provides profound challenges and difficulties, stimulating revisionist demands for redress of injustices. But Muslims also recognize that it may produce useful consequences which in the end sustain, rather
than radically undermine, the basic systemic framework in which claims and
counter-claims have long been negotiated. Even when new competitive
dimensions are added, and in spite of an obvious weakness relative to the
West, Muslim elites may still largely regard it as natural that the game should
be played out by interstate rules. In this way, they would best be able to control globalizing challenges and to mould these forces to their own benefit, not
the least of which is the consolidation of existing regimes.

---

[46] See Robert O. Keohane and Joseph S. Nye, Jr, 'Power and Interdependence in the
Information Age', *Foreign Affairs*, 77/5 (1998).

[47] The terminology belongs to Manuel Castells, *The Information Age: Economy, Society
and Culture, Volume 1: The Rise of the Network Society* (Oxford: Blackwell Publishers,
1996), 52.

3. THE ISLAMIST REVOLT?

The rise of radical Islamism, however, may bring such complacency into question. There is no doubt that a multiplicity of groups and movements are attacking the status quo throughout the world. The Bin Laden network is thought to stretch virtually across the globe, its intent to be anarchical, its effect radically destabilizing. This movement and others are devoted to the cause of jihad and, unlike many Muslims who prefer to distinguish between spiritual and physical 'struggle', they do not shy away from seeing it in terms of force. The Islamic Jihad movement in Egypt is a notable exponent of this point of view. According to 'Abd al-Salam Faraj in his *al-Farida al-Gha'iba* (The Neglected Duty), written in 1981 to justify the assassination of President Sadat,[48] jihad is not simply a vaguely collective obligation of the Muslim community. It is an individual duty (*fard 'ayn*) which no Muslim can avoid. The impulse sometimes seen in Muslim history to withdraw from an impure society in the hope of creating a purer society (*hijra*) is an abdication of responsibility. It would also not make sense to form a political party to advance one's goals, for the system itself is the problem. Scriptural authority and the teachings of learned scholars make it clear that militant engagement is a necessity, particularly when it is directed at rulers who have deviated from the path of Islam.

This approach is also endorsed by the Hizb al-Tahrir al-Islami, the Islamic Liberation Party, which began in Palestine and Jordan but is now a discernible presence on university campuses in Britain and elsewhere in Europe. It expresses strong hostility in particular to the modern Turkish state owing to its abolition of the caliphate and its slavish dedication to Western ways. For such groups, Muslims are endlessly caught up in a web of governmental complicity with such hegemonic institutions as the IMF and World Bank. Globalization is skewed in favour of the rich, and in fact the differential between the top 20 per cent and the lowest 20 per cent of the world's population has dramatically widened, doubling in the past 40 years. Despite the immense wealth of the US to its great discredit, such disparities also exist inside it. In addition, the WTO has sided with large pharmaceutical companies to deny affordable medication to the world's poor.[49]

Joint manoeuvres between American and Muslim military forces, such as the Egyptian army, or between Turkey and Israel, are *haram* (forbidden) because, in contradiction of the Qur'an (4:141), they allow unbelievers to have authority over believers given that the outside force almost always assumes

---

[48] This was first published in *al-Ahrar* (Cairo: 14 December 1981).
[49] *Khilafah Magazine* (Dhul Qa'dah 1422/January 2002), 5.

the operational lead. Moreover, such joint exercises strengthen the hand of the
unbelievers, thereby, in this reasoning, lending cooperation to sin and trans-
gression against Qur'anic command (5:3).[50] Unbelief (*kufr*) is thus imposed
by the West and, significantly, by its henchmen at home who seek to separate
religion from politics in contravention of Islamic imperatives. Indeed, when
Pakistan's General Musharraf denounces Kashmiri and other valid jihadist
groups as extremists, he espouses a value system at odds with Islam:

> The word 'extremist' is a Western invention that is used as a label for anyone that is
> opposed to the norm. Those who carry Islam are opposed to the norm throughout the
> Muslim world because they are convinced that the rulers of Muslims are Western-
> backed agents that continue to implement Western kufr systems of government in
> order to impose Western kufr colonialism on the world. In such a situation it is cor-
> rect to be opposed to the norm, whether or not the West and their puppet rulers then
> insist [on calling] such people 'extremists'.[51]

The solution is restoration of the Islamic caliphate, rejoining politics to religion
and providing a beacon to all Islamic lands. Muslims should not shy away from
recourse to force in order to carry out this mission; jihad is necessary to overthrow unjust rulers and to advance the cause of eventual Muslim unification.

As this suggests, the events of 11 September 2001 and their aftermath have
brought to the fore a set of criticisms of the international order that has been
growing since at least the 1970s. Osama Bin Laden, although not noted for
his theological originality, nonetheless exploited the fragmentation of authority that lies behind much of the modern Islamic experience and appointed
himself a religious interpreter for the times. Although he demonstrated in the
process a public relations genius that caught many by surprise, his arguments
were merely an update of the powerful critique of the Islamic Jihad and a borrowing from Hizb al-Tahrir. The former is more weighty, and was perhaps
made known to him through the tutorial mediation of Ayman al-Zawahiri, the
amir of the Jihad group and the deputy leader of al-Qa'ida. The thrust of this
world view, often remarked upon, is subversive: does not the Qur'an say that
polytheists should be fought until they cease to exist (9:5) and that those who
do not rule according to God's law are unbelievers and, by implication, should
be resisted (5:44)? The radicals use the first Qur'anic reference to delegitimize
non-believers standing outside of Islam, while they apply the second internally as an attack on the rulers of the Muslim world who are corrupt and
dependent on infidel power. Although both arguments rely on interpretations of scripture that other Muslims contest, they derive much of their force

[50] 'A Series of Thoughts II: 3. Joint Manoeuvres Between a Muslim Army and a Kaafir
Army', http://www.hizb-ut-tahrir.org (31 January 2002).
[51] Letter to the [Pakistani] Religious Affairs Minister Dr Mahmood Ahmed Ghazi,
http://www.hizb-ut-tahrir.org (23 January 2002).

from the direct appeal to 'tradition'. This appears to validate a timeless moral framework that collapses the boundaries between external and internal and relies on built-in notions of justice and injustice.

For those who subscribe to this view, world politics is pre-eminently, but not exclusively, fixed on peoples. Muslims have constant aspirations to unity and faith regardless of the international balance of power or the character of their own regimes, but the same political factors of system and state inevitably thwart these aspirations. American hegemony, institutionalized in an order centred on the United Nations and reliant upon client states, has perverted the goals of the *umma*. Moreover, like 'Muslims', Christians, and Jews are categories of international political analysis, and 'Crusaders' (*al-salibiyyin*) exist today as they did in the medieval period. But so, too, do heroic *mujahidin*, who, in the late twentieth century in Afghanistan, Bosnia, Chechnya, and Kashmir among other places, defied the godless powers of the age.

In this world view, world politics is both territorial and de-territorialized. On the one hand, the conventional nation-state category finds a matter-of-fact place in the analysis. Iraq, for instance, is thought to be under Western attack precisely because it is the most powerful of the Arab states. And Russia, of course, sought to extend its domain over Afghanistan, which then became the first line of Muslim defence. On the other hand, the juridical bifurcation of the world into Islamic and non-Islamic realms has gained new currency as purportedly Muslim states fall into the non-Islamic category. States like Saudi Arabia or Pakistan may proclaim themselves to be Islamic, but they are actually 'allies of Satan' (*a'wan al-Shaytan*). The very name of Saudi Arabia tends to be avoided in this radical discourse, and vaguer, though resonant, designations are used, such as 'peninsula of the Arabs' (*jazirat al-'arab*) or 'the land of the holy places' (*bilad al-haramayn*). The language is often symbolic, but Muslims everywhere would understand, for example, that calls for the liberation of the al-Aqsa mosque and of the Grand Mosque (Masjid al-Haram) mean the demise of Israeli control over Palestine and of Saudi control over the Saudi kingdom. Some groups such as the Muhajirun in Britain, an offshoot of the Hizb al-Tahrir, go so far as to say that, because no regimes can be considered Islamic today, there is no such thing as *dar al-islam*. Yet the common radical formulation 'lands of Islam' (*aradin al-islam*) reveals perhaps more than was intended: on the one hand, the sense of a wider community bound together by common belief and traditions, but, on the other, the implicit acknowledgement that internal differences persist.

Islamist radicals unsurprisingly single out the US as the latest and most aggressive imperialist. Bin Laden's statement of 7 October 2001 dated the current troubles of the Muslim world to 80 years before that date.[52] The reference

---

[52] *The Times* (8 October 2001).

is not precise, but it is likely that it refers to the demise of the Ottoman Empire after the First World War and to the specific abolition of the caliphate in 1924. This interpretation is consistent with a general Islamist account that links European, specifically British, intervention with local secularizing regimes—in this case, Atatürk—to explain the collapse of Muslim unity. The American presence is particularly harmful because it is both economic and religious or 'ideological'; its attempt to attain market domination is dependent on the curtailing of Islam to a kind of safe, conservative, and largely privatized Islam such as that practised by the ruling elites of the Muslim world. Like all imperialists, the US seeks the fragmentation (*tamziq*) of the Islamic world and the creation of 'paper statelets' (*duwaylat waraqiyya*) that can be turned into 'bases' (*qawa'id*) for foreign penetration and control. Individual Americans, civilian as well as military, are thus legitimate targets of jihad.[53] The UN, which properly belongs in the realm of the 'hypocrites' (*munafiqun*), a term often used in Islamist discourse to delegitimize opponents, can never be the promoter of international consensus. Rather, it is as culpable as the US because it assists America in its designs on the Islamic world. The true believer could not expect this body to be impartial given its role in the partition of Palestine, and Muslim governments that continue to maintain a UN seat have made themselves infidels.

Bin Laden and his supporters believe the resort to terrorism is justified for a set of closely-linked reasons. The US has been aggressive and unjust and, on both counts, this calls for defensive action. Overlapping with other Muslim criticisms cited earlier, this view singles out for condemnation American support for Israel, but also the introduction of troops in the holy peninsula of Arabia since the Gulf war of 1990–1. The former has denied Muslims their legitimate rights—pre-eminently the right to self-determination—and the latter has turned Saudi Arabia into an 'American colony'. In these circumstances, terrorism is a legitimate 'response to injustice':[54]

They [tyrants and oppressors] rip us of our wealth and of resources and of our oil. Our religion is under attack. They kill and murder our brothers. They compromise our honor and dignity and dare we utter a single word of protest against the injustice, we are called terrorists. This is compounded injustice. And the United Nations insistence to convict the victims and support the aggressors constitutes a serious preceden[t] which shows the extent of injustice that has been allowed to take root in this land.[55]

---

[53] Bin Laden's fatwa against Americans is found in *al-Quds al-'Arabi* (London: 23 February 1998).

[54] Bin Laden video, al-Jazira Channel (26 December 2001). The 'American colony' quotation is in an interview with Bin Laden, *The Independent* (10 July 1996).

[55] May 1998 interview with Bin Laden, reproduced in: http://www.pbs.org/wgbh/pages/frontline/shows/binladen/who/interview.html (9 January 2002).

It is thus imperative to strike American power at its heart: 'It is important to hit the economy [of the US], which is the base of its military power ... If the economy is hit they will become reoccupied [*sic*]'.[56]

4. EXTERNAL AND INTERNAL CHALLENGES

Two major trends coexist simultaneously today. First, as we have just seen, radical Islamists like Bin Laden have formulated, in word and deed, an anti-Western programme that calls into question Muslim acceptance of, and acquiescence in, the prevailing international order. In this perspective, association with the world's superpower taints all. To a significant extent, this view overlaps with broader Muslim complaints about hegemonic globalization. America, in particular, is seen as exploitative, aggressive, and militantly secular. The war against terrorism since late 2001 is particularly viewed with alarm, suggesting to many that the US desires unbridled power and aims to control the Muslim *umma*. It appears no less than a new Western crusade against Islam. Bin Laden's reputation as a *mujahid* against the Soviets in Afghanistan has assured him of personal popularity throughout the Muslim world, but his political message also resonates widely. Even some Saudi religious officials have defied their government by endorsing his world view: 'America does not want the full implementation of Islam's values and principles ... It does not want there to be a free Islamic economy ... America doesn't want to have any competitors.'[57] Although most Muslims would dissociate themselves from the violent means used to counter the purported Western interventionism, particularly the targeting of civilians, they would subscribe to the general complaint. Even a Saudi-influenced convocation of specialists in Islamic law, who met to offer an Islamic definition of terrorism, made it clear that, although they wished to censure the September attacks, they were also concerned about state terrorism such as practised by the Israelis in Palestine or the Serbs in Kosovo and Bosnia. In fact, 'this is the most dangerous kind of terrorism to world peace and security, and to confront it is just self-defence and *jihad* in the path of God'.[58]

---

[56] Al-Jazira Channel (26 December 2001).

[57] The comments of 'Abdullah bin Matruk al-Haddal from the Saudi Ministry of Islamic Affairs, on al-Jazira Channel, 'Al-Ittijah al-Mu'akis' programme (22 January 2002). The Saudi dissident religious scholar, Safar al-Hawali, issued a fatwa justifying the 11 September attacks on New York and Washington as legitimate targets and condemned the Northern Alliance for its support of the 'unbelievers'.

[58] This was the resolution of the Islamic Fiqh Academy of the Muslim World League meeting in Mecca in January 2002: *al-Sharq al-Awsat* (11 January 2002).

In this sense, a fundamental shift has occurred from the earlier pattern of accommodation to the international order. It is true that, particularly when it comes to the Palestinians, the ideas of nationalism and state sovereignty are reaffirmed as their due. But the combined challenges of globalization and radical Islamism have clearly induced many Muslims to wonder how the encompassing liberal international economic order can ever respond to Muslim needs, or how a state system dominated by the US and the UN can ever be sympathetic to Muslim claims to justice.

Second, however, the larger picture demonstrates that the Muslim challenge to and rejection of international society has not always been revolutionary. One reason why this is the case is the ongoing adaptation of Muslim political elites to the existing structure of order in international relations, which was discussed earlier. Both erosion of state autonomy and the reaffirmation of state power have taken place. The former is often assumed, but there is also no doubt that existing elites have recognized the power of transnational and globalizing forces and have sought to harness these to buttress their rule. They have had successes in doing so. But they are conscious of their own connectedness and resentful that they are made to feel irrelevant or peripheral in the global configuration. This speaks to a kind of politics of identity that is perhaps more discernibly emerging than it did at the time of the supposed Third World 'revolt' against the West. But, at the same time, the very same consciousness and resentment reaffirm to the conservative political elites the benefits to be derived from the conventional system. In short, they find redress for their grievances and legitimization of their right to rule in the process through participation in the system. Such a utilitarian calculation of one's interests helps to shape the normative view that systemic order is desirable as the precondition for an adjustment of relations between Muslim and non-Muslim states. Order, therefore, sets the stage for justice claims.

In addition to this continuing accommodation, there has also been a significant turning inwards which further complicates the simple notion of an Islamic confrontation with international order. This inner turning comes from two sources. The first source is the Islamists' criticism of their own governments and society as having become un-Islamic. The vast majority of Islamists, whether radical or moderate, have directed their ire at targets at home. Just as the secular Arab nationalists a generation earlier had concluded that they would never prevail over Israel as long as their own governments were corrupt, Islamists have put at the heart of their programme both the overthrow of secular and impious governments and a vaguely defined Islamization of society. Part of this approach has led, in effect, to a tacit acceptance of the interstate model. The immediate and medium-term struggle is to make Egypt or Indonesia more Islamic rather than to displace either with an unattainable caliphate. The lessons of the 1920s and 1930s have been remembered: disagreements over who should become the new caliph and the unseemly competition among solidifying national elites made the goal of political union seem unattainable. The task became to implement the *shari' a* in national legal systems, to deflect harmful cultural Westernisation, and to meet the social needs of believers.

It has been argued that Islamism is the natural consequence of stratification and division which modern capitalist development generates.[59] The product of modernization, it inhabits the framework of modernity. It represents the natural voice of protest, the reaction to perceived injustices, in societies where Islamic symbols and language dominate the political arena. Bryan Turner carries the implications of this to a conclusion that may seem startling given what has been the conventional public image. If Islamists are engaged in revolt, it is in *favour* of modernity. What is resented, he argues, are the uncertainties, multiple meanings, and shifting goal posts of postmodernity.[60] This interpretation is not entirely unproblematic, but it does suggest that the majority of Islamists, for all their fiery rhetoric and at times violent action, implicitly accept the accustomed, structured order to which the political elites adapted long ago. International society is but one facet of this familiar milieu.

Islamists form part of a wider move to pluralism within Muslim societies. They are not necessarily committed to the values of tolerance of diversity and the acceptance of pluralism; but they are self-consciously organized in opposition to, or at least competition with, other groups. This de facto pluralism is, in part, the result of the fragmentation of authority that has characterized the modern Muslim world. This de-monopolization has been going on for a long time and was first associated with the spread of literacy and direct access to religious texts. New kinds of interpreters—Islamist movements, individuals like Bin Laden, government bureaucracies, non-state organizations—have therefore emerged, claiming a right to *ijtihad* (independent judgement) and possessing scriptural literacy. Governments and opposition groups are often in direct competition for control of the symbolic discourse of Islam, thereby creating a 'politics of language' in which the stakes are high: who speaks authoritatively for what is proposed as the definitive religious tradition? States no longer have information monopolies, and many of the main Islamist groups today, such as Hizbullah in Lebanon, Hamas in Palestine, and even the Taliban in Afghanistan, have had their own web sites. They have been able to spread their message, if not universally, then at least to computer-literate student, professional, and intellectual elites.

But other groups are also emerging, and they constitute the second source of internal attention. These women's groups, human rights groups, and other

[59] Mustapha Kamal Pasha and Ahmed I. Samatar, 'The Resurgence of Islam', in Mittelman (ed.), *Globalization: Critical Reflections*, 198.
[60] Bryan S. Turner, *Orientalism, Postmodernism and Globalism* (London: Routledge, 1994), 89–90, 92–4.

special interest groups are increasingly making their views known and heard. Indeed, a great many Muslims now argue that Islam and democracy are compatible. Muslims who do not share this view find democracy an alien system at variance with a normative order based on divine, not popular, sovereignty and a complete, revealed law that makes a legislative body superfluous. But for an increasing number of Muslim intellectuals in societies as diverse as Jordan, Iran, Turkey, and Malaysia, the debate is over how Islam is, or can be, democratic, not over whether it incorporates the values of pluralism, tolerance, and civic participation. The Muslim minorities of Europe, North America, and Australia, daily living with the demands of a participatory society, are especially important to this process of intellectual change. Moreover, the process is no doubt abetted by the close connections between societies of origin and Muslims in the West, the availability of relatively cheap publications, the wide reporting of the ideas of such influential thinkers as the Iranian Abdolkarim Soroush or the Syrian Muhammad Shahrur, and the ability to download recent speeches or writings from the Internet.

The multiple voices which are being heard, facilitated, and enhanced by the new technologies may be disharmonious and not necessarily lead to the normative triumph of pluralism. But the de facto diversity that they represent is pertinent to the development of civil society in the Muslim world. Clamorous voices and serious claims are being heard and, to some extent, recognized, and new civic bonds of trust and responsibility are promoted. These in turn are productive of 'social capital' that may, though not necessarily, be translated into more durable structures of civil society. In so doing, this process may well undermine the state as it undermines the old political elites. Yet this result is by no means certain, and the argument can be made, in line with democratic theory, that a healthy civil society would only strengthen the state. What is indisputable is that, in so far as the discourse of justice is now firmly setting the agenda, it has been in significant part internalized: that is, operating at the level of counter-elites within states of international society.

5. CONCLUSION

So entrenched has the nation-state been in our political imagination that much of the discussion of transnationalism and now globalization has focused on its survival or demise. It is, in a way, a concession to the enduring nature of that towering institution, which has been accepted as the core of international order since the mid-seventeenth century. It is not accidental that religion has been present but invisible, for it was the Peace of Westphalia (1648) that, in endorsing territorially based sovereignties, also presumed to move diplomacy to the safer ground of secular relationships. The religious dimension was never entirely missing, of course, and churches, missionaries, and religious ideologies often played a complicating role. But it is clear that religious factors have generally been understated in analyses of the international or global order.

The increasing interdependence of the world has brought profound challenges to the primacy of the territorial state, and globalizing economics as well as Islamist transnational networks have contributed to the uncertainty. It is indisputable that the state is not about to disappear; one could even argue that, in a world of multiple actors and diffuse economic power, with its command of force and bureaucratic cohesion, it has had a renewed lease on life. Yet what is also apparent is that alternative communities of affiliation and identity have emerged and lie in uneasy coexistence with the state. These may be smaller—ethnic or sub-national—or larger—cultural or religious—but they all have in common the articulation of shifting social and political aspirations, if not exactly allegiances. In essence, a politics of identity has become central and new solidarist conceptions of order and justice are enhanced. In the specific case of Islam, a sense of victimization has taken on concrete meaning. This has led some Muslims to see in globalization the means for domination of the *umma*, and led a number of these as well as others to turn to a programme of Islamization—radical or moderate—in order to implement a new basis for social and political solidarity. The state remains firmly rooted, therefore, but other forms of political community are imaginable and, to a certain extent, imagined.

Contrasting trends are simultaneously at work. Globalization is vehemently denounced as unfair and unequal, yet Muslims, including Islamists, see in it some possibility of creating a new order. The state as an institution is under challenge, and yet it reasserts power. Islam is resurgent, but it contributes to a fragmentation of cultural and political authority at home. Two axes—one territorial, the other related to governance—now seem intimately linked. The first speaks of interstate order and has tended to equate justice with systemic equilibrium or harmony, whereas the second invokes justice in a more complex way. Indeed, justice appears Janus-faced, challenging what is perceived as a hegemonic and secular order yet also inherently accepting that order as attention is principally directed to the reform of Muslim societies themselves. To invoke Hedley Bull again, two of his ideal types of international proponent may be combined. Conservatives espouse, or see, order above all; revolutionaries seek to establish, or purport to see, the New Jerusalem; and liberals square the circle by finding the two necessarily interconnected as a matter of hope or fact.[61] Using these categories in the analytical sense, we are left with

---

[61] Bull, *The Anarchical Society*, 94.

revolutionary possibilities within a conservative framework. The balance between accommodation to international society, and challenges to it, is under pressure, and the order-justice debate in the Muslim world has grown discernibly more complex in the post-Cold War world. Claims to justice have become both insistent and more urgent.

Select Bibliography

ALDERSON, K. and HURRELL, A. (eds), *Hedley Bull on International Society* (Basingstoke: Macmillan, 2000).

ALSTON, P. (ed.) with BUSTELO, M. R. and HEENAM, J., *The EU and Human Rights* (Oxford: Oxford University Press, 1999).

ALSTON, P. and CRAWFORD, J. (eds), *The Future of UN Human Rights Treaty Monitoring* (Cambridge: Cambridge University Press, 2000).

ANADKAT, N., *International Political Thought of Gandhi, Nehru and Lohia* (Delhi: Bharatiya Kala Prakashan, 2000).

ARMSTRONG, D., *Revolutions and World Order* (Oxford: Oxford University Press, 1993).

BANDYOPADHYAYA, J., *North Over South: A Non-Western Perspective of International Relations* (New Delhi: South Asian Publishers, 1984).

BARBER, B. R., *Jihad vs. McWorld* (New York: Times Books/Random House, 1995).

BEITZ, C., *Political Theory and International Relations* (Princeton: Princeton University Press, 1979).

BENTHAM, J., *An Introduction to the Principles of Morals and Legislation* (London: Athlone Press, [1780] 1970).

BILLINGTON, J., *The Icon and the Axe: An Interpretive History of Russian Culture* (New York: Vintage, 1970).

BISHIKAR, C. P., *Pandit Deendayal Upadhyaya, Ideology and Perception* (New Delhi: Suruchi Prakashan, 1991).

BOHMAN, J., 'International Regimes and Democratic Governance: Political Equality and Influence in Global Institutions', *International Affairs*, 75 (1999).

BOZEMAN, A., *The Future of Law in a Multicultural World* (Princeton: Princeton University Press, 1971).

BROWN, C., 'International Political Theory and the Idea of a World Community', in K. Booth and S. Smith (eds), *International Relations Theory Today* (Cambridge: Polity Press, 1995).

BROWNLIE, I., *Basic Documents on Human Rights*, 3rd edn (Oxford: Clarendon Press, 1992).

BUCHANAN, A., 'Rawls's Law of Peoples: Rules for a Vanished Westphalian World', *Ethics*, 110 (2001).

BULL, H., *The Anarchical Society: A Study of Order in World Politics*, 2nd edn (Basingstoke: Macmillan, 1995).

—— and WATSON, A. (eds), *The Expansion of International Society* (Oxford: Oxford University Press, 1984).

BUNT, G. R., *Virtually Islamic: Computer-Mediated Communication and Cyber Islamic Environments* (Cardiff: University of Wales Press, 2000).

CHAN, G., *Chinese Perspectives on International Relations: A Framework for Analysis* (Basingstoke: Macmillan, 1999).

CHAN, S., 'Chinese Perspectives on World Order', in T. V. Paul and John A. Hall (eds), *International Order and the Future of World Politics* (Cambridge: Cambridge University Press, 1999).

CLARK, I., *The Post-Cold War Order: The Spoils of Peace* (New York: Oxford University Press, 2001).

COCHRAN, M., *Normative Theory in International Relations: A Pragmatic Approach* (Cambridge: Cambridge University Press, 1999).

CULPEPER, R. and PESTIEAU, C. (eds), *Development and Global Governance* (Ottawa: International Development Research Centre, North-South Institute, 1996).

DALLIN, A., *The Soviet Union at the United Nations* (New York: Praeger, 1962).

DEMARTINO, G. F., *Global Economy, Global Justice. Theoretical Objections and Policy Alternatives to Neoliberalism* (London: Routledge, 2000).

DENG, Y., 'The Chinese Conception of National Interests in International Relations', *The China Quarterly*, 154 (June 1998).

DUNNE, T. and WHEELER, N. J. (eds), *Human Rights in Global Politics* (Cambridge: Cambridge University Press, 1999).

EICKELMAN, D. F. and ANDERSON, J. W. (eds), *New Media in the Muslim World: The Emerging Public Sphere* (Bloomington: Indiana University Press, 1999).

ELSTER, J., *The Cement of Society. A Study of Social Order* (Cambridge: Cambridge University Press, 1989).

FISK, M., *The State and Justice. An Essay in Political Theory* (Cambridge: Cambridge University Press, 1989).

FOOT, R., *Rights Beyond Borders: The Global Community and the Struggle over Human Rights in China* (Oxford: Oxford University Press, 2000).

GADDIS, J. L., *Strategies of Containment: A Critical Appraisal of Postwar American National Security Policy* (New York: Oxford University Press, 1982).

—— *Russia, the Soviet Union, and the United States: An Interpretive History*, 2nd edn (New York: McGraw Hill, 1990).

—— *We Now Know: Rethinking Cold War History* (New York: Oxford University Press, 1997).

GANDHI, M., *The Selected Works of Mahatma Gandhi, Volume 6: The Voice of Truth* (Ahmedabad: Navjivan Trust, 1968).

GARTHOFF, R. L., *Détente and Confrontation: American-Soviet Relations from Nixon to Reagan*, revised edition (Washington: Brookings, 1994).

GARTON ASH, T., *In Europe's Name: Germany and the Divided Continent* (New York: Random House, 1993).

GOLWALKER, M. S., *Bunch of Thoughts*, 3rd edn (Bangalore: Sahitya Sindhu Prakashana, 1996).

—— *We or Our Nationhood Defined* (Nagpur: Bharat Publications, 1939).

HABERMAS, J., *L'Intégration Républicaine* (Paris: Fayard, 1998).

HAMPSHIRE, S., *Justice is Conflict* (London: Duckworth, 1999).

HARRISS, I., 'Order and Justice in "The Anarchical Society"', *International Affairs*, 69/4 (1993).

HELD, D., *Models of Democracy*, 2nd edn (Cambridge: Polity Press, 1996).

HILL, C., 'The Capacity-Expectations Gap, or Conceptualizing Europe's International Role', in S. Bulmer and A. Scott (eds), *Economic and Political Integration in Europe: Internal Dynamics and Global Context* (Oxford: Blackwell, 1994).

HOFFMANN, S., 'Conference Report on the Conditions of World Order', *Daedalus*, 95/2 (1966).

——*Duties Beyond Borders: On the Limits and Possibilities of Ethical international Politics* (Syracuse: Syracuse University Press, 1981).

—— 'Is There an International Order?', in S. Hoffmann, *Janus and Minerva* (Boulder, CO: Westview, 1987).

HOLBROOKE, R., *To End a War* (New York: Modern Library, 1998).

HOPF, T. (ed.), *Understandings of Russian Foreign Policy* (University Park: Pennsylvania State University Press, 1999).

HOWSE, R. and NICOLAIDIS, K., *The Federal Vision: Legitimacy and Levels of Governance in the United States and the European Union* (Oxford: Oxford University Press, 2001).

HUNTINGTON, S. P., 'The Clash of Civilizations', *Foreign Affairs*, 72/3 (1993).

HURRELL, A., 'Norms and Ethics in International Relations' in W. Carlsnaes, T. Risse, and B. Simmons (eds), *Handbook of International Relations* (London: Sage, 2002).

JACKSON, J. H., *The World Trade Organization. Constitution and Jurisprudence* (London: Pinter for Royal Institute of International Affairs, 1998).

JACKSON, R. *The Global Covenant: Human Conduct in a World of States* (Oxford: Oxford University Press, 2000).

JETLY, N. (ed.), *India's Foreign Policy: Challenges and Prospects* (New Delhi: Vikas Publishing House, 1999).

KAPLAN, R. D., *The Coming Anarchy: Shattering the Dreams of the Post Cold War* (New York: Random House, 2000).

KAPUR, D., 'Expansive Agendas and Weak Instruments: Governance Related Conditionalities of the International Financial Institutions', *Journal of Policy Reform*, 4/3 (2001).

KISSINGER, H., *A World Restored* (New York: Houghton Mifflin, 1957).

——*Does America Need a Foreign Policy? Toward a Diplomacy for the 21st Century* (New York: Simon and Schuster, 2001).

KOSKENNIEMI, M., 'The Police in the Temple. Order, Justice and the UN: A Dialectical View', *European Journal of International Law*, 6 (1995).

KOTHARI, R., *Transformation and Survival: In Search of Humane World Order* (Delhi: Ajanta, 1988).

KRUEGER, A. O. (ed.), *The WTO as an International Organization* (Chicago: Chicago University Press, 1998).

LEVIN, N. G., *Woodrow Wilson and World Politics: America's Response to War and Revolution* (New York: Oxford University Press, 1968).

LEWIS, B., *The Middle East and the West* (New York: Harper Row, 1964).

—— 'The Roots of Muslim Rage', *The Atlantic Monthly* (September 1990).

LIGHT, M., *The Soviet Theory of International Relations* (Brighton: Harvester Wheatsheaf, 1988).

LINKLATER, A., *The Transformation of Political Community: Ethical Foundations of the Post-Westphalian Era* (Cambridge: Polity Press, 1998).

—— 'The Evolving Spheres of International Justice', *International Affairs*, 75/3 (1999).

LIST, F., *The National System of Political Economy* (Fairfield, NJ: Augustus M. Kelley, [1885] 1977).

MACFARLANE, S. N., 'NATO in Russia's Relations with the West', *Security Dialogue*, 32/3 (2001).

MAZRUI, A. A., 'Globalization: Homogenization or Hegemonization', *The American Journal of Islamic Social Sciences*, 15/3 (1998).

MILLER, D. L., *On Nationality* (Oxford: Clarendon Press, 1995).

—— 'Introduction', in D. Miller and M. Walzer (eds), *Pluralism, Justice and Equality* (Oxford: Oxford University Press, 1995).

——*Principles of Social Justice* (Cambridge: Harvard University Press, 1999).

MILLER, J. D. B. and Vincent, R. J., *Order and Violence: Hedley Bull and International Relations* (Oxford: Oxford University Press, 1990).

MOTTAHEDEH, R., 'The Clash of Civilizations: An Islamicist's Critique', *Harvard Middle Eastern and Islamic Review*, 2/1 (1995).

MUZZAFAR, C., 'Globalisation and Religion: Some Reflections', in J. A. Camilleri and C. Muzzafar (eds), *Globalisation: The Perspectives and Experiences of the Religious Traditions of Asia Pacific* (Petaling Jaya: International Movement for a Just World, 1998).

NARDIN, T., *Law, Morality and the Relations of States* (Princeton: Princeton University Press, 1983).

NEHRU, J., *India's Foreign Policy: Selected Speeches, Sept. 1946–April 1961* (New Delhi: The Publications Division, Ministry of Information and Broadcasting, Govt. of India, 1961).

NEUMANN, I., *Russia and the Idea of Europe* (London: Routledge, 1996).

O'BRIEN, R., GOETZ, A. M., SCHOLTE, J. A., and WILLIAMS, M., *Contesting Global Governance: Multilateral Economic Institutions and Global Social Movements* (Cambridge: Cambridge University Press, 2000).

O'NEILL, O., *Towards Justice and Virtue: A Constructive Account of Practical Reasoning* (Cambridge: Cambridge University Press, 1996).

PASHA, M. K. and SAMATAR, A. I., 'The Resurgence of Islam', in J. H. Mittelman (ed.), *Globalization: Critical Reflections* (Boulder, CO, and London: Lynne Rienner Publishers, 1996).

PAUL, T. V. and HALL, J. A., *International Order and the Future of World Politics* (Cambridge: Cambridge University Press, 1999).

PISCATORI, J., *Islam in a World of Nation-States* (Cambridge: Cambridge University Press, 1986).

RAJAEE, F., *Globalization on Trial: The Human Condition and the Information Civilization* (Ottawa: International Development Research Center, 2000).

RAWLS, J., *A Theory of Justice* (Cambridge: Harvard University Press, 1971).

——*The Law of Peoples* (London: Harvard University Press, 1999).

RENGGER, N. J., *International Relations, Political Theory and the Problem of Order* (London: Routledge, 2000).

REYNOLDS, D., *One World Divisible: A Global History Since 1945* (London: Penguin, 2000).

ROBERTS, A. and KINGSBURY, B. (eds), *United Nations, Divided World: The UN's Roles in International Relations*, 2nd edn (Oxford: Oxford University Press, 1993).

ROBINSON, T. W. and SHAMBAUGH, D. (eds), *Chinese Foreign Policy: Theory and Practice* (Oxford: Oxford University Press, 1994).

RUGGIE, J., 'Territoriality and Beyond: Problematising Modernity in International Relations', *International Organization*, 47/1 (1993).

SCHEDLER, A., DIAMOND, L. J., and PLATTNER, M. F. (eds), *The Self-Restraining State: Power and Accountability in New Democracies* (Boulder, CO: Lynne Rienner, 1999).

SCHOLTE, J. A., 'The IMF meets Civil Society', *Finance and Development*, 35/3 (1998).

SCHRAM, S. R., *The Political Thought of Mao Tse-tung* (Harmondsworth: Pelican, 1969).

SEN, A., *Inequality Reexamined* (Oxford: Oxford University Press, 1992).

SHAMBAUGH, D., *Beautiful Imperialist: China Perceives America, 1972–1990* (Princeton: Princeton University Press, 1991).

SHKLAR, J. N., *The Faces of Injustice* (New Haven: Yale University Press, 1990).

SIMMA, B. (ed.), *The Charter of the United Nations: A Commentary* (Oxford: Oxford University Press, 1994).

SINGH, J., *Defending India* (Basingstoke: Macmillan, 1999).

SMITH, M., 'The European Union and a Changing Europe: Establishing the Boundaries of Order', *Journal of Common Market Studies*, 34/1 (1996).

SMITH, T., *America's Mission: The United States and the Worldwide Struggle for Democracy in the Twentieth Century* (Princeton: Princeton University Press, 1994).

SPENCE, J. D., *The Search for Modern China*, 2nd edn (New York: W. W. Norton, 1999).

STEPHANSON, A., *Manifest Destiny: American Expansionism and the Empire of Right* (New York: Hill and Wang, 1995).

SURANOVIC, S. M., 'A Positive Analysis of Fairness with Applications to International Trade', *The World Economy*, 23/3 (2000).

VAN NESS, P., *Revolution and Chinese Foreign Policy: Peking's Support for Wars of National Liberation* (Berkeley: University of California Press, 1970).

WALDRON, A., *From War to Nationalism: China's Turning Point, 1924–1925* (Cambridge: Cambridge University Press, 1995).

WALZER, M., *Spheres of Justice* (New York: Basic Books, 1983).

WELCH, DAVID A., *Justice and the Genesis of War* (Cambridge: Cambridge University Press, 1993).

WHEELER, N. J., *Saving Strangers: Humanitarian Intervention in International Society* (Oxford: Oxford University Press, 2000).

WIGHT, M., 'Why Is There No International Theory?', in M. Wight and H. Butterfield (eds), *Diplomatic Investigations* (London: Allen and Unwin, 1966).

WILLIAMS, M. A., *International Economic Organisations and the Third World* (Hemel Hempstead: Harvester/Wheatsheaf, 1994).

WOHLFORTH, W., 'The Stability of a Unipolar World', *International Security*, 24/1 (1999).

WOODS, N., 'The Challenge of Good Governance for the IMF and World Bank Themselves', *World Development*, 28/5 (2000).

XINBO, W., 'Four Contradictions Constraining China's Foreign Policy Behaviour', *Journal of Contemporary China*, 10/27 (2001).

ZIMMERMAN, W., *Soviet Perspectives on International Relations, 1956–67* (Princeton: Princeton University Press, 1969).

Index

Bold page numbers indicate chapters. The suffix n after a page number indicates a footnote.